CLASSICAL PRESENCES

General Editors

Lorna Hardwick James I. Porter

CLASSICAL PRESENCES

Attempts to receive the texts, images, and material culture of ancient Greece and Rome inevitably run the risk of appropriating the past in order to authenticate the present. Exploring the ways in which the classical past has been mapped over the centuries allows us to trace the avowal and disavowal of values and identities, old and new. Classical Presences brings the latest scholarship to bear on the contexts, theory, and practice of such use, and abuse, of the classical past.

Madly after the Muses

Bengali Poet Michael Madhusudan Datta and his Reception of the Graeco-Roman Classics

ALEXANDER RIDDIFORD

OXFORD
UNIVERSITY PRESS

OXFORD
UNIVERSITY PRESS

Great Clarendon Street, Oxford, OX2 6DP,
United Kingdom

Oxford University Press is a department of the University of Oxford.
It furthers the University's objective of excellence in research, scholarship,
and education by publishing worldwide. Oxford is a registered trade mark of
Oxford University press in the UK and in certain other countries

First Edition published in 2013

Impression: 1

British Library Cataloguing in Publication Data
Data available

ISBN 978-0-19-969973-5

Printed in Great Britain by
MPG Printgroup, UK

For Beatrice –

yathā padārpan tumi karo, madhumati,
keno nā hoibe sukhī sarbajan tathā?
(Meghnādbadh kābya, 4.221f.)

Preface

In Calcutta, on 15 May 1860, while he was preparing for the Sudder examination with a view to training for the Bar in London, Michael Madhusudan Datta (1824–73),[1] the Bengali poet and playwright, conventionally referred to as Madhusudan, wrote in a letter to a friend:

> I have a great deal to do. I have my office-work to attend to. I generally devote four or five hours to Law; I read Sanscrit, Latin and Greek and scribble. All this is enough to keep a man engaged from morn to dewy eve . . . .[2]

Busy though he was with these studies, Madhusudan also found time to produce a prodigious quantity of Bengali poetry and drama. Indeed, May 1860 was the middle of his most creative period (1859–62), a time during which he would produce an epyllion, an epic, several dramas, including a tragedy, as well as various elegiac and lyric works. Just as his examination preparation focused on the reading of 'Sanscrit, Latin and Greek', so too his Bengali works figured a fusion of Graeco-Roman and Sanskrit sources (among others): his epic masterpiece the *Meghnādbadh kābya* (1861) was an 'Iliadic' reworking of the Hindu epic *Rāmāyaṇa*; his *Bīrāṅganā kābya* (1862) represented an Ovidian transformation of the Sanskrit epic and puranic tradition; his drama, the *Padmābatī nāṭak* (1860), staged the 'Greek story of the golden apple Indianised'.[3] Madhusudan's description of his preparation for the Sudder law examination—'I read Sanscrit, Latin, and Greek and scribble'—could have described just as aptly his contemporary literary practice.

[1] I follow Seely (2004) 3, n. 1, in using the form 'Datta' rather than 'Dutt', or other variations of the name. Throughout this study I shall follow the Bengali convention (*contra*, for example, Clark (1967)) of referring to the poet as 'Madhusudan' rather than 'Datta'.

[2] See Murshid (2004) 121. Note that Madhusudan paraphrases Milton here. See the latter's description of Mulciber's fall (*Paradise Lost* 1, 742f.): 'From morn/ To noon he fell, from noon to dewy eve'.

[3] Madhusudan's own description of the *Padmābatī nāṭak*, found in the same letter as that cited in n. 2 above.

For Madhusudan, as a Bengali poet, the appropriation of the Graeco-Roman classics was less a matter of slavish admiration of the West than of enhancing the prestige of Bengali national culture. Describing his purpose in applying his classical education to the composition of the *Meghnādbadh kābya* (1861), he stated to a Bengali friend: 'It is my ambition to engraft the exquisite graces of the Greek mythology on our own.'[4] By the 1860s, when Madhusudan was at the height of his literary powers, Indian nationalism was still an embryonic ideology, and it would not be until the 1870s and beyond that it would gain real traction. The proto-nationalism of the 1860s had not yet thrown off the belief that the national cause would be best served by Bengalis competing with the West on its own terms, by incorporating the most hegemonic artefacts of European high culture into the texture of a 'reformed' vernacular tradition. Madhusudan's oeuvre was nationalistic only in this embryonic sense, but in this sense it was fervently nationalistic. As the poet himself declared to his friend Rajnarain: 'There never was a fellow more madly after the Muses than your poor friend! Night and day I am at them'.[5]

Self-aggrandisement through emulation is an inherently problematic project: the nationalist purpose could hardly be served by Bengal meekly aping the West, or by its poets becoming crass epigones of their Western literary heroes. Madhusudan was quite alive to this tension. In a typically colourful expression of self-analysis, the poet declared:

> In matters literary, old boy, I am too proud to stand before the world, in borrowed clothes. I may borrow a neck-tie, or even a waist coat, but not the whole suit.[6]

This metaphor is a striking one, and draws the reader irresistibly towards comparisons between Madhusudan's literary works and his unconventional and iconoclastic biography.[7] This was a Bengali gentleman[8] who renounced Hinduism in favour of Christianity; who habitually dressed like an Englishman and drank brandy; who

[4] Murshid (2004) 125. [5] Murshid (2004) 130.

[6] Murshid (2004) 107.

[7] The best biography of Madhusudan in English is Murshid (2003), an abridged translation of Murshid's definitive Bengali biography.

[8] For the notion of Madhusudan and his contemporaries as Bengali 'gentleman poets', see R. Chaudhuri (2002).

travelled to London where he was called to the Bar by Gray's Inn; who married an Anglo-Indian woman in Madras but then abandoned her and their children and spent the rest of his life living with an English woman in Calcutta, London, and Versailles; who, in 1873, died a Romantic poet's death from consumption and alcoholism in a Bengali library. Madhusudan had a mania for appropriating Western habits of thought and behaviour: both his life and his literary works were underpinned by cross-cultural borrowings, often as ironic as they were enthusiastic, which led to a hybridity of cultural identity with ultimately tragic consequences.

This is a book about the first Indian vernacular poet to commingle Indian and Western sources in the creation of a cosmopolitan literary aesthetic. It is also an account of a man with an indefatigable instinct for subversion and iconoclasm. The book's central thesis is that Madhusudan's appropriation of the Graeco-Roman classics, a topic which has only received piecemeal treatment even in works of Bengali scholarship and less still in the Anglophone academy, was subversive of almost every kind of prevailing cultural norm, both Hindu and British, popular as well as elite. Madhusudan deployed his literary cosmopolitanism to defy not only the indigenous Sanskrit pundits, whom he dismissed as 'old rascals',[9] but also the Western literary establishment, and many others besides. Madhusudan is one of the most extraordinary and surprising figures in the whole of Indian literary history, and as such he deserves much greater attention from Western scholars than he has so far attracted. The aim of this book is to help redress the balance.

Alexander Riddiford

[9] Murshid (2004) 107.

Acknowledgements

In the course of writing this book, and researching for the doctoral thesis out of which it has grown, I have enjoyed the good fortune of receiving a great deal of assistance from various people and institutions. Without the generous financial support of the Arts and Humanities Research Council, which sponsored me through both a Master of Studies and a D.Phil. at Oxford University, I could not have undertaken my research into Madhusudan's works and this book could not have been written. The AHRC, along with Magdalen College and the Faculty of Classics of the University of Oxford, provided much-appreciated funding for a research trip to Kolkata in 2007, an opportunity which enabled me both to access archives and libraries relevant to my research and to further my study of the Bengali language. I am also most grateful to Hanne-Ruth Thompson of the School of Oriental and African Studies in London for her generous assistance in 2006/7 as I attempted to scale the Mount Kailās of the Bengali language before going to Kolkata. I am much indebted to William Radice for introducing me to Hanne and for his generous advice and assistance at all junctures of my doctoral research and my preparation of this book for publication. I am also much obliged to Clinton B. Seely for the many helpful comments in his review of my typescript, and to Claudio Moscatelli for kindly giving me permission to reproduce on the front cover of this book an image of a painting held in his collection.

During my researches in Kolkata I met various academics, librarians, and archivists who were generous in offering me their time and help. Among these I owe most to Rosinka Chaudhuri, who was kind enough to take an interest in my project and to introduce me to colleagues at the Centre for Studies in Social Science, Kolkata, and who has continued to be most generous with her help and advice. I am grateful to the staff of the National Library and of Bishop's College, Kolkata, for permitting me to access their archives. I extend particular thanks to the United Society for the Propagation of the Gospels and the Bodleian Library of Commonwealth and African Studies at Rhodes House, Oxford, for allowing me to publish transcriptions of their archival material. During my doctoral researches at

Oxford I was most fortunate in my colleagues and am especially grateful to Nina Mirnig, Peter Szanto, and Bihani Sarkar for their advice on various Indological matters, and to Bihani and her family for their kind hospitality during my stay in Kolkata.

There are a great many colleagues and former tutors to whom I am indebted. Above all I owe an immense debt of gratitude to Stephen Harrison, the supervisor of my M.St. and D.Phil. theses, who could not have been more sympathetic, helpful, and responsive in his supervision of my work, and who helped me to shape my vision for this project from its earliest beginnings. Jaspreet Singh Boparai, a fellow aficionado of Madhusudan's oeuvre, is responsible for first introducing me to Madhusudan's life and works, and I am sincerely grateful to him for having done so. I would like to thank Fiona Macintosh for her incisive guidance at numerous stages in the evolution of my researches. I should also take the opportunity to express my profound thanks to Gerard Kilroy and Cath Finch for first introducing me to the study of classical antiquity, and to Oliver Taplin and Adrian Kelly for encouraging me to pursue the research which underpins this book.

Hilary O'Shea, Catherine Steele, and Taryn Campbell of Oxford University Press have been unfailingly helpful and supportive throughout the publication process. I am most grateful to Lorna Hardwick and James Porter, the Classical Presences series editors, for accepting my proposal for a contribution to their series, and to the two anonymous reviewers of the proposal for their encouraging comments and their invariably incisive suggestions for improvement. I am particularly grateful to Lorna Hardwick for taking the time to read the doctoral thesis out of which this book has grown, and for her detailed advice as to how to develop the work and open it out to engage with broader scholarly contexts; and to Elleke Boehmer for giving so generously of her time and help during the process of composing the book proposal and for helping me to frame the work's central themes.

All of those named above, and many more besides, have helped make this book much better than it would otherwise have been. For all of its remaining defects, needless to say, I am entirely to blame.

Finally, though I hesitate to mention debts that cannot be adequately described let alone acknowledged, there are some whose help and support have sustained me in much more than my work on this project. To my parents, Debbie and Paul, I am profoundly grateful for their generous and unflagging encouragement, and to my father for his assistance with photography and in editing the illustrations presented in the book. My wife Beatrice's family have also been steadfast in their support. However, I dedicate this book to Beatrice herself, without whose help I could not have written it, and without whose love I would have nothing.

Contents

List of Illustrations xvi
Note on the Transliteration of Bengali and Sanskrit into Roman Script xvii

1. Madhusudan: a Classicizing Oeuvre in Context 1
2. The *Padmābatī nāṭak* (1860) and the Judgement of Paris 62
3. The *Meghnādbadh kābya* (1861), Homer's *Iliad*, and Vergil's *Aeneid* 93
4. Further Receptions of Vergil's *Aeneid* 122
5. The *Bīrāṅganā kābya* (1862) and Ovid's *Heroides* 140
6. The *Hekṭor-badh* (1871) and Homer's *Iliad* 167

Conclusion: 'Above all Greek, above all Roman Fame' 189

Appendix 1 Madhusudan's New Testament examination Script (9 June 1847) 204
Appendix 2 Editions of Classical Texts Possibly Encountered By Madhusudan 219
Appendix 3 Judgement Scene in *Padmābatī nāṭak* 224
Appendix 4 Synopsis of the *Padmābatī nāṭak* 230
Appendix 5 *Siṃhal-bijay kābya* 235
Appendix 6 Synopsis of the Poems of the *Bīrāṅganā kābya* 237
Appendix 7 Sources Of The *Bīrāṅganā kābya* And The *Heroides* 241
Appendix 8 Preface to the *Hekṭor-badh* 242
Appendix 9 Madhusudan's Orientalist Indo-Europeanism 246

Bibliography 247
Index 269

List of Illustrations

Figure 1.1 Image of Madhusudan, reproduced from a photograph 3

Figure 1.2 Photograph of Madhusudan's tomb, Park Street, Kolkata (author's collection) 4

Figure 1.3 Image of Madhusudan's emblem, taken from Sanyal (*c.* 1917) 37

Note on the Transliteration of Bengali and Sanskrit into Roman Script

The Sanskrit language is mostly written in Devanāgarī, the script in which various modern north Indian languages such as Hindi are also written. Bengali, though it derives primarily from Sanskrit in its basic grammar and lexicon no less than Hindi does, is not one of these languages but instead has its own script, similar to Devanāgarī but distinct from it in various respects. It is a convention, when writing about Bengali or Sanskrit literature in English, not to quote from the languages in their original scripts but to transliterate the Indian words into the Roman script. This way the Anglophone reader who lacks knowledge of the Indian scripts may not only approximate the sounds of Bengali and Sanskrit words but also learn and recall them more readily.

The approach taken in this book with regard to transliterating Sanskrit words reflects the standard method used by Western Indologists. This method, essentially phonetic in nature, involves the use of diacritical marks to make distinctions unknown to the Roman alphabet. For example, the letters 'ś', 'ṣ', and 's' represent three kinds of sibilant (palatal, retroflex, and dental respectively), and should be pronounced (very roughly) as 'sh', 'sh', and 's' (with the second 'sh' formed with retroflexion of the tongue, that is with the tongue curled back on itself as in the US pronunciation of 'purdy'). The most important diacritical marks are the bar above a vowel (as in 'ā'), which indicates lengthening, and a dot below a consonant indicating retroflexion (the curling back of the tongue as in 'ṣ' above). It should be noted that I transliterate the names of Hindu gods, mythological characters, and other traditional Hindu terms and concepts in the Sanskrit way rather than the Bengali (thus Meghanāda and Rāvaṇa, instead of the Bengali Meghnād and Rābaṇ). However, the titles of Bengali works which include the names of such characters are transliterated in the Bengali way (thus *Meghnādbadh kābya*). I have decided to do this so that readers with a knowledge of Hindu mythology but without any Bengali may more easily recognize those Hindu figures and concepts familiar to them.

The prevailing conventions for transliterating Bengali words are rather more complicated, and in fact there is some variation between the transliteration methods adopted by different scholars (see for example Clark (1967), Seely (2004), or Radice (2010)). My own method for transliterating Bengali is an attempt at synthesizing the various prevailing methods and falls somewhere between the phonetic and the orthographically conservative. In some instances, the conventional system of transliteration preserves letters which are not in fact pronounced as such in spoken Bengali. For example, the Bengali name of Madhusudan's dramatic heroine Padmābatī (this is the conventional transliteration of the name, and the form used throughout this book) is in fact pronounced approximately as *Poddaboti*. The conventional transliteration preserves the Sanskritic 'm', which in spoken Bengali is assimilated to the preceding 'd' to form a long consonant 'dd'. I adopt this and other such conservative (i.e. Sanskritic) orthographical conventions on the basis that they are by now so well-established that it would be perverse to depart from them. However, save to the extent that convention dictates that certain unpronounced Sanskritic letters should be preserved in the transliteration of Bengali, I have chosen to adopt a broadly phonetic method of transliteration. For example, I transliterate Bengali's Sanskritic 'inherent vowel' (in Sanskrit a 'schwa' sound but conventionally transliterated 'a'; in Bengali pronounced, unless it is silent, as one of two 'o' sounds) only where it is in fact pronounced, and I do not transliterate it at all where it is silent (as in the final but silent inherent vowel of *laṅkār*, 'of Laṅkā', written thus rather than *laṅkāra* or *laṅkāro*). However, where this inherent vowel is in fact pronounced, I transliterate it phonetically (that is with a Bengali 'o' rather than a Sanskritic 'a') only at the end of a word, and elsewhere with a Sanskritic 'a': thus *jāgaraṇ* (pronounced *jagoron*), but *āścaryo* (pronounced *ashchojjo*). The only exception I make is for the names of Bengali literary works. Madhusudan's epic masterpiece, *Meghnādbadh kābya*, is conventionally transliterated with the final inherent vowel written with a Sanskritic 'a' rather than the Bengali 'o', *viz.* '*kābya*', even though the spoken Bengali pronunciation of the word approximates *kabbo*. I follow this convention for the benefit of those readers who are already familiar with the traditional method for transliterating Madhusudan's Bengali works.

Whilst a purely phonetic system for transliterating Bengali may in some ways be preferable (and would certainly be much simpler), the method adopted in this book has the virtue not only of approximating the methods used in other English books on the subject but also of conveying some of the Sanskritic archaeology preserved in Bengali orthography. This is a feature of the written language which an Anglophone reader may compare with the English phenomenon of preserving 'silent' letters in English spellings such as the 'k' and 'gh' in 'knight'. In this way, it is hoped that the Anglophone reader without any Bengali may acquire a sense not only of the sound but also of the Sanskritic flavour of Madhusudan's Bengali register which, as will be explained in Chapter 1, represents a self-consciously Sanskritized form of the language, with the vast majority of the Bengali lexicon's rich Persian stratum all but erased.

1

Madhusudan: a Classicizing Oeuvre in Context

INTRODUCTION

In Indian West Bengal and in Bangladesh, which before partition formed a single region within India known as Bengal, Madhusudan is a fixture in the literary firmament, a well-known and respected nineteenth-century poet and playwright. His position has been an unusually unsettled one in Bengal's evolving literary discourse. Early nationalist critics once scorned his love of European culture and later Marxist readers have often deplored his unabashed elitism. However, as the first fully 'Westernized' Bengali poet to compose works in the Indian vernacular, Madhusudan can claim to be the first major 'modern' literary figure not only of Bengal but of India *tout court*. On this basis alone, and quite apart from the charm and iconoclasm of his literary oeuvre, the importance of his place in Indian literary history can hardly be doubted.

In the West, by contrast, Madhusudan is not a name to conjure with. Nor is his cultural context familiar to many. The Western reader may be expected to know something, perhaps, of the later Bengali poet Rabindranath Tagore, the first Asian to win the Nobel Prize for Literature (and to date the only Indian to have done so), but is otherwise unlikely to know much about the so-called Bengal Renaissance, the socio-political and cultural context out of which emerged the works of Madhusudan, Bankim, Tagore, and numerous other Bengali writers and artists. A study of Madhusudan's response to the Graeco-Roman classics must not only provide a sense of scholarly context for the texts under analysis, but also offer some orientation regarding the poet's biography, his historical context, and the cultural trends that informed his literary outlook.

1. BIOGRAPHY AND OEUVRE

Madhusudan, son of the lawyer Rajnarayan and his wife Jahnabi, was born on 25 January 1824 in Sagardanri, a remote village in Jessore district (now in Bangladesh) and some eighty miles to the east of Kolkata, then Calcutta.[1] See Figure 1.1 below for an image of the poet. Madhusudan converted to Christianity, much against his family's wishes, on 9 February 1843,[2] but only took the Christian name Michael some time later.[3] It is unclear precisely when he took the name: apparently not before 9 June 1847, and certainly no later than the announcement in the Madras *Athenaeum* on 18 January 1848 of his arrival in Madras.[4]

[1] The precise date of his birth is somewhat uncertain: in contemporary rural Bengal it was not unusual for the date of a child's birth to go unrecorded. However, Ghulam Murshid, Madhusudan's most recent biographer, has settled on 25 of January as the most likely date: see Murshid (2003) 11. Throughout this book I shall refer to the English translation of Murshid's biography (2003), except where the Bengali original of this work (1995, 1997 [revised edition]) offers necessary further detail. It should be noted that, while Murshid's biography is very nearly definitive, it is still sometimes helpful to consult Madhusudan's 'primary' biographers, Basu (1893) and Som (1916) who, in certain respects, go into greater detail.

[2] For the dates and details of his conversion, see Murshid (2003) 48.

[3] The long-held view that Madhusudan took the Christian name Michael upon conversion to Christianity in 1843 is mistaken (*pace* Radice (2010)): see Seely (2004) 20f. for the definitive demonstration of this error. For the evidence relied on by Seely in this connection, see Murshid (1995; 1997) 66, 88 and 102. I am grateful to Professor Seely and Dr. Radice for drawing my attention to this controversial issue.

[4] Madhsuduan's answer script to a New Testament examination, written on 9 June 1847 at Bishop's College, Calcutta soon before he moved to Madras, bears the name (apparently written in Prof. Rev. Street's hand) 'Modhoo Soodden Dutt', and is signed (in the student's own hand) with 'M. Dutt'. This evidence corroborates, in my view conclusively, the view expounded by Seely (2004) 20f. that Madhusudan did not take the Christian name Michael until after his departure from Bishop's College in 1847 (i.e. not upon converting to Christianity in 1843). Professor Seely has kindly drawn my attention to the first hard evidence of Madhusudan's use of the Christian name Michael in the 'Arrivals and Departures' section of the Madras *Athenaeum* on 18 January 1848 (where he is announced as 'M. M. Dutt of Bishop's College'), a source referred to in the original Bengali version of Murshid's biography (1995; 1997). See Appendix 1 below for transcripts of the question paper and Madhusudan's answer script (see USPG Archive, housed in the Bodleian Library of Commonwealth and

Figure 1.1. Photograph of Madhusudan.

The family moved to Calcutta in 1833–4, where Madhusudan was educated in various institutions. In particular, as will be seen in Section 3 below, his education at Hindu College and Bishop's College in Calcutta would lay the intellectual and cultural foundations for his later literary career. Hindu College, which provided young Bengali Hindus with a British-style education, was a hotbed of radical ideas which gave rise to Young Bengal, a movement of young Hindu gentlemen, primarily students of Hindu College, which was characterized by the adoption of Western habits and attitudes, a nascent patriotism for 'India' as a nation, and the application of Enlightenment scepticism to Hindu religious orthodoxy. Despite his later parodying of the worst excesses of Young Bengal in his famous farce, *Ekei ki bale sabhyatā?* ('Is This What You Call Civilization?') (1860), Madhusudan was very

African Studies at Rhodes House, Oxford, C.Ind.I(6)32 and C.Ind.I(6)32G respectively). For further documents in the USPG archive relevant to Madhusudan's studies there, see especially C.Ind.I.12.111, C.Ind.I.13.134, and C.Ind.I.13.140.

Figure 1.2. Madhusudan's tomb.

much a part of this movement (arguably its apogee),[5] and his later literary and cultural iconoclasm had its genesis in his time at Hindu College.

Madhusudan led an extraordinary life even by the extraordinary standards of nineteenth-century Calcutta. He achieved enduring fame as a poet and playwright composing in the Bengali language (from the late 1850s onwards), having previously written poetry in English, though with only limited success.[6] Before this, however, he worked in Madras (as a schoolteacher and as a newspaper editor), having moved to that city from Calcutta for complex personal reasons. Here, he married Rebecca McTavish, one of his students at the Asylum and a white woman of Scottish extraction,[7] with whom he fathered four

[5] See Section 2 below for further examination of the phenomenon of Young Bengal and Madhusudan's relationship to it.

[6] For a good recent treatment of some of his early English works, see R. Chaudhuri (2002).

[7] She was in fact a 'Eurasian' (partly of Indian extraction): see Murshid (2003) 78ff.

children while still in Madras.[8] In the end, he abandoned his wife and their children when he began an affair with Henrietta White, another white woman, who thereafter lived with him as his mistress and with whom he raised three further children.[9] Upon returning to Calcutta in the late 1850s he turned his efforts towards composing literary works in Bengali rather than in English, and it was during this brief period (1859–62) that he produced most of his Bengali poems and plays. His Bengali oeuvre as a whole, and his masterpiece, the epic *Meghnādbadh kābya* (1861), in particular, are considered to mark the beginning of the 'modern'[10] period of Bengali literature and, given Bengal's cultural leadership within the subcontinent at the time, of Indian literature generally.

In June 1862, Madhusudan left Calcutta for London, thus fulfilling a lifelong ambition to travel to England, and there he trained to become a barrister, finally being called to the Bar by Gray's Inn on 17 November 1866.[11] This journey to Europe interrupted his literary career and was ill-fated in various ways, though some minor works and most of his highly accomplished sonnets were composed during this time abroad. Upon his return to Calcutta on 20 February 1867,[12] Madhusudan would not rekindle the great literary success he achieved in the early 1860s. Although he trained for the Bar in London, he in fact moved his family to Versailles—largely for financial reasons but perhaps in part to escape the racial taunts meted out to them in London[13]—and added to his already formidable stock of languages. In France, he learned to speak French (all his children by Henrietta were raised to be fluent in the language) and German, and improved his Italian. Before leaving India, Madhusudan had already learnt English, Bengali, Italian, Latin, Greek, Sanskrit, Hebrew,

[8] Such marriages (between Indian men and white women) were very rare, and the parties to them were, as Madhusudan discovered (see Murshid (2003) 208), socially stigmatized by the white community. His children by Rebecca were called Bertha, Phoebe, George, and Michael: see Murshid (2003) 107.

[9] See Murshid (2003) 160, 168, 183f.

[10] See, for example, Seely (2004) 3.

[11] Murshid (2003) 183.

[12] Murshid (2003) 187.

[13] It is unclear whether the difference in culture between London and Paris was merely perceived rather than real, but it is interesting to note that, writing to his friend Gour from Versailles, and contrasting the attitudes prevalent in London and Paris, Madhusudan remarked of Parisian culture that: 'Every one, whether high or low, will treat you as a man and not a "damned nigger"'. see Murshid (2004) 223.

Telegu, and Persian. During this time in Versailles he also developed a distinct sympathy for French culture: he began to write a series of fable poems in Bengali inspired by La Fontaine, and quite remarkably he even gave his son, who was born in France, the Christian name 'Napoleon'.

Madhusudan returned to Calcutta after being called to the Bar, and set up his legal practice there in a room at Spence's Hotel. However, his legal career was only a limited success. His financial extravagance, which had always been marked, took a disastrous turn. He and Henrietta, who had both developed a morbid drinking habit whilst living in France,[14] contracted consumption and died within days of each other in 1873.[15] For a recent picture of Madhusudan's tomb, located in the Park Street cemetery in Calcutta, see Figure 1. 2. above.

Madhusudan is best known in Bengal, and in India more generally, for the Bengali poems and plays he produced during a remarkably productive period between 1859 and 1862, after his return to Calcutta from Madras (1856) and before his departure for Europe (1862). Of all his Bengali works, he is best known for his epic masterpiece, the *Meghnādbadh kābya* (1861).[16] However, his first published work in Bengali was the play, the *Śarmiṣṭhā nāṭak* (1859), which was also the first of his Bengali *nāṭak* or dramas.[17] *Ekei ki bale sabhyatā?* ('Is This What You Call Civilisation?') and *Buṙo sāliker ghāre roṃ* ('New Feathers on the Old Bird') (1860), his only two *prahasan* or farces, were the next works. Shortly thereafter he published the *Padmābatī nāṭak* (1860), his second Bengali drama, which begins with an

[14] Both drank alcohol regularly before their sojourn in Europe, but it seems to have been the stresses of life in Europe that drove them to alcoholism: see Murshid (2003) 194.

[15] For a much fuller account of Madhusudan's extraordinary life than can be conveyed here, see Murshid (2003).

[16] Throughout this book I refer to the *Meghnādbadh kābya* (*MBK*), as critically edited by Sanyal (1917), reprinted in the edition of Majumdar (2004). For English translations of this work, see Seely (2004) and Radice (2010).

[17] He also published his own English translation of this work (1859). Note that the first work he published after arriving back in Calcutta in 1856 was, in fact, his English translation of the Bengali drama *Ratnābalī* (1858): see Murshid (2004) 314. For all Madhusudan's Bengali works (save the *MBK* (see n.16 above)) the edition I refer to throughout this book is Bandyopadhyay (1945–51). From time to time, I also refer to the editions of Patra (1989), (2004), and (2005), which contain some useful commentary. There are no readily available English translations of any of Madhusudan's Bengali works (save the *Śarmiṣṭhā nāṭak*, which the playwright himself translated and the *MBK*).

Indianization of the Judgement of Paris, and which will be the focus of Chapter 2 below. Next came the *Tilottamā-sambhab kābya* (1860), an epyllion, that is to say, a relatively short epic narrative poem, in four *sarga* (or cantos), and the first Bengali work to be composed entirely in blank verse. It was, therefore, after the production of a number of Bengali works that Madhusudan composed and published his masterpiece, also in blank verse, the *Meghnādbadh kābya* (1861), an epic in nine cantos, and the subject of Chapter 3 below. The end of his most productive period of literary composition was marked by three works: the *Kṛṣṇakumārī nāṭak* (1861), his first of two tragic dramas; the *Brajāṅganā kābya* (1861), a collection of odes, devotional hymns celebrating the god Kṛṣṇa and his consort Rādhā; and the *Bīrāṅganā kābya* (1862), a collection of epistolary poems written by Hindu heroines to their heroic husbands and lovers, the subject of Chapter 5 below. In addition to these works, Madhusudan went on to publish the *Caturdaśpadī kabitābalī* (1866), a collection of 102 Bengali sonnets (the first sonnets composed in the Bengali language), written over an extended period (before and during his time in Europe). Finally, he published the *Hekṭor-badh*, 'The Slaying of Hector' (1871), a Bengali prose 'version' of *Iliad* 1–12, and the subject of Chapter 6 below. One last play, the tragedy *Māẏākānan* (1874), was published posthumously. In addition to the above, Madhusudan also composed various minor and occasional pieces, and many fragments of, and plans for, further Bengali works have also survived: sketches, for example, of additional epistolary poems to be included in a revised edition (never published) of the *Bīrāṅganā kābya*; and a plan for, and fragments of, a national epic to be called the *Siṃhal-bijay kābya*. Madhusudan's Bengali works have, since their first publication, attracted no little scholarly interest in Bengal (as well as a broader cultural interest)[18] and, since the 1960s, a small but significant body of Western scholarship has also emerged treating these works.[19]

[18] Scholarly works of particular importance include Basu (1893), Sanyal (1917), Bhattacharya (1962), and Murshid (1995, 1997 [a revised edition]), an abridged English translation of which was published as Murshid (2003); other works will be consulted in the following chapters, including Majumdar (2004), an excellent collection of Bengali essays and commentaries on the *MBK*. For further Bengali studies of Madhusudan see also, for example, Sen (1959) and Das (1973).

[19] See esp. Clark (1967), Seely (1982), Seely (2004), and Radice (2010).

At this juncture, the reader should note that Madhusudan has generally been poorly served by translations. His masterpiece, the *Meghnādbadh kābya* (1861), is the only exception, with two very good English translations having appeared in the last 10 years.[20] For almost all his other Bengali works, save the *Śarmiṣṭhā nāṭak* (1859), which Madhusudan translated into English himself, there are no English translations at all. This is in itself an unhappy state of affairs but it also poses obvious practical difficulties when it comes to writing about these works for readers who cannot reasonably be assumed to have access to the Bengali originals. Therefore, I have included in appendices at the end of this book various synopses and my own translations from passages of the Bengali works and, in the course of the following chapters, I have translated every Bengali citation into English for the reader's benefit. Full translations into English of his entire oeuvre, the inclusion of which in this volume would have made it impractical and unwieldy, would represent a very desirable contribution to the field.

Although Madhusudan is best known for these Bengali works, he also wrote a number of works in English earlier in his life.[21] He began composing English verse around 1841 during his time at Hindu College (1837–43), and continued to harbour ambitions for his English poetry until 1849, when he published 'The Captive Ladie', which met with acclaim in Madras but not in Calcutta. His English *juvenilia*, the poems he wrote whilst at Hindu College, are of mixed quality and are little studied. Many of them follow quite clearly in the traditions of the English verse of Henry Louis Vivian Derozio, the Anglo-Indian poet and pedagogue, and are thus marked, above all, by the influence of English Romantic poetry and the British Orientalist tradition.[22]

Two of the earliest of these English poems, both composed in 1841, amply demonstrate the poet's early aspirations towards Western culture, first inculcated in him by his education at Hindu College (see Section 3 below), and indicate the kind of hybridity of cultural identity which would underpin his self-image throughout his life. One of

[20] See Seely (2004) and Radice (2010).

[21] For an analysis of these English poems in the context of emergent Indian nationalism and the discourse of Orientalist scholarship, see R. Chaudhuri (2002).

[22] These poems are thus of some significance regarding the reception of English education by Indian students and the emergence of Indian identity through the medium of English poetry, see R. Chaudhuri (2002).

these, a short poem beginning 'I sigh for Albion's distant shore', and ending 'I sigh for Albion's strand/ As if she were my native land!', attests to an early desire to travel to Europe and to a love of English culture. Of a piece with this poem is another, 'My fond sweet blue-eyed maid', a love poem fantasizing about an imaginary European girl: 'Though in a distant clime I roam,/ By fate exiled from thee . . .' In the event, Madhusudan would indeed travel to Europe (a time, by and large, of bitter disappointment and suffering), and would marry a woman of European extraction and then take another as his mistress, remaining with the second up until her death just days before his own. These two early poems attest amply to a profound sense of exile-at-home, a kind of cultural displacement which would condition much of Madhusudan's life and literary oeuvre.[23] Moreover, while other aspects of his love for the West were eroded by hard experience, such as the racial abuse he and his family suffered during their time in London, his respect for the cultural riches of the West, and indeed his love for Henrietta, seem to have endured until the very end of his life.[24]

The reasons for Madhusudan's turn away from English and to Bengali as the medium for his literary endeavour are instructive for an interpretation of his oeuvre. If any one event precipitated Madhusudan's turn to the Indian vernacular, it seems to have been the advice of J.E.D. Bethune, the famous British civil servant and Anglicist.[25] Bethune had been sent a copy of Madhusudan's English poem, *The Captive Ladie* (1849), composed by the poet while he lived in Madras. Although Bethune did not bother to read the work, which is by some way the most sophisticated of his extant English poems, nonetheless he felt qualified to advise Madhusudan in the following terms (this seems to have been his stock response to all native Indian poets with literary aspirations):

[23] This kind of displacement, whereby the colonial subject feels 'exiled even when one is at home', is a phenomenon frequently observed by postcolonial critics: see, for example, Huddart (2007) 31. See also Boehmer (1995) 8.

[24] The dedicatory letter written to the dedicatee of the *Hekṭor-badh* (1871), the Bengali prose version of *Iliad* 1–12, composed after the poet's return from Europe and examined in Chapter 6 below, attests to this enduring love of Western, especially Graeco-Roman, culture.

[25] For the crucial distinction between Anglicist and Orientalist ideologies and policies in the British administration of India, see Section 2 below.

he could render far greater service to his country and have better chance of achieving a lasting reputation for himself, if he will employ the taste and talents, which he has cultivated by the study of English, in improving the standard and adding to the stock of the poems of his own language . . .[26]

Soon after Madhusudan received this advice, he began to turn to the cultivation of Bengali as a literary language, and it was later that year, on 18 August 1849, that the poet wrote to a friend: 'Am I not preparing for the great object of embellishing the tongue of my fathers?'[27] Madhusudan's turn to Bengali no doubt had a more complex genesis than the remarks of one civil servant, however important he may have been. Indeed, in a sonnet composed much later in his literary career, Madhusudan would re-imagine this turn to Bengali in exclusively Indian terms, specifically as his response to the call of Lakṣmī herself (patron goddess of the Bengali language),[28] an image more in keeping with the rhetoric of the emerging nationalism of the time. However, one should keep in view the surprising fact, elided by this sonnet, namely that the Anglicist advice of a British civil servant seems to have been at least one trigger for Madhusudan's embrace of the Bengali language.[29]

2. HISTORICAL AND CULTURAL CONTEXT

Before other issues can be considered in any depth, various historical and cultural contexts need first to be introduced, since many of them are likely to be unfamiliar to the Western reader. The close readings of Madhusudan's oeuvre in Chapters 2–6 below presuppose a certain level of knowledge of the following topics, and they are essential for understanding the texts under analysis.

[26] Cited by Murshid (2003) 89.

[27] Murshid (2004) 78.

[28] The first version of this sonnet, titled *kabi-mātṛbhāṣā* ('the poet's mother tongue'), appears in a letter to Madhusudan's friend, Rajnarain, dated September 1860 (see Murshid (2004) 152) but it was later included, in a slightly different form, in his collection of 102 sonnets published in 1866. See A. Chaudhuri (2008) 39–56 for an analysis of the sonnet in terms of the poet's turn to the Bengali language.

[29] Indeed, see R.Chaudhuri (2002) for Madhusudan's combination of both Anglicist and Orientalist ideas in his literary works.

It should be noted that the flowering of culture and the arts in the long nineteenth century is often referred to as the Bengal Renaissance, a rather infelicitous and misleading phrase.[30] I am of the view that this label is better avoided and I do not use it myself. If a label must be applied to the phenomenon, then *nabo-jāgaraṇ* ('new awakening'),[31] endorsed by Tapan Raychaudhuri,[32] is certainly better, though even this imports various unfortunate ideas. In any event, the reader should note that the aspects of social and cultural change discussed in this section are often considered as influences on, or aspects of, the so-called Bengal Renaissance.

When his parents brought Madhusudan from the Bengali countryside to Calcutta in 1833/4 as a young child, the city had already been transformed by the British colonial presence in various political, cultural, and social respects. As Kaviraj has observed, Calcutta had long been established as the first city of British India and as the centre of British trade on the subcontinent. From 1764, when Britain's East India Company had defeated Mir Kasim, the *Nawab* of Bengal,[33] Britain's political and military dominance in the region had grown from strength to strength. Before this British victory, the region had been wracked by tensions between the various competing colonial and indigenous powers. In this context, the East India Company's emergence as Bengal's dominant political and military power was initially welcomed by the Bengali elite, and relations between the Company and the indigenous population remained relatively cordial for some decades. Indeed, Calcutta enjoyed a privileged position within the political and cultural order of British India throughout the nineteenth century, with Britain co-opting English-educated Bengalis to serve in its administration in other parts of the subcontinent. This abiding state of affairs goes some way towards explaining why, for example, the news of the Sepoy Uprising (or Indian Mutiny) of 1857–8 was received with little enthusiasm by the Bengali elite.[34] This indigenous elite, known

[30] For the genesis of the concept of the Bengal Renaissance, see Sarkar (1946).

[31] See, for example, Gupta (1959).

[32] See Raychaudhuri (1988).

[33] This victory marked a watershed in the British ascendancy within the region: see Kaviraj (2003) 532.

[34] See, for example, the analysis of Pal (1932) iii. This contradicts the popular opinion that all Indians welcomed the Sepoy Uprising. It certainly became a source of inspiration to twentieth-century Indian nationalism but it is anachronistic to think that the Bengali elite welcomed it at the time. While Bengali 'nationalism' emerged

in Bengali as the *bhadralok* (or 'gentlefolk'), had a vested interest in the preservation of the political status quo,[35] and only began to resist it in any coherent way from the 1870s onwards.

In its early stages, the Company's administration of Bengal was predicated on cooperation and diplomacy rather than coercion and force. The good will of the Bengali *bhadralok* was essential to the stability of British control in the region. Various British scholar-administrators of the late eighteenth century, known collectively as the 'Orientalists',[36] most famously Sir William Jones (or 'Oriental Jones'), made strenuous and sympathetic efforts to study indigenous Indian languages and cultures.[37] They edited, printed, and translated various works of Sanskrit literature. Jones' scholarly journal *Asiatick Researches* (first volume 1788), with its focus on Indian culture and antiquity, was part of a broader British attempt to reconstruct and distil an idea of an authentic (that is, pre-Mughal and therefore pre-Muslim) Hindu culture.[38] The most famous result of this period of Orientalist scholarship is Jones' proposal of Sanskrit's linguistic kinship with Greek and Latin, the theory marking the beginning of Indo-European comparative philology.[39]

Sir William Jones considered the kinship between the Graeco-Roman and the Hindu worlds to be linguistic, but also cultural and intellectual. In his famous discourse, delivered in 1786 on the third anniversary of the establishment of his *Asiatick Society* in Calcutta, Jones expressed the view that:

gradually during the course of the mid- to late nineteenth century, the idea of an India independent of British rule did not emerge in the political consciousness of Bengal until much later, certainly not before 1875: see R. Chaudhuri (2008) 128ff.

[35] For broad treatments of Calcutta's growth as a city and of the Bengali elite in the early stages of the British period, see Sinha (1978) and Mukherjee (1977).

[36] 'Orientalist' in this sense is not to be confused with Said's use of the term, though it is hard to use it today without Saidian connotations: see R. Chaudhuri (2002) 2, n. 2. In the course of this book I use the term 'Orientalist' in its pre-Saidian sense except where stated otherwise.

[37] For the role of early British 'Orientalism' in the broader attempts made by the colonial power to understand indigenous Indian systems of knowledge and information, see Bayly (1996).

[38] See Kejariwal (1988).

[39] It is crucial to note that Jones and the other early British Orientalists looked for and discovered kinship between Indian and European cultures, a fact which challenges Saidian arguments that these scholar-administrators conspired in a project to classify the 'Oriental' as 'Other': see Kejariwal (1988) ix–xi, 221–33. For broader criticism of Said's position see, *inter alia*, Irwin (2003).

> ...we now live among the adorers of those very deities, who were worshipped under different names in Old Greece and Italy, and among the professors of those philosophical tenets, which the Ionic and Attic writers illustrated with all the beauties of their melodious language.

With a Romantic's fascination with origins, Jones discerned aspects of contemporary Hindu culture and religion that he identified with features of Roman and especially Greek antiquity. For Jones, Calcutta was, in a sense, a second Athens. Given that Britain's former American colonies, lost just ten years before this speech was made, imagined their new Republican identity in Roman terms,[40] it is interesting that Jones identified Britain's recently secured Indian colony particularly with the Hellenic world. Scholars have argued that the adoption of Roman models by the new Republics of the USA and France was a key trigger for Britain's abandonment of its Augustan predilection for Rome and for the turn towards a Hellenism that would dominate nineteenth-century British taste.[41] The shift in the British Empire's centre of gravity in the late eighteenth century from America to India was, so to speak, a shift from Rome to Greece.

This late-eighteenth-century phase of British engagement with Indian culture had an enduring status in the imagination of the indigenous Hindu elite in Bengal.[42] The nostalgia for early British Orientalism among Bengalis in the nineteenth century indicates that this had been a high point of the British involvement in India, at least from the point of view of British relations with the Hindu community, and that British policies in the nineteenth century had tended in the direction of an increasing disengagement from indigenous Indian culture (both Hindu and Muslim).[43] Rosinka Chaudhuri has shown that nineteenth-century Bengali poetry in English, starting with Henry Louis Vivian Derozio, the Anglo-Indian poet of Portuguese extraction, reprised themes from Jones' scholarship and poetry in its patriotic treatment of Indian culture.[44] Indeed, Madhusudan's early

[40] See Stray (1998) 12ff., Richard (1994) and (2009), and Winterer (2002). For explicit notions of the United States as the New Rome in the late nineteenth century, see esp. Malamud (2010).

[41] See Stray (1998) 12ff.; also Jenkyns (1980), Turner (1981) and (1989).

[42] See R. Chaudhuri (2002).

[43] See Bayly (1996).

[44] Note that the recent researches of historians including Bayly (1996), Trautmann (1997), and Irschick (1994) have emphasized what Irschick has called the 'dialogic' and 'heteroglot' nature of the interaction between colonized and colonizer in the first

English poems also showed this keen interest in British Orientalist scholarship, references to scholarly articles by Jones and other Orientalists appearing in the poet's own footnotes to his poetry, and in his later Bengali works Orientalist Indo-European scholarship would serve as a key cultural filter through which the poet read Graeco-Roman and indeed Sanskrit literature. The Bengali poet's favourite Sanskrit works were more or less coextensive with those which most appealed to the early British Orientalists.

The late eighteenth century was the heyday of British Orientalists like Jones but the nadir of the British missionary's success in Bengal. It is a surprising fact that, at this time, British missionaries had to work in the Danish colony of Serampore (near Calcutta) since missionary activity had been forbidden by the East India Company and would continue to be so until 1813.[45] The Company's 1698 Charter had permitted missionary work but, especially after the Battle of Plassey in 1757, the Company came to see evangelism as apt to upset the delicate understanding that had been established between the British and the indigenous elite.[46] Missionary activity was thus forbidden on the basis that attempts to interfere with native culture and beliefs were likely (at best) to discomfit the Hindu elite whose support underpinned the Company's business interests in the region.

When the Company's Charter came up for renewal in 1792/3 there was a move by evangelical elements in the Company and Parliament, instigated by the 'philanthropist' Charles Grant, to amend the Charter to permit missionary work in British India and to provide funds for the establishment there of schools offering a Western-style education.[47] In the event, this move was, at least for the time being, unsuccessful: the Company held out against parliamentary pressure and, on 7 September 1808, it even issued a despatch declaring strict religious neutrality and refusing to lend authority to

phase of British imperialism in India. Such approaches, which challenge extreme versions of the postcolonial position, are beginning to be manifested in the works of literary historians as well: see R. Chaudhuri (2002) esp. 32. For a fuller exposition of my own methodological position, see Section 4 below.

[45] For an overview of Company policy regarding missionary activity and Indian education, see Ballhatchet (1965) 565-9; for an overview from a postcolonial perspective, see Vishwanathan (1990); for the most useful primary sources, see Sharp (1920) and Richey (1922).

[46] Sharp (1920) 4.

[47] Sharp (1920) 16ff.

any attempt to propagate the Christian religion.[48] But in 1813 the Charter came up for renewal once more and this time the evangelical element was successful. The East India Company Act of 1813 lifted the prohibition on missionary activity in British India and provided for the funding of educational institutions. The business-minded British authorities, still anxious that imposing Western culture on the indigenous population could upset the very community on whose good will their business interests depended, began by setting up institutions to instruct Hindus in Sanskrit and Muslims in Arabic and Persian.[49] At the same time institutions offering a Western education were established, not by the Company itself but by private individuals and missionaries, and indeed even by certain members of the Hindu elite.[50] The Hindu College, which Madhusudan would himself attend from 1837 to 1843 (see Section 3 below), was founded in 1817 at the instigation of certain grandees of the conservative Hindu community. The rationale of the Hindu founders of the College turned on a wish to take from Europe 'that which they found good and liked best'.[51] Against Company policy at the time, indeed in the teeth of Chief Justice Edward Hyde East's protestations, the Hindu community resolved to establish a College to give its sons a Western education.[52]

As Irschick (1994) has observed, if the first phase of British colonial involvement in Bengali society had been based on mutual accommodation, then from 1813 onwards British India evolved into a domain of competing alternatives. British missionaries promoted Christianity while the Company continued to foster respect for indigenous religion. Some members of both communities promoted Western modes of learning while others promoted indigenous Indian modes. This was

[48] Decree reprinted in Kaye (1859) 513.

[49] Sharp (1920) 16ff.

[50] It is notable that enthusiasm for Western education was weaker among the Muslim population, whose elite members were in any case much fewer in number. Notable exceptions include Nawab Abdul Latif (1828–93), a friend of Madhusudan (see Murshid (2004) 71, n. 6) and one of the early Bengali Muslims to be educated in the 'English' fashion, who founded in 1862 the Mahommedan Literary Society which played a significant role, amongst other things, in promoting English education among Bengali Muslims.

[51] See A. Chaudhuri (2008) 73f. and 106f.

[52] A fact, as is noted by R. Chaudhuri (2002) 11, which the influential essay by Bhabha (1994) 145ff. altogether omits to consider in his account of early-nineteenth-century 'psychodynamic resistance' to Western culture.

the period of Raja Rammohun Roy, the formidable polyglot theologian who founded the Hindu reformist Brahmo Samaj movement (and was perhaps the first Bengali to have learnt ancient Greek). Rammohun tried to bring these competing religious positions together in his Unitarian doctrine, attacking first the position of the Hindu pundits and then that of the Christian missionaries.[53] The equal footing on which Rammohun engaged with the British Serampore missionaries (in the course of his pamphlet war with them he even managed to convert one to his own religion) illustrates an important point elided by most postcolonial scholars, namely that indigenous Indian responses to the culture of the British colonial rulers were not limited to silent acts of passive aggression but were capable of an independent and strident engagement.

By the early 1820s, some Company officials and members of Parliament had become frustrated with the Company's policy of promoting and supporting only vernacular education in India, and it was around this time that the famous 'Anglicist'/'Orientalist' controversy emerged. Against the Orientalist position, the ideological legacy of Oriental Jones and the late-eighteenth-century British Orientalists, the Anglicists argued that Britain had a duty to offer Indians the perceived benefits of a Western-style education, and promoted a curriculum based on the study of English language and literature. It is a well-known irony that the systematic study of English literature began in British India several decades before it began in England,[54] the impetus for the early introduction of English literary studies in Indian schools being the Anglicist vision of a Christianized British India. The Anglicist position was given canonical expression in Macaulay's famous 'Minute on Indian Education' (1835), which thereafter formed the basis of the Company's educational policy,[55] in which the Whig politician argued: 'What the Greek and Latin languages were to the contemporaries of More and

[53] For more details see R. Chaudhuri (2002) 14ff.

[54] See Vishwanathan (1990). Note that, even by 1831, at least 3,000 'native' youths were being educated in the English language and 'becoming acquainted with the valuable stores of European literature and science in general'. See the editorial of the *East Indian* (the editor of the journal being Derozio), dated 14 September 1831.

[55] In fact it was specifically Lord Auckland's 'Minute', written in 1839 and broadly endorsing the views of Macaulay which passed into practical policy: see Richey (1922) 1. A despatch of the Company's Court of Directors dated 20 January 1841, made it clear that Company policy would apply the suggestions of Auckland's 'Minute'.

Ascham, our tongue is to the people of India'.[56] William Bentinck's arrival in Calcutta in 1829 as Governor-General of Bengal boosted the Anglicist cause and his policies anticipated the philosophy of Macaulay's 'Minute'. Under Bentinck's administration (1829 to 1835), the Asiatick Society, the material embodiment of the Orientalist vision, was put under severe financial pressure, while the College of Fort William, where much important work had been done in the analysis and propagation of Hindu learning, was disbanded altogether.[57]

Macaulay's highly influential notion of English language and literature as a catalyst for an Indian cultural revolution is precisely why, especially in the context of a discussion of the Graeco-Roman classics in contemporary Bengali culture, the phrase 'Bengal Renaissance' is so infelicitous; and why, if a label must be used, as was argued above, the phrase *nabo-jāgaraṇ* or 'new awakening' is certainly preferable. The kind of Renaissance envisaged by British educational policy, and in some senses carried into effect by it, was of a subsidiary, secondary kind. Whereas a Renaissance in its European sense refers to the rediscovery of Europe's indigenous ancient cultures (and the notional revival of contemporary culture by means of such rediscovery), the so-called Bengal Renaissance refers to the apparent enlivening of Bengali culture through contact with the contemporary culture of a foreign colonial power: a culture neither indigenous nor ancient. Moreover, the cultural artefacts of the Graeco-Roman world, where they were made available to Indians at all, were usually mediated for the contemporary Bengali through the prism of the English language. Madhusudan was unusual for his generation of Bengalis in acquiring unmediated access to Graeco-Roman culture through his knowledge of Latin and Greek.

Postcolonial scholars have caricatured Britain's promotion of English language and literature in the educational domain as a cynical instrument for the oppression of her Indian subjects. Vishwanathan's *Masks of Conquest* (1990), for example, examines and emphasizes the connection between the evangelical movement and the English literary curriculum, focusing on Rev. Alexander Duff's role in pressing English literary studies into the service of evangelism and conversion.

[56] Macaulay (1835), cited in Sharp (1920) 107ff.

[57] See Kopf (1969) 241. At the same time, moreover, the Serampore College 'Anglicized' its curriculum, while the Calcutta School and School Book Societies, Orientalist institutions both, were severely undermined (see Kopf (1969)).

To some extent, the English literary curriculum did indeed serve British colonial purposes: it certainly provided a stratum of Bengali society that the Company could use to assist in the administration of the rest of the subcontinent. However, Vishwanathan's thesis elides crucial details: that, for example, Hindu College, the first and most prestigious institution teaching English language and literature in Calcutta, forbade the promotion of Christianity and excluded any Hindu youths who did convert.[58] Indeed, Madhusudan was expelled from Hindu College for this very reason in 1843.[59] Moreover, the first Principal of the College was the avowed atheist, David Hare.[60]

In 1839 Rev. Alexander Duff remarked of the young Hindus receiving English education at the time:

> Their great authorities ... were Hume's *Essays* and Paine's *Age of Reason*. With copies of the latter, in particular, they were abundantly supplied ... It was some wretched bookseller in the United States of America, – basely taking advantage of the reported infidel leanings of a new race of men in the East, and apparently regarding no God but his silver dollars, – despatched to Calcutta a cargo of that most malignant and pestiferous of all anti-Christian publications ....[61]

This 'new race of men in the East', the recently 'Westernized' Bengali elite, was turning its knowledge of English language and literature to purposes of which British Christians like Duff deeply disapproved.[62] There was a great spectrum of responses to this English education among its Bengali recipients, and even the most ardent Westernizers, such as Madhusudan, in Raychaudhuri's words, 'accepted from that vast storehouse only what appealed to them in the light of their historical experience and cultural preferences.'[63] Indeed, as Raychaudhuri went on to observe, 'at one point, the educational policy makers who introduced "the tyranny of poetry" ... considered

[58] As noted by R. Chaudhuri (2008).

[59] Murshid (2003) 48ff.

[60] See R. Chaudhuri (2008).

[61] Duff (1839) 616.

[62] The thesis of Vishwanathan (1990) is much weakened by her claim that 'it is entirely possible to study the ideology of British education quite independently of an account of how Indians actually received, reacted to, imbibed, manipulated, reinterpreted, or resisted the ideological content of British literary education ...' (Vishwanathan (1990) 11). See, *contra* Vishwanathan (1990), Ahmad (1992) 172, whose point is pressed further by R. Chaudhuri (2002) esp. 9 and 90ff.

[63] Raychaudhuri (2002) 355.

removing English history from the syllabus lest *babus* get ideas unsuitable to their station in life.'[64]

Arguably the most insidious aspect of British educational policy in India was not so much the promotion of English language and literature in itself (Bengalis could and did turn this knowledge to their own ends) but the fact that it went no further than teaching the modern Western vernacular. The educational tool necessary at that time for advancement in almost every elite British profession was a knowledge of Greek and Latin, and this extended to British India too.[65] Most Indian schools omitted this elite and privileged mode of Western learning from their curricula.[66] This omission had a real effect on the professional possibilities open to the Bengali elite. Vasunia has recently shown that successful entry into the Indian Civil Service (ICS) was virtually impossible without an extremely high level of competence in Latin and Greek.[67] As a consequence, it was not until 1864 that a native Indian, the Bengali Satyendranath Tagore, one of Rabindranath's elder brothers, succeeded in winning a place in the colonial bureaucracy that ran his own country.[68] The significance of this success for Bengal was hardly lost on Madhusudan who, himself in Europe at the time, composed a celebratory and patriotic sonnet for Satyendranath Tagore (Sonnet 78) comparing the latter's triumph with Arjuna's successful mission to the city of the gods (ll. 1–5). In this connection, moreover, it is significant that Manomohan Ghosh, who failed in his first attempt at the ICS examination, in fact visited Madhusudan in Versailles for coaching in Latin and Greek.[69] The Bar was similarly off-limits to the native Indian without Western classical languages, these forms of knowledge being

[64] Raychaudhuri (2002) 355.

[65] Thomas Gaisford, the nineteenth-century Dean of Christ Church at Oxford, famously advised the congregation from the pulpit of Christ Church Cathedral that the study of Greek would lead to 'positions of considerable emolument': see Stray (1998) 60.

[66] But not all educational institutions (*contra* Trivedi (2007) 287): it will be shown in Section 3 below that Bishop's College Calcutta, which Madhusudan attended in the 1840s, offered an admirably rigorous classical syllabus.

[67] See Vasunia (2005a) and (2005b). The self-same Macaulay who successfully advocated the Anglicist cause with respect to Indian educational policy, which envisaged no instruction in Latin and Greek, also spoke in 1833 in defence of the emphasis on Greek and Latin in the ICS entrance examinations: see Stray (1998) 53.

[68] See Murshid (2003) 171 and 178.

[69] See Murshid (2003) 171 and 178.

the key to accessing all elite British institutions including the Inns of Court.[70] Indeed, both the achievements for which Madhusudan's life was distinguished—his attempt to 'reform' Bengali literature and his call to the Bar by Gray's Inn—were underpinned, enabled, and shaped by his classical education at Bishop's College.[71]

Indians thus received an education in English rather than an English education. This aided the colonial administration: it provided a sector of Bengali society capable of mediating between the British rulers and the Indian masses.[72] But the withholding of Graeco-Roman knowledge from most Indians effectively imposed a glass ceiling on their career prospects within the British colonial system. This should be borne in mind throughout the following chapters since it gives a powerful socio-political significance to Madhusudan's application of his advanced Western classical education to his Bengali oeuvre.

The educational policies of the British administration were, moreover, the foremost catalyst for cultural, social, and political transformation in Bengali society, though the transformations were not always those envisaged or desired by British policy makers. As was noted above, Bengalis themselves led the way in establishing educational institutions that promoted Western learning. Hindu College, founded in 1817, was one such institution and its effect on the young Hindus who studied there was profoundly transformative.[73] By the 1830s, when Madhusudan enrolled there, the students of Hindu College had become synonymous with a Westernizing reform movement known as the 'Derozians' (named after the charismatic and iconoclastic Anglo-Indian teacher Derozio) or 'Young Bengal' (a term apparently modelled on 'Young Italy' and other contemporary European movements of this kind).[74] Young Bengal stood for the rejection of Hindu

[70] Stray (1998) 60ff.

[71] See Murshid (2004) 121; and see the comments in my Preface, above, for Madhusudan's study in 1860 of Sanskrit, Latin and Greek in preparation for the 'Sudder' law examinations.

[72] This role of 'mediation' between British rulers and Indian masses was in fact explicitly envisaged in Macaulay's famous 'Minute' (1835), reprinted in Sharp (1920) 107ff.

[73] For a treatment of the impact of Hindu College on its students, and on the wider Bengali community, see R. Chaudhuri (2002).

[74] Mazzini founded Young Italy as an Italian patriotic movement in 1831 while in exile in Marseilles; the term 'Young Bengal' probably entered journalistic parlance in the 1830s: see R. Chaudhuri (2008) lix ff.

orthodoxy in favour of an enlightened secularism (not usually in favour of Christianity), for the adoption of Western habits (drinking alcohol, smoking, eating beef), for the celebration of Western culture (especially English literature and moral philosophy), and for social reform (especially regarding women's rights).[75]

Young Bengal came in for some derision from the English community in Calcutta,[76] and no little suspicion from the orthodox Hindu community (the students' parents in many cases). Indeed Madhusudan's Bengali farce, *Ekei ki bale sabhyatā?* ('Is This What You Call Civilization?') (1860), is a light-hearted and bawdy satire parodying the worst excesses of 'Young Bengal', depicting its adherents as Westernized dilettantes rather than ardent social reformers. And yet Madhusudan was very much a part of this movement, arguably its apogee.[77] Indeed the first recorded use of the expression 'Young Bengal' yet found is in a description of Madhusudan himself.[78]

It is important to be clear about precisely what is meant in this context by 'Hindu orthodoxy' (the concept against which Young Bengal defined itself), especially since Madhusudan's own response to, and reactions against it will recur as a theme throughout the following chapters. Hinduism (the English word for the many religions of the 'Hindus', which is itself a term derived from Persian and imposed from the outside)[79] refers to the wide variety of religious beliefs and practices indigenous to the Indian subcontinent (apart

[75] R. Chaudhuri (2008) lix ff. On the focus on women's rights in Bengali social reforms, see Bandyopadhyay (2004) 381, esp. n. 198 for further bibliography.

[76] Henry Meredith Parker, in 'A Bengali Eclogue' (1851), a parodic treatment of two young 'Derozians', implies that the appeal of the West for these young Hindus lay above all in the sensual pleasures it condoned (beef-eating, smoking, drinking): see R. Chaudhuri (2000).

[77] It has been thought that the dissolute and Westernized character Nimchand Datta, the erudite hero of the play *Sadhabar Ekadasi* by Dinabandhu Mitra, in fact stands for Madhusudan; though it was denied by the playwright: see R. Chauduri (2008) lix.

[78] R. Chaudhuri (2008) lx, while arguing that the phrase must have been coined in the 1830s, could not find any attestations of it before 1849. However, I have discovered an attestation two years earlier. On 23 July 1847, Rev. Street, Principal of Bishop's College, wrote of Madhusudan (just after his final examinations): 'He came here with the airs and notions of liberal young Bengal - though not its bad practices . . .' (It is perhaps significant that the word 'bad' is added as an afterthought in superscript.) See Rhodes House Archive, Oxford, C.Ind./I13/134.

[79] See Flood (2003) 3.

from certain discrete religions such as Buddhism, Sikhism and Jainism). These beliefs and practices have changed very much over time and vary greatly from region to region within India. The use of the single term 'Hinduism' to encompass such divergent and distinct concepts is clearly somewhat inadequate.[80] Hinduism as defined above is therefore a hall of mirrors that serves, sometimes confusingly, to signify both the part and the whole: there is Hinduism *qua* Bengali Vaishnavism, which falls within Hinduism *qua* the totality of Bengal's distinct varieties of Hinduism, which in turn falls within a much looser Hinduism in the broad pan-Indian sense described above. It is to be noted, then, that the phrases 'Hinduism' and 'Hindu orthodoxy' in the context of this book connote Hinduism in its regional Bengali sense, with particular reference to the religious cultures of the elite pundits and Hindu reformists of Calcutta.

Hindus today typically worship one or several of the Hindu gods, different sects emphasizing the status of different godheads within the pantheon, or asserting that there is truly only one or more such godheads. They generally locate the genesis of their religious doctrine in the 'god-authored' Sanskrit Scripture of the ancient Veda, also known as *śruti* ('revelation'), and in the later 'man-authored' Sanskrit Scripture known as *smṛti* ('recollection').[81] A part of this 'man-authored' *smṛti* literature comprises the Sanskrit epic tradition, Vālmīki's *Rāmāyaṇa* and Vyāsa's *Mahābhārata*.[82] These two epics, which had their origins in a heroic oral tradition, were overlaid with a later priestly or Brahmanical layer in which the epic heroes were celebrated as avatars of various gods (this is how the texts became 'Scriptural'):[83] most notably Rāma, eponymous hero of the *Rāmāyaṇa*, is thus celebrated as an avatar of the supreme god Viṣṇu. These Sanskrit epics, of which various influential vernacular 'versions' were composed in the mediaeval period (including mediaeval

[80] For a discussion of the historical problem in defining 'Hinduism' see Flood (2003) 2; for the political dimensions involved in the definition of 'Hinduism' see esp. Smith (2000) 741f.

[81] See Flood (2003) 4ff. But note, for example, that there are also non-Brahmanical traditions such as Shaivism which considers the Tantric texts rather than the Veda as their doctrinal starting-point: see Smith (2000) 201ff.

[82] See Brockington (2003). These epics are, however, just part of the long and rich tradition of Sanskrit *purāṇas* ('ancient [stories]'), which continued to be composed until the mediaeval period: see Matchett (2003).

[83] See Smith (1980).

Bengali versions), in fact dominate the popular Hindu conception of Scripture in Bengal as in most regions of India. The status of the Hindu epics as Scripture, and their centrality in popular conceptions of Scripture as such, must be borne in mind when we consider how Madhusudan 'secularized' the Hindu epic tradition by, for example, turning his readers' sympathy (in a consciously Miltonic fashion) against the hero Rāma (whom Hindus hold to be an avatar of the supreme god Viṣṇu).[84]

One ought also to remark on Bengal's particular varieties of Hinduism, which, as in all Indian regions, have their own distinctive aspects. Since the mediaeval period Bengali Hindus have mostly practised Vaishnavism (the *bhakti* or 'devotional worship' of Kṛṣṇa, another avatar of Viṣṇu),[85] and the cult worship of the pan-Hindu goddess Durgā (also known as Debī or Kālī), the Hindu mother goddess and (at the same time) the fierce goddess of destruction.[86] Indeed Calcutta's most sacred Hindu site is the Kalighat or 'pool of Kālī', and its greatest Hindu festival the Durgāpūjā or 'Durgā worship'.[87] In the nineteenth century, as was noted above, Bengali Hinduism was subject to the reforming efforts of the theologian Raja Rammohun Roy, founder of the Brahmo Samaj (or 'Society of Brahma'), which sought to 'reform' Hindu doctrine by reinterpreting Hindu Scripture and by incorporating aspects of Islam and Christianity into this reinterpretation. While the Brahmo Samaj appealed to many Bengali Hindus, above all to those educated in the Western style, traditional Hindu orthodoxy remained the norm at least outside the society of Westernized high-caste Bengalis.

Hindu culture is distinctive not only in its religious aspects but also in its art and, of particular relevance to the themes of this book, in its poetry and poetics. Many of Madhusudan's works represent a response to, and in some respects a reaction against, the Hindu tradition of Sanskrit literary aesthetics. Aside from Hindu Scripture,

[84] Indeed see A. Chaudhuri (2008) 111 for the watershed marked by Madhusudan's oeuvre: this was arguably the first time in Bengali literary history that subject matter of a religious nature (Hindu epic, and so on) was 'transplanted from the domain of religion into the domain of culture'.

[85] For the origins and development of Hindu devotionalism in Bengal, known as the *Gauḍīya Vaiṣṇaba* tradition, see Flood (1996) 138ff.

[86] For the pan-Hindu status of Durgā (contrasted with the regional nature of the *Gauḍīya Vaiṣṇaba* tradition), see Flood (1996) 182ff.

[87] For the rituals and sites of Bengali Goddess-worship, see Kinsley (1998) 106ff.

Sanskrit boasts a highly sophisticated poetic and dramatic tradition originating, apparently, in the centuries before the Common Era.[88] The most celebrated exponent of Sanskrit *kāvya* ('poetry') and *nāṭaka* ('drama') is Kālidāsa, a poet and playwright of the fourth or fifth century CE,[89] best known for his drama *Abhijñānaśakuntalam* and poems such as the *Meghadūtam*.[90] In addition to this canon of Sanskrit poets and playwrights, at the head of which Kālidāsa is generally imagined to stand,[91] there is also a highly sophisticated tradition of Sanskrit poetics and dramaturgy.[92] Sanskrit literary aesthetics is largely phenomenological, focusing on the mechanisms by which a literary text induces its readers or audience to experience certain emotions. In this context the theory of *rasa* (or 'flavour') arose and came to dominate the discourse of Hindu poetics. A *rasa* is defined as a literary quintessence of a 'stable [*viz.* real-life] emotion' (or *sthāyibhāva*), an 'objective correlative' to use the English phrase coined by T.S. Eliot (a concept which may have been informed by Eliot's own Sanskrit readings),[93] which a poet or playwright may embed in his work in order to provoke the correlating 'real-life emotion' in his audience.[94] Thus a poem must notionally display, for example, the *śṛṅgārarasa* ('erotic flavour') if it is to elicit the *bhāva* or 'emotion' of arousal in its reader. This tradition of Sanskrit aesthetics is not descriptive, as Western classical aesthetics usually purports to be,[95] but prescriptive: it codifies, differently according to the

[88] See De (1976) 1ff.

[89] For the scant evidence regarding the dates of Kālidāsa's life, see Vasudeva (2006) 16f.

[90] For the importance of Kālidāsa in the history of Sanskrit poetry and drama see Vasudeva (2006) esp. 15.

[91] See, for example, *Dhvanyāloka* 1.6, an important Sanskrit aesthetics treatise, which states that only five or six Sanskrit poets, headed by Kālidāsa, may be classed as great; see also Vasudeva (2006) 15.

[92] For an introduction to Sanskritic aesthetic theory, see De (1976) esp. 18ff. and Ingalls (1990).

[93] See Eliot (1919). For the thesis (compelling, in my view) that Eliot's notion of the 'objective correlative' was inspired, at least in part, by *rasa* theory, see, for example, Rayan (1965).

[94] Note that there is also the competing theory of *dhvani* or 'vibration' propounded by Ānandavardhana, the mediaeval Kashmiri aesthetician who authored the *Dhvanyāloka* (see Ingalls (1990)); but the theory of *rasa* is the dominant one and the more relevant to the present study.

[95] For a comparison between Western classical aesthetics and the Hindu aesthetic tradition, see Gupt (2006). Note, above all, that whereas Western classical aesthetic theories focus on the relationship between the literary text and the reality it represents

different aestheticians, precisely which verbal and thematic features comprise each *rasa* or 'flavour'; and the success of a Sanskrit work is judged by the criteria laid out in these 'aesthetical treatises' (*alaṅkāraśāstra*).

The Bengali branch of Sanskrit aesthetics, by contrast with other regional branches, and mirroring Bengal's particular branch of Brahmanical Hinduism, developed its own distinct characteristics during the mediaeval period. The inclusion of the *bhaktirasa* or 'flavour of devotion', which Bengali aestheticians placed at the head of all 'flavours',[96] reflects the proliferation of religious devotional poetry in mediaeval Bengal, a phenomenon which itself reflects the turn towards *bhakti* or 'devotional worship' that is distinctive of mediaeval Bengali Vaishnavism (the worship of Krishna (see above)). Indeed, when Madhusudan refers in his correspondence to Sanskrit aesthetics, a discourse which will be of recurring importance in the following chapters, he invariably cites the *Sāhityadarpaṇa* of Viśvanātha, a treatise composed in Sanskrit during the medieval period in the Bengal/Orissa region, rather than earlier (more pan-Indian) treatises of Sanskrit aesthetics.

The authority of the Sanskrit tradition had a marked effect on the development of Bengali as a literary language in the mediaeval period. The Sanskrit for 'vernacular' is *apabhraṃśa* ('falling off', 'departure [from Sanskrit]'), and Sanskrit's sense of its own superiority over the vernacular had an enduring effect on Bengal's cultivation of its own vernacular language.[97] Mediaeval and modern Bengali, like most other North Indian languages, derive principally from Sanskrit rather as the modern Romance languages derive from Latin. When Bengali vernacular literature began to emerge in the Mediaeval period (a tradition which reached its apogee in Vaishnava devotional poetry and the Bengali 'versions' of the *Rāmāyaṇa* and *Mahābhārata*) it was from the outset 'inextricably associated with the universalizing presence of Sanskrit'.[98]

(Plato's *diagesis* (modes of narration) and Aristotle's *mimesis* (modes of representation)), by contrast the Sanskrit tradition is primarily concerned with the phenomenological matter of the audience's response to a literary text. For these Western classical ideas, see esp. Woodruff (1992).

[96] See esp. S. Sen (1971).

[97] S. Sen (1971) 10ff.

[98] Kaviraj (2003) 513.

The Indian vernacular's relationship to its ancient antecedent is rather more problematic than an analogy with the Latin and the Romance languages might imply. Above all, we must note that the basic Sanskritic substrate of the Bengali language was overlaid with Persian (and some Arabic) influences due to lengthy contact with Persian during the centuries of Mughal rule. In addition to this layer of Persian lexical items one might note the later smattering of Portuguese and the proliferation of English words that entered the Bengali language from an early stage of colonial contact. From the late eighteenth century onwards the British began to frame grammatical rules for Bengali, to edit Bengali texts of cultural significance, and they introduced print culture.[99] This process, especially the introduction of print culture,[100] entailed a pressure towards the standardization of literary Bengali. This new 'high Bengali' or *sādhubhāṣā* emerged and displaced, with surprisingly little resistance, the various dialects which had traditionally been used for literary purposes and, broadly speaking, this new standard dialect reflected a mixture of Calcutta speech and the dialect of the Nadīẏa-Śāntipur region of Bengal.[101]

William Carey, the Serampore missionary later employed as a scholar in Fort William, did much to contribute to this process of standardization through his Grammar and Dictionary of the Bengali language. The question of Bengali's twin inheritance of both Persian and Sanskrit lexica complicated the process of standardization. In the first edition of Carey's *A Grammar of the Bengalee Language* (1801) the missionary stated:

> The language in which the classical books of the Hindoos are written is principally derived from the Sangskrito [*viz.* Sanskrit]. This is called pure Bengalee: but multitudes of words, originally Persian or Arabic, are constantly employed in common conversation, which perhaps ought to be considered as enriching rather than corrupting the language.[102]

Carey's identification of the Sanskritic aspects of the vernacular as 'pure Bengalee' no doubt had much to do with the advice of the

[99] For a good overview of this process, see Kaviraj (2003) 533ff. For the transformations entailed by these processes, see Sastri (1956) 171–96, 211–83.

[100] For the limits of the applicability of the notion of 'print capitalism' (see Anderson (1991)) to the Bengali context, see Kaviraj (2003) 533, n. 42.

[101] See Kaviraj (2003) 533, n. 42.

[102] Carey (1801) 1.

Hindu Pundits employed by Carey to assist him in his study of the vernacular language (Sanskrit being the Hindus' sacred language), and with his own study of Sanskrit under these Pundits. In any case, the notion that the Sanskritic elements of the Bengali language were more 'pure' than the Persian elements had an important impact on the standardization of a 'high Bengali' dialect.[103] One of the most significant developments in the process of standardization was the deliberate adoption of a 'modified' Sanskritic version of precolonial Bengali, and the deliberate 'Sanskritization' of the language (including the coining of new Sanskritic terms, rather as Latin and Greek were used to coin new terms in various European vernacular languages during the Renaissance and subsequently).[104] Indeed, efforts were made in some quarters to 'cleanse' the Bengali language altogether of Persian forms.[105] Thus, as the Bengali language became standardized and was adapted to meet the demands of modern culture, it was somewhat paradoxically the ancient Sanskrit language to which Bengalis turned to bolster their vernacular idiom. Furthermore, we should note that, in parallel to this Sanskritization of 'high' Bengali, there was an increasing engagement among certain Bengalis with the English language, and a consequent proliferation of English terms in the Bengali lexicon. Thus, in their efforts to meet the new challenges of a modern India, Bengalis turned above all to English and Sanskrit - of which one was not modern and the other not Indian.[106]

The linguistic relationship between Sanskrit and nineteenth-century 'high' Bengali or *sādhubhāṣā* (which may be identified, more or less, with the language in which Madhusudan composed his literary works)[107] was thus very complex. In addition to such linguistic complexity the authority of the Sanskrit literary tradition continued

[103] For a Marxist analysis of this 'standardization' of an elite dialect see Banerjee (1989) 154f.

[104] For a detailed historical analysis of this process of 'Sanskritization', see Murshid (1992).

[105] For example, the 1838 *phārsik abhidān*, or 'Persian Dictionary', of Jaygopal Taralankar gave Sanskritic alternatives to common Bengali words of Persian origin. For *śaram* (a word of Persian origin meaning 'shame'), for example, the reader is advised to substitute the Sanskritic word *lajjā* ('shame').

[106] An irony noted by Kaviraj (2003) 533.

[107] For Madhusudan's particular innovations in Bengali language and prosody, see esp. Bera (2004).

to exert great influence on Bengali literary culture in the nineteenth century.

Madhusudan himself complained of the Hindu Pundits, who initially criticized his experimental and 'Westernizing' poetry, that 'as for the old school, nothing is poetry to them which is not an echo of Sanscrit . . .'[108] Of the *Meghnādbadh kābya* (1861), Madhusudan's celebrated epic and masterpiece, the poet said to his friend: 'Do not be frightened, my dear fellow, I don't trouble my readers with vira ras [*vīrarasa*, "the heroic flavour"] . . .'[109] Madhusudan's Bengali oeuvre represents a reaction against (but not an unqualified rejection of) this Sanskritic tradition of literary aesthetics. The poet's resistance to indigenous Indian forms of cultural authority represents a crucial respect in which Madhusudan's oeuvre may stand as a corrective to the postcolonial fixation on Indian resistance to Western colonial authority.

However, the Bengali author's cultivation of the vernacular language was only anti-Sanskritic to a certain extent. His early Bengali plays, the *Śarmiṣṭhā nāṭak* (1859) and the *Padmābatī nāṭak* (1860), are self-consciously modelled in formal terms on the Sanskritic paradigm. The crucial observation to make is that Madhusudan's Bengali oeuvre stood as a reaction not only against Hindu orthodoxy but also against popular Bengali literature: in the prefatory poem of the *Śarmiṣṭhā nāṭak* the playwright laments what he calls Bengal's *alik kunāṭyo* or 'false, bad theatre'.[110] In the service of 'reforming'[111] Bengali literature Madhusudan took what he deemed best from the Sanskrit tradition (a reaction against popular culture) while importing a variety of forms and concepts from Western literary culture (a reaction against Hindu orthodoxy).

As a final note on the Sanskrit literary tradition, one should emphasize the importance of the early British Orientalist interest in Sanskrit literature for the development of Bengali cultural self-consciousness.[112] Hindu mythology, as embodied in Sanskrit Scripture and non-liturgical literature (like poetry and drama), was and indeed

[108] Murshid (2004) 179. [109] Murshid (2004) 118.

[110] For recent Marxist criticism of *bhadralok* artists like Madhusudan as having suffered from an 'alienation from the masses', see Banerjee (1989) esp. 14.

[111] Madhusudan's expression: see Murshid (2004) esp. 118.

[112] For the influence of the early Orientalists on nineteenth-century Bengali poetry in English, see R. Chaudhuri (2002).

remains an integral part of a living religion (unlike the dead but reclaimed mythologies of Greece and Rome in the West). The British Orientalists, by comparing Hindu mythology and theology with those of Greece and Rome, indicated a new way of reading Sanskrit poetry and epic, not as a part of the living Hindu religion but as texts of secular interest. One scholar has recently argued that the Graeco-Roman classics were never taught in British India because the Hindus already had their own 'classics' in the form of the Sanskrit canon.[113] The analysis in Section 3 below of Madhusudan's rigorous classical education at Bishop's College will disprove the first half of this thesis (the Graeco-Roman classics were indeed sometimes taught in British India). Moreover, the other half of the thesis is also somewhat misconceived: Sanskrit literature did not represent a Hindu 'classical' inheritance in the Western sense of the term. It was not until the publication of Madhusudan's Bengali oeuvre that the Sanskrit tradition would be, to use Amit Chaudhuri's phrase, 'transplanted from the domain of religion into the domain of culture',[114] an act prefigured by the Orientalist discourse but executed by Madhusudan in his vernacular poetry and plays. Definitionally, the term 'classics' denotes a cultural rather than a religious artefact. Inasmuch as the Sanskrit corpus includes a great deal of what might more properly be described as Scripture, it is not strictly appropriate or realistic to talk of that corpus as 'classical'.

A further contextual issue necessary for a proper appreciation of Madhusudan's oeuvre concerns the emergence in mid-nineteenth-century Bengal of the nationalist discourse. Again it was Young Bengal, the Hindu reform movement considered above, that first promoted patriotism for India as a country. Indeed, one may observe the genesis of this patriotism in the English poetry of Derozio himself (the inspiration for the Young Bengal movement), who was the first to celebrate India[115] in patriotic terms (and with recourse, interestingly, to tropes borrowed from British Orientalists like Sir William Jones).[116] The patriotism of Young Bengal was thus in some ways a

[113] Trivedi (2007).

[114] As noted by A. Chaudhuri (2008) 111.

[115] Note that early Indian 'patriots' like the Anglo-Indian Derozio referred their patriotism to 'India' rather than to Bengal specifically: see R. Chaudhuri (2002) 109ff.

[116] R. Chaudhuri (2002) 109ff.

necessary condition for, or at least a precursor to, the Indian nationalism which would begin to emerge from the 1860s onwards.

It is worth recalling at this juncture an observation set out above, that from the late eighteenth century onwards the Presidency of Bengal, with Calcutta as its administrative centre, served as the centre for British involvement in India as a whole. As a consequence of Calcutta's primacy within British India, the Bengali *bhadralok*, or 'gentlefolk', gained a privileged position not only within Bengal but also within British India generally.[117] Of all Indian elites it was the Bengali *bhadralok* who were most radically 'Westernized' by British educational policy; this enabled them to serve in other regions of India as mediators between the British administration and its Indian subjects (whether as clerks, administrators, journalists or schoolteachers—recall Madhusudan's work in the Presidency of Madras in the 1850s). And yet Britain's co-option of the Bengali elite as a proxy for itself in other parts of India had unforeseen consequences. Just as early Indian patriots like Derozio referred their patriotism to the notion of 'India' (rather than the narrower idea of Bengal), so too the early Bengali nationalists referred their nationalism to the broad idea of 'India'.[118] The fact that Bengalis felt, perhaps rather paternalistically, that they could speak on behalf of India as a whole had much to do with Britain's historical use of a Bengali elite in its administration of the rest of the subcontinent.

There were various subtle but distinct ideological shifts between the sort of patriotism espoused by Young Bengal (an attitude which also embraced Western values and rejected Hindu orthodoxy) and the fully-fledged nationalism which would not only celebrate India's nationhood but imagine and argue for an India independent of foreign rule and reject all things Western.[119] The shifts were gradual

[117] Emphasized by Vishwanathan (1990); see Banerjee (1989) for a treatment of the elite status of the Westernized *bhadralok* within Bengali society.

[118] The concept of 'India' (or *Bhārata*) had long existed in the discourses of Sanskrit literature as a unified and cosmopolitan cultural space (subject to regional variation) stretching the length and breadth of the Indian subcontinent: see Pollock (2003) 105, esp. n. 143. However, the concept of 'Indianness' in the sense of a unified political and ethnic identity, eliding discrete creeds and regional differences, was a nineteenth-century invention. For an exploration of the invention of 'Indianness' in this sense, see A. Chaudhuri (2008) 105ff.

[119] For the emergence of nationalist thought in colonial Bengal see P. Chatterjee (1993); for its link with literary culture see esp. R. Chaudhuri (2002) and Bhatia (2004).

and Madhusudan's Bengali oeuvre (composed from the late 1850s onwards) was produced at a particular stage within this process of evolution.

By the late 1850s, Bengalis had begun to feel 'abandoned' by the British community. Girish Chundra Ghosh, the contemporary Bengali playwright, wrote in 1862:

> As regards Indian literature . . . history, antiquities, the present race of Anglo-Indians [British residents in India] . . . are lamentably ignorant . . . Jones, Colebrooke, Wilson . . . respected our fathers and looked upon us hopefully at least with melancholy interest, as you would look on the heir of a ruined noble. But to the great unwashed abroad today, we are simply niggers – without a past; perhaps, without a future. They do not choose to know us.[120]

By the late 1850s, the British had lost that 'patrimonial' and 'affective'[121] knowledge of India which they had enjoyed before (and which had reached its zenith in the Orientalist scholarship of the late eighteenth and early nineteenth centuries). It was this underlying withdrawal of the British from Indian society that sowed the seeds of Bengali resentment against Britain, and thus the emergence of Indian nationalism in Bengal. It should be noted, furthermore, that this withdrawal was accompanied and exacerbated by the flourishing both in Europe and among the British in India of so-called 'racial science', the dogmatic classification of different races whereby the European was deemed to be biologically and culturally superior to all other races: ' . . . to the great unwashed abroad today, we are simply niggers'.[122] Previously, beginning with the discoveries of Sir William Jones in the late eighteenth century, there had been a pervading belief in a necessary connection between language and race, the corollary of which was that the status of Sanskrit as a linguistic cognate with Latin and Greek (among other European and non-European languages) necessarily entailed an ethnic kinship, a shared Indo-European or Aryan identity between the Indian and the European. This linkage, referred to pejoratively by European opponents of it as the 'tyranny of

[120] Cited by R. Chaudhuri (2002) 149.

[121] See Bayly (1996). This shift in behaviour and attitude seems to be why, by the mid-nineteenth century, the early British Orientalists of the late eighteenth and early nineteenth centuries had acquired a 'mythical' aspect in the minds of the Bengal elite: see R. Chaudhuri (2002) 148f.

[122] Cited by R. Chaudhuri (2002) 149.

Sanskrit', was shattered in the 1850s by works like Gobineau's notorious *Essai sur l'inégalité des races humaines*.[123] From then on, racial science's development could advance unimpeded by the notion that Sanskrit's kinship with European tongues entailed a racial kinship between Indians and Europeans. In India, as well as in Europe, the relationship between linguistic and racial forms of kinship proved to be problematic. The new Orientalism of Friedrich Max Müller, though apparently of no interest to Madhusudan (who preferred the old Orientalism of Sir William Jones), attracted the intense interest of various mid-nineteenth-century Bengali intellectuals.[124] Bankimchandra Chattopadhyay in particular, but also Swami Vivekanda, wrote at length on the matter and did so, in Trautmann's words, 'with both deep admiration of Orientalism and sharp criticism of the distorting force of prejudice in even the most able of its practitioners'.[125]

Nationalist and postcolonial scholars have located the origins of the Indian nationalist movement in the events of 1857/8, the so-called 'Indian Mutiny' or 'Sepoy Uprising',[126] the upshot of which was that governmental control of India passed from the East India Company to the Crown (a key milestone in the history of British India).[127] However, it is well documented that in Calcutta, where Indian nationalism would indeed emerge a few years later, these bloody events were greeted with ambivalence or antipathy:[128] the Bengali *bhadralok* had a vested interest in preserving the status quo since they still enjoyed a privileged position within it. The Mutiny/Uprising cannot properly be described as the 'first war of Indian independence', as later nationalist scholars have sometimes dubbed it,[129] since it was in no way directly connected with the nationalist discourse that emerged

[123] Notorious in no small part for its influence on the development of twentieth-century ideologies of racial hatred: see Trautmann (2004) xxv and Poliakoff (1974).

[124] See Raychaudhuri (1988) 178 and Trautmann (2004) 220.

[125] Trautmann (2004) 220.

[126] For contemporary sources for, and later historical studies of, the Mutiny/Uprising, see Taylor (1996).

[127] The trauma of the Mutiny/Uprising caused a hardening in British attitudes towards India, a shift in attitude which, according to some analyses, spelt the beginning of the end of British control over the subcontinent: see esp. Metcalf (1960).

[128] See esp. Pal (1932) iii.

[129] For an analysis of the 'reclaiming' of the Mutiny/Uprising for the later nationalist cause, see esp. Embree (1963).

afterwards in quite a different social and geographical space within British India.

Bayly's analysis argues that the Mutiny/Uprising and the nationalist discourse which would emerge in Bengal a little later were connected not directly but indirectly, that is to say by a common underlying cause.[130] According to this view, it was the withdrawal of the British from Indian society (which entailed a rise, from the 1860s onwards, of feelings of resentment among the previously respected Bengali elite) that had earlier crippled Britain's military intelligence capabilities by the late 1850s to the extent that it failed to foresee or forestall the Mutiny/Uprising. It would only be at a later stage of the nationalist discourse that the 'Sepoy Uprising' would be reclaimed and re-imagined as the first moment of a nationalist awakening. After the events of 1857/8 and the consequent establishment of Crown rule, the process of British withdrawal from Bengali society evidently accelerated. As one scholar has put it, 'British attitudes rigidified into separate enclosures that did 'not choose to know' Indians').[131] But this process of withdrawal had in fact begun some time beforehand. In any event, it would certainly be anachronistic to view Madhusudan's Bengali oeuvre, which shows various subtle intimations of anti-British and nationalist feelings,[132] as a commentary on the Mutiny/Uprising as such. Madhusudan himself does not refer to the events of 1857/8 in any of his correspondence or elsewhere. In the early 1860s the emerging nationalist discourse and the events of 1857/8 were still quite separate in the minds of the Bengali intelligentsia; nor indeed had the notion of an India independent of Britain yet emerged.[133] At this early stage in the development of Indian nationalism, the moment at which Madhusudan's oeuvre was composed, Britain and the West still had a part to play in the formation of an Indian national identity.

The discourse of nationalism in India, as in contemporary Europe,[134] was inextricably bound up with the idea (or ideal) of a

[130] Bayly (1996). [131] R. Chaudhuri (2002) 149.

[132] A point argued by Radice (1998).

[133] See R. Chaudhuri (2008) 128ff.

[134] But note that Indian nationalism, though it may have taken the discourse of European nationalism as an ideological starting point, diverged in radical ways from its European counterpart: see Raychaudhuri (2002) 345ff.

'national literary culture':[135] indeed, the literary sphere was arguably the central crucible for the formation and development of Indian nationalist ideology in Bengal.[136] In the 1850s and 1860s, the nationalist 'reform' of Bengali vernacular literature meant not rejecting the West but drawing on the forms and ideas of a notionally 'superior' Western culture in order to enhance Bengali national pride.[137] In a speech delivered in 1869, Bankim, the important Bengali novelist and early nationalist ideologue, expressed his position clearly:

> Those who can teach their country, consider it beneath their social position to do so. It is degrading for the dashing young Bengali who writes and talks English like an Englishman, to be caught writing a Bengali book... There are a few honourable exceptions, and these men have done an immense good to Bengali literature. It is a fact that the best Bengali books are the productions of Bengalis who are highly cultivated English scholars. The matter for regret is how few these books are, and how few the scholars who have written them.[138]

[135] Note that it was not really until the 1870s, in journals such as Bankim's influential *Baṅgo-darśan*, that 'a literary public sphere' would fully emerge: 'the disputations in their pages determined the formation of canonical criteria for literary production'; see Kaviraj (2003) 536. For the European idea (or ideal) of the 'national literary culture' ('imagined communities' of readers sustained by a 'print capitalism' which had been enabled by the Industrial Revolution), see esp. B. Anderson (1991). But note once again that the Indian counterpart to this European phenomenon was radically distinct from it in crucial respects: see Chakrabarty (2000) and, in response to this, A. Chaudhuri (2008) 57-68. One key difference between the idea of a 'Bengali national literature' and comparable European phenomena concerns the question of education. Only a very few Bengalis had acquired a 'Western' education, and this entailed the 'disastrous' consequence of the 'Westernized' intelligentsia's 'total alienation from the masses' (Sarkar's phrase, cited by Raychaudhuri (2002) 353). The 'Westernized' Bengali intelligentsia's turn away from English and to the Bengali language (in Bankim's journal *Baṅgo-darśan* and in the literary works of figures like Madhusudan) thus represented, in part, an attempt to remedy that 'alienation' and to bring Western forms and ideas to a wider Bengali community.

[136] For examinations of the role of the literary sphere in the formation and development of Indian national identity, see esp. Chakrabarty (2000), R. Chaudhuri (2002), and Kaviraj (2003).

[137] See R. Chaudhuri (2002) 113. Again this nationalist idea seems to have had much to do with the British 'withdrawal' (described earlier) from Indian society. The sense of being 'abandoned' by the British is evident in the exasperation of Bankim: 'There is no Hindu history. Who will praise our noble qualities if we do not praise them ourselves?' (cited in R. Chaudhuri (2002) 147f.).

[138] From a lecture given by Bankim Chandra Chatterjee (Bankim), printed in *Bengal Social Science Association Transactions*, Vol. 3 (1869) 41.

One of the 'few honourable exceptions' to whom Bankim refers is, presumably, Madhusudan.[139] Indeed, Bankim would later celebrate Madhusudan, in his obituary of the poet in 1874, as a *jātīẏo kabi* or 'national poet'.[140]

Madhusudan's own account of his literary ambitions makes it clear that the creation of a 'national literary culture' lay at the heart of his cultivation of Bengali literature;[141] and Bankim's contemporary evaluation takes Madhusudan's literary purpose at his own estimation of it.[142] However, the later reception of Madhusudan's oeuvre would fall victim to further shifts and revisions within the nationalist discourse. By the late 1870s, the nationalist celebration of India was coming necessarily to imply the exclusion of anything Western (whereas before, figures like Madhusudan and Bankim had deemed the aggrandizement of India and the adoption of Western ideas to be two parts of a common project). It was at this later moment in the development of Indian nationalism that Madhusudan's friend Rajnarain would criticize his late friend's Bengali oeuvre precisely for its lack of *jātīẏo bhāb* or 'national feeling'.[143] The Western influence on Madhusudan's oeuvre was considered by Rajnarain, *contra* Bankim, to detract from its Indianness rather than enhance it. Rajnarain's criticism is of course persuasive in its own context; but when Madhusudan composed his Bengali works some years earlier he was engaging with and contributing towards an earlier (indeed embryonic) stage of the nationalist discourse, one which did not define Indianness necessarily against the West but strove to Westernize Indian culture (in Madhusudan's case, Bengali literature) in such a

[139] Writing to Gour from Versailles in January 1865, Madhusudan would prefigure Bankim's later call to arms, declaring: 'If there be anyone among us anxious to leave a name behind him . . . let him devote himself to his mother-tongue.' See Murshid (2004) 241.

[140] See Murshid (2003).

[141] See esp. Murshid (2004) 118.

[142] Madhusudan's view that the influence of Western literary sources did not diminish the 'Indian' or 'Hindu' character of his work is made clear, for example, when he states: 'You shan't have to complain of the un-Hindu character of the Poem [the *Meghnādbadh kābya*]. I shall not borrow Greek stories but write, rather try to write, as a Greek would have done.' See Murshid (2004) 125.

[143] See Murshid (2003). Rajnarain took this rejection of the West in the domain of language and literature almost to an absurd level: his Society for the Promotion of National Feeling, for example, would fine members who used English words. See Raychaudhuri (1988) 12ff.

way that it could compete with Britain.[144] It is critical, in assessing the proto-nationalist endeavours of Madhusudan's oeuvre, to eschew teleology and anachronism and to foreground the particular moment within the evolution of Indian nationalism at which that oeuvre was first published.[145]

Nothing embodies Madhusudan's complex proto-nationalism better than the literary emblem that he appears to have devised for himself, and the symbolism of this emblem provides a helpful guide to any reading of his oeuvre. See Figure 1.3 below for a facsimile of the emblem as it is presented in the Sanyal (*c.* 1917) edition of the *MBK*. The emblem is first attested in the ornate letter which the poet sent to King Victor Emmanuel II of Italy, in which he presented a Bengali sonnet, plus his own French translation of it, written in honour of the sixth centenary of Dante's birth.[146] Rarely, if ever, as Radice has recently commented, has a poet left behind a 'more succinct and diagrammatic indication of how he wished his works to be read'.[147] The Sanskrit motto beneath the Saint George's Cross (the facsimile reproduced below does not capture the fact that the cross was originally red),[148] speaking to the passion which had always sustained Madhusudan's cross-cultural literary ambitions, reads: *śarīraṃ vā pātayeyaṃ kāryaṃ vā sādhayeyam*, 'May my body collapse or my purpose be achieved'. Radice has parsed Madhusudan's emblem in the Introduction to his recent translation of the *MBK*, suggesting, quite compellingly, that the sun stands for the Bengali poet's personality, the elephant and lion for his Indian and European literary inspirations respectively, and the lotus for his opus itself—the *kāryam* or purpose to be achieved on pain of death.[149] And yet, at the centre of this metaphorical kaleidoscope, hidden in plain view, is the key to the diagram: the Saint George's Cross.

[144] For the attempts of Madhusudan and his Bengali contemporaries to 'compete' with their British contemporaries, see Dharwadker (2003) 231.

[145] I follow R. Chaudhuri (2002) in locating Madhusudan's oeuvre in a moment which may be labelled 'emergent nationalism' or 'proto-nationalism'.

[146] For a discussion of this sonnet and the context in which it was written, see Radice (2010) xii–xiii and Radice (2008) 149–72.

[147] Radice (2010) xiv.

[148] Note that the Bengali words outside (above and below) the oval emblem read: *meghnād-badh kābya/ maikel madhusudan datta praṇīt*, 'the *Meghnādbadh kābya*/ composed by Michael Madhusudan Datta', and refer to the context in which the emblem is presented in Sanyal (*c.* 1917).

[149] See Radice (2010) xli–c.

Figure 1.3. Madhusudan's emblem.

Madhusudan's life and works were underpinned by a desire, embarrassing to some later Indian nationalists but patriotic in its own way, to compete with British culture rather than to deny it altogether. His emblem asserts boldly what his literary oeuvre implies: *civis Britannicus sum*.[150]

[150] A Latin expression used almost a century later in the dedication prefacing N. Chaudhuri (1951), a famous work reflecting on Bengali attitudes towards Britain and the West. Note also that Madhusudan incorporated into his emblem the Saint George's Cross rather than the Union Flag: a suggestion, perhaps, that his aspiration was for India to hold a place alongside England analogous to that of the other constituent nations of the United Kingdom. Madhusudan's emblem was, in a sense, a flag to unify England and India, just as the Union Flag sought to combine the national identities of the British Isles. For the comparable and comparably ambiguous experiences of Ireland and India vis-à-vis English literary culture in the context of the emergence of nationalist ideology in the nineteenth century, see, in particular, Wright (2007).

3. MADHUSUDAN'S CLASSICAL EDUCATION

The path which led Madhsudan to a Western classical education was an unusual one, the product of certain hasty and exceptional decisions (in particular his conversion to Christianity), and it is important to stress that the depth of his appreciation of the Graeco-Roman world and its languages was not by any means typical of his generation of Bengali intellectuals. Atypical though his experience may have been, the rigorous classical curriculum which he and his fellow students (some of whom were converts originally from the Hindu community like Madhusudan) followed at Bishop's College disproves the claim recently made that 'no Greek or Latin texts were ever taught in India, not even in the most elite government or missionary institutions'.[151]

Madhusudan's formal education did not in fact begin in Calcutta. Before his family's arrival in the city in 1833/4, he is thought to have attended two elementary schools in the district of Jessore (eighty miles to the east of the city). Here, the curriculum seems to have been that of a *pathshala*, a traditional Hindu school, with a curriculum based on the elementary study of Bengali and Persian, the latter still being at the time the *lingua franca* in many professional and administrative domains in Bengal.

Between the arrival of the Datta family in Calcutta in 1833/4 and Madhusudan's enrolment at Hindu College in 1837, he attended an elementary school in the city, though the identity of this school is unknown. Whichever school this was, it seems possible that, in addition to English, he also learnt some Latin and even a little Greek here. Before enrolling at Bishop's College on 9 November 1844 (at the age of 20),[152] Madhusudan evidently knew some Latin and Greek: on the twentieth of that month the Principal of Bishop's College, Professor Withers, reported of Madhusudan that he had 'a creditable knowledge of Latin, and of the elements of Greek'.[153]

[151] Trivedi (2007) 287.

[152] For the date of Madhusudan's enrolment at Bishop's College, see the note written by Rev. Street, dated 17th February 1846 (USPG archives: C.Ind. I.13/107). See also Murshid (2004) 11, n. 25. For the ambiguity surrounding Madhusudan's exact age, see Murshid (2003) 11.

[153] See USPG C.Ind.1/12/11. This letter was first discovered by Murshid: see Murshid (2003) 60.

Neither Latin nor Greek were taught at Hindu College (where Madhusudan studied between 1837 and 1843),[154] and so the poet's most recent biographer, Ghulam Murshid, has inferred that he gained this classical knowledge at the school he attended before 1837.[155] This may well be correct, but we might also consider the evidence of a letter written by Madhusudan to his friend Gour Dass Bysack (Gour) in May 1843 (soon after his expulsion from Hindu College for converting to Christianity but over a year before enrolling at the missionary college).[156] Here, Madhusudan pleads with Gour, who still attended Hindu College, to ask a mutual friend to return his 'Eutropius' and 'Eton Grammar'.[157] These two texts, commonly used at the elementary stage of a classical education in some contemporary British schools,[158] may have been those used by Madhusudan at the school he attended before Hindu College, and which he was now revisiting before enrolling at Bishop's College. However, given his later appetite for autodidactic study (see below), it may be that Madhusudan's 'creditable' knowledge of Latin and Greek when he arrived at Bishop's College was the fruit of a year of self-instruction.

The details of Madhusudan's education become rather clearer after his enrolment at Hindu College in 1837. As was noted in Section 2 above, Hindu College was founded in 1817 at the initiative of certain grandees of the Hindu community (among others), and its curriculum was Anglicist but entirely secular in outlook.[159] A climate of rational scepticism prevailed, thanks largely to the dynamic teaching of the atheist David Hare and later the prodigious Anglo-Indian Derozio (himself accused of atheism);[160] and classes focused on the

[154] For the date and circumstances of Madhusudan's enrolment at and departure from Hindu College, see Murshid (2003) 18 and 45ff.

[155] For the uncertainty surrounding the date of Madhusudan's arrival in Calcutta, see Murshid (2003) 18.

[156] Note that the date of this letter is uncertain (see Murshid (2004) 39, n. 1), but there is good internal evidence for placing the date soon after the departure of D.L. Richardson from Calcutta in April 1843.

[157] Murshid (2004) 39.

[158] The Eton Grammars (of Latin and Greek) were written with a view to making Latin and Greek accessible to a wider range of students: see the review in *The Gentleman's Magazine*, 'Miscellaneous Reviews' (1840) 403; and also Stray (1998) 56ff.

[159] A fact which, as R. Chaudhuri (2002) 95 notes, disrupts the notion maintained by certain postcolonial scholars of 'the complicity between the evangelists and the literary curriculum'.

[160] See R. Chaudhuri (2008).

'humanistic' study of English literature, European literature (ancient and modern) in translation, and Enlightenment moral philosophy. The religious scepticism of the College's early pedagogues infected the attitude of the students towards their own religion and, though few converted to Christianity, many rejected the orthodox Hinduism of their parents. Peary Chand Mittra illustrates nicely the rationalistic and sceptical spirit of the College in an account of some Brahmin boys who, during a prescribed Hindu ritual when 'they were required to utter *mantras* or prayers, [instead] repeated lines from the *Iliad*'.[161]

The iconoclastic climate of Hindu College was dampened in 1839 by the arrival, as Principal, of Captain David Lester Richardson (DLR as he was known), a good friend of Macaulay himself. Whereas Derozio before him had agitated his students in favour of social reform, DLR positively discouraged any attitudes or actions on the part of his Hindu students that might irritate the conservative Hindu community or indeed the British authorities.[162] DLR took a special interest in the young Madhusudan, who even at this stage showed both academic and literary talent, and it was thanks largely to his encouragement that Madhusudan began to write English poetry at this time (from 1841 onwards).

Details have survived of the actual syllabus taught at Hindu College while Madhusudan studied there, and contemplation of it gives one a flavour of the intellectual landscape to which the College's young Hindu students were introduced. The junior branch studied Abercrombie's *Intellectual Powers*, Waitley's *Easy Lessons in Reasoning*, Russell's *Modern Europe*, Tytler's *Universal History*.[163] The senior branch read the *English Reader* of the 'Text Book Society', Murray's *English Grammar*, Crombie's *Etymology and Syntax*, Marshman's *History of Bengal*, and Hume's *History of England*.[164] Although the Latin and Greek languages were not taught, students were introduced to Gibbon's *The Decline and Fall of the Roman Empire* and Mitford's *History of Greece*.[165]

DLR was invited by Macaulay to compile an anthology of British poetry, addressed specifically to a readership of young Hindus such as

[161] Mittra (1877) 16, quoted in R. Chaudhuri (2002) 25.
[162] See Murshid (2003) 22ff.
[163] I owe these details to Murshid (2003) 23f.
[164] Murshid (2003) 23f.
[165] Murshid (2003) 23f.

the students of Hindu College, and this was published in 1840 under the title *Selections from the British Poets*.[166] This anthology, which we know Madhusudan read with particular alacrity,[167] was immediately incorporated into the syllabus of Hindu College. In addition to a broad range of English passages ranging from Chaucer to the young Tennyson (then just thirty-one years old), the anthology contained a substantial section of Greek and Latin poetry in translation (pp. 1529–75). This selection of Graeco-Roman passages reflected not the contents of a British schoolboy's classical curriculum but contemporary British literary taste in classical poetry: most space was allocated to the Homeric epics (seventeen out of the forty-six pages: pp. 1529–46);[168] and only one brief passage of Ovid was included.[169] By contrast, the contemporary British schoolboy typically began his classical education with large quantities of authors like Ovid, Caesar, Euripides, and Xenophon in the original languages.[170]

DLR's anthology also affords us a tantalizing insight into the material availability of the Graeco-Roman classics in contemporary Calcutta. DLR justifies his choice of Homeric translations in the following terms:

> In the preceding pages I have given a greater number of extracts from Cowper's translation of Homer, than from Pope's, for two reasons – because Cowper's is generally allowed to be far more faithful to the original (though less musical and ornate), and because Pope's translation is already in almost every hand and is easily and cheaply procurable in the native bazaars of Calcutta, while a copy of Cowper's is rarely obtainable even in the European shops here . . .[171]

Scholars have shown that Calcutta's trade in copies of Western literary works was lively even at this early stage (and not only in

[166] Richardson (1840).

[167] Murshid notes the anecdote that Madhusudan, having read DLR's anthology and impressed by the erudition of its Introduction, exclaimed to friends 'If only *I* could write such an Introduction!' (see Murshid (2003) 23).

[168] For the historical causes of Victorian 'Hellenism', a preference for Greek rather than Latin literature, see esp. Turner (1989).

[169] The anthology also included passages of Hesiod, Simonides, Sappho, Anacreon, Moschus, Lucretius, Vergil, Horace, Phaedrus, and Lucan.

[170] See Stray (1998) 46ff. For the ironic position of Ovid, an elementary staple of contemporary British education but rejected by prevailing British taste as a 'degenerate in a degenerate age', see Vance (1997) 154.

[171] Richardson (1840) 1542.

'European shops');[172] DLR's comment shows that this trade extended to English translations of classical works.

Although, at Hindu College, Madhusudan encountered a significant quantity of Western classical literature in translation, it was not until he enrolled at Bishop's College in 1844 that he began to master the Greek and Latin languages. As was noted above, Madhusudan had to leave Hindu College after converting to Christianity on the 9 February 1843.[173] His conversion seems to have evolved from complex personal circumstances: it was in part a rash attempt to avoid marriage to a Hindu girl, which was being arranged by his father; but it also served to further his long-held ambition to travel to England. His initial reasons for conversion therefore appear to have been rather insincere but within months of conversion he seems to have discovered a genuine faith in Christianity, to the extent that for a time he even considered becoming a missionary.[174] Madhusudan's rather headlong embrace of Christianity threw his life into turmoil: his formal education stalled[175] and it was not until 9 November 1844 that it was resumed at Bishop's College, a missionary institution just outside Calcutta, where he would remain until the end of 1847.[176]

Bishop's College was the first missionary college set up in British India. In 1818, five years after the suspension of the Company's prohibition on missionary activity (see Section 2 above), the Society for the Propagation of the Gospel in Foreign Parts (SPG), a missionary movement headquartered in Oxford, offered £5,000 to Middleton, the Lord Bishop of Calcutta, and recommended the founding of a missionary college in the immediate vicinity of Calcutta. Bishop Middleton duly founded Bishop's College and it opened in December 1820.[177] From the first it became the centre for missionary activity in

[172] See R. Chaudhuri (2008). Indeed, note that Calcutta was printing more books at this time than any other city in the world save London: see R. Chaudhuri (2002) 1ff.

[173] See Murshid (2003) 48.

[174] During the hiatus in Madhusudan's formal education between Hindu College and Bishop's College he spent some time as a houseguest of a Mr Thomas Smith of the Scottish Church. Smith's company seems to have triggered in Madhusudan a genuine interest and faith in Christianity. See Murshid (2003) 56.

[175] Note, however, that while he was Smith's houseguest, Madhusudan was informally taught by his host a great deal about Shakespeare: the clergyman had an expert's knowledge of the subject. See Murshid (2003) 56.

[176] For the date of Madhusudan's enrolment at Bishop's College, see Murshid (2004) 11.

[177] See Murshid (2003) 59 and Murshid (1995) 76.

Bengal: the conversion to Christianity of 1,800 Bengalis in the Tollygunge and Barripore missions by 1840, within twenty years of the college's foundation, was directly attributable to the influence of Bishop's College.[178]

The College was founded by Middleton to instruct 'the Native and other Christian youth . . . in the doctrines and discipline of the Church, in order to their becoming preachers, catechists, and schoolmasters',[179] and also to receive British missionaries and teach them the oriental languages that would be necessary to the success of their work. From the very beginning there was a mixture of English, 'Anglo-Indian', and 'native' Christian converts in attendance at the college. Bishop Middleton dreamt that the college would become a 'University of the East',[180] and of course this meant the inclusion in the College syllabus of a large amount of classics.[181] Latin and Greek were sacred languages, essential to the task of Christian ministry, but instruction in these languages was not limited to what was strictly necessary for study of the Bible.[182] The curriculum taught at the College was thus basically threefold: study of the Bible and related literature; instruction in Latin and Greek and the reading of the Graeco-Roman classics; and teaching in various oriental languages (Bengali, Sanskrit, Tamil, and even Chinese).[183]

The syllabus studied at the College during Madhusudan's attendance, and even one of Madhusudan's examination scripts (which is transcribed in full for the first time in Appendix 1 below), and a report on his academic performance in 1847, have survived in the archives of the United Society for the Propagation of the Gospels (USPG). The 'List of Studies' for 1844, Madhusudan's first year at the

[178] See O'Connor (2000) 78.

[179] Bishop's College statutes, cited by Pascoe (1901) 475.

[180] Pascoe (1901) 475.

[181] For the emphasis on classics in school and university curricula in contemporary Britain, see Stray (1998).

[182] Oxford and Cambridge, institutional paradigms for Bishop's College in certain respects, were also Anglican institutions at the time. Here too, the study of the Graeco-Roman classics, as a discipline distinct from the study of Scripture, was deemed a central part of clerical training: classics and Anglicanism were two sides of the same coin. See Stray (1998) 60ff.

[183] The curriculum of the college in the late 1830s and 1840s was a little (though not hugely) different from what Middleton envisaged in 1818. I have garnered information on the subjects studied in the college around the time of Madhusudan's attendance from the college's 'Lists of Studies' (1835–1844), which may be found at the USPG archive, Rhodes House, Oxford: C.Ind/I(6)30A-C.

College (when he was in the Second Division, the lower of two), shows how central was the study of the Graeco-Roman classics:[184]

LIST OF THE STUDIES DURING THE YEAR.

The First Division

Grk. Test. Last 18 chh. of Acts & E. to Cor. I & II.
Pearson on the Creed—From Art. VIII to Art XII (both inclusive)
Hooker's Eccl. Pol. Book V S. 1–34.
Grotius—Last Book
St. Chrysostom de Sacerdotio Libb. I. II. III. IV. V.
Herodotus Clio & Euterpe
Jubenalis [*sic*] Satires V.V. sqq.
Persii Satires
Lucretius I. II. III.
Platonis Crito & Phaedo.
Algebra—to the end of Annuities.[185]

The Second Division

Virgils Georgics & six of the Eclogues—twice over.
Whewells Bridgewater Treatise

[184] USPG archives C.Ind/I(6)30B: I retain original spelling and punctuation. See also Murshid (1995) 79.

[185] The first item refers, in abbreviated form, to the New Testament, Acts and Paul's Letters to the Corinthians. John Pearson's *An Exposition on the Creed* (1659) is a classic in Anglican theological exposition, as is Hooker's *On the Laws of Ecclesiastical Polity* (1593), both evidently used here as textbooks on Anglican doctrine. 'Grotius', given the context, presumably refers to Grotius' *De Veritate Religionis Christianae* (1627), or 'On the Truth of the Christian Religion', a famous apology for Protestant doctrine; while *De Sacerdotio Dialogi*, 'Dialogues about the Priesthood', by Saint Chrysostom (*c.* 347–407) is a six-book defence of the ministry. 'Clio' and 'Euterpe', names of two of the nine Greek Muses, refer to Books 1 and 2 of the *Histories* (divided into 9 Books) of the Greek historian Herodotus. Juvenal is a Roman poet of the late first and early second centuries CE: his *Satires* comprise five Books and are composed in dactylic hexameter. The *Satires* of Persius (mid-first century CE) are earlier works following in the same genre. Lucretius' *De Rerum Natura*, or 'On the Nature of Things', is an epic poem expounding the theories of Epicureanism in poetic form; while *Crito* and *Phaedo* are two Greek philosophocal dialogues of Plato respectively treating justice and the nature of the afterlife (among much else).

Abercrombie on the Moral Feelings (parts of)
Noelli Catechismus
Horatic Odes & Epodes
Xenophontis Cyropedia Bks. I. II. III. IV. V.
Cicero de Senectute & Somnium Scipionis
Euripidis Medea, throughout
Aurelii Victoris Histor. Rom.—the commencement.
Eton Exempla Minora—throughout.
[. . . . .][186] Latin—commenced.
Neilsons Greek composition—commenced.
Latin Nonsense Verses.
Wordsworths Greek Grammar.
Euclid Bks I. II. III. IV. VI. & part of XI.[187]

The 'Lists of Studies' which survive for other years (1835, 1837, and 1838) include further works of Graeco-Roman classical literature: Cicero's *De Finibus*, Thucydides' *Histories* 1, three works of Tacitus (*Germany*, his *Life of Agricola*, and the *Annals*), Vergil's *Aeneid* (Books 1, 2, 6, and 7), and Xenophon's *Anabasis* (1835); Homer's *Iliad*, Plato's *Phaedrus*, Ovid's *Metamorphoses*, and Aristotle's *Rhetoric* (1837); and Sophocles' *Philoctetes* (1838). It is also interesting to note the inclusion on the syllabus of various Greek and Latin textbooks (the *Eton Exempla*, *Neilson's Greek Composition*, and so on).

186 Text illegible here.

187 Vergil's *Eclogues* and *Georgics*, collections of Latin bucolic and didactic poems respectively, predate the *Aeneid*, the Augustan poet's celebrated epic. William Whewell's *Bridgewater Treatise* (1833) is a text arguing that science, the study of the laws of nature, is indicative of the existence of a divine law-giver, while *The Philosophy of the Moral Feelings* by John Abercrombie (1835) builds from first principles a treatise on the nature of morality. *Noelli Catechismus*, or the 'Catechism of Noell', takes the form of a dialogue in Latin between a *Praeceptor* ('Teacher') and his *Discipuli* ('Students') and figures a broad discussion of Christian doctrine. 'Horatic Odes and Epodes' refers to the famous Latin *Odes* and *Epodes* of the Augustan poet Horace, while Xenophon's *Cyropedia*, or 'Education of Cyrus', is a Greek work treating the education of the Persian King Cyrus. *De Senectute* ('On Old Age') and *Somnium Scipionis* ('Dream of Scipio') are two prose texts by Cicero, Roman politician and treatise-writer of the first century BCE, the greatest exponent of Latin prose; while the *Medea* of Euripides is one of the most famous Greek tragedies (fifth century BCE). The *Histories* of Aurelius Victor, a Roman historian of the fourth century CE, provide a wide-ranging synopsis of Roman history from Augustus to Julian. 'Euclid', presumably shorthand for Euclid's *Elements*, is a seminal Greek treatise on geometry and other mathematical topics while Wordsworth's Greek grammar and Neilson's Greek composition were textbooks used in the Victorian period for instruction in classical Greek language.

Textbooks of this kind were the works in which the pedagogical ideology of the classics, to use Stray's phrase, was 'materially embodied' in the Victorian period.[188]

The range of classical texts studied at the College reflected the curricula of contemporary British public schools: Ovid, Euripides, Xenophon, and Cicero were the elementary staple of the public school classical diet.[189] The College was not offering the depth or breadth of classical education offered at Oxford or Cambridge, and this was a contrast which the teachers at the College seem to have felt keenly. As Rev. Street, the Principal of the College, wrote (rather defensively) in 1847 to a correspondent in Oxford:[190]

> Let it be remembered that the students are not young men who have passed an University Exn, or even have been at a Public School in England, but lads who come to us in too often the very lowest state of preparation classical & theological alike.

However, the standard of instruction in Latin and Greek at the College was evidently very high. As Wilson, the evangelical Bishop of Calcutta and founder of Calcutta Cathedral, commented in 1838:

> It was delightful to see these lads, only fourteen months at the College, vying with those of European extraction, who had been two or three years. These young Hindoos have not only cast off all idolatrous usages and habits, but are steadily acquiring Christian knowledge. They are quick in their apprehension of truth, with tenacious memories and great piety. They translate Homer, Xenophon, Cicero, and Ovid in a manner perfectly surprising, and with a justness of English pronunciation which increases the pleasure[191]

Given this atmosphere of intensive classical learning, which was of a standard to impress the visiting Bishop, it is significant that Madhusudan stood out even in this context as an exceptional student. After the College examinations of June 1847, Madhusudan was ranked third overall in the College out of twenty-five students, the top student not 'of European extraction'.[192] Indeed, he was deemed

[188] Stray (1998) 54. [189] Stray (1998) esp. Chapter 3.

[190] USPG archives, C.Ind./I/13.140, p. 3: a letter from Rev. Street to a Mr Rogers, dated 29 December, 1847.

[191] As cited in Pascoe (1901) 475f.; see also O'Connor (2000) 78, and n. 8.

[192] USPG archives, C.Ind./I13/134.

worthy of special mention in a letter written by Rev. Street, the Principal of the College, on 23 July 1847:[193]

> He [*viz.* Madhusudan] is very intelligent, a good Greek & Latin scholar and thorough master of English, as you may suppose when I mention that before coming here he affected fame as an English poet.

Furthermore, we have one of Madhusudan's examination scripts from June 1847 (his final year at the College):[194] his answer paper (dated 9 June) for the 'New Testament' examination.[195] No transcription of this examination script has ever been published and so, with the kind permission of the United Society for the Propagation of the Gospels and the Bodleian Library, Oxford, I include a full transcription of it in Appendix 1 below, prefaced with a brief introduction to the context of the manuscript's production. As may be seen from my transcription of this examination script, Madhusudan's handling of Greek terms, and his ability to cite passages of the New Testament from memory (and with fair observance of Greek accentuation),[196] indicates a sound knowledge of the language. In answer to question eleven of this examination, which asked for the citation in the original language of a passage of the Greek Testament,[197] Madhusudan wrote: 'As I cannot remember the words as they are in the Greek text, I refrain from translating these sentences in my own way'.[198] Given his training at the College, and his apparent facility as a classical scholar, it is quite credible that Madhusudan could have translated these Biblical phrases into his own Greek prose. Greek prose composition was a central part of the classical syllabus at Bishop's College, and indeed an aspect of the contemporary British classical education that distinguished it from the classical educations offered in most

[193] USPG archives, C.Ind./I13/134.

[194] This examination script was first discovered by Ghulam Murshid but he does not discuss it in his biography of Madhusudan.

[195] USPG archives, C.Ind.I.(6)32A-G.

[196] Citation or composition of Greek without accents was referred to in the Victorian period as 'ladies' Greek' (see Stray (1998) 81), and the ability to handle Greek with good observance of accentuation was deemed to indicate a mastery of the language.

[197] Specifically, the question asked for the original Greek for the following New Testament passages: *If I wash thee not, thou hast no part with me.* (St. John xiii. 8); and, *Jesus saith to him, He that is washed needeth not save to wash* his *feet, but is clean every whit: and ye are clean, but not all.* (St. John xiii. 10). See USPG archives, C.Ind.I.(6)32.

[198] See Appendix 1 for a discussion of Madhusudan's slightly flippant tone here and his attitude towards Christianity.

other European countries.[199] In this way, then, Madhusudan's 1847 examination script is of no little importance to this book's basic thesis[200] since it shows beyond doubt what has not previously been clear, namely that from the mid-1840s onwards the poet was quite able to read classical Greek texts in the original language.

We also know which editions of the classical texts taught on the syllabus are likely to have been held in the College library: see Appendix 2 for a tabulation of these editions. Their identity is significant since they represent Madhusudan's first exposure, in the original languages, to Graeco-Roman works that would later come to influence his Bengali oeuvre. In the chapters to come this textual aspect of his reception of the Graeco-Roman classics will be included in the broader literary analysis. In 1822, Oxford University Press (OUP) and Cambridge University Press (CUP) each made the extraordinary donation to the college of a copy of every publication currently in print.[201] These generous gifts formed the backbone of the College library[202] and, indeed, they were the material enabler of the College's classical curriculum.[203] Unfortunately, the College

[199] Latin and Greek prose and verse composition were basic to a classical education in Victorian Britain; schools in other European countries put much less emphasis on composition. See Stray (1998) 68ff.

[200] The document is important in various other ways too, perhaps particularly in that it shows conclusively that Madhusudan did not take the Christian name Michael before leaving Bishop's College in 1847 (see Murshid (2003) 78ff.). See also nn. 3–4 above.

[201] See Murshid (2003) 59; Murshid (1995) 76. The OUP and CUP donations were made in late 1822 (or somewhat later), *contra* Murshid who implies that they were made in 1820. The request from the USPG, communicated to the Publishing Houses by the Archbishop of Canterbury himself, was received and discussed only in June 1822. Interestingly, the Delegates of the OUP were rather reluctant to make the gift and referred the request to Convocation, which, in the event, agreed to it (see minutes from meeting of the Delegates, 14 June 1822).

[202] But note that Bishop Middleton donated 500 books to the College in 1820. These books were presumably scriptural in the main; indeed in the archives of the College itself (which still remain though in a rather bad state of repair) I found a remarkable (and valuable) *Novum Testamentum Graecum e Codice MS Alexandrino*, with a *praefatio* in Latin (printed in 1786), which may perhaps have been a part of Middleton's donation.

[203] Note that Calcutta Cathedral, whose foundation stone was laid in 1839 and which was consecrated in 1847, also boasted a large library thanks to the endowment of Bishop Wilson. According to a survey of that library's stock carried out in 1922, of the 1,696 feet of books in that library, at least 110 feet came under the category of 'Classics, etc.'. See the archives of Bishop's College, Calcutta, in a box labelled 'Box 1, Library (1839-47): Report from 1922'.

library seems no longer to exist as such[204] but a consideration of those texts in print at OUP and CUP in 1822 gives one a fair impression of the editions held by the College (see Appendix 2). It will be of interest in later chapters that, for example, the edition of Homer's *Iliad* at Bishop's College was probably the OUP Heyne edition, which included Alexandrian *scholia* (marginal comments which have informed much modern scholarship on the Homeric epics). And it will be relevant to the close reading in Chapter 5 that the only edition of Ovid's *Heroides* then in print at either Press was the early eighteenth century Delphine edition.

Madhusudan completed his formal education in June 1847, at the age of 23 but throughout his life he showed an enormous capacity for autodidactic study. After finishing at Bishop's College, Calcutta, Madhusudan moved to Madras where he would find work in various capacities: as a teacher at the Madras Orphan Asylum; as 'Second Tutor' at Madras University, and as editor of and contributor to a variety of journals. Here, he socialized mostly with the English and Anglo-Indian community (a habit reflected in his marriage to Rebecca and relationship with Henrietta: see Section 1 above).[205] Although he complained that Madras University had 'nothing in the shape of a good library',[206] his friendship with George Norton, the Madras Advocate General, evidently eased matters: 'We correspond like friends, and he has given me a most valuable number of classical works, as a "token of his regard"'.[207] These classical texts, gifted by Norton in 1849, are quite likely the editions consulted by Madhusudan in the composition of his Bengali works from the late-1850s onwards. Appendix 2, which tabulates the editions likely to have been stocked at Bishop's College Calcutta, also lists the most prominent editions of relevant classical works which were in print before 1849, and which may thus have been included in Norton's gift.

Madhusudan's scholarly preparations for his later Bengali oeuvre began at this time, a decade before he actually began to compose in

[204] I visited the college in December 2007: the library no longer existed as such, though I did find an archive which contained a few eighteenth and nineteenth century books, including the *Novum Testamentum Graecum* (1786) and various old manuscripts of Bengali and Sanskrit literature.

[205] Note also that his English lecture, 'The Anglo-Saxon and the Hindu' (1854), was dedicated to his late friend, the Englishman C.E. Kennet.

[206] Said in a letter dated 6 July 1849: see Murshid (2004) 74.

[207] Murshid (2004) 74.

the language. In a letter dated 18 August 1849 (soon after Norton's generous gift of 'classical works'), he stated:

> My life is more busy than that of a school boy. Here is my routine: 6–8 Hebrew, 8–12 School, 12–2 Greek, 2–5 Telegu and Sanskrit, 5–7 Latin, 7–10 English. Am I not preparing for the great object of embellishing the tongue of my fathers?[208]

It will be seen in the chapters to come that this remarkable timetable of autodidactic study, carried out ten years before Madhusudan began to 'embellish' the Bengali language with his own compositions, in fact reflects to a large extent the cultural elements brought together in his later Bengali oeuvre. The purpose to which Madhusudan had now begun to turn his classical education, the enhancement of Bengali 'national' pride through literature, was very different from the purpose envisaged by the missionaries at Bishop's College (namely the propagation of the Gospel). Madhusudan's Bengali oeuvre thus fits a pattern of creative and subversive 'misappropriation' which came to define the Bengali response to the British educational policies of the period.

4. BROADER ISSUES AND DEBATES

The following chapters examine Madhusudan's response to the Graeco-Roman classics in his Bengali oeuvre. The book's purpose is to describe and analyse this response, but also to highlight the multifarious subversiveness which underpins it: Madhusudan's classicizing works show from time to time a kind of proto-nationalist antipathy towards the West. In almost all cases his readings of the Graeco-Roman classics went against the grain of contemporary British tastes and, moreover, he used these texts as a tool to resist and undermine the hegemony of elite Hindu culture.

The texts studied in the following chapters are quite extraordinary and worthy of receiving in the West the high level of scholarly attention that they have attracted in India. Each text is a complex web of literary incorporations. For example, Madhusudan's epic masterpiece, the *Meghnādbadh kābya* (1861), fuses the Western and Indian

[208] See Murshid (2004) 78.

epic traditions with liberal samplings from Homer, Vergil, Dante, Tasso, and Milton, but also from the Sanskrit and mediaeval Bengali *Rāmāyaṇas* among other sources. His play the *Padmābatī nāṭak* (1860) dramatizes the Judgement of Paris using Indian characters and deities and employing theatrical motifs and devices drawn particularly from Kālidāsa's Sanskrit *Abhijñānaśakuntalam* and various Shakespearean plays. The *Bīrāṅganā kābya* (1862) comprises a series of Ovidian epistolary elegiacs, modelled structurally and thematically on the Latin *Heroides*, but 'written' by heroines from Hindu mythology to their husbands or lovers, and thus drawing extensively on the Sanskrit and mediaeval Bengali epic traditions.

In Madhusudan's classical appropriations one detects a distinct, though often subterranean, tendency to resist the West and its values. A striking example of the subtle subversion which characterizes much of his work is the exploitation of the curious but marked mid-nineteenth-century reluctance of Britain to embrace Rome as a model for Empire.[209] In his 1854 lecture 'The Anglo-Saxon and the Hindoo' (see Chapter 4), Madhusudan emphatically associates the 'Anglo-Saxon' with Aeneas and the 'Hindoo' with Dido: not only is the link between Britain and Rome made explicitly (against the grain of contemporary British self-image), but the specific link between the Anglo-Saxon and Aeneas could hardly be more damning of Britain's dalliance with India. Indeed, Madhusudan insinuates that the British Aeneas has essentially violated the Indian Dido, and that his metaphor falls short only in that the Hindoo never had the tender feelings for the Anglo-Saxon which Dido once felt for Aeneas. Moreover, this emerges as a particularly stark instance of colonial dissent when considered in the context of Rome's status at this time as a political symbol. Rome was largely avoided by mid-nineteenth-century British propagandists as a source for political symbols and iconography since Rome's possibilities in this connection had been exhausted and tainted by a succession of radical movements and regimes deemed threatening to British sovereignty: the French Revolution, the foundation of America's democratic institutions, the Napoleonic Empire.[210] Indeed, one might recall at this juncture that, some years

[209] See, for example, Vance (1997) 141. However, for early uses of Rome in Britain's imperial self-fashioning, see esp. Mantena (2010) 54–73.

[210] See Goff (2005) 17; and Vance (1997). See also Vasunia (2005b) who considers some late Victorian works connecting the Roman and British Empires.

later, the poet would name one of his sons Napoleon. Furthermore, Madhusudan later disrupts this analogy between Rome and Britain in his draft version of a Bengali 'national epic' (see again Chapter 4) in which the Bengali hero Vijaya stands for Aeneas: a fact which reinforces the recent scholarly contention that the British reluctance to embrace Rome may be explained in part by the 'indeterminacy' of Rome as a symbol for empire and nationhood. As Majeed has argued, Britain felt a strong anxiety regarding its own former status as a Roman colony and the 'fearsome capacity' of both Rome and India 'to assimilate British national identity on different levels'.[211] Madhusudan's response to the *Aeneid* goes to the very quick of this anxiety.

This Vergilian moment of colonial resistance is especially marked, but the dissenting and unorthodox nature of Madhusudan's appropriation of the Western classics also operates on a far subtler level: his readings of the Graeco-Roman classics almost always went against the grain of contemporary British taste. In certain broad respects it may appear that Madhusudan's Bengali response to European classical culture was not entirely divorced from the prevailing trends and tastes in contemporary Britain. For example, Madhusudan's Hellenism—despite his surprising taste for Roman authors it was Homer's *Iliad* to which he reverted most frequently and responded in the most thoroughgoing way—is broadly in tune with contemporary British Hellenism. And yet, even in this respect, his literary preferences may be explained without recourse to contemporary British influence. While Madhusudan's recurrent engagement with Homer and with Greek culture at its earliest stages may be compared with contemporary British trends, the frequent Indo-European links, which he makes between Homer and traditional Hindu mythology and theology, point to a Hellenism borne out of the late-eighteenth-century Orientalist identification of ancient Greece and Hindu India. Contemporary British and Indian artists had distinct reasons for identifying themselves and their respective cultures with the Greeks of antiquity. What is clear, however, is that, if the Bengali poet was not influenced to a great extent by contemporary British tastes, this was a deliberate choice on his part rather than a function of his ignorance of them. It is clear that Madhusudan followed the British literary scene closely, holding a subscription to periodicals such as *Blackwood's Magazine*

211 Majeed (1999) 108. See also Goff (2005) 14f.

and, had he wished to do so, he could certainly have aped the contemporary trends in British classicizing poetry in his Bengali compositions. The independence of Madhusudan's response to the Graeco-Roman classics—his more or less unmediated appropriation of the West's ancient cultures—is noted from time to time in the course of the following chapters, and the implications of this independence is explored in the Conclusion. However, notwithstanding the broad independence of the Bengali poet's engagement with Europe's classical authors from contemporary British influence, Madhusudan's reading of various classical texts is often coloured by the responses to them of earlier British poets (Milton and Pope in particular) and, indeed, from time to time there are moments when the influence of contemporary poets such as Tennyson or Arnold is at least arguably present in his Bengali works. In particular, there is something arguably Arnoldian in Madhusudan's dual treatment of Homer as an object not only for emulation (see especially Arnold's *Sohrab and Rustum* and his *Balder Dead*)[212] but also for translation (see Arnold's famous quarrel with Newman over how best to translate Homer).[213]

Finally, a third strand of subversiveness, perhaps the most conspicuous and all-pervasive throughout his oeuvre, may be detected in Madhusudan's use of the Graeco-Roman classics to resist and undermine the hegemony of elite Hindu culture. Indeed, it is a primary purpose of this book to emphasize what many postcolonial histories suppress, namely that it was not uncommon for Bengali intellectuals of the mid-nineteenth century to resist the hegemony not only of imperial Britain but also of the indigenous elite culture of the Hindu pundits and the perceived corrosive effects of popular Bengali culture. It was the view at least of this particular Bengali poet that these were the primary obstacles standing in the way of the development of an intellectually respectable indigenous Bengali literary culture. In Chapter 3, for example, there will be an analysis of the most obvious example of this trend: here it will be seen that the poet drew on Homeric and Vergilian paradigms in his epic *Meghnādbadh kābya* to

[212] For Arnold's use of Homer's *Iliad* as a structural and thematic model in these poems, and his contrasting use of subject matter drawn from non-Greek cultures, see Harrison (2007d).

[213] See esp. Porter (2004) 338; also 'Homeric Translators and Critics', *The Saturday Review* (27 July, 1861) p. 96; cited in Bermann (2005) 250.

cast the Hindu demon Rāvaṇa as a Hector figure and the Hindu god Rāma as an unsympathetic Agamemnon, an effect which represents an inversion of traditional Hindu sympathies. However, Madhusudan drew upon the Graeco-Roman classics to challenge elite or popular Hindu assumptions in many other respects. Madhusudan's oeuvre was directed towards the creation of a modern Bengali national literature, and this involved a 'reclaiming' of traditional Hindu narratives and myths stripped bare of the hyper-traditional literary sensibilities of the priestly elite. However, it also meant resisting the popular arts, such as popular drama or *alik kunāṭyo*, 'false, bad theatre', as Madhusudan considered it. Thus for the Bengali poet, Western literary culture, and the Graeco-Roman classics in particular, served the dual purpose of helping to oust elite Hindu taste from the apex of Bengali literary culture and of elevating the modern Bengali vernacular from what was in his view the base and unsophisticated culture of the Hindu masses.

It is because of this multifarious subversion, which was directed at almost every kind of prevailing cultural norm—Western, indigenous, elite, popular—and which underpins Madhusudan's reception of the Graeco-Roman classics, that the works of this prominent nineteenth-century Bengali poet, and the following readings of them, can claim to be of interest to various broader scholarly discourses. Indeed, Madhusudan's classical education (see Section 3 above), and his later use of it in his literary oeuvre, place Madhusudan at the very beginning of a long line of colonial and postcolonial poets whose rigorous classical educations came to inform their attitudes towards art, the West, and their own cultures. Derek Walcott, of course, is arguably the most prominent contemporary link in this long chain of resistance-through-classics.[214] Indeed Walcott's analysis of his own subversive postcolonial practice in engaging with the Western cultural heritage[215] offers a critical vocabulary that can be productively applied to Madhusudan as well. The two poets are comparable in using their classical educations, despite the purposes of British educational policies, as a potential source of creativity; or, as Walcott has said, '[the education]

[214] For Walcott's creative practices in handling the classics see, for example, Prince (2007) and Taplin (1991).

[215] See especially the attitudes towards postcolonial hybridity articulated in Walcott's *What the Twilight Says: an Overture* (1970).

was cruel, but it created our literature'.[216] While Madhusudan's experiences of education both at Hindu College and Bishop's College were in fact fairly positive on a personal level, there is a strong parallel here between Walcott and the Bengali poet in their claiming of the Graeco-Roman classics as a tool for shaping their own cultural and literary identities. Moreover, there will be occasion in the course of the following chapters to compare Madhusudan's self-appointed role as 'reformer' of Bengali literary culture, and the prominent position he gave to the Western classics in this project, with Walcott's use of the classics in examining and addressing the 'broken' African tradition of black Caribbean culture.[217]

Madhusudan's role in this notional 'reform' of Bengali literature will be construed in its specific Bengali and Indian contexts, and here Madhusudan will emerge as a representative, possibly even the apogee, of various contemporary cultural trends. It was seen in Section 2 above that he belonged to the Westernizing, secular movement known as 'Young Bengal', whose patriotism for India was channelled into aping British mores and taking from the stock of Western art and literature what they thought would most aggrandize their own culture. In addition, however, the following chapters will show that Madhusudan's literary endeavours represent an interesting point of comparison for the works of later Bengali literary figures including, for example, novelist and social reformer Bankim Chandra Chatterjee and Rabindranath Tagore. Madhusudan can claim to be the first to attempt a 'reform' of Bengali literature, and he has always been a literary presence to be taken into account by later Bengali and other Indian authors. For example, in an early essay (1888) Tagore criticized Madhusudan's commingling of Homeric and Hindu epic traditions in his masterpiece the *Meghnādbadh kābya* (1861), characterizing this literary fusion as a case of fatal impurity, a text falling between two stools.[218] Interestingly, as a mature artist, Tagore reviewed his attitude towards Madhusudan and came to appreciate

[216] Walcott in Hamner (1997) 50. For an analysis of Walcott's classical education and his attitude towards it, see Prince (2007) esp. 179.

[217] See, for example, Walcott's *Ruins of a Great House* ('Stones only, the *disjecta membra* of this Great House . . . ').

[218] For a discussion of the 'youthful bravado' (later recanted) that led Tagore to attack Madhusudan's literary legacy in this way, see Radice (2010) xcvi–xcvii and Radice (2005).

his work warmly,[219] albeit as the product of an earlier generation with values distinct from his own. Madhusudan's Graeco-Roman samplings were not echoed in Tagore's work, but the older poet's presence at the head of a 'modern' Bengali tradition was one which the new standard-bearer of that tradition could hardly ignore. Indeed, Tagore learnt to forge a certain Bengali lightness and clarity through his response to Madhsuduan's dense and sometimes obfuscatory style.

While Madhusudan's cultural context is a distinctively Indian one, and the distinctiveness of this cultural backdrop will never be far from view in the following chapters, it is hoped that this book may also contribute something to the exciting new discourse of 'black classicism'. Over the past few years, various scholars, both from within and outside the field of Classical Studies and Classical Reception, have published works addressing the engagement of African or African American artists and scholars with the Graeco-Roman Classics.[220] What this book will take from the nascent field of 'Classica Africana'[221] is a paradigm for analysing challenges to the 'whiteness' of the Graeco-Roman Classics. Indeed whereas, for example, the later African American scholar William Sanders Scarborough (1852–1926)[222] worked not so much to stake out a 'black classicism' as to show that the classics figured as part of a shared humanity (colour-blind to racial difference), Madhusudan at times seemed to go further than this and to claim the Western Classics to be especially germane to Hindu culture.[223] Madhusudan's reception of the Greek and Latin texts, as will emerge in the course of the book, was deeply marked by the comparative scholarship of the early British Orientalists, Sir William Jones in particular. The poet used this discourse to align Graeco-Roman theology and myth extensively with its Hindu counterparts. This Indo-European method of reading the Graeco-Roman past carried with it an implicit suggestion that the Western Classics were in fact less germane to contemporary Western culture than to the still-living polytheism and mythology of Hindu culture. Madhusudan's *Hekṭor-badh* (1871), a Bengali prose 'version' of the *Iliad*,

[219] See esp. Radice (2010) xcvi.
[220] For an overview of this recent trend, see Greenwood (2009).
[221] Ronnick (2005) 5.
[222] See Ronnick (2005) for an edition of the autobiography of this scholar.
[223] A feature of Madhusudan's appropriation of the Classics which we might in fact compare with the close cultural identification seen in the mid-twentieth-century drama of Ola Rotimi (see esp. *The Gods are Not to Blame*, 1969): see Goff (2007) 111f.

replaces the Olympian deities with Hindu deities like Śiva, Durgā, Rati and so forth. It is insinuated that Modern India is a more natural home than modern Europe for the cultural heritage of ancient Greece and Rome. In this particular attitude, always subterranean and implicit, Madhusudan seems to attest to the embryonic Hindu nationalism of his time. Indeed, an analysis of this early moment of the nationalist discourse is relevant to a contextualized understanding of the modern politics of Hindu nationalism, which still draw heavily on arguments concerning Hindu culture's Aryan purity and orginality. Furthermore, there is arguably a racial aspect to Madhusudan's interest in Hindu culture's comparability with classical Europe. The connection between Indo-European studies and so-called 'racial science' was a crucial and much-contested one in the mid-nineteenth century. Madhusudan's profound interest in Indo-European scholarship, and his habit of reading the Graeco-Roman classics through a Sanskritic lens (and vice versa), may be seen in this 'languages and nations' context,[224] and will be considered from this point of view in the Conclusion.

Furthermore, Madhusudan's sustained Indo-European method of cultural appropriation stands as an engaging point of comparison to the kinds of material relevant to the discourse of 'black classicism'. Madhusudan's repeated use of the Indo-European comparisons of the early British Orientalists suggests a route to the appropriation of the Graeco-Roman classics that stands in marked contrast to the 'map' proposed in the context of black classicism by Goff and Simpson in *Crossroads in the Black Aegean*. Goff and Simpson construct the 'Black Aegean' as a 'triangle... projected from within the Black Atlantic and symmetrical with it, but with its third point radiating eastwards so that it links Africa to ancient Greece...',[225] but the web of cultural interrelations suggested by Madhusudan's Indo-European Classicism is more suggestive of a four-dimensional space, in which the historically cognate status of Hindu and European culture only becomes apparent when the clock is turned back. Thus the relationship between Hindu India and the Western classics is one of

[224] See Trautmann (2004) for a study of the 'languages and nations project', and the reaction of intellectuals such as Gobineau in the 1850s against the 'tyranny of Sanskrit', i.e. against the view that linguistic kinship necessarily entailed racial kinship. See also Poliakov (1977), Lincoln (1999), and Olender (1992).

[225] Goff (2007) 38f.

horizontal kinship, the sharing of a common ancestor: a notion, incidentally, reinforced by the still vibrant discourse of Indo-European studies.[226] Madhusudan's awareness, through the Orientalist scholarship of figures such as Sir William Jones, that the Graeco-Roman and Hindu mythologies are in fact cousins, sprung from a common origin, means that his Indian reception of the Western Classics figures an attempt to identify India with Europe in quasi-genetic terms (with possible racial connotations, as indicated above). This identification stands in contrast to many of the African and African American receptions of Greece and Rome which have been studied so far by scholars working in the field of black classicism: in that context the classical European heritage is often deracinated and recast as a human rather than a culturally delimited artefact.[227] That said, Madhusudan's proprietorial attitude to the Western classics provides an interesting point of comparison for the stance of artists such as Wole Soyinka, a postcolonial winner of the Nobel Prize for Literature who, in his *Art, Dialogue and Outrage*, speaks with great swagger about appropriating rather than sharing the Greek heritage.[228]

Just as the themes and topics of this book are located at the interface between Indian culture and the Graeco-Roman classics, so too its methodological and theoretical position stands at the interface between postcolonial studies and classical reception. On the postcolonial side, my methodological thrust takes its inspiration particularly from the technique of close reading practised by Edward Said (see especially *Culture and Imperialism* and the readings in *The World, the Text and the Critic*).[229] Edward Said has argued that certain 'cultural forms' like the novel were 'immensely important in the formation of imperial attitudes',[230] and Elleke Boehmer has extended this notion by imagining Empire and the movements which emerged in opposition to it as essentially 'textual undertaking[s]'.[231] Similarly, my own close readings in the following chapters aim to reveal and analyse cultural and political discourses. My approach is especially like Boehmer's method of postcolonial practice (as opposed to postcolonial

[226] As opposed to the controversial (indeed largely discredited) vertical relationship of African (i.e. Egyptian and North African) precursors and Greek successors postulated in the African context most notably by Bernal in *Black Athena* (1987).

[227] See Greenwood (2009).

[228] Soyinka (1988).

[229] Said (1993) and Said (1983).

[230] Said (1993) xii.

[231] Boehmer (1995) 5.

theory),[232] with its emphasis on 'hybrid' identities[233] and its attempt 'to introduce more texts and contexts into the discussion of colonial and postcolonial issues'.[234] Madhusudan's location between (and transcending) colonizing and colonized cultures gave rise to a very particular aesthetic, separate from but informed by both cultures, which repays close analysis. My readings of Madhusudan's Graeco-Roman appropriations aim to enrich the polyphony of the postcolonial discourse by examining the creative practices of an artist little known in the West but justly prominent in Indian literary histories. The Bengali poet's oeuvre is frequently elided in postcolonial studies, or encapsulated in a brief generalizing paragraph, not because of its lack of interest (Madhusudan's is one of the most surprising voices in all of Indian literature), but probably because of its inaccessibility to almost all Western scholars (most of his Bengali works have yet to be translated into English). A further reason for Madhusudan's comparative neglect by postcolonial scholarship is his use of elite Western culture not only as a tool for resisting the hegemony of Western cultural values (which is undoubtedly detectable in his oeuvre, albeit usually at a subterranean level), but also as a means of challenging the supremacy of elite Hindu culture. This book is thus in part intended as a corrective to the postcolonial fixation on Indians' resistance to the West, and will endeavour to highlight Madhusudan's challenges to indigenous forms of cultural hegemony as well.

The other main discourse, in addition to the postcolonial, to which this book aims to make a contribution is that of classical reception. Indeed, the discourse of black classicism, considered above, is in part a recent emanation of classical reception, the relatively new field of classics scholarship dedicated to analysing responses to Graeco-Roman literature and culture. This book positions itself at the interface of classical reception and postcolonial studies, two disciplines first fused in pioneering works such as Barbara Goff's *Classics and Colonialism* and Lorna Hardwick's *Classics in Post-Colonial Worlds*.[235] These works have trodden a delicate path, the 'classics' being in some senses precisely the kind of hegemonic body of knowledge on which notions

[232] Key figures in the field of postcolonial theory include Bhabha and Spivak (see esp. Bhabha (1994) and Spivak (1999)), and of course Edward Said. See also Ahmad (1992) where it is argued that postcolonial theory is nothing more than another manifestation of the West's 'will to power'.

[233] Boehmer (1995) 8.

[234] Boehmer (1995) 8.

[235] See Goff (2005) and Hardwick (2007).

and justifications of Empire were once based. They have taken pains to show that the Graeco-Roman heritage has been pressed into service against Empire as well as on its behalf.[236] This book has much to say in this context, in particular with regard to Madhusudan's overt political statements (his alignment of Britain with Aeneas and India with Dido being a prime example), but also in his covert subversion of British classical taste (his unorthodox interest in Roman authors, for instance). It should also be stated, on a more theoretical note, that my readings reject the school of thought that sees classical reception as the project of stripping away post-Classical exegetical accretions to reveal the ancient world in its 'original' form.[237] Rather, the book is located squarely within Martindale's formulation of the discipline, which sees classical reception as the study of the engagement between two cultures, the receiving and the received, and which gives an equal weight to each in its analysis of this engagement.[238] This book endeavours to give equal weight to the two cultural contexts, the Bengali and the Graeco-Roman, and to be alive to the subtleties and tensions within each of them. In particular, the differences between Greek and Roman culture, and the significance of these differences in the context of nineteenth-century British India, are foregrounded and examined at various junctures in the following chapters.

The discourse of classical reception also offers a fruitful way of analysing Madhusudan's surprising classical tastes. For example, Madhusudan's interest in Ovid, whilst virtually unparalleled in the mainstream of contemporary British poetry, finds a point of comparison (a coincidental rather than causative one, but of interest nonetheless) in the work of the female Liverpudlian poet Emma Garland. In 1842, Garland produced a translation of Ovid's *Heroides* designed specifically for a female readership and twenty years later Madhusudan produced his Hindu *Heroides* for a specifically Bengali readership. This parallel, along with moments of possible resonance with Elizabeth Barrett Browning (especially in her love of Pope's *Homer*, which Madhusudan shared) and the Bengali poet's citation of the work of Felicia Hemans, indicates the comparably subaltern

[236] Though I agree with Hardwick that one must avoid an 'uncritical sense of relief' that classical texts have recently been recognised as a source of resistance as well as oppression: see Hardwick (2007) 2.

[237] See Rowe (2003) 3.

[238] See, for example, Martindale (2006) esp. 11f.

status of the colonial and the female in the sphere of nineteenth-century British culture. During this period, the classics represented, as indeed they still do, a rich source of inspiration, and provided paradigms of resistance against cultural hegemony, for those readers who were not strictly meant to be reading them—readers, that is, who were not well-educated white men. Madhusudan's literary interest in Western women, which calls to mind the well-known contemporary caricature of the effeminate Bengali,[239] will be a recurrent theme in the course of the following chapters.

Finally, it should be noted that the scope of this book does not extend to a thoroughgoing examination of Madhusudan's reception of Sanskrit or mediaeval Bengali literature. The topic of the poet's traditional Hindu sources will be crucial throughout the following chapters for a proper understanding of the nature of his response to the Graeco-Roman classics (since very often the two traditions are juxtaposed and impliedly compared or contrasted) and, indeed, for a nuanced appreciation of how the poet used the Western classics to challenge and undermine elite Hindu culture. However, it would be impractical to attempt a complete survey and analysis of all these Indian sources in this context, and moreover it would distract from the focus of the present study, which has been circumscribed by specific reference to the Western classical canon. A full treatment of Madhusudan's reception of these sources, which has not yet been attempted in English, would be an interesting complement to the present study, and would represent a very welcome contribution to the field.[240]

[239] In this connection see esp. Sinha (1995).

[240] I should note, however, that the Source Notes in Radice (2010), the excellent new translation of Madhusudan's *MBK*, represent a most helpful survey of the Indian literary influences on that particular poem. For the reader with Bengali, the study of Indian sources in Bhattacharya (1962) offers a helpful guide to the Sanskrit and Bengali influences on the poet's Bengali oeuvre as a whole.

2

The *Padmābatī nāṭak* (1860) and the Judgement of Paris

INTRODUCTION

The *Padmābatī nāṭak* (1860) was Madhusudan's second Bengali *nāṭak* or drama (see Appendix 3 for a translation of Act One, and Appendix 4 for a synopsis of the whole play). It is the first of his Bengali works in which we see a wholesale engagement with a *topos* drawn from the Graeco-Roman tradition. Madhusudan himself described Act One of the play as the 'Greek story of the golden apple Indianised',[1] and indeed, Act One is the primary locus for explicit engagement with classical figures and tropes. However, the whole play represents a radical reworking of the Greek model, beginning with the 'Judgement of Indranīl' in Act One, which resonates very clearly with the scene on Mount Ida, but ending in Act Five with the happy conclusion of an amusingly warped 'Trojan War'. The play begins with this cornerstone Graeco-Roman mytheme dropped into the world of traditional Indian drama, with its strict Sanskritic rules of dramaturgy, and the following four acts serve as a kind of literary and cultural experiment: How would the Judgement of Paris have played out, the author asks, had it taken place in ancient Hindu India and unfolded in compliance with these Hindu dramaturgical rules? The answer to this question, as embodied in the drama, is ripe with literary and cultural conceits to provoke and amuse the playwright's cosmopolitan Bengali audience.

[1] See Murshid (2004) 121.

1. THE *PADMĀBATĪ NĀṬAK* (1860)

Madhusudan composed the *Padmābatī nāṭak* in 1860, and it was first published in April or May of that year.[2] The publication of the play came hard on the heels of his two farces, *Ekei ki bale sabhyatā?* ('Is This What You Call Civilisation?') and *Buṙo sāliker ghāre roṃ* ('New Feathers on the Old Bird'), and preceded the publication of the complete *Tilottamā-sambhab kābya.*[3] It was composed during a period of intense innovation: the two *prahasan* (farces) of that year represent Madhusudan's first foray into this comic genre, and they quickly established themselves as paradigms for later Bengali farce. The *Tilottamā-sambhab kābya* was Madhusudan's first Bengali poem to be composed in blank verse (*amitrākṣar-chanda*: 'non-rhyming verse'), a metrical system that would later be used to great effect in the epic *Meghnādbadh kābya* (1861) and the *Bīrāṅganā kābya* (1862) (see Chapters 3 and 5 below). Madhusudan is famous for being the first poet to compose blank verse in Bengali,[4] a most successful and serendipitous literary experiment, which, as it happens, seems to have had its origins in a semi-serious wager with Yatindramodan Tagore in 1859. Indeed, in his pioneering of blank verse there is a curious parallel with the origins of English blank verse. Just as blank verse was introduced into English prosody in the sixteenth century as a way of rendering Western classical texts into the modern vernacular,[5] so too Madhusudan's works of Bengali blank verse turn repeatedly to Western classical sources and thereby seek to renew them for a contemporary audience or readership.

The *Padmābatī nāṭak* (*PN*), though first published in 1860, was not in fact performed until 1865 after the author had gained celebrity for

[2] See Bandyopadhyay (1945–51) [*Padmābatī nāṭak*] 2: first published at 'the end of the month of April or in the first week of May 1860 . . .' (my translation from the Bengali). The edition of the *Padmābatī nāṭak* referred to throughout is Bandyopadhyay (1945–51), and the translation into English is my own.

[3] For the relative chronology of Madhusudan's works, see Murshid (2004) 314f. The first two cantos of the *Tilottamā-sambhab kābya* in fact appeared in consecutive issues of the journal *Bibidhārtha saṃgraha* in 1859, but the whole poem was published in book form only later in 1860: see Radice (1987) 92f.

[4] See Radice (1987) 92f. and Basu (1893), Appendix, p. 30.

[5] See the Earl of Surrey's blank verse translations of Vergil's *Aeneid* 2 and 4. Indeed the Earl of Surrey's first use of blank verse, like Madhusudan's, began as a kind of literary experiment: see Shaw (2007) 34ff.

his poetic works, in particular the *Meghnādbadh kābya* (1861). But, although the play began its life as a text more read than performed, it did eventually reach the stage,[6] and this performative aspect of the work should be kept in mind when reading the text.[7] Formally, the *PN* is a drama (*nāṭak*) divided into five acts (*aṅka*), and it is a work of remarkable innovation. For example passages of the play, which is otherwise a work of prose, are composed in the blank verse which Madhusudan first developed in the *Tilottamā-sambhab kābya*.[8] These passages, furthermore, are generally 'purple patches' such as the god Kali's Euripidean 'prologue' at the beginning of Act Four:[9] a further indication, perhaps, that blank verse and the concept of the 'classical' were curiously yoked in Madhusudan's mind.

Act One dramatizes an Indian version of the Judgement of Paris, while Acts Two to Five relate this Judgement's rather surprising consequences. Much of the play—the characters and basic plot—is of the poet's own invention,[10] but it owes a great deal to various literary models. Although various aspects of the play bear the marks of Western influence, above all the 'Judgement' in Act One, nonetheless the language and various dramatic conventions are markedly Sanskritic (the word *nāṭak* itself is a term derived from the Sanskrit aesthetic tradition). The *PN* represents, as noted above, a literary speculation: how would the Judgement of Paris, if staged in Hindu mythological costume, play out in the hands of a traditional Hindu dramatist? However, while Madhusudan's works of Sanskritic *nāṭak*

[6] The play was not performed until 1865, when it was staged in the homes of the Calcutta elite. It was produced at Calcutta's 'Public Theatre' for the first time in 1874, a year after the playwright's death: see Bandyopadhyay (1945–51) *Padmābatī nāṭak* 4. The early performance history of Madhusudan's dramas (*nāṭak*) and farces (*prahasan*) is quite complex: his plays were composed for performance, and although some of them later gained some celebrity (especially the *Ekei ki bale sabhyatā?* (1860)), most of them were first performed some time after their first publication.

[7] See in particular Chatterjee (2008) for a treatment of the rich demotic theatrical tradition of nineteenth-century Bengal, and the mid-century emergence of elite responses to and reactions against it.

[8] This play is not (*contra* Patra (1989) and Bandyopadhyay (1945–51) 1ff.) the first instance of 'blank verse' in the Bengali language: the *Tilottamā-sambhab kābya*, published in book form after the *PN* but serialized in *Bibidhārtha saṃgraha* in 1859, claims this distinction (see n. 3 above).

[9] Kali's prologue to Act Four is redolent of Aphrodite's speech at Euripides' *Hippolytus* ll. 1–57: see Section 3 below.

[10] The play, for example, was described by Nyayaratna as 'the creation of the poet's own imagination' (quoted in Bandyopadhyay (1945–51) 1).

did indeed represent an attempt to 'elevate' Bengali drama above the *alik kunāṭyo* ('false, bad theatre': Madhusudan's words)[11] which was then popular among less well-educated audiences by returning the genre to its Sanskritic roots, we should not forget that his adoption of Sanskritic forms and structures was also a literary pose, underpinned by a wry irreverence towards India's cultural heritage. As is so often the case in his works Madhusudan's *Padmābatī nāṭak* is loosely clothed in Sanskritic respectability, but strict adherence to the rules and norms of the Hindu tradition is wilfully abandoned in favour of an uninhibited cross-cultural free play: Shakespearean drama and even Attic tragedy emerge into full view from time to time. These broader features of the play will be considered in greater depth in Section 4 after the close readings of the next two sections.

2. ACT ONE: THE 'GREEK STORY OF THE GOLDEN APPLE INDIANISED'[12]

The Indianization of the Greek story of the golden apple in Act One of the PN involves a much more radical and complex transformation of the Greek myth than earlier critics have noticed.[13] Not only does the Judgement scene, for example, substitute Hindu goddesses for Greek, but it also transforms the Greek myth itself into an allegory for the Hindu 'trichotomy' (*trivarga*) of the 'goals of man' (*puruṣārtha*). Paris has a choice between three worldly boons (varying somewhat in different versions) but King Indranīl must effectively choose between *kāma* (desire), *artha* (wealth), and *dharma* (law), the well-known triad of the Hindu *trivarga*.[14] In both stories, the judge favours the goddess of love, his prize is a superlatively beautiful female, and war

[11] See Chapter 1, n.110 above. [12] See n. 1 above.

[13] The *PN*, and indeed Madhusudan's *nāṭak* ('dramas') in general, have received less critical attention than the author's *kābya* or 'poetry'. The influence of Greek mythology on Act One of the *PN* has been noted in passing by various scholars (see, for example, Dasgupta (1933–5), Dasgupta (1969), and Radice (1987)), but the subject has never been addressed in any detail. The fullest treatment of the engagement of the *PN* with Greek mythology is in Basu (1893), Madhusudan's 'primary' biography, and even this is fairly superficial and shows little appreciation of the Graeco-Roman context.

[14] We will examine the meanings of all these Sanskrit terms below.

breaks out over this woman with the judge's city ultimately coming under siege. However, in the Bengali play, the judge's prize is not a married queen but a virgin princess. This girl turns out to be the long lost daughter of one of the slighted goddesses and, thanks to the mother's timely recognition of her daughter towards the end of the play, the couple go on, after the ravages of war, to live happily ever after. The Bengali play ends with its Paris and Helen set to rule as king and queen of their Indian Troy. As we shall see in Section 3 below, this radical transformation of the Greek myth may be understood, at least in part, as a function of the Bengali play's engagement with Sanskritic models: a consequence of the Indianization of the Greek myth.

The 'Judgement of Indranīl' is a scene dominating the first half of Act One.[15] Yogindranath Basu, one of Madhusudan's 'primary' biographers, pointed out the obvious correspondences between the *PN* and the 'Greek story of the golden apple':

> Śacī, Ratidebī, Nārad, King Indranīl, and Princess Padmābatī of the play *Padmābatī* are modelled, respectively, on Greek legend's Juno, Venus, Discordia, Paris and Helen. Among the differences is that instead of the goddess Pallas, whose province concerns knowledge and wisdom, in the *Padmābatī* Madhusudan introduces the goddess Murajā, the Chief Queen of the King of the Yakṣas.[16]

This critic is largely correct to identify the play's characters in this way. However, Basu's treatment of the play's response to Greek myth, being such a cursory one, is lacking in nuance. For example, he refers repeatedly to the *grīk kabi* ('Greek poet') whom he supposes to have related the Judgement of Paris.[17] It is not clear which 'Greek poet' he has in mind, but one suspects he is thinking of Homer. However, it is one of the peculiar features of the Judgement of Paris story that, despite its fame and cardinal position in the mythological canon, we have no single authoritative version of it, no extended narration of it

[15] For a translation of the relevant passage, see Appendix 3; and for a synopsis of the whole of the PN, see Appendix 4. The numbering of the lines, designed for ease of citation, is my own and refers specifically to my English translation.

[16] Basu (1893), as cited by Bandyopadhyay (1945–51) 2 (my English translation of the original Bengali).

[17] For example: *grīk kabir nyāẏ*, 'like the Greek poet'; *grīk kabir apekṣā baram surucir*, 'more refinement than the Greek poet'; etc. (see Basu (1893), as cited by Bandyopadhyay (1945–51) 2 (my English translation of the original Bengali)).

in the Homeric poems (though it seems to be assumed by the plot of the *Iliad*),[18] and no account of the myth with reference to which other accounts might be called 'variations'.[19] It is in fact a multifarious myth, related or alluded to in various classical texts, subject to both minor and major differences between distinct versions, and is first mentioned in a single brief allusion towards the end of the *Iliad*.[20] Indeed, some of the most thoroughgoing extant versions of the story are not Greek at all, but by Roman poets or mythographers.[21] It is, then, a classical myth without a classical version.

The Judgement of Indranīl, as dramatized in Act One of the *PN*, has some features common to almost all ancient versions, both Greek and Roman, of the Judgement of Paris; others shared only with some ancient accounts but not with others; and some features entirely departing from all Graeco-Roman models. It is quite possible that Madhusudan approached the Greek myth partly through English digests of Graeco-Roman mythology,[22] or other contemporary responses to the story. However, we know that in his composition of other works (the *Meghnādbadh kābya* and *Bīrāṅganā kābya* in particular) Madhusudan consulted ancient texts in which the Judgement of Paris is related or mentioned. Given that two renditions of the

[18] I take *Il.* 24.25ff. to be an allusion to the Judgement of Paris, and the myth to be assumed by the plot of that poem. This passage has entailed vexed questions, which I can but leave open. Σ A *Il.* 24.25ff. (v 522 Erbse) claims that the passage is interpolated, arguing that if Homer had known the story of the Judgement of Paris, he would have mentioned it often (and not just once). Reinhardt (1938) shifted the burden of proof on to those who would see the passage as interpolated: see Davies (1981) esp. 56; also Stinton (1965) 2ff. for a summary of Reinhardt's excellent critique of this Iliadic scene. I follow, amongst others, Macleod (1982) 88f. in taking the passage to be authentic, and as the first reference to the Judgement of Paris.

[19] As noted by Stinton (1965). See ibid. for an excellent overview of these differing accounts, the tradition of the myth in general, and specifically its treatment in Attic tragedy.

[20] See n. 18 above.

[21] Among the fullest and most important ancient renditions of the myth we might count *Il.* 24.23–30 (despite Aristarchus' objections); the *Cypria* (see Procl. *Chrest.* 80.4–8 Severyns); Euripides *Andr.* 274–308, *Tro.* 924–32, *Hec.* 644–6, *Hel.* 23–9, 676–81, *I.A.* 182–4, 580, 1299–1309 (Euripides returns to the *topos* extremely often): on his special preferences in representing the Judgement, see Stinton (1965), Stinton (1990); Isoc. *Hel.* 41–44; Catul. 61.17–19; Verg. *Aen.* 1.26f.; Prop. 2.2.13f.; Ovid *Her.* 5.33–6, 16.53–88, *Rem.* 711f.; Lucian *Dear. Iudic.*; Hyginus *Fabula* 92; Colluthus *Harpage Tes Helenes*, l. 123; see also Frazer (1921) vol. 2, 172, n. 1, Clairmont (1951), Raab (1972), and Michalopoulos (2006) 3.

[22] For example, Thomas Bulfinch's *The Age of Fable*, first published in 1856, contains a brief version of the story.

Greek myth are related in Ovid's *Heroides* (5.33ff. and 16.53ff.), and that we know from an analysis of Madhusudan's *Bīrāṅganā kābya* (1862) that the Bengali poet had read this Latin work closely (see Chapter 5 below), we may bear it in mind especially as a possible source for the *PN*.[23] In the event, however, it will emerge that no one Graeco-Roman source text seemed to be especially favoured by the Bengali playwright. Quite possibly the myth was so well known to Madhusudan, given the depth of his classical education and the elementary stage at which he would have been introduced to the Judgment of Paris, that even he could not have indicated the precise source for his version of it.

Before treating the episode's particular identifications between the Hindu and Graeco-Roman characters in detail, we should note that Madhusudan's implicit identifications of Rati with Aphrodite, and of Śacī with Hera, bear the marks of an engagement with the discourse of Indo-European comparative mythology (as inaugurated by the British Orientalists in the late eighteenth century).[24] In earlier English works Madhusudan would note correspondences of this kind in scholarly footnotes (an Orientalist affectation)[25] as when, in one poem, he glosses 'swerga' (*viz.* Sanskrit *svarga*) as 'The Hindu Olympus'.[26] But later in his Bengali works he forgoes this procedure and leaves such correspondences implicit. In the *PN* there are only two identifications which map directly on to this Indo-Europeanist

[23] Madhusudan worked very closely with the *Iliad* in his masterpiece, the *MBK* (1861), and he composed a loose Bengali prose 'version' of *Iliad* 1–12 in the *HB* (1871): see Chapters 3 and 6 respectively.

[24] For the great influence of the British Orientalists (like Sir William Jones and H. H. Wilson) on the Bengali *bhadralok* of the mid nineteenth century, see R. Chaudhuri (2002). Around this time, Friedrich Max Müller, Professor of Sanskrit at Oxford, was reviving British interest in Indo-European comparative mythology, and was taking steps to move this discipline beyond the earlier (rather intuitive and unscientific) theories of Sir William Jones: see Stone (2002). But for Madhusudan, like many of his Bengali *bhadralok* contemporaries, it was this earlier Orientalist tradition to which he turned. For a fuller treatment of the influence of Sir William Jones on Madhusudan's oeuvre (in particular, the *Hekṭor-badh* (1871)), see Chapter 6. Note that the discipline of Indo-European comparative mythology, though perhaps not as active a field of inquiry as Indo-European comparative philology, is still very much alive today. Watkins (1995) and, more recently, West (2007) have made major contributions to the field.

[25] It was a hallmark of the poetry of the British Orientalists that they would qualify any Indian sources, or points of Graeco-Roman and Sanskritic similarity, with scholarly footnotes: see R. Chaudhuri (2002).

[26] See *The Captive Ladie* (1849), Canto 1, n. 't', printed in Patra (1989).

discourse (Śacī as Hera, Rati as Aphrodite). The other correspondences are more or less ad hoc: Indranīl, for example, plays the role played by Paris in the myth's plot, but the character 'Indranīl' was in fact invented for this drama. In Madhusudan's later Bengali works, especially in the *Hekṭor-badh* (1871), these correspondences are more extensive, with a wide array of Graeco-Roman deities being equated with Hindu counterparts, and they map more directly onto the discourse of Indo-European comparative mythology. Indeed it will be seen in Chapter 6 below, which is a close reading of the *Hekṭor-badh* (1871), that a particular article by Sir William Jones seems to be a primary source for Madhusudan's method of equating Graeco-Roman and Hindu gods.[27]

Basu was right to note that Rati plays the role of Aphrodite in the Judgement scene of the *PN*. Like the Greek goddess Aphrodite, Rati governs the province of love and sex,[28] and the bribe she offers to Indranīl relates to sexual gratification. Rati will go on to make Indranīl a gift of a beautiful woman, the Princess Padmābatī, just as Aphrodite goes on to give Helen to Paris; Rati's gift will ultimately entail no little trouble for Indranīl, as does Aphrodite's for Paris, though there is no sense (*contra* many accounts of Helen's role in the Greek myth) that this trouble is in any way Padmābatī's fault. Rati's 'bribe' at Act 1, 68 is vague and insinuating: she talks of the supreme pleasure of the bee in drinking from flowers, and says that such women as bloom like flowers in the world are devoted to her service.[29] Here we might call to mind *Iliad* 24.29-30 where Aphrodite gives Paris *alegeine mokhlosune*, 'grievous randiness'.[30] Rati's bribe in the *PN* fits this Iliadic passage better than any other version of the

[27] Specifically, Jones (1788): see Chapter 6.

[28] For Aphrodite's connections with sex and the loss of virginity (setting her role in marriage apart from the roles of Hera and Demeter), see Cancik (2002) 832. Note, however, that Aphrodite's sphere of operation was not limited to sex. She was also worshipped, for example, as the seafarer's guardian (see IG II^2 2872; Pausanias 2.34.11). For the influential structuralist notion of the Greek deities as defined by their 'powers', as opposed to their 'spheres of influence' (as the positivists argued), see Vernant (1991) esp. 272ff. Thus Aphrodite, according to Vernant's thesis, is not so much a goddess of sex (a sphere of influence) as a goddess defined by a power (harmony, concord) that she uses in various spheres (sex, seafaring, civic relations).

[29] Note that, like Madhusudan's Rati, Aphrodite was worshipped by virgins: see Pausanias 2.32.7, 2.34.12, 3.13.9; also Cancik (2002) 832.

[30] For comment on this passage see Macleod (1982) *ad loc.*

Greek myth:[31] the 'gift' of the goddess of love, as initially offered in both cases, refers to a vague kind of sexual titillation rather than to any woman in particular.[32]

Similarly, Śacī is to be identified with Hera. As the queen of the gods, and inasmuch as she tries to bribe the judge with an offer of supreme kingship, Hera is quite evidently Śacī's model in the Judgement scene of Act One. Again, this correspondence, like that between Rati and Aphrodite, seems to be informed by Indo-European comparative mythology. Śacī's presentation of herself in regal terms (her emphasis on her marriage to Indra, king of the gods) is consistent with Hera's personality, as at *Il.* 4.59ff. where she asserts her superiority by emphasizing, *inter alia*, her marriage to Zeus.[33] Furthermore, in her great anger towards Indranīl when his judgement goes against her (see Act 1, 74), and in her nursing of that anger through the persecution of the King and her attempts to ruin him (see Section 2 below), Śacī is very reminiscent of the queen of the Greek gods, who was famous for her great anger towards Paris and Troy. Note that Śacī's proposed bribe in the *PN* is specifically *sasāgar pṛthibīr indratvapad* 'overlordship of the earth and the oceans' (1, 64); we might compare this with Juno's offer in Hyginus (*fabula* 92): *in omnibus terris eum regnaturum, divitem praeter ceteros praestaturum*, 'that he [*viz.* Paris] rule over all the earth, and be pre-eminent in wealth'.[34] In the *Padmābatī nāṭak* these two discrete bribes, unlimited earthly power and pre-eminent wealth, are put in the mouths of two separate deities: while Śacī (the Hera-figure) offers Indranīl boundless kingship, it is the goddess Murajā who offers him pre-eminent wealth.

[31] But note that, in another respect, Rati recalls especially the Cypris of Colluthus (see ll. 86–98): both Collouthus' Cypris and Madhusudan's Rati recapitulate, for rhetorical effect, the bribes of the two other goddesses before presenting their own.

[32] We might also note that Rati, the play's Aphrodite-figure, speaks rather as Sappho does in fr. 16 Voigt. Rati dismisses the bribes of kingship and wealth and, in her bee metaphor (68), implies that the best thing is what one loves (as bees love flowers, so men love women). Similarly, Sappho says (ll. 1–5) that different people like different things, but that the most beautiful thing is what one loves. Indeed, Sappho illustrates this idea with the *exemplum* of Helen (ll. 6ff.) who left her child and parents to be with Paris.

[33] See Stinton (1990) 34.

[34] This offer of unlimited kingship, as related in Hyginus' account, is to be contrasted with Hera's offers of kingship over specific territories as found in other versions of the myth: see Stinton (1990) 34.

The participation of Murajā in the Judgement of Indranīl, as Basu notes (see above), seems to go against the syncretistic logic of the scene: Murajā is not comparable with Athena in the same way that Śacī (queen of the gods) and Rati (goddess of love) are comparable with Hera and Aphrodite. Murajā is the queen of the Yakṣas and wife of Kubera, the god of wealth; and, unlike Athena who offers Paris wisdom in some versions of the myth and military prowess in others,[35] this Hindu goddess offers Indranīl material riches. Basu argues: 'Madhusudan, by not making the goddess of knowledge and wisdom like a common woman vain about her beauty, displays more refinement than the Greek poet.'[36] In other words, the playwright could have shown Sarasvatī, the Hindu goddess of wisdom engaging in the beauty competition and offering a bribe of wisdom, akin to Athena's offer of wisdom in some accounts of the Judgement of Paris, but the playwright chose not to blaspheme against the most revered goddess Sarasvatī, and instead had the minor goddess Murajā play Athena's role in the beauty competition. Basu's argument, though its regrettable misogyny is of its time, may not be entirely wrong: Madhusudan's awareness of Hindu sensibilities may be in play in preventing Sarasvatī from engaging in such a competition in the *Padmābatī nāṭak*. However, it is to be noted that Madhusudan, in the Judgement of Paris as he related it briefly in the 'Preface' to the *Hekṭor-badh* (1871), describes Athena as (Preface (3)): *jñānadebī arthāt sarasvatī* . . ., 'the goddess of wisdom, that is Sarasvatī . . .'. Here Madhusudan shows little compunction about associating Sarasvatī with Athena's 'common' behaviour in the beauty competition.

My own interpretation of Murajā and her bribe would be rather different from Basu's. It seems to me that Murajā's participation in the Judgement of Indranīl serves to turn the 'Greek story of the golden apple' into an allegory for the three *puruṣārtha* ('goals of man') of the Hindu *trivarga* ('trichotomy', 'threefold set'), a radical transformation of the Greek model. The Judgement of Paris consists not only of a beauty competition but also of an 'allegorical choice' for the judge,[37] and in order to 'Indianize' this allegorical choice,

[35] See Stinton (1990).

[36] Basu (1893), cited in Bandyopadhyay (1945–51) 2: my translation from the Bengali. For my concern about his use of the phrase 'the Greek poet', see n. 17 above.

[37] This distinction between the two aspects of the myth is made, for example, by Stinton (1990) 21ff. The allegorical choice is brought to the fore in Sophocles' satyr drama *Krisis* (see fr. 361 P; cf. Call. *Lav. Pall.* 15ff.), in which Aphrodite evidently

Madhusudan has a Hindu goddess of wealth replace the Greek goddess of wisdom. According to Hindu scripture,[38] the legitimate 'goals of man' (*puruṣārtha*), considered as a 'set of three' (*trivarga*),[39] are as follows: *kāma* (desire); *artha* (wealth); and *dharma* (law or religious duty).[40] A man should, if at all possible, devote himself to all three *puruṣārtha* together, and this devotion to the *trivarga* as a whole is deemed better than devotion to just one of the three.[41] However, the three are hierarchized: if one cannot attain *kāma* (desire) and *artha* (wealth) without offence to *dharma* (law or religious duty), and if one can choose to pursue only one out of the three, then one should choose *dharma*.[42] The *dharma* of a king (a member of the *kṣatriya* or 'warrior' caste), as opposed to the *dharma* of a Brahmin (the 'priestly' and highest caste), includes all duties relating to the proper administration of a kingdom (see *MDhŚ* 7.26ff.). The three offers made by the three goddesses thus represent the three *puruṣārtha* of the *trivarga*. Śacī offers the King *sasāgar pṛthibīr indratvapad* 'the overlordship of the earth and the oceans' (*PN* 1, 64), and because Indranīl is a king,

stands for *hedone* ('pleasure') and Pallas for *phronesis* ('wisdom'): see Stinton (1990) 23.

[38] The touchstone text for this issue is the famous Sanskrit *Mānavadharmaśāstra* (*MDhŚ*), or 'Law Code of Manu'. For a critical edition and translation of this work, and a good introduction to the *Dharmasūtra* tradition from which this text emerged, see Olivelle (2005). This Sanskrit work (already highly influential in Hindu India and further afield in South-East Asia by the time of the establishment of British colonial rule in India) was the first Indian work on 'law' that Sir William Jones chose to translate into English, and was consulted by the British colonial administration as they began to carry out the administration of justice in India: see Olivelle (2004) xvi.

[39] In fact, there is sometimes a fourth term added to the *trivarga* (making it the *caturvarga* or 'fourfold set'), namely *mokṣa* or 'liberation'. This fourth term is not in play in the Judgement of Indranīl; but see Malamoud (1982) 33–9 for a treatment of the *caturvarga* compared with the *trivarga*.

[40] The Sanskrit word *dharma* is very hard to render into English since its semantic range is wide and complex. In this context *dharma* refers to the 'law', or to one's '(religious) obligation'; but in other contexts it may encapsulate a variety of other ideas, and in modern spoken Bengali it is used simply to mean 'religion'.

[41] It is made clear in various texts (including at *MDhŚ* 2.176) that the best *puruṣārtha* is the combination of all three. See also *Mahābhārata* 5.124, 34.36 and *Arthaśāstra* 1.7, 3–5, the latter indicating that exclusive devotion to any one of the three is detrimental to the other two and to itself. (See Malamoud (1982) 39.) But note that in some passages of Kālidāsa we find a *dharma* 'extremism': the king of Kālidāsa's *Raghuvaṃśa*, for example, engages in acts of *kāma* or *artha* only if they relate directly to *dharma* and appear as 'simple instruments' of *dharma*. See *Raghuvaṃśa* 1.25; also Kālidāsa's *Kumārasaṃbhava* 5.38; and Malamoud (1982) 33–9.

[42] See *MDhŚ* 4.176; *Yajñavalkya* 2.21; *Bṛhaspati* 1.111 and 113. See also Derrett (1968) 201, Kane (1973) 8–10, and Malamoud (1982) 39f.

this bribe is relevant to his *dharma*. Rati offers him sexual gratification, which is a bribe relevant to *kāma* (desire). Murajā's bribe is quite different from Athena's offer of military glory or wisdom and her divine office is quite distinct from Athena's, for this Hindu goddess must offer a bribe relevant to *artha* (wealth) if the episode is to function as an allegory of the Hindu *trivarga*.

Thus Murujā's role in the Judgement scene, which at first may seem an idiosyncratic aberration from the Greek model, is in fact crucial to the 'Indianization' of the allegorical level of the Greek myth. Indeed, the explicit terms of the *trivarga* are invoked later in the scene when Śacī addresses Indranīl (1, 74):[43] *re duṣṭo mānab, tui kāmer baś haẏe dharmo naṣṭo karli?*, 'O wicked man, have you succumbed to desire [*kāma*] and destroyed the law [*dharma*]?' Indeed, it is interesting to note that Śacī's representation of Indranīl's judgement here as a simple choice between *kāma* (desire) and *dharma* (law), in its suppression of the middle term *artha* (wealth), is akin to ancient representations of Paris' judgement as a straight choice between *hedone* (pleasure) and *phronesis* (wisdom).[44] Furthermore, Madhusudan's implicit reading of the Judgement of Paris as an overtly allegorical myth is akin to some Western analyses of the Greek story, both ancient and modern.[45] Recently, for example, Merkelbach has read this Greek myth as *die Wahl... zwischen mehreren Lebenswegen*, 'the choice.... between different lifestyles', aptly comparing it with the more clearly allegorical tale of Hercules at the crossroads.[46] The Judgement of Indranīl, like the Judgement of Paris, figures a choice of 'lifestyles', but the Bengali playwright has transformed this Greek choice into a markedly Hindu one.

However, it should also be noted that, although the Bengali scene represents a choice between lifestyles, it is also cleverly implied in the play that Indranīl's choice, although it favours the unworthy life goal

[43] See also Śacī's emphasis on *dharma* (the king's obligations with respect to it, and her associations with it) at Act 1, 35 and 59.

[44] See esp. Sophocles' Satyr-play, of which only one fragment survives: Fr. 361P; cf. Call. *Lav. Pall.* 15ff. Here Aphrodite represents *Hedone*, Pallas *Phronesis*. See also Stinton (1990) 23, esp. n. 27.

[45] For the ancient tradition of reading the Judgement of Paris in allegorical terms, see Stinton (1990).

[46] See Merkelbach (1970), reprinted in (1996) 1ff. For the relevant story of Herakles, see Prodicus B 2 DK = Xenophon, *Memorabilia* 2.1.29ff. See also Davies (2003) 33.

of desire, is objectively a fair assessment of the three goddesses' relative beauty. If Nārada is to be believed when he says to the three goddesses (at 1, 30) that anyone other than the most beautiful of them will, immediately upon touching this flower, turn to stone and spend a thousand years in the grove of mount Vindhya, then the fact that Rati does not turn to stone in Act One is a vindication of the King's judgement.[47]

It is clear by now that Indranīl stands for Paris in this Bengali scene: indeed, Indranīl's interview with the three Hindu goddesses is even set against a mountain backdrop (Mount Vindhya), just as the Judgement of Paris takes place on Mount Ida. However, the Indian hero's behaviour and characterization engage in a complex manner with their Greek model. Indranīl panics as soon as he is appointed judge (1, 59) but this alarm is in marked contrast to the King's initial response to the appearance of the three goddesses. The king's first reaction to the theophany is one of delight (1, 46): . . . *ẽder animeṣ cakṣu ār chāẏāhīn deho ẽder debatva-sandeha dūr nā kalyeo, ẽder aparūp lābaṇye āmār se saṃśaẏ bhañjano hato* . . . , 'Even if their unblinking eyes, their bodies that leave no shadow, did not dispel doubt about their divinity, any uncertainty I might have would be resolved by their incomparable loveliness . . . ' This expression of delight, incidentally, may put one in mind of the Vergilian Aeneas' inadvertent flirtation with his own divine mother: *namque haud tibi voltus/ mortalis, nec vox hominem sonat: O, dea certe* . . . , 'for your appearance is not mortal, nor does your voice sound human: O, surely a goddess . . . ' (*Aen.* 1.327f.).[48] But Indranīl's initial joy is soon replaced by fear when he is appointed as judge. This mixture of delight and alarm—or rather the progression from the former to the latter as the scene unfolds—locates the Bengali scene between different versions of the Judgement of Paris myth. In many ancient versions of the story, including some paintings of it, Paris is depicted as alarmed upon seeing the goddesses and reluctant to make a judgement: Colluthus 123 and Ovid *Heroides* 16.67f. imply such alarm, as perhaps did the *Cypria* from which Colluthus' account

[47] Moreover, the King claims that in giving judgement he is giving his honest opinion: see 1, 70 and 72. Rati's fate may be taken to justify the King's claim.

[48] Indeed the resonance between Aeneas' words and Odysseus' address to Nausicaa at Hom. *Od.* 6.168 (for which see Austin (1971) *ad loc.*) deepens the uncomfortable suggestion of a sexual frisson here between mother and son. For more on Madhusudan's reception of Vergil, see Chapter 4 below.

may ultimately be derived.[49] Indeed, it is generally a difficult experience for mortals, even heroes, to behold deities in early Greek literature.[50] In one type of black-figure vase painting, Paris' alarm and reluctance are especially well illustrated: Paris is shown turning to flee and being physically restrained by Hermes.[51] However, the Bengali hero is frightened and reluctant not upon seeing the goddesses, but only upon receiving instructions to act as judge between them: in this way one may wonder whether Madhusudan projects on to Indranīl his own awareness of the Greek myth and its consequences for the hapless judge, and anticipates his audience's recognition of the Judgement of Paris myth in the unfolding scene. Initially, in any case, Indranīl is quite confident in their presence, a feature of the scene reminiscent, perhaps, of the brazen behaviour ascribed to Paris at *Il.* 24.25ff.

Indranīl's initial fearlessness before the goddesses may also have to do with his status as a king and as the *nāyak* ('hero') of a traditional Hindu *nāṭak* ('drama').[52] The hero is not a solitary shepherd like Paris, but a Hindu *rājā* ('king') engaged in hunting. Stinton says of Paris' alarm, referring to his dual status as shepherd and prince, that 'it is less appropriate to the prince of Troy than to the solitary herdsman, fearful at the invasion of his privacy'.[53] Indranīl, being unambiguously the *rājā* and *nāyak* of a Bengali *nāṭak* modelled on the Sanskritic paradigm, responds to the conventions of that ancient genre. One of these conventions is that the hero is usually a *rājā*,[54] who should retain *gāmbhīrya* ('composure') even in frightening

[49] See Stinton (1990) 25, esp. n. 48. Note that there is doubt whether Colluthus actually knew the *Cypria* (see ibid.), but even if working with an epitome it was likely fuller than what we have (*viz.* the excerpts of Proclus): see Bethe (1914) ii, 205f.

[50] The apparition of Iris causes Priam to tremble: see *Il.* 3.131 and 24.169–71. Gods often disguise themselves to avoid alarming mortals in this way: see Aphrodite's appearance before Anchises at *H.Hymn.Aph.* 51. See Stinton (1990) 25, n. 46. It may be significant that the appearance of a god may frighten mortals in the Hindu tradition too: the most famous example of such alarm is probably Arjuna's reaction to Kṛṣṇa's theophany in the second book of the *Bhagavad Gītā*, on which see Dhavamony (1982) 26.

[51] This type of painting is specifically Attic: see Hampe (1954) 549. For the motif of Paris' alarm and reluctance, see Stinton (1990) 25, esp. n. 44.

[52] On the profound influence of Sanskritic dramaturgy on this Bengali play, see Section 3 below.

[53] Stinton (1990) 25 esp. n. 49. In Greek paintings, if not in literature, heroes are not usually alarmed by the presence of gods: see ibid.

[54] This is a convention rather than an absolute rule: see Keith (1924) 39.

circumstances.[55] Indranīl's initial reaction to the goddesses' theophany may be in contrast to Greek tradition but it accords well with the hero's Hindu identity. His panic later in the scene, however, is perhaps less dignified than traditional Sanskrit dramaturgy would normally allow.

Basu identifies the divine sage Nārada as an Eris-figure (see above), and in many respects this is correct. Indeed, the golden lotus (*kanakpadmo*), which he mentions at *PN* 1, 56, is, quite literally, the 'golden apple Indianised',[56] the lotus being a markedly Indian symbol. Nārada's desire to inculcate strife between the three goddesses (*PN* 1, 15) resonates clearly with the pique of Eris/Discordia at not being invited to the wedding of Peleus and Thetis: in Hyginus 92 and Colluthus 39ff.,[57] for example, this motif is related explicitly. However, whereas Eris has a particular grievance against the goddesses, Nārada's attitude is more mischievous than aggrieved, and his mythological reputation (note his epithet *kalahapriyo* or 'fond of quarrels') is for sparking playful rather than serious disputes. From the very beginning, then, the nature of the goddesses' quarrel is more trivial in this Bengali version than in the Greek paradigm.

As regards the cause underlying the Judgement of Paris, the Graeco-Roman tradition in fact splits two ways: of the two accounts of this cause, one is simple and the other complex. Some accounts, like Hyginus 92, present the Judgement of Paris as a straightforward reflex of Strife's pique; but others, like the *Cypria* and Ovid *Her.* 16, have Strife acting in the furtherance of the *Dios Boule* ('Plan of Zeus').[58]

[55] See, for example, *Daśarūpaka* 2.15 and Haas (1962) *ad loc*,; also *Sāhityadarpaṇa* 89. For more detail, see Section 2 below.

[56] Note that the apple of discord is not found in Graeco-Roman literature before Hyginus *Fabula* 92. For possible depictions of an apple in pictorial representations of the Judgement of Paris in the archaic period, see Stinton (1990) 22, n. 24.

[57] See Stinton (1990) 22, esp. n. 25. Note that in the Preface to Madhusudan's *Hekṭor-badh* (1871) the grievance of Eris is the reason given for her institution of the beauty contest.

[58] *Cypria* Fr. 1K, cf. Proclus, *Chrest.* i., p.17K, Σ *Il.* 1.5, Cramer, *Anecd.* 4. 406: Euripides also alludes to this idea (see *Helen* 39f. and *Orestes* 1614f.). See also Tzetzes on Lyc. 93 and Apollod. *Epit.* iii. 1. According to Hesiod fr. 96 Rzach = Merkelbach H 57ff., Zeus acted to preserve the gods' 'racial purity' (see Stinton (1990) 22, n. 26). But the whole story of the *Dios Boule* ('Plan of Zeus') may, as is suggested by the *scholium*, be generated by *Il.* 1.5: see Stinton (1990) 57 and Bethe (1914) (vol. 2) 213, 241, and 282. Note that in the later *Hekṭor-badh* (1871), in whose Preface Madhusudan briefly relates the Judgement of Paris, the simpler rather than the more complex version of divine motivation is given.

According to this second tradition, Zeus felt that the world was overburdened with people, and upon consultation with Themis he hit upon the remedy of a great war (to be triggered, rather elaborately, through the ministrations of Eris/Discordia and the Judgement of Paris). In the *PN*, too, there is the suggestion that the beauty competition is motivated by a higher divine authority. Nārada, in conversation with the three goddesses, tells of an ominous event which unfolded when he picked the golden lotus (1, 26): all of a sudden a divine voice (*daibabāṇī*), claiming to be or to speak for the great goddess Pārvatī, rebuked him for picking the lotus and told him that, unless he gave it to the most beautiful female in the three worlds, he would be scorched by her husband Śiva. Note that Pārvatī/Debī and Śiva are of a higher order of divinity than the three quarrelling goddesses:[59] Hindu theology departs from an analogy with the Greek in respect of this notion of divine hierarchy. Much of this detail, of course, departs from all Graeco-Roman models: in no extant account does Eris steal the Golden Apple, nor is she in any account threatened with destruction if she does not give the prize to the correct female. However, Nārada's words here do recall those of Discordia (Eris), for example, in the account of Hyginus *Fabula* 92: *quae esset formosissima, attolleret*, 'she who is the most beautiful should take [the apple]'.[60] Nārada's establishment of a beauty competition seems here to be entailed by the will of a higher

[59] Indra, husband of Śacī, is the warrior god of the Vedic pantheon (i.e. at the earliest stage of attested 'Hindu' religion), associated with storms and thunder (Michaels (2004) 202–5). In the later 'Puranic' stage of Hinduism, and especially in the *Mahābhārata*, Indra is represented as king of the gods and is still remarkable for his valour. However, his importance seems to be declining in the Sanskrit epic (see Gonda (1962) and Gajendragadkar (1946)), and his kingship over the gods seems really to be a kind of guardianship of the universe (see Michaels (2004) 213), rather than a transcendent power. Indeed in later stages of Hindu belief, Indra's status is increasingly sidelined. The decline in Indra's importance is commensurate with, and caused by, the increasing importance of new divinities: in particular Brahmā, Viṣṇu, and Śiva. These three gods come to comprise the '*trimūrti*' ('threefold embodiment') of later Hindu theology: three discrete aspects of the same transcendent divinity, each representing the distinct forces (respectively) of creation, maintenance, and destruction (see Matchett (2003) 139 and Michaels (2004) 205). Pārvatī is the consort of the great god Śiva (one of whose names, *Mahādeva*, means literally 'great god'); and in Śākta theology, especially prominent in Bengal, Pārvatī and Śiva are deemed to figure two aspects of the same godhead.

[60] Note that this command is said in some later accounts (see Lucian, *Dial. Deorum* 20.7 and Tzetzes on Lyc. 93) to be inscribed on the Golden Apple itself: see Roscher (1884ff.) [vol. 1] 1338, *ad* 'Eris', and Stinton (1990) 22, n. 24. Indeed, this motif is found in the *Hekṭor-badh* account of the Judgement of Paris.

deity, and thus the Bengali Judgement seems to favour the more complex Graeco-Roman tradition: Pārvatī's action through Nārada's agency echoes Zeus' action through Eris' agency. However, the question whether the beauty competition has truly been entailed by Pārvatī's command or is in fact simply Nārada's own plan is left open for the audience,[61] for we only have Nārada's word for it that he did indeed hear a 'divine voice', as he claimed (1, 26). Indeed, this ambiguity may be said to reflect the variation attested in the Graeco-Roman sources. Madhusudan, as it were, thematizes the very bifurcation at the heart of the Greek myth: he has his quarrel caused by an Eris-figure who may or may not be acting on the authority of a higher deity.

Nārada corresponds with Eris, as was noted above, only in certain respects. His status as a 'divine sage' (*debarṣi*) rather than a god, not to mention his masculinity, complicates a straightforward identification of the character with the Greek Eris. Nārada is known for sparking quarrels in a playful way, whereas Eris' actions in sparking the quarrel are far from jocular. Indeed, in some ways Nārada is rather more like Hermes/Mercury than Eris. Just as this god leads the goddesses to Paris on Mount Ida—as for example at Ovid's *Her.* 16.61ff. or Hyginus *Fabula* 92—[62] so too, in the *PN*, Nārada brings the three Hindu goddesses to King Indranīl on Mount Vindhya and effectively appoints him as judge (1, 43).[63] Indeed, Nārada is not only like Hermes/Mercury but also in some respects like Zeus/Jupiter: just as the king of the Graeco-Roman gods excuses himself from settling the beauty competition, so too Nārada astutely passes the task on to a hapless mortal.

The Judgement of Indranīl is far from being a straightforward 'version' of the Greek myth. The transposition of the story to the Bengali stage and its 'Indianization' entail various transformations both superficial and radical, the most radical transformation being the conversion of Paris's 'allegorical choice' into an allegory for the Hindu *trivarga*. We know from observations made in later chapters

[61] But note that Mount Vindhya, where Act One sets its scene, has strong associations with Pārvatī.

[62] Note that the motif of Hermes leading the goddesses to Paris is depicted frequently in early Greek black-figure: see Hampe (1954) 549.

[63] Note that this kind of multiple identification, whereby one or more Hindu deities/heroes may be identified with one or more Graeco-Roman counterparts, is also a marked feature of Madhusudan's later works: the *MBK* (1861), the *BK* (1862), and the *HB* (1871). See Chs. 4–7.

(see Chapters 3, 5, and 6) that Madhusudan knew at least two classical texts in which this myth is related (Homer's *Iliad* and Ovid's *Heroides*), but Madhusudan's 'Indianization' of the story does not fully accord with any one classical rendition and, indeed, it shows some remarkable departures from them all. Act One of the *PN* is indeed the 'Greek story of the golden apple Indianised', but this 'Indianization' is much more transformative and complex than has previously been acknowledged.

Finally, it is important to note that, quite apart from the play's unprecedented Indianization of the Judgment of Paris, Madhusudan's dramatization of the myth is itself a surprising and unusual feature of the work. Although in antiquity the story was the subject, for example, of a Cratinus comedy, the *Dionysalexandros* (*c.* 430 BCE),[64] which used the Greek myth as a platform for political parody,[65] the myth has rarely found its way on to the European stage. The closest thing we find to a precedent for Madhusudan's dramatization of the Judgement story is probably the seventeenth-century French tragicomedy by Sallebray, *Le Jugement de Pâris et le Ravissement d'Hélène*, composed in 1639.[66] (This play shares a variety of features with the Bengali play: both figure an irreverent skit on the Greek original; both end with 'Paris' and 'Helen' together; both are punctuated with various kinds of song and music.) Earlier English works, such as Congreve's masque, *The Judgement of Paris* (1701), have staged the Judgement of Paris.[67] And yet none of these Western dramatizations seems to have had any direct influence on the Bengali play. The *PN* is a unique work of Indian drama, but it is also a unique episode in the history of the reception of the Judgment of Paris myth.

3. THE REST OF THE *PADMĀBATĪ NĀṬAK*

The ultimate consequences of the Judgement of Indranīl are drastically different from those of the Judgement of Paris. While there are

[64] See Kassell (1983–95) (vol. 4) frr. 39–51.

[65] See Sommerstein (2002) 92ff.

[66] See A. Cook (1981) for a good overview of seventeenth-century French drama and further bibliography.

[67] A libretto set to music by various composers, most famously by John Eccles (1701) and later (and most successfully) by Thomas Arne (premiered 1740).

some basic similarities between the stories as they unfold (the awarding of a beautiful woman to the judge as a prize; the ensuing war that is waged against the judge's city over that woman), the two narrative arcs in fact conclude very differently.[68] Whereas Troy falls and Paris is stripped of his prize, the Bengali hero defeats the forces investing his city and the play ends with King Indranīl and Queen Padmābatī, the plot's Paris and Helen figures, set to rule happily over their Indian Troy.

The rest of the play, then, diverges sharply from the consequences that the node of Greek mythology, with which the drama begins, might lead one to expect. For the play's intended audience, the Western-educated and cosmopolitan Bengali man of letters with an eye for European high culture, Indranīl's judgement in Act One raises the fear of a Greek consequence. But, as the rest of the Bengali play unfolds, the audience's fears are allayed as the Bengali hero's bad action leads not to a Greek but to a markedly Indian consequence. The playwright drops the Greek myth into the world of traditional Sanskrit drama (the opening lines and stage directions of the Bengali play are extremely evocative of Kālidāsa's Sanskrit play *Abhijñāna-śakuntalam*, and the influence of that Sanskrit work throughout the Bengali play is frequently felt). In turn, that Hindu world radically reshapes the Greek myth in the image of its own literary tropes and customs. The cross-cultural conceit which underpins the play, the happy ending of an Indian Judgement of Paris, is largely a function, as will be seen, of the play's flirtation with the prescriptive rules of Sanskritic dramaturgy. This conceit in turn figures an implied comparison and contrast between the literary tastes of the Greek and Hindu traditions: the latter's distaste for the catastrophic downfall of the hero, at least in the mainstream Sanskritic *kāvya* and *nāṭaka* traditions,[69] is the diametric opposite of the former's appetite for it, at least in Attic tragedy.

The divergences of the Bengali play, after Act One, from the paradigm of the Greek myth are many and varied. However, there are striking respects in which the play continues to follow the Greek paradigm, or at least to touch it tangentially. First of all, one's

[68] See Appendix 4 for a detailed synopsis of the plot of the whole of the *PN*.

[69] Note that these Sanskrit terms, from which the modern Bengali words *kābya* and *nāṭak* are derived, are properly transliterated as *kāvya* and *nāṭaka*.

expectation of a Helen-figure is to some extent fulfilled.[70] Rati, goddess of love, gives Indranīl a pre-eminently beautiful woman, Princess Padmābatī, as a reward for his judgement (2, 1, 17), just as Helen is offered to Paris by Aphrodite.[71] Note that, as with the 'Paris' figure Indranīl, Padmābatī is a character created by the playwright rather than one taken directly from Hindu mythology. Helen is the fairest woman in the world,[72] and so too (at least according to Śacī) is this Indian princess (2, 1, 67): *padmābatīr matan sundarī nārī pṛthibīte nāi*, 'there is no woman on earth as beautiful as Padmābatī'.[73] Rati gives Padmābatī to Indranīl in exchange for the Golden Lotus, and indeed the very name of the Princess identifies her with the Golden Lotus. 'Padmābatī', if analysed as a *yaugika* ('etymologically significant') noun, breaks down into the elements *padma* ('lotus') and the feminine inflexion of the possessive suffix *-bat-*: 'the Girl with the Lotus'. This identification between the Golden Lotus and the Princess is appropriate enough (and alerts one's attention to the transaction involved in the Greek myth): the former passes from judge to goddess, the latter from goddess to judge, the beauty prize in exchange for the world's most beautiful woman.

Unlike Helen, of course, Padmābatī is a virgin Princess rather than a married Queen. Thus Padmābatī's marriage to Indranīl (which occurs in the break between Acts Three and Four) is not adulterous like Helen's seduction/abduction by Paris.[74] However, even in this respect, the Bengali play does not diverge absolutely from the Greek myth; for there is a secondary tradition of the Helen story in which

[70] Indeed, Basu (1893) notes that Padmābatī is a Helen figure: see Section 2 above.

[71] The idea of Helen as the 'gift of Aphrodite' is especially prominent, for example, in Euripides' *Helen* ll. 27f., 238f., 364f., 1098–100. See Burian (2007) 274.

[72] This is a famous *topos* beginning with Homer: see Hom. *Il.* 3.154–158; contrast Ovid's *Met.* 15.232f. where the elderly Helen complains of the loss of her beauty. See Cancik (2005) 63.

[73] Note, however, that such hyperbole is a common trope in Sanskrit drama and in Madhusudan's other Bengali plays: Kṛṣṇakumārī, for example, is described by the courtesan Madanikā in just the same way at 4, 2, 10 of Madhusudan's *Kṛṣṇakumārī nāṭak* (1861).

[74] The distinction between seduction and abduction did not operate in ancient Greece as it does in the modern world. See, for example, Herodotus' *Histories* 1.4.2, where it is presented as traditional wisdom that a woman will not be 'snatched away' unless she wishes to be. On Herodotus' interest in sexual issues see Asheri *ad* Herodotus' *Histories* 1.4.2 and Walcot (1978) 137–47. However, the question of Helen's willingness to follow Paris to Troy is explored in careful detail by the Roman poet Ovid in *Heroides* 16 and 17.

the Spartan Queen, like Queen Padmābatī in the Bengali play, was never anything but a chaste wife. In addition to the Helen who went with Paris to Troy, the Helen whom we find in the Homeric poems and elsewhere, there was a tradition of a Helen who did not in fact go to Troy at all: this Helen was replaced by an *eidolon* ('phantom') which accompanied Paris to Troy in her place, while she herself was transported by Hermes to Egypt where she remained faithful to Menelaus.[75] There are various striking similarities between Padmābatī and this second Helen: above all note that, like this Helen, the Bengali heroine is a chaste wife and not a promiscuous adulteress. Furthermore, just as this Helen is removed from Paris by Hermes, so too at *PN* 4, 1, 24, Padmābatī is taken from Indranīl by the god Kali. And just as it was Hera who arranged for Hermes to remove Helen to Egypt in order to deprive Paris of his prize (in pique at losing the beauty competition),[76] so too it is Śacī (the Hera figure of Act One) who arranges for the god Kali to take Padmābatī away from Indranīl in Act Four Scene 1. The resonance between the heroine Padmābatī and this second Helen in fact deepens towards the end of the play: just as this Helen is reunited, after a painful separation, with her lawful husband (Menelaus) in Euripides' *Helen*,[77] so too Padmābatī is reunited with Indranīl after the war of Vidarbha at the end of the *PN* 5, 2.

Another intriguing respect in which the figure of Padmābatī may be said to engage with her Spartan model is her divinity. The Bengali heroine, apparently a mortal Princess, turns out at *PN* 5, 2 to be in fact the long lost daughter of the goddess Murajā. She had been born on earth as a human *avatar* of Murajā's daughter, the goddess Vijaẏā, and it is only at the end of the play that the goddess recognizes Padmābatī as her own daughter. This transcending of the boundary between mortal and immortal echoes Helen's status in the Graeco-Roman tradition. In the Greek epic tradition Helen is generally considered to be the daughter, though raised by mortal parents, of

[75] See Stesichorus fr. 192 PMG (the palinode), Herodotos 2, 113–5, and Euripides' *Helen*. See Burian (2007) 4, esp. n. 7. General studies of the complex myth of Helen, from antiquity through to the present day, include Ghali-Kahil (1955), Lindsay (1974), Clader (1976), Meagher (1995), Suzuki (1989), and Maguire (2009).

[76] See Burian (2007) 2.

[77] See Eurip. *Helen* 541ff. for the 'recognition' scene between husband and wife, which begins, in Burian's words *ad loc.*, in a 'tragicomedy of errors': see Burrian (2007).

the great god Zeus[78] and the goddess Nemesis:[79] the goddess gave birth to an egg which she delivered to, or which was found by, Leda the wife of the Spartan King Tyndareus.[80] Each heroine is raised in a royal household as a mortal Princess while in reality being of divine parentage.

The War of Vidarbha, which occurs as a direct consequence of Indranīl's marriage to Padmābatī, figures a basic respect in which the Beṅgali play continues, after Act One, to engage with the Greek paradigm. Although Padmābatī's relationship with Indranīl is not adulterous, nonetheless it does represent an 'elopement' of sorts, since their marriage is in breach of the protocol of *svayaṃvara*. The *svayaṃvara*, literally '[the bride's] own choice', is the ninth form of Hindu marriage,[81] and is in some respects not unlike the *mnestus* ('suit') of early Greek poetry.[82] The Hindu *svayaṃvara* is a form of marriage as old as the *Rig Veda* but it seems to have become a mere literary trope rather than a cultural reality early in the Common Era.[83] The *svayaṃvara* either involves the bride making a straightforward selection from a number of suitors or, as in the Greek tradition of *mnestus*, is predicated on a competition between the suitors (the winner of which marries the bride).[84] When, in the *PN*, Indranīl marries Padmābatī after the suitors have been disbanded due to the Princess' ill health, they are aggrieved that the *svayaṃvara* has not been carried out as prescribed. It is thus Indranīl's violation of the *svayaṃvara* that entails the suitors' campaign against Vidarbha (*PN* 4, 1, 1). Helen's *mnestus* or 'suit', on the other hand, passes off without such complication. Menelaus wins Helen legitimately according to the rules of *mnestus*. It is only when his wife is then abducted/seduced by his guest Paris that the Trojan War is provoked. Schematically, then, Indranīl stands as a Menelaus figure: he is the first husband, the winner (albeit illegitimate) of the suit for his bride's hand. However, as the man who provokes the anger of the thwarted

[78] See Hom. *Il.* 3.418 and *Od.* 4.184, 219, 227. See, *contra*, Hes. Cat. fr. 24 H where Helen is considered to be the daughter of the god Oceanus. For an overview of Helen's place in the Graeco-Roman tradition, see Cancik (2005) 62f.

[79] See *Cypria* fr. 9.1 PEG I.

[80] See, for example, Sappho fr. 166f. Voigt, Cratinus fr. 115 PCG IV = Ath. 9.373e.

[81] For a treatment of *svayaṃvara* in the Hindu tradition, see Chatterjee (1961) 603–15.

[82] Indeed, Madhusudan uses the word *svayaṃvara* to describe Helen's *mnestus* in the Preface to his *Hekṭor-badh* (1871). For a good recent study of the early Greek *mnestus*, see Haubold (2000) esp. 140ff.

[83] See Chatterjee (1961) 614f.

[84] See Chatterjee (1961) 608ff.

suitors, Indranīl plays the role of Paris: for the Achaeans who sailed against Troy were contracted to fight by their status as former suitors for Helen's hand. At the beginning of Helen's *mnestus*, her father Tyndareus made the suitors swear an oath to support his daughter's future husband in battles over her.[85] When Paris ran off with the Spartan queen, the Achaeans were obliged to act on their oath and join Menelaus and Agamemnon in their expedition against Troy.[86] Like the kings besieging Vidarbha, the Achaeans may be said to have assaulted Troy in their role as failed suitors. And just as the Trojan War may be seen as an horrendous extension of Helen's *mnestus*, so too the Vidarbhan War is described later in the Bengali play as *svayaṃbarsaṃgrām*, 'the war of the *svayaṃvara*' (4, 2, 23).

Furthermore, the depiction of Padmābatī standing on top of the Gate of Vidarbha in *PN* 4, 1 is reminiscent of the Iliadic *Teikhoskopia*, Helen's conversation with Priam on the walls of Troy in *Il.* 3. Specifically, the Indian queen's lament over all the deaths caused by her marriage (4, 1, 5) is suggestive of Helen's self-rebuke at *Il.* 3.180 and her wish that she had died before following Paris to Troy (ll. 173–6).[87] Each woman expresses these feelings of regret whilst standing on the walls of a city that is under siege for her sake. This Bengali scene (4, 1), in fact, seems to be a marked locus for Greek influence. In addition to this possible Iliadic resonance, the opening of Act Four, the darkest episode of the whole play, is full of resonances from prologues to Attic tragedies. The scene of a besieged city might make one think of Aeschylus' *Septem*, an early Attic tragedy set in the besieged city of Thebes.[88] And just as the Chorus of Theban women complain of the terrifying din of the thud of hooves, the clashing of shields, and so forth (ll. 83ff.), so Padmābatī and her friend reel at the terrifying sounds of war. At *PN* 4, 1, 9 Padmābatī exclaims to her

[85] See Hesiod *Cat.* fr. 19646w–200; 202; 204; Hyg. *Fabulae* 81. For a treatment of this *mnestus* in early Greek hexameter poetry, see Haubold (2000) 140f. It is clear that Madhusudan was aware of the suitors' oath at the *mnestus* of Helen: he narrates it himself in the Preface to his *Hekṭor-badh* (1871).

[86] See Haubold (2000) 140f. The suitors' oath brings the *mnestus* of Helen into line with a broader pattern in early Greek hexameter poetry, namely the logic of 'marriage or death' (ibid. 141). All the Achaeans who competed for Helen's hand (save Odysseus who, knowing the outcome in advance, woos from a distance: see ibid. 141, n. 434) eventually die as a consequence of their failed suit. Just as Helen's suitors die, so Padmābatī's would-be suitors are ultimately defeated in the Bengali play.

[87] For a treatment of the *Teikhoskopia*, see Kirk (1985) 286ff.

[88] See Hutchinson (1985) 41f. for the scene-setting at the beginning of this play.

friend: *uh! ki bhaẏaṃkar śabdo!...ei dekho bīrdaler pāẏer bhāre basumatī yeno kēpe kēpe uṭhchen*, 'Oh! What a terrifying sound!... behold how the Earth seems suddenly to be trembling, as it were, under the weight of the warriors' feet'. Furthermore, the Bengali scene opens with a soliloquy by the god Kali (4, 1, 1) which is markedly reminiscent of Aphrodite's prologue at *Hippolytus* ll. 1–57: the two speeches share a tone of spite, a stated malevolence towards particular mortals, and the feature of self-definition. Aphrodite begins her speech by proclaiming her power (her first word is *polle*, 'mighty'), her renown among mortals and immortals, and her name.[89] Kali's speech begins (*PN* 4, 1, 1): *āmi kali; e bipul biśve ke nā kāpe/ śuniẏā āmār nām?...*, 'I am Kali; in this wide universe who does not tremble upon hearing my name?' Thus in at least two respects Act Four of the Bengali drama, the darkest episode of the play, opens as an Attic tragedy might open. If the audience had forgotten its foreboding that Indranīl's judgement might entail a terrible Greek consequence, then Act Four's ominous samplings from Attic tragedy rekindle that foreboding quite emphatically.

Further resonances with Western drama, especially Shakespeare and other later European works, may be detected in the course of the *PN*. One wonders, in particular, whether the plot of the discovery of a long-lost child, Murajā's 'recognition' of Padmābatī as her own daughter, might owe something to Shakespeare's *Twelfth Night*. However, in generic and formal terms, the *PN* is a drama composed, above all, on the paradigm of Sanskritic dramaturgy. In his correspondence at the time of the play's composition, the playwright is quite explicit that this play, like the *Śarmiṣṭhā nāṭak* (1859) before it, is composed on the 'classical model'[90] (Indian rather than Greek).[91]

[89] For a treatment of this Euripidean prologue, see Halleran (1995) 145ff.

[90] In a letter to a friend, Madhusudan remarked: 'I don't know if you have seen 'Sermista', or if you have what you think of it. There is another Drama of mine [*viz.* the *PN*], which will be soon acted by a company of Amateurs. It is also written on the classical model... If I am spared, I intend to write 3 or 4 more plays of the classical kind, just to give our countrymen a taste for that species of the drama...' (see Murshid (2004) 118).

[91] As is made explicit by Madhusudan when, in another letter, he wrote (after the composition of the *Padmābatī nāṭak*): 'If I should live to write other dramas, you may rest assured, I shall not allow myself to be bound down by the dicta of Mr Viswanath of the Sahitya-Darpan'. (See Murshid (2004) 121.) The playwright here refers to the mediaeval Sanskrit treatise on literary aesthetics (the *Sāhityadarpaṇa*) by the Orissan called Viśvanātha. Madhusudan's two earlier plays (the *Śarmiṣṭhā nāṭak* (1859) and the *Padmābatī nāṭak* (1860)) were indeed 'bound down' by the 'dicta' of Sanskrit dramaturgy; his later dramas (the *Kṛṣṇakumārī nāṭak* (1861) and the *Māẏākānan*

This influence of Sanskrit dramaturgy on the play (as well as the specific model of the *Abhijñānaśakuntalam*, Kālidāsa's famous Sanskrit drama), goes some way to explain the radical departures of the Bengali drama from the narrative arc of the Greek myth. It was contended above that the Bengali play figures a kind of transcultural experiment: how would this most famous, cornerstone Greek myth (the 'Greek story of the golden apple') play out on the traditional Hindu stage? The rules of Sanskritic dramaturgy dictate that the story will unfold in a manner radically different from any Western version of the Greek story.

We know that we are in the world of Sanskritic *nāṭak* from the very opening of the Bengali play. The manner in which King Indranīl bursts on to the stage at the beginning of Act One, and the words he uses when doing so, are strikingly reminiscent of King Duṣyanta's entrance at the beginning of Kālidāsa's *Abhijñānaśakuntalam* (henceforth *AŚ*), or 'The Recognition of Śakuntalā': each enters bow in hand, hunting a stag, and comments on how far off course the pursuit has taken him.[92] *PN* Act Two, Scene 2 recalls Act Six of the Sanskrit play: in each scene two girls question a *Kañcuki* or 'Brahmin Chamberlain', who then goes on to give them the information they need. Indranīl's leap to assist the swooning Padmābatī at *PN* 3, 1, 70 is strikingly reminiscent of Duṣyanta's assistance to the swooning Śakuntalā in the first act of the Sanskrit play. Padmābatī's words at *PN* 5, 2, 18 (the final scene of the Bengali play) recall Śakuntalā's in the final scene of the Sanskrit play (cf. *AŚ* 7 (7.130)): each heroine reflects on how Fate, having neglected her for so long, has finally turned in her favour. Each play culminates in a dramatic *abhijñāna* or 'recognition': Duṣyanta recognizes Śakuntalā as his wife at the end of the Sanskrit play, and the goddess Murajā recognizes Padmābatī as her daughter at the end of the *PN*.[93] Furthermore, the specific character of Gautamī, the wife of the *maharṣi* ('great sage') Aṅgīra, is shared by the two plays: in the

(1874)) follow in a more Western tradition, drawing in particular on the model of Shakespearean tragedy.

[92] Compare *PN* 1, 1 and *AŚ* 1 (1.1); for a good introduction to an edition of this famous Sanskrit play, see Vasudeva (2006): I refer to the line references of this edition.

[93] 'Recognition' or *anagnorisis* is, of course, an important concept in Aristotle's *Poetics*: see esp. 52a22ff. Note that Murajā's 'recognition' of her daughter in the *PN*, being a bodily reaction (the swelling of the mother's breasts upon seeing the daughter), falls outside the Aristotelean categories (though it is closest to the third kind of 'recognition', by means of 'memory': ibid. 54b19ff.). For commentary on this famous

Sanskrit play, this female character facilitates the reunion of the two lovers and, in the *PN*, it is Gautamī who cares for the heroine until her husband finally comes for her at *PN* 5, 2. Perhaps most interestingly of all, the Bengali play is imagined to occur, as it were, contemporaneously with the Sanskrit drama: in the Bengali *PN* Śacī's opening speech alludes to the continuing struggle of the god Indra against the Daitya clan (1, 2); and, between the penultimate and final acts of the Sanskrit play, the hero Duṣyanta is imagined to have been fighting alongside Indra against the Daitya clan.[94] The Bengali drama thus inhabits the very same literary time and space as the imagined world of this Sanskrit play.

In addition to the play's intertextual relationship specifically with Kālidāsa's drama, the *PN* is also underpinned and shaped by the broad 'dicta' of Sanskrit dramaturgy. The most radical departures of the Bengali play from the model of the Greek myth may be accounted for in terms of Madhusudan's compliance with these dramaturgical rules. The Sanskrit tradition of dramaturgy comprises a very subtle and intricate system of rules concerning how a *nāṭak* (along with other dramatic productions such as the *prahasan* or farce) is to be constructed.[95] The Bengali play by no means complies with all of the Sanskrit tradition's prescriptions and prohibitions: in its introduction of blank verse (used in certain passages), among other things, the play is clearly very innovative; and it even departs sometimes from the Sanskrit tradition in the kinds of subject matter it treats.[96] However, the play does comply quite self-consciously with very many of the

Aristotelean concept, see Else (1957) *ad loc.*, and also Halliwell (1986) esp. 212–7. For a comparison between Aristotle's *Poetics* and Bharata's *Nāṭyaśāstra* see Gupt (2006).

94 At the end of Act Six, Duṣyanta is summoned to fight for the gods against the Daityas; at the beginning of Act Seven he returns to earth, mounted on his sky-chariot, after six years of fighting: see Vasudeva (2006) *ad loc.*

95 For an introduction to Sanskrit drama see B. Keith (1924); for an introduction to Sanskritic aesthetic theory, see De (1923) and (1925), and Ingalls (1990). The topic of Sanskritic literary aesthetics has been introduced in some detail in Chapter 1 above. The three pre-eminent works of Sanskritic dramaturgy are considered to be the *Nāṭyaśāstra* of Bharata, the *Daśarūpaka* of Dhanañjaya, and the *Sāhityadarpaṇa* of Viśvanātha (the last of which Madhusudan refers to by name in his correspondence).

96 A salient example is the depiction of the siege of Vidarbha in Act Four, Scene 1: see *Daśarūpaka* 3.39 where Dhanañjaya forbids the onstage representation of various actions including long journeys, murder, fighting, revolt of a kingdom or province or the like, a siege, eating, bathing, intercourse, anointing the body, and putting on clothing. See also Haas (1962) *ad loc.* It was noted above that this scene, *PN* 4, 1, bore the marks of Greek influence (the Iliadic *Teikhoskopia*; Aeschylus' *Septem*; Euripides'

rules of the Sanskrit tradition; and the author himself made it clear in his correspondence that this compliance was a part of his compositional methodology.[97] For example, as was noted in Section 2 above, Indranīl's behaviour in Act One upon meeting the goddesses on Mount Vindhya seems to be dictated by the necessity, as prescribed by various texts of Sanskrit literary aesthetics, for the *nāyaka* or *netā* ('hero') of a Sanskritic *nāṭaka* ('drama')[98] to show *gāmbhīrya* ('composure') at all times.[99] The Bengali play's very division into five *aṅka* or 'acts' follows the Sanskritic model.[100] And the playwright's inclusion of characters such as a *bidūṣak* ('jester') is in compliance with the conventions of the Sanskrit tradition.[101] The influence of Sanskrit dramaturgy on the Bengali play is wide-reaching and extends to very many aspects of the drama's composition.[102]

However, the 'dicta' of Sanskrit dramaturgy most relevant to our interpretation of the *PN* are those concerning what may or may not occur to the *nāyaka* or hero. According to the Sanskritic tradition, the death of the principal character may occur neither onstage nor offstage, nor even be reported in an explanatory scene.[103] Thus

Hippolytus): perhaps this Greek influence is due to the Scene's subject matter (a city under siege) being proscribed by Sanskritic dramaturgical theory.

[97] See n. 91 above.

[98] For the proper transliteration of this Sanskrit word, see n. 69 above.

[99] See Section 1 above, esp. n. 55.

[100] A regular *nāṭaka* comprises five *aṅka*, whereas a *mahānāṭaka* ('great drama') may comprise ten (so *Daśarūpaka* 3, 43; see also *Sāhityadarpaṇa* 510, Lévi (1890) 140, and Haas (1962) *ad loc*). I refer to the Röer (1851) edition of the *Sāhityadarpaṇa*, which may indeed have been the edition Madhusudan worked from; and the Haas (1962) edition of the *Daśarūpaka*.

[101] See *Daśarūpaka* 2.13; see also *Sāhityadarpaṇa* 77–9, and Haas (1962) *ad loc.*

[102] I have found no systematic treatment of the *Padmābatī nāṭak* from the point of view of its engagement with the Sanskrit dramaturgical tradition. Such a study would be welcome: it would be especially interesting to examine the play's engagement with the discourses of *rasa* theory (see Chapter 1 above), and the ways in which the behaviour of Indranīl as the 'hero' of the play, and of Padmābatī as the 'heroine', conform to the Sanskrit tradition.

[103] See *Daśarūpaka* 3.40; also *Sāhityadarpaṇa* 215, 316. Haas (1962) notes, judging from actual Sanskrit dramas rather than Sanskrit dramaturgy, that 'this canon may be violated provided the dead person is restored to life in the course of the play'. This prohibition on the hero's death either onstage or offstage figures a crucial distinction between classical Greek and traditional Hindu dramaturgy: in Attic tragedy the death of the hero does not occur onstage, but often does so offstage and is reported onstage. For a comparison of Aristotle's theory of aesthetics with the Indian tradition, see Gupt (2006).

Indranīl, unlike Paris, may not be ruined as a result of his Judgement, at least not on the Hindu stage. Furthermore, in his selection of a plot, which may come from a well-known story or be invented by the playwright,[104] the Sanskritic playwright must omit or rearrange anything from the original story that might be inappropriate to the dignity of the play's *nāyaka* ('hero').[105] It seems to be in compliance with this dictum of Sanskrit dramaturgy that Madhusudan, in transposing the Greek story of Paris and Helen to the Indian stage, omits or rearranges features of the Greek narrative that do not sit well with the dignity of the Indian hero. Thus Paris' devious abduction/seduction of another man's wife becomes Indranīl's marriage (albeit somewhat illegitimate) of a virgin. Unlike Paris, Indranīl is depicted, by and large, as heroic and manly,[106] Paris' ultimate defeat by the enemy is replaced by Indranīl's successful lifting of the siege against his city, and Indranīl, unlike Paris, lives to enjoy the prize he received from the goddess of love. The shape of the Bengali play's narrative arc is thus conditioned by the rules of Sanskrit dramaturgy, and the hero is spared the anticipated Greek consequences of his action in Act One.

[104] If the playwright takes the plot from an earlier story, then further rules are entailed. Sanskrit tradition prescribed that when the 'hero' of the play is, like Indranīl, of the *dhīrodātta* (self-controlled and exalted) type, the *ādhikārika* ('principal subject') chosen by the playwright must be that incident for which the hero is renowned. (See, for example, *Daśarūpaka* 3.28.) One might say that for Paris this incident would be the 'Judgement of Paris'; and so this rule of Sanskrit drama may explain why the *ādhikārika* of the *PN*, given that Indranīl is a 'Paris' figure, comprises the details of and fallout from the Judgement of Indranīl.

[105] See *Daśarūpaka* 3.29; and *Sāhityadarpaṇa* 304, 409. A salient example of this 'rearrangement' of a traditional story to avoid offending the dignity of a play's hero is the omission of Rāma's treacherous killing of Vāli by Māyurāja in the drama *Udāttarāghava* (see Haas (1962) *ad Daśarūpaka* 3.29): here Vāli is depicted, *contra* earlier versions of the story, as coming to slay Rāma on account of his friendship with Rāma's enemy Rāvaṇa; Rāma then slays Vāli in self-defence rather than treacherously.

[106] See Section 2 above on Paris' reaction on seeing the three goddesses on Mount Ida. For Paris as an ambiguous hero see, for example, his conversation with his brother at Hom. *Il.* 6.312ff., 3.37ff, 6.325ff., and 515ff.; see also Collins (1988).

4. *PADMĀBATĪ NĀṬAK*: INDIANIZATION IN CONTEXT

Quite apart from being worthy of scholarly attention for its inherent charm and qualities as a work of drama, the *PN* is of great significance in at least one major respect: apart from certain translations and versions of Western classical texts,[107] the Bengali play seems to be the first work of literature in the oeuvre of any major Indian vernacular author to engage directly and unambiguously with the Graeco-Roman classics. It is not until the *PN* that we find the Bengali vernacular used as a vehicle for the treatment of Western classical themes. And despite possible moments of classical resonance in Madhusudan's roughly contemporaneous *Tilottamā-sambhab kābya*, it is not until the *PN* that the Graeco-Roman world bursts unambiguously onto the Bengali literary scene. Furthermore, in addition to being the first major Bengali work to engage with the Western classics in this way, the play also marks the beginning of Madhusudan's ongoing project to combine and reconcile the Graeco-Roman and Hindu traditions in the creation of a new cosmopolitan vernacular aesthetic. Throughout his oeuvre, and in all the other works examined in the following chapters, Madhusudan returned again and again to the interplay and connections between the ancient worlds of Hindu India and classical Europe. The *PN* represents the first step in this frequently recurring cross-cultural project, and as such it anticipates later works such as his justly celebrated masterpiece, the epic *Meghnādbadh kābya* (1861).

And yet, the *PN* is unlike any of Madhusudan's other works. In later pieces, the poet went on to recast traditional Hindu material using appropriated classical forms (a mode of appropriation not unlike, for example, Matthew Arnold's near-contemporary *Balder Dead* and *Sohrab and Rustum*, and suggestive more generally of the far-reaching notion of the aesthetic superiority of Western classical form). However, in the *PN* we see precisely the reverse. In this earlier work, it is Western classical material which succumbs to traditional Hindu forms. The kernel of Greek myth with which the play begins is

[107] See, for example, Vasunia (2007) on Dalpatram's *Lakshmi*, an 1840s Gujarati version of Aristophanes' *Wealth*, co-authored by a Briton and an Indian.

transformed into an allegory of the markedly Hindu *trivarga*, or the choice between three different life goals (Section 2). And the trajectory followed by the play after the Judgement of Indranīl is overtaken by Hindu literary prescriptions: the anticipated Greek consequence of the hero's bad choice is averted by the intervention of the discourse of traditional Hindu aesthetics (Section 3).

The *PN* was composed not long after the 'Sepoy Uprising/ Indian Mutiny' (1857/8), and some sixteen years before the Dramatic Performances Censorship Act 1876.[108] Dinabandhu Mitra's *Nil Darpan* (1858/9), the *Indigo Mirror*, a controversial and inflammatory Bengali play which revealed the British oppression of Indian indigo planters to elite urban audiences in Calcutta,[109] may not in the event have been translated by Madhusudan,[110] although some believe that he was its translator.[111] And yet it is clear, in any case, that Bengali drama in 1860, the year of the *PN's* publication, was a locus of tense and increasing political contestation,[112] and a very interesting cultural space in which to examine and probe elite Western culture. In this context, and notwithstanding that the *PN* was not in fact staged until some years after its first publication, Madhusudan's irreverent assimilation of the cornerstone mytheme of the Graeco-Roman classics to Hindu forms and generic modes necessarily takes on a political colour. It would be going too far to suggest that there was anything overtly subversive about the play. And yet there is something covertly subversive, in a light-hearted and subterranean way, in the *PN*'s depiction of a cardinal moment of elite Western mythology being engulfed and transformed by traditional Hindu literary values: Greek mythology's arch-seducer becomes a noble, if comically foppish, Hindu King; a rather sordid Western narrative of seduction or even abduction is turned into a romantic and noble Hindu love story.

The *PN* endeavours to improve the 'Greek story of the golden apple' as it Indianizes it; and it is instructive that Madhusudan marshals in service of this project the Sanskrit play which the British orientalist Horace Wilson had described as the 'jewel' of Indian

[108] See, for example, Bhatia (1994) 1.

[109] The play was the subject of a famous libel suit brought by the white indigo planters, and was widely seen as a scandalous and seditious piece: see Oddie (1999).

[110] See Radice (2010) xlv, n. 54.

[111] See esp. Oddie (1999) 119. Note, however, that the evidence on which Oddie bases his view may be doubtful: see Radice (2010) xlv, n. 54.

[112] Bhatia (1994) 1ff.

literature,[113] Kālidāsa's *Abhijñānaśakuntalam*. This most celebrated of Sanskrit plays, along with the aesthetic tradition connected with it, is used to rehabilitate a morally dubious Western classical myth. This is the cultural status quo of mid-nineteenth-century British Bengal turned upside down: this was a period when Indian texts were generally disapproved of as subjects of study in Bengali schools, and it was typical for Western commentators to hold that 'the more popular forms of [oriental literature] are marked with the greatest immorality and impurity'.[114] And yet here we have traditional Hindu literature as an agent of moral rehabilitation, and the object of that rehabilitation is none other than a cardinal Graeco-Roman myth.

Thus, in a subtle and understated way, the *PN* defies contemporary British assessments of Hindu literary values, whilst at the same time retaining throughout a light-hearted and generous cosmopolitan taste for the 'best' of both Hindu and European literary influences. In this way, the play represents a notable case in point for Dharwadker's thesis that nineteenth-century Anglo-Indian political tensions were, at least among the Bengali elite, often sublimated to the purely literary level:

> The aestheticization of Indian-English writing in the long nineteenth century thus was an integral part of the dynamics of cultural contestation . . . It displaced the ongoing real-world conflict between India and Great Britain from the political and economic spheres into the aesthetic sphere, so that the war of colonization and resistance was now fought – and lost – by the 'other means' of pure literariness.[115]

However it is not at all clear that the *PN*, as a notional battle in the context of this metaphorical war, was in fact lost. This was a play that dared to impose Indian form on Western substance, and to insinuate that, at least in some respects, even the elite Graeco-Roman classics could be improved upon with an appropriate admixture of Indian literary taste.

[113] For a discussion of Wilson's view, and the evolving British attitude towards Sanskrit literature in the nineteenth century, see Vishwanathan (1990) 5ff.

[114] See *Parliamentary Papers*, 1852–3, Evidence of Charles Trevelyan, 32, 198; and Vishwanathan (1990) 5f.

[115] Dharwadker (2003) 268.

3

The *Meghnādbadh kābya* (1861), Homer's *Iliad*, and Vergil's *Aeneid*[1]

INTRODUCTION

After the *Śarmiṣṭhā nāṭak* (1859), the *Tilottamā-sambhab kābya* (1860), and the *Padmābatī nāṭak* (1860), the drama discussed in the previous chapter, Madhusudan published what would come to be seen as his masterpiece, the epic *Meghnādbadh kābya* (1861) (henceforth *MBK*).[2] This epic poem, prefigured and prepared for in certain respects by Madhusudan's earlier Bengali poem, the epyllion *Tilottamā-sambhab kābya* (1860),[3] has received the most academic attention of all Madhusudan's oeuvre and is the work for which he is best

[1] This chapter appeared in embryonic form in an article in the Bulletin of the School of Oriental and African Studies: see Riddiford (2009).

[2] The first part of the *MBK* (Cantos 1–5) was first published on 4 January 1861 CE The second instalment (Cantos 6–9) is harder to date with precision but seems to be around the beginning of the Bengali new year of 1268, in other words somewhat later in the first half of 1861 CE For the evidence supporting these dates, see Bandyopadhyay (1943), reprinted in Majumdar (2004) 294. The period of 1859 to 1862, and particularly 1860–1, was a frenetically productive period for Madhusudan and saw the production of most of his Bengali works.

[3] As contended, for example, by Radice (1987) 92. In particular, the earlier work prefigures the *MBK* in its sustained use of blank verse, its narration of a Puranic story, and its division into 'cantos' (*sarga*). Madhusudan himself came to see the earlier poem as *kancha* ('raw', 'immature'), and began to revise the work: see Murshid (2004) 173. The *Tilottamā-sambhab kābya* arguably takes Keats' *Hyperion* as its formal model: like this English work it narrates a battle between gods and Titans which, ultimately, the gods win. The poem's engagement with the Western classics is thus mainly indirect (mediated by Keats' epyllion); but it may be said to prefigure the direct engagement of the *MBK* with the Western Classics.

known in India today.[4] It is also the only one of his Bengali works of which English translations are readily available, apart from the *Śarmiṣṭhā nāṭak* (1859), which Madhusudan translated into English himself. Two English translations, in fact, are now available, both of which will give the reader a good sense of the Bengali original.[5] Both translations come with detailed and helpful notes and prefatory material exploring the literary texture of the *MBK* and the significance of Madhusudan's wider oeuvre. This chapter, which treats narrower themes than those examined in Seely (2004) or Radice (2010), is intended above all to complement the observations made in those two works.

The *MBK* narrates an episode from the Hindu *Rāmāyaṇa*, the famous Hindu epic tradition telling of the war waged by Rāma to rescue his wife Sītā from the Rākṣasas or demons.[6] The Hindu Rāmāyaṇa tradition relates the whole story of the lengthy war waged by the divine hero Rāma against the city of the demon king Rāvaṇa, but for his epic poem Madhusudan chose to relate just a short episode towards the end of that war. This choice of episode is a springboard for the poem's profound engagement with Western epic traditions. The events covered by the nine cantos of the Bengali epic, a series of events near the end of the great war, which culminate not in the end of strife but in the death of the besieged city's greatest warrior, deliberately echo the episode of the Trojan war selected by Homer in the *Iliad*. Above all, the *MBK* takes Homer's *Iliad* as its structural and

[4] There is an excellent new edition of the poem, Majumdar (2004), which includes a variety of Bengali essays and commentaries (both early and recent) on the *MBK*, and which is indispensable to any student of the *MBK*. Madhusudan's work, especially the *MBK*, has attracted increasing attention from the Western academy over the last few decades: see, above all, Clark (1967), Seely (1982), (1988), and (2004), and Radice (2010).

[5] See Seely (2004) and Radice (2010). The Bengali text used here is the edition of Sanyal (1917), reprinted in Majumdar (2004).

[6] The episode narrated equates roughly to a passage of the Sanskrit epic *Rāmāyaṇa*, Book 6 (of 7), Chapters 68–105. For an introduction to the Sanskrit poem, see Brockington (1998) esp. 34–40; for the *Rāmāyaṇa* tradition (both classical and vernacular), see Richman (1992). Madhusudan was able to read Sanskrit and claims to have read the Sanskrit original by the poet Vālmīki but he also read the mediaeval Bengali 'version' of the epic by Kāśīrāmdās (Serampore edition): see Murshid (2004) 63 for Madhusudan's reference to this particular edition of this mediaeval Bengali *Rāmāyaṇa*, and see Seely (1982) for Madhusudan's response to this work in *MBK* 8. In this chapter I will refer, where necessary, to the Sanskrit rather than Bengali *Rāmāyaṇa* since the Sanskrit poem is more readily available (both in the original and in English translation) to the English reader.

generic paradigm. As will be seen in Section 2, specific characters and passages of the Bengali epic are distinctly modelled on the Greek epic (such as a version in *MBK* 2 of the 'Deception of Zeus' in *Iliad* 14),[7] and on a structural level the poem's narrative arc and narrative strategies take that Greek epic as a point of departure. Speaking of the relationship between his poetic model and his Indian subject matter, Madhusudan himself said that his aim was not to 'borrow Greek stories[8] but write, rather try to write, as a Greek would have done'.[9] His ambition, so he went on to say in the same letter, was to 'engraft the exquisite graces of the Greek mythology on our own . . .'[10] If the MBK is Indian in subject matter then it is above all Greek in form and style: Vālmīki's *Rāmāyaṇa*, or an episode taken from it, recast in an Iliadic mould.

1. *MBK* 8 AND *AENEID* 6

Although the *MBK* is marked more profoundly and extensively by the influence of Homer's *Iliad*, the most sustained and obvious sampling from the Graeco-Roman classics in the Bengali epic is from the sixth book of Vergil's *Aeneid*. In a letter to a friend, Madhusudan wrote of his work on the eighth canto of his Bengali epic:

> I have finished the sixth and seventh Books of Meghanad and am working away at the eighth. Mr Ram is to be conducted through Hell to his father, Dasaratha, like another *Aeneas*.[11]

The poet's own description of *MBK* 8, cited above from one of his letters, points the way to a reading of the passage as a reception of *Aen* 6.[12] The influence on *MBK* 8 of *Aen*. 6, Aeneas' journey to the

[7] Referring to *MBK* 2.265ff., Madhusudan said in a letter to Rajnarain: 'As a reader of the Homeric Epos, you will, no doubt, be reminded of the Fourteenth *Iliad*, and I am not ashamed to say that I have intentionally imitated it—Juno's visit to Jupiter on Mount Ida'. See Murshid (2004) 144.

[8] This was Madhusudan's technique in the *Padmābatī nāṭak* (1860): see Chapter 2 above.

[9] See Murshid (2004) 125.

[10] Murshid (2004) 125.

[11] See Murshid (2004) 160. Emphasis original.

[12] The first edition of Vergil's *Aeneid* that Madhusudan is likely to have encountered, i.e. the edition most likely kept at Bishop's College Calcutta, is that of P. Pett (1820): see Chapter 1 above; also Appendix 2. By the time Madhusudan came to

underworld to visit his father Anchises, is in fact well documented,[13] and the reader may consult Clark (1967) for a more or less comprehensive list of the Bengali passage's Vergilian correspondences. In brief, the god Śiva suggests to his wife Durgā that she instruct the goddess Māẏā (who thus stands for the Vergilian Sibyl) to conduct Rāma, the leader of the Rāghava forces investing the city, who has just lost his beloved brother Lakṣmaṇa in battle, to the City of the Dead (*MBK* 8.78ff.) where he can consult his dead father Daśaratha (here, then, an Anchises figure) as to how he might revive Lakṣmaṇa (ll. 100–12).[14] Rāma is conducted there by the goddess and, in various respects (both specific and broad), the episode is highly redolent of the Vergilian model. Most strikingly, the manner in which Daśaratha greets his son in the underworld contains almost verbatim quotations from *Aeneid* 6. The reactions of the two fathers upon seeing their sons are especially comparable: both stretch out their hands (8.741f., 6.685); each sheds profuse tears (8.742, 6.686).[15] Daśaratha addresses Rāma (8.743-5): *āili ki re e durgam deśe/ eto dine, prāṇādhik, deber prasāde,/ juṛāte e cakṣudvaẏe?*, 'Have you come, finally, to this inaccessible land, O [my son] dearer than life, by god's grace, to please my two eyes?'[16] This is virtually a Bengali rendering of Anchises' famous words to Aeneas at 6.687f. (*venisti tandem* . . .): 'Have you come at last, and has the devotion your father expects defeated the harsh journey? Am I granted, son, to see your face . . . ?'[17]

compose the *MBK* he may also have encountered, for example, the edition of J. Conington (1859); see Chapter 1 above, also Appendix 2. Throughout this chapter my citations from Vergil's original Latin, as well as the line references given, are based on the edition of Mynors (1972).

[13] See Clark (1967). There have also been various piecemeal treatments by Bengali scholars of Vergil's influence on *MBK* 8: see esp. Sen (2004). However, Clark's is the most thoroughgoing treatment. Seely (1982), a response to Clark (1967), concedes the influence of Vergil on *MBK* 8 (see esp. pp. 467 and 476), but argues that much of Madhusudan's description of the underworld in fact comes from depictions of the Hindu underworld in mediaeval Bengali literature.

[14] Clark (1967) 339. For the purpose of Aeneas' *katabasis* in *Aen.* 6, and the thorny issue of the 'reality' of the journey and the 'truth' of what Aeneas sees in the underworld, see Williams (1990) 206 (the journey as a 'dream', personal to Aeneas), and *contra* West (1990) 230ff. and Horsfall (1995) 146f. No such ambiguity underpins Rāma's *katabasis*: the Indian hero does not exit the underworld through an ivory gate.

[15] Clark (1967) 350.

[16] For the theme of the father-son relationship in the *Aeneid*, and of Aeneas' filial *pietas*, see esp. Lee (1979).

[17] Clark (1967) 350.

However, even before Rāma reaches his father, there is a series of incidents that recall the Roman paradigm. For example, Māẏā carries Śiva's trident (*triśūla*: *MBK* 8.109) as a totem allowing safe passage to the underworld in a manner that recalls the Sibyl's bearing of the 'golden bough' (6.183–211).[18] Furthermore, the first obstacle for Rāma, once the descent has been made, is the river Vaitaraṇī (8.162ff.), the river of 'Hell' as described in the Sanskrit *Bhāgavata Purāṇa* and in mediaeval Bengali texts,[19] which gushes through a narrow gorge (8.166–9) rather as the river Acheron is depicted as a whirlpool (6.295–7). Rāma crosses this river using a 'marvellous bridge' (*adbhut setu*: 8.175), whereas Aeneas crosses the Acheron in Charon's boat. The bridge discriminates between the virtuous and the sinful (ll. 185ff.), just as Charon does between the buried and unburied.[20] In these, and in various other respects, the Bengali passage is closely modelled on its Vergilian paradigm.[21]

Seely (1982), whilst substantially conceding Clark's thesis of a Vergilian model, has argued that much of the eschatological detail of *MBK* 8 in fact comes from the mediaeval Bengali tradition. Clark (1967) and Seely (1982) are to be read as complementary studies rather than as mutually exclusive propositions.[22] Madhusudan builds a Bengali answer to Aeneas' *katabasis* using the building blocks made available to him by the Hindu tradition. Where there is overlap between the Roman and Indian sources this is a reflex, in effect, of Madhusudan's interest in the comparability of European and Indian antiquity.[23] Like much of Madhusudan's literary oeuvre,

[18] Clark (1967) 340. For the specific purpose of the golden bough, to be laid on Proserpina's threshold as a *munus* ('gift'), rather than the vague purposes ascribed to it by, for example, Austin (1977) 83, see West (1990) 234ff.

[19] See also Seely (1982) 473 and n. 28.

[20] Clark (1967) 342.

[21] For further details Clark (1967) is a useful resource.

[22] See Radice (1987) who argues that both articles should be read together rather than in opposition to each other.

[23] *Contra* Seely (1982), who argues that where there is overlap (possible Roman and Hindu sources for the same passage of the *MBK*), we may discount the Latin source in favour of the Indian: '[Madhusudan's] own Bengali epic literature provides model enough' (p. 473). So, for example, Seely argues, *contra* Clark (1967), that the vultures tearing at the spirits at *MBK* 8.308–12 (which Clark compares with *Aen.* 6.597–600), come from the Bengali *Mahābhārata*: 'no reaching to European sources is necessary'. I would suggest that the very coincidence that such birds occur in both eschatological traditions is precisely what this passage of the *MBK* is pointing to.

MBK 8 is a continuation by other means of 'Orientalist' Indo-European comparativism.[24]

A crucial point to note about Rāma's *katabasis* in *MBK* 8 is that it represents a significant departure from the *Rāmāyaṇa* tradition.[25] Several 'journeys to the underworld' are narrated in the Hindu epic tradition but never at this point in the *Rāmāyaṇa* narrative.[26] Indeed, at *MBK* 8.143ff., this fact of innovation is itself aptly thematized. In *Aen.* 6, the Sibyl leads Aeneas to the underworld through the *antro ... aperto* ('open cave': 6.262) of Avernus, a path to the underworld already established before Aeneas' arrival.[27] Māẏā, by contrast, has to dig a tunnel for Rāma to access the City of Yama (8.143): *sṛjibo suṛaṅgapath* ..., 'I shall create a tunnel path ...'. Just as Māẏā must excavate her own tunnel to the underworld in the absence of a pre-existing path, so the Bengali poet breaks new ground for the *Rāmāyaṇa* tradition by inserting a *katabasis* at this point in the narrative.

The departure from the *Rāmāyaṇa* tradition represented by Rāma's *katabasis* in *MBK* 8 is striking: it is the only extended episode of the *MBK* which departs entirely from all earlier accounts of the story. The insertion of the *katabasis* episode may be explained, at least on one level, in terms of generic expectation. An epic poem, if

[24] See esp. Chapter 6 below (a comparison between Madhusudan's theological and mythological 'syncretism' and the scholarship of Sir William Jones). For the nostalgic reverence for the early British Orientalists felt by the Bengali *bhadralok* in the 1850s and 1860s, see R. Chaudhuri (2002).

[25] The mediaeval Bengali *Rāmāyaṇa* has a lengthy description of the events surrounding Lakṣmaṇa's resuscitation (the Sanskrit epic gives a rather brief account of it): see Seely (1982) 468f. In this mediaeval Bengali *Rāmāyaṇa*, the physician Suṣeṇa instructs Hanumān to fetch curative plants from Mount Gandhamādana and much detail is lavished on the description of this journey. In the *MBK*, this journey to the mountain is elided (though we must assume that it takes place between the end of *MBK* 8 and the beginning of *MBK* 9) and replaced by Rāma's journey to the underworld. The instruction of the physician Suṣeṇa is replaced by the advice of Rāma's father Daśaratha.

[26] In the mediaeval Bengali *Rāmāyaṇa*, the hero Hanumān, Rāma's ally, makes two journeys to Pātāla, a 'Hell' distinct from the City of Yama (Rāma's destination in *MBK* 8). For the distinction between Pātāla and the City of Yama, see Seely (1982) 471, n. 17. The first is made in search of Sītā (Rāma's wife), the second in search of Rāma and Lakṣmaṇa (who have been abducted by Mahīrāvaṇa, one of Rāvaṇa's sons).

[27] Indeed, the cave at Avernus has been identified with the so-called *Antro della Sibilla* discovered by Maiuri in 1932; see Austin (1977) 48ff. Parts of the complex (including a long tunnel and features distinctive of an *adytus* ('temple')) have been dated to the fifth or sixth centuries BCE.

properly constructed on Western classical principles, may be expected to have a *katabasis*. Indeed, in correspondence, Madhusudan said of the structure of the *MBK*: 'I think I have constructed the Poem on the most rigid principles, and even a French critic would not find fault with me.'[28] His inclusion of a *katabasis* in the narrative of the *MBK* is perhaps the most obvious example of the poet's adherence to Western classical canons of epic composition. One might recall the playful comment of Lord Byron, one of Madhusudan's favourite English poets, in *Don Juan* (I.100): 'A panoramic view of Hell's in training,/ After the style of Virgil and of Homer,/ So my name of Epic's no misnomer . . .'[29] One might note, incidentally, that Vergil's inclusion of his own *katabasis* narrative in *Aen.* 6 was itself an innovation in Aeneas lore, suggesting perhaps that, like Byron, the Roman poet himself felt that such an episode was required of an authentic epic poem.[30] Madhusudan's very disruption of the *Rāmāyaṇa* tradition in *MBK* 8 may thus be seen as a Vergilian trope, most likely unwitting, which echoes the Roman poet's innovative insertion of a *katabasis* in *Aen.* 6.

Madhusudan's reception of *Aen.* 6 also has important implications for our interpretation of the Bengali poem as a whole. The Vergilian panel of *MBK* 8 serves, like other aspects of the poem assessed in Section 2 below, to diminish or at least complicate the glory of Rāma, the unequivocal and indeed divine hero of the *Rāmāyaṇa* tradition. Madhusudan was frank about his blasphemous treatment of the Hindu divine hero, once commenting to a friend: 'I despise Ram and his rabble; but the idea of Ravan elevates and kindles my imagination; he was a grand fellow.'[31] While this notion of using epic as a vehicle for raising a demonic figure and diminishing the divine in the eyes of the reader is rooted in Madhusudan's passionate interest in Milton's *Paradise Lost* (in *The Marriage of Heaven and Hell* William Blake famously described Milton as being 'of the Devil's party without knowing it'), in fact the Bengali poet used both Vergil and Homer to assist in this inversion of traditional tropes. The *katabasis* of *MBK* 8 contributes to this process in subtle ways. For example, in addition to the close verbal and thematic resonances between *MBK* 8 and *Aen.* 6

[28] Murshid (2004) 166. See also Radice (2010) lxvi and Majumdar (1947) 120.

[29] For Byron's use of classical epic in *Don Juan*, see Jeffrey (1971); and for the poem as an 'anti-epic', see Lauber (1968).

[30] See Camps (1969) 75ff.

[31] See Murshid (2004) 169.

outlined above, we may also detect many significant contrasts between the two passages, most of which are unflattering to the Indian hero. In *MBK* 8, Rāma may indeed be 'another Aeneas',[32] but in many ways he is also a lesser Aeneas. Clark argues that both Daśaratha and Anchises 'tell their sons what the future holds in store for them, and advise them what immediate action they should take'.[33] Certainly, we might compare Daśaratha's prophecy at *MBK* 8.791 ('. . . the land of Bhārata will be filled, o renowned one, with your good renown!') with the extended 'Parade of Heroes' at *Aen.* 6.756ff.[34] However, there are also marked differences between the prophecies: Anchises tells Aeneas of the glory that will be entailed by the mingling of Trojan and Italian stocks (*Aen.* 6.756f.: Trojan Aeneas will marry Italian Lavinia),[35] whereas Daśaratha advises Rāma (*MBK* 8.784-6): *nāśibe samaẏe tumi biṣam saṃgrāme/ rābaṇe; sabaṃśe naṣṭo habe duṣṭamati/ tabo śare . . .*, 'In time you will slay Rāvaṇa in fierce combat; the wicked one will be slain by your arrows along with his whole lineage . . .'. Rāma will conquer Rāvaṇa completely. And yet, the Vergilian allusion brings clearly to mind the contrast between the future glory of Aeneas' descendants (of which the *Aeneid* is a mere foreshadowing)[36] and the obscurity of Rāma's descendants. The close Vergilian allusion at this point in *MBK* 8 alerts the reader to an aspect of Aeneas' glory which Rāma cannot match.

There may be no 'Parade of Heroes' in *MBK* 8 but, at 8.585ff., there is a catalogue of the Daityas ('Titans') of the Satyayuga (the 'true age', an earlier era of Hindu mythology). Clark notes that this may be compared with the *Titania pubes* (6.580ff.): the Titans who in the *Aeneid* (as Clark observes) find themselves in Hell rather than Elysium.[37] One might

[32] Madhusudan's phrase: see n. 10.

[33] Clark (1967) 351.

[34] See also *Aen.* 6.889f. For a discussion of the rhetorical intent of the Parade of Heroes, see Horsfall (1995) 144ff. For a close, line-by-line reading of this passage, see Austin (1977) 232ff.

[35] Note that the fusion of Trojan with Italian stock is given 'significant prominence' in this passage: see Austin (1977) *ad* l. 756.

[36] On the 'Parade of Heroes' and its relationship to Roman history (as imagined proleptically in the 'Parade'), see West (1988) esp. 284ff. For further passages relevant to later Roman history, see also *Aen.* 1.257ff. 8.626–728; also Austin (1977) 232–4 and Griffith (1967–8) 57ff.

[37] See Clark (1967) 349. Indeed, the tradition of the Titans being punished in Tartarus is very old indeed: see *Il.* 14.279 ('those who dwell under Tartatus, who are called Titans'). Note that the Titans are the 'old gods' (*genus antiquum*, *Aen.* 6.580: see Hesiod *Th.* 424 and 486, and M. West (1966) *ad Th.* 133 and 167f. and Austin (1977)

especially compare the brothers Sunda and Upasunda—Daityas who tried to overthrow the king of the gods (ll. 592f.)—with the *Aloides gemini* (twin sons of Aloeus), who tried to thrust Jove down from his realm above (*Aen.* 6.582ff.). What is most significant here is that this catalogue of 'Titans' stands in for Vergil's 'Parade of Heroes'.[38] The context is highly Vergilian: Rāma enters *sañjībanī purī*, Hindu Elysium, and beholds *kṣetro—raṅgabhūmirūpe*, 'a field—like a battlefield' (*MBK* 8.567), in which some warriors wrestle and spar (ll. 571f.) while others listen to a *kabi* (poet) charming them with the *bīṇā* (the Indian lyre) and singing of the glorious deeds of heroes (*bīrkulsaṃkīrtane*) (ll. 575ff.). We might aptly compare this passage, as Clark does, with *Aen.* 6.640ff. Here too, the warriors in Elysium vie in sports (ll. 642ff.) and the poet Orpheus charms them with his lyre (ll. 645ff.). We might expect, given Rāma's markedly Vergilian entrance into this Hindu Elysium, that like Aeneas he should go on in due course to inspect a Parade of Heroes. However, instead of an extended passage treating of future heroes of the Rāghava line, we find a catalogue of Titans or Daityas from the mythological past. These figures are not only from the past (contrasting with the Roman heroes of the future), but they are infamous rather than glorious, vanquished rather than victorious. Niśumbha, for example, was a champion (*śūreśe*, 'lord of heroes': l. 587), but after menacing the gods he was laid low by a deity (ibid.). Contrast Augustus Caesar, a son of a god (l. 792), who will establish another golden age (ll. 792ff.) and advance his empire *super et Garamantas et Indos* (beyond the Garamants and Indians) (ll. 794f.).[39]

ad Aen. 6.580), whereas the Daityas do not predate the prevailing gods of the Hindu epic (and puranic) tradition, but are a younger generation.

[38] The absence of a 'Parade of Heroes' in *MBK* 8 is, of course, also a function of the very different contexts in which the *Aeneid* and the *MBK* were composed. The *MBK*, after all, is not a 'national epic' (on Madhusudan's ideas for a Bengali 'national epic' see Chapter 4 below) and is not composed for any political patron, whereas the family of the *Aeneid's* patron (Augustus Caesar's Julian clan) receives a large proportion of the verses of Vergil's 'Parade of Heroes' (89 verses, or 96, depending on one's reckoning). For an analysis of the context of Vergil's 'Parade' see West (1993) 284ff. On the attitude of the *Aeneid* towards, and for the poem as a product of its Augustan context, see Camps (1969), Gold (1982), Galinsky (1996), Tarrant (1997) 177–87, Stahl (1998), and Thomas (2001) 25–54.

[39] For the important Julian element in Vergil's 'Parade of Heroes', see esp. D. West (1993) 284.

Madhusudan's use of the *Aeneid* as a paradigm thus plays its part in lowering our estimation of 'Ram and his rabble':[40] the disruption of the Vergilian ordering of events (replacing a Parade of Heroes with a catalogue of 'Titans') figures an implicit but stark contrast between the glories of Aeneas' descendants and the obscurity of Rāma's. Such Vergilian resonances induce us to conclude that Rāma is no *pater Aeneas* ('father Aeneas').[41] Nor, moreover, would the mantle of 'father' be an especially illustrious one for Rāma to inherit given the shameful deeds of his father (emphasized at *MBK* 8.792–3).

The Vergilian panel of *MBK* 8 represents a bold disruption of the *Rāmāyaṇa* tradition. The passage performs a twofold function: on the one hand it aligns the Bengali poem with the Western classical epic genre through the generic marker of the *katabasis* trope and, on the other hand, it contributes, in a subtle and understated way, to a broader process (which underpins the work as a whole) of diminishing the traditionally heroic and divine character of Rāma in the eyes of the reader. However, while this Vergilian passage is, perhaps, the most obviously Graeco-Roman moment in the whole poem, and is certainly a rich locus of intertextual meanings, it is in fact Homer's *Iliad* which lends the Bengali poem its broader structural and generic shape, and indeed which contributes more profoundly to the reversal of key tropes of the Rāmāyaṇa tradition.

2. THE *MBK* AND HOMER'S *ILIAD*

When Madhusudan wrote in one of his letters that he intended, in the *MBK*, not to 'borrow Greek stories but write, rather try to write, as a Greek would have done',[42] the Greek he had in mind was, of course, the epic poet Homer.[43] This would be the first of two occasions on

[40] Madhusudan's description of the Rāghavas: see Murshid (2004) 168.

[41] For a treatment of Aeneas' role as leader and *pater* in the *Aeneid*, see, for example, Quinn (1968) 1–24, 112–35, 150–59, Otis (1964) 241–64, and Lloyd (1957) 133–51.

[42] See Murshid (2004) 125.

[43] Madhusudan's first exposure to the Greek *Iliad* at Bishop's College was, most likely, the second edition (1821) of C. G. Heyne's *Ilias* (an OUP edition in two volumes with Latin commentary and references to Scholia): see Chapter 1 above and Appendix 2 below. While it is clear that Madhusudan was able to read the *Iliad* in the original, his response to the poem was also mediated by translations and other poetic responses to Homer. In a letter to a friend, for example, he quotes Cowper's

which Madhusudan would engage with Homer's *Iliad* in an extended Bengali piece. The *Hekṭor-badh* or 'The Slaying of Hector', which was published ten years after the *MBK* in 1871 and which will be the subject of Chapter 6 below, may be read as an 'Orientalist' (in the sense that it was underpinned by the comparative insights of Indo-European scholarship) 'version' of *Iliad* 1–12 composed in experimental Bengali prose.

Madhusudan's use of the *Iliad* as a model for the *MBK* was fundamental to the shape and structure of the Bengali poem, and it is an influence which has often been noted. Chaudhuri, in his famous *Autobiography of an Unknown Indian*, says of Madhusudan that: 'Ravana was to him another Priam, Ravana's son Meghanad a second Hector, and Ravana's city, which to us was the Citadel of Evil, was to Dutt a second Holy Troy.'[44] The Iliadic model is certainly crucial, as will be seen, to Rāvaṇa's elevation in the reader's sympathies. However, the means by which Homer's *Iliad* is assimilated into the fabric of the Bengali poem are highly subtle, as is the way in which this assimilation contributes to the complication of the traditional roles of hero and villain in the epic.

Homer's *Iliad* is a palpable presence throughout the *MBK*. The most obvious way in which the reader becomes aware of this presence, as Chaudhuri's observation intimates, is by means of the nexus of character correspondences between the two poems. Since the episode selected by Madhusudan for the *MBK* fits the narrative arc of the *Iliad* so neatly, with the narration starting *in medias res* towards the end of a lengthy city siege, the correspondences emerge quite obviously. Rāvaṇa king of the Rākṣasas, as Chaudhuri indicates above, is evidently modelled on King Priam, and the king's Rākṣasas are thus analogous to Priam's Trojans. Both are kings of a besieged city, Laṅkā and Troy respectively. Both suffer the loss of a great warrior son, whose obsequies are performed at the end of the poem.[45] Meghanāda, Rāvaṇa's son, is in turn a Hector figure: he is the stalwart of his city's defences, the greatest warrior of Laṅkā. His family life in particular and his character in general are depicted with great sympathy: Meghanāda's farewell to his wife Pramīlā at *MBK*

translation of *Il.* 1.8–9 comparing it with Milton's *Paradise Lost* ll. 33–4: see Murshid (2004) 125.

[44] See N. Chaudhuri (1951) 191; also Kaviraj (2003) 534.

[45] See Dasgupta (1933–5) 128.

3.523-34, for example, recalls Hector's farewell to Andromache at *Il.* 6.369–502.[46] Meghanāda's wife Pramīlā, by extension, thus corresponds to Andromache.[47]

Rāma, as the leader of the invading Rāghava forces, may be compared with Agamemnon; and his Rāghava warriors with the Achaeans. Like Agamemnon, Rāma conducts the siege of a city with a view to reclaiming a woman. Rāma's mission is to recapture his own wife Sītā, which also aligns him with Menelaus, Helen's husband and Agamemnon's brother. Rāma's despondency about the war (he declares from time to time that the Rāghavas should go home: see *MBK* 6.47–67 and 8.49–78) recalls Agamemnon's exhortation (insincere, unlike Rāma's) of his army to return home at *Il.* 2.110–41.[48] Madhusudan's alignment of Rāma with Agamemnon in this way is a striking aspect of the poet's reversal of the traditional attitude towards the conflict (in which Rāma represents good and Rāvaṇa evil). Few critics have ever considered the Iliadic Agamemnon to be a sympathetic character,[49] and the Bengali poet's alignment of Rāma with the Greek leader emblematizes the poem's antipathy towards the traditional hero of the *Rāmayaṇa* story.

Sītā, wife of Rāma, corresponds to the Iliadic Helen.[50] Like Helen, she has been abducted from her husband, and the war of the poem is waged in her name. Indeed, at *MBK* 9.185–200, her lament is similar to Helen's at *Il.* 3.399–412, each woman being presented as censuring herself in vehement terms.[51] Lakṣmaṇa, Rāma's younger brother, is

[46] See Dasgupta (193–5) 119f., 122, 124.

[47] See Dasgupta (1969) 85. She is, however, also rather like Vergil's Camilla or Homer's Penthesilea in that she is a female warrior (cf. esp. *MBK* 3.67–159); see Dasgupta (1933–5) 121.

[48] For treatment of the *Diapeira* of *Il.* 2, see Cook (2003) and Katzung (1960) esp. 48.

[49] Cf. Schadewaldt (1943) 37-9, esp. 38, n.1, Lohmann (1970) 35, 76, 221, and esp. Taplin (1990); *contra* Donlan (1971–2) 109–15.

[50] Indeed, in his own commentary to his poem, *The Captive Ladie* (1849), Madhusudan calls Sītā the 'Indian Helen'; see Gupta (1974) 487, note 'p'. The poet goes on to say: 'Seeta was taken away from the forest where Rama resided during his banishment from his kingdom. The consequence is known.' Thereupon, he quotes (in Latin) Horace *Odes* 3.3.18–21: *Ilion, Ilion/ fatalis incestusque iudex*.... It is significant for our understanding of Madhusudan's project in the *MBK* that he considers the fall of Troy to be, as it were, the consequence of the abduction of Sītā: for Madhusudan, Indian and Graeco-Roman mythology are directly analogous.

[51] See Dasgupta (1933–5) 128. Note, of course, that in Sītā's case, unlike Helen's, this self-censure is quite unfair.

aligned with Agamemnon's younger brother, Menelaus. In a divergence from the Iliadic paradigm, it is, in fact, Rāma whose wife has been abducted. However, as the champion of the invading army, and the hero who vanquishes the besieged city's greatest warrior, Lakṣmaṇa also plays the role of Achilles.[52] His subsequent slaying at the hands of Meghanāda's father, in retaliation for his son's death, recalls Hector's revenge-killing at the hands of Achilles. Vīrabhadra's preservation of Lakṣmaṇa's corpse (*MBK* 7.757–61) likewise recalls Apollo's preservation of Hector's corpse in *Il.* 24 (see esp. *Il.* 24.18–21).[53] Lakṣmaṇa is thus the locus of complex and competing Iliadic roles.

The character correspondences between the two poems are not limited to the human plane but extend to the gods as well. It is clear, for example, that Madhusudan's Śiva is equivalent to the Iliadic Zeus.[54] Like Zeus, he has the greatest power of all the gods[55] and, like Zeus, he has a wife, the goddess Durgā, whose will is in conflict with his. Furthermore, Durgā corresponds with Hera: she is set against her husband's plans, supporting the invading army (while her husband favours Rāvaṇa), just as Hera supports the Achaeans in contrast to her husband's partiality for the Trojan side. In both poems, the side supported by the goddess will ultimately be triumphant, though on the back foot for much of the poem. The goddess Māẏā is equivalent, in different ways, to both Athena and Iris. She protects Lakṣmaṇa from the enemy's weapons at *MBK* 6.607–10, just as Athena protects Menelaus from the Trojan assault at *Il.* 4.130–3.[56] But at times she also recalls the Iliadic Iris: at Śiva's command, she sends a dream to Lakṣmaṇa at *MBK* 5.109–25 in much the same way as Iris, on Zeus' orders, communicates with Priam at *Il.* 24.143ff. and with other characters elsewhere. In addition, it should be noted that her name, meaning literally 'deception' or 'illusion', in fact recalls that of the Iliadic Ate.

It should be noted, of course, that such divine correspondences (between the Hindu and Homeric theologies) map on to the discourse of Indo-European comparative mythology: this is a strategy we have

[52] Dasgupta (1933–5) 124. [53] Dasgupta (1933–5).

[54] Dasgupta (1933–5) 120, 124; Dasgupta (1969) 79f.

[55] For a treatment of the power of Zeus, cf. Lesky (2001) esp. 174-6.

[56] Indeed the simile used to describe the goddess' protection is especially resonant with the Iliadic passage; see Dasgupta (1933–5) 124.

already seen deployed in the *Padmābatī nāṭak* (1860), where various Hindu deities were implicitly aligned with Graeco-Roman counterparts (see Chapter 2 above), and is one which will recur in later works. In fact it will be demonstrated in Chapter 6, in the analysis of the *Hekṭor-badh* ('The Slaying of Hector') (1871), that Madhusudan's syncretistic practices throughout his Bengali oeuvre figure a specifically Orientalist effect, a reflex of Madhusudan's response to the scholarship of the Orientalist Sir William Jones in particular, as well as a broader engagement with the broader Indo-European discourse in general.[57]

While these character correspondences are suggested above all by the comparable narrative arcs of the two poems (in both cases an episode towards the end of a long war at the end of which the champion of the besieged city is laid low), the passage which is perhaps most strikingly Iliadic occurs in the second canto of the Bengali poem and temporarily disrupts the Iliadic narrative arc. Śiva's seduction at the hands of his wife on mount Kailāsa (*MBK* 2.265ff.) was described by Madhusudan himself in a letter to Rajnarain as being modelled on Hera's deception of Zeus at *Il.* 14.197ff.: 'As a reader of the Homeric Epos, you will, no doubt, be reminded of the Fourteenth Iliad, and I am not ashamed to say that I have intentionally imitated it—Juno's visit to Jupiter on Mount Ida'.[58]

The similarities between the Bengali passage and the Iliadic model are readily visible. Like Hera, the goddess Durgā decides to use erotic allure to manipulate her husband, the most powerful of the gods, and calls upon the goddess of love to assist her in this purpose (compare *MBK* 2.265ff. and *Il.* 14.187ff.).[59] The goddesses of love, Aphrodite and Rati, provide Hera and Durgā respectively with the seductive means required (*Il.* 14.214ff. and *MBK* 2.287ff.). In both cases, moreover, the queen of the gods calls upon the assistance of a lesser male deity (compare *MBK* 2.306ff. and *Il.* 14.262ff.): Hypnos, the Greek

[57] See Chapter 1 above for an introduction to early British Orientalism.

[58] Murshid (2004) 144. The comment has been noted by various critics, but see esp. Dasgupta (1969) 79.

[59] For the context of Hera's decision to seduce and deceive Zeus, see Janko (1992) 168.

god of sleep, and Kāma, a Hindu god of desire, akin to a Cupid figure but in fact the husband of Rati, the goddess of love. Both Kāma and Hypnos are initially reluctant to help the goddess. Each recalls an occasion when the king of the gods had punished him in the most terrifying way: Kāma remembers when he was once incinerated for shooting Śiva with one of his flower-arrows (*MBK* 2.309ff.);[60] and Hypnos reminds Hera how she had once induced him to send Zeus to sleep so that she could wreak mischief on Heracles, an action which provoked Zeus to try to find Hypnos and do him untold violence (*Il.* 14.271ff.). However, both gods are finally persuaded to help: Hypnos through bribery (the offer to have his favourite Grace as his wife: *Il.* 14.270ff.); Kāma through gentle persuasion and reassurance (*MBK* 2.330ff.).

Finally, in both instances, the goddess's seduction works as planned, and the consummation of their desire is met with the spontaneous appearance of flowers. However, whereas clover, saffron and hyacinth spring forth from the ground beneath Zeus and Hera (*Il.* 14.347fff.), by contrast red lotuses, jasmine, and various other flowers in fact rain down (in accordance with the Indian erotic trope) upon Śiva and Durgā (*MBK* 2.441ff.).

The differences between the two passages are, in a sense, more significant than the various close similarities indicated above. Durgā does not endeavour to deceive Śiva, whereas Hera's seduction of Zeus is designed to distract him so that the Achaeans may receive Poseidon's assistance without Zeus preventing it (*Il.* 14.197ff.). Durgā's intention is simply to rouse Śiva from his deep meditation and, indeed, Durgā is quite frank with Rati (the Hindu Aphrodite) that this is her purpose (*MBK* 2.278ff.). The Bengali passage is thus not a Dios Apate, a 'Deception of Zeus', so much as a straightforward seduction. Indeed, in the Iliadic scene, Hera deceives almost everyone (except Hypnos, whom she instead bribes), whereas in this passage of the *MBK* Durgā is honest in all her dealings. Moreover, when Durgā has achieved her object through her seductive techniques, and her husband regains consciousness, the latter in fact concedes that Durgā's desire to assist Rāma is morally right and acquiesces in her plans

[60] See Radice (2010) *ad loc.* for an explanation of this allusion. See also Sanyal (1917) *ad loc.* for detailed observations on linguistic and thematic resonances between this passage of the *MBK* and Homer's *Iliad*.

(*MBK* 2.425ff.).[61] The scene is an inversion of the Iliadic model: seduction deployed to effect a transition from unconsciousness to waking (rather than from consciousness to sleep), and to establish a consensus between husband and wife (rather than to deceive the husband as to the wife's true purpose). Indeed, Durgā could not have deceived Śiva even if she had wished to: before she has the opportunity to discuss her purpose with him he tells her (l. 426f.): *āmi jāni, debi, tomār maner kathā* . . . , 'I know, o goddess, what is in your mind'.

More broadly, the differences between the two scenes are significant for the reader's response to the plight of Rāma and Rāvaṇa. Whereas in the *Iliad* the divine characters are partisan towards those mortals who are their devotees (and are so on the basis solely of this devotion), in the *MBK*, the gods as a community back Rāma for moral rather than partisan reasons and only Śiva supports Rāvaṇa (and does so, in a Homeric fashion, because he is his ardent devotee). Unlike the Homeric gods, however, Śiva readily admits that this support is contrary to a proper moral view of the conflict (see *MBK* 2.425ff.) and, once roused from his meditation by Durgā, he is easily persuaded to give up his immoral protection of him. Thus, once Durgā manages to wake Śiva and persuade him to assist Rāma, all the characters on the divine plane reach a consensus in favour of Rāma. Thereafter, Rāvaṇa's fate is sealed. In this way, the egregious odds faced by Rāvaṇa in fact heighten both the tragedy of his own downfall and more particularly that of Meghanāda, the besieged city's champion, who later in the poem will be laid low in a war brought down upon his city through no fault of his own, but by his own father's immoral acts. Moreover, the unanimous divine support for Rāma from this point of the poem onwards makes his achievement somewhat less impressive: whereas Hera achieves only a brief respite for the Achaeans by making Zeus fall asleep, Durgā permanently seals the fate of Rāvaṇa and his army by waking Śiva from his meditation. Thereafter Rāma is little more than the instrument by which all of the gods put their collective intention into effect.

[61] For the broad differences between the Homeric gods and the Hindu gods in the *MBK* (especially the fact that the Homeric gods act less from moral causes than as a response to human flattery and adulation), and for Śiva's exception to this rule in favouring Rāvaṇa largely on the basis of his extreme devotion, see Radice (2010) 323.

Madhusudan's location of this Bengali version of the Dios Apate so early in his poem is a curious feature given that in the Greek poem it occurs in the second half of the narrative. This is the longest and most significant Iliadic passage of the *MBK*, and it certainly serves to announce the Bengali poem's Homeric credentials early on in the narrative. Therefore, one may reasonably ask why, when the rest of the poem's narrative arc follows such a markedly Greek trajectory, this most striking Iliadic passage is out of kilter. The prominent positioning of this passage serves, among other things, as an apologia for the Bengali poem's relative lack of battle narrative. Madhusudan himself stated in a letter to a friend that 'Homer is nothing but battles . . . I have, like Milton, only one'.[62] By placing front and centre in his Bengali epic, a Homeric scene in which, as Janko has noted, 'Homer parades his mastery of the other [i.e. non-martial] types of epic composition in his repertoire',[63] Madhusudan indicates, first, that Homer himself is not, in fact, 'nothing but battles' and, secondly, that his own Bengali epic is Iliadic in subtler ways than a straightforward emulation of Homeric battle scenes could achieve. The Bengali poet's Homeric appropriations are surprising, and they represent a reading of the Greek poem that is sensitive to the varied textures of its poetry. Indeed, the Bengali passage in question is not a 'bedroom farce', as the Iliadic passage has been aptly described:[64] it is an erotic but quite serious scene. It is striking that Madhusudan should take an episode from Homer's *Iliad*, an epic known for its gravity and seriousness, and make it less rather than more light-hearted. In any event, by placing this Iliadic scene so prominently within the *MBK* the Bengali poet indicates the presence within Homer's famously weighty and serious poem of a more frivolous and farcical generic strand.

If the Seduction of Śiva in *MBK* 2 disrupts the Iliadic narrative arc of the Bengali poem, then in many and varied respects the Homeric structure is adhered to throughout the *MBK*. It has already been noted above that the *MBK*, following the *Iliad's* lead, narrates a brief episode towards the end of a war. Furthermore, like the Homeric epic, the Bengali poem points forward to the end of the war of Laṅkā in passages of external prolepsis. Just as Troy's fall (*Il.* 17.406f.) and Achilles' death (*Il.* 22.358–60) are foreshadowed in the *Iliad* whilst

[62] Murshid (2004) 171.
[63] Janko (1992) 168.
[64] Janko (1992) 168.

falling outside of the scope of the main narrative,[65] so Rāma's success and the fall of Laṅkā (*MBK* 8.784–6) are foreshadowed in the *MBK*. By contrast, in the Sanskrit and Bengali *Rāmāyaṇas*, Madhusudan's primary sources for the substance of the *MBK*, these events are narrated chronologically and in full.[66]

Moreover, at a microtextual level, certain structural devices underpinning the *MBK* seem to be modelled on the *Iliad*. Many of the books of the *MBK* begin with an indication of time.[67] *MBK* 2.1–2, 3.17ff. and 8.1–6 all bear indications of nightfall, echoing *Il.* 2.1ff., 10.1ff., and 24.2ff.[68] Similarly, certain books of the *MBK* begin with an indication of dawn, as at *MBK* 7.1ff. and 9.1, recalling the book openings at *Il.* 8.1, 11.1ff. and 19.1ff.[69] Another subtle aspect of the Bengali epic's narrative strategy, which takes Homer's *Iliad* as a source of inspiration, is its similes.[70] The poem's use of the Homeric simile has been shown by Seely to be a particular locus for the poet's subtly subversive literary practices,[71] but it may also be seen as a part of a broader incorporation of Iliadic narrative patterns into the fabric of the Bengali poem. Moreover, scholars have already noted the striking relationship of the simile at *MBK* 6.607–10 to *Il.* 4.130–3.[72] The allusion is unmistakable: in both passages a goddess protecting a favoured warrior from missiles is compared with a mother protecting her sleeping son from flies/mosquitoes. This Iliadic simile is *sui generis*, the vehicle's subject being found only here and nowhere

[65] See de Jong (1987) 81–6 and Alden (2000) 150, n. 81, 175, 178.

[66] See the Sanskrit *Rāmāyaṇa*, 6.110.

[67] For the book divisions of the Homeric poems and their Alexandrian date, cf. esp. Taplin (1992) 285–93, Stanley (1993), and Jensen (1999) 5–91.

[68] Cf. also *Od.* 20.1ff. and *Aen.* 5.10f.

[69] Descriptions of dawn are even more frequent at the beginning of the books of the *Odyssey*; cf. *Od.* 2.1ff., 3.1ff., 5.1ff., 8.1ff., 13.18ff., 16.1ff., 17.1ff. (and *Od.* 23 (371f.) with an unusual variation); also *Aen.* 4.6f., 7.25f., 11.1ff.

[70] The similarity between Homeric similes and certain similes in the *MBK* has been noted before, the most thorough account so far being S. Bhattacharya (1962) 19–36 (but see also Sanyal (1917) in his commentary *ad MBK*). See, *contra*, D. Bhattacharya (1972) 197ff., who detects what he sees as *bibhrānti* or 'errors' in the earlier work, arguing (rather pedantically) that S. Bhattacharya was over-enthusiastic in his desire to identify Homeric and other Western influence in the *MBK*.

[71] See Seely (1988).

[72] See Dasgupta (1933–5) 124 and S. Bhattacharya (1962) 35. Note that Seely (1988), despite his title ('Homeric Similes, Occidental and Oriental . . .'), only treats the *MBK's* debt to Tasso and Milton, not to Homer.

else in the poem.[73] However, what is just as striking as this kind of one-to-one correspondence is the poet's imitation of whole Iliadic simile types. Thus the *MBK* departs from the rather plodding and monotonous types of simile found in the Sanskrit and Bengali *Rāmāyaṇas* and takes the Homeric paradigm as a starting point: the images are drawn from nature (lions, birds, fire, cattle, boars, wind, water),[74] and deployed in a manner that is sensitive to their thematic context (a particularly Homeric feature), and with the introduction now and then of an Indian tiger or elephant to add variety and a Bengali stamp to the Greek source.[75]

At a more obvious and macroscopic level, the story arc of the *MBK* is modelled in miniature on that of the *Iliad*. The *MBK*, a poem narrated in nine *sargas* (or 'cantos'), falls essentially into three triads. The first of these begins, as at *Il.* 1.1–7, with a poetic invocation.[76] The march of the Rākṣasas at *MBK* 1.555ff., which has the effect of a catalogue of warriors, is narrated early in the poem just as the Catalogue of Ships occurs at *Il.* 2.484–877. The end of *MBK* 3, concluding the poem's first triad, narrates a deliberation among the gods, an echo of the council of the gods held at *Il.* 8.350–488 (occurring at the end of the poem's first third). Furthermore, at *MBK* 4.21ff., just after the second proem, the defenders of the city exult in their success, echoing the Trojans' confidence at *Il.* 8.542–63.

At the end of the second triad, the sixth canto of the poem, the death of Meghanāda is narrated. At the equivalent point in the *Iliad*'s narrative (the sixteenth book, two thirds through the poem) Patroclus is killed by Hector (cf. *Il.* 16.829–63). This is immediately followed by the revenge killing of Meghanāda's slayer by his father Rāvaṇa. In the *Iliad*, this second death comes later (in the twenty-second book) but the sequence is analogous: A kills B and C kills A (where C's love of B motivates his killing of A).[77]

[73] For the thirty other subjects found in only one Iliadic simile, cf. Lee (1964), Edwards (1991) 34, esp. n. 39. For an overview of recent scholarship on the Homeric simile, see Buxton (2004).

[74] See Lee (1964) 65–73; also Edwards (1991) 34, and Fränkel (1921).

[75] See Riddiford (2009) 342–50 for further details.

[76] There is a second invocation at *MBK* 4.1–20 similar to the second invocation at *Aen.* 7.37–45.

[77] Cf. Janko (1992) 310 for the 'traditional incident' whereby 'A kills B and C kills A'.

MBK 7 is a compression of *Il.* 18–22: Vīrabhadra reports Meghanāda's death to Rāvaṇa (*MBK* 7.95ff.) just as Antilokhus reports Patroclus' death to Achilles (*Il.* 18.2ff.); Rāvaṇa musters the troops (*MBK* 7.153ff.) just as Achilles inspires the Achaeans by showing himself to them again (*Il.* 18.215ff.); a 'theomachy' intercedes in the narrative (*MBK* 7.516ff.), just as in the *Iliad* (*Il.* 20.54ff.); and, finally, the revenge killing is narrated (*MBK* 7.729ff. and *Il.* 22.249ff.). Finally, the *MBK* ends with the cremation of Meghanāda (*MBK* 9.209–end) just as the *Iliad* closes with the burial of Hector (*Il.* 24.718–end). In both cases, the funeral follows, and is made possible by, something of a rapprochement between mortal enemies: Rāma and Rāvaṇa (*MBK* 9.103ff.); and Achilles and Priam (*Il.* 24.217ff.).[78]

The Bengali epic models its story arc on that of the Homeric epic, and is broadly divisible into episodes or movements, which map on to the Greek model. And yet, the way in which the Bengali narrative arc relates to the *Iliad*, especially in the final four cantos of the *MBK*, rather complicates our interpretation of the Iliadic identities of the Hindu characters as outlined above, and this complication in turn colours our interpretation of the Bengali poem as a whole. As noted earlier, the death of Meghanāda in *MBK* 6 occurs at the end of the poem's second third, just as Patroclus dies at the end of the *Iliad*'s second third, at *Il.* 16.829–63. The problem raised by this correspondence is, as it were, one of identity: with which Homeric character are we to identify the hero Meghanāda? Nirad Chaudhuri felt that, for Madhusudan, Meghanāda was 'a second Hector'. This view refers to Meghanāda's status as principal hero and defender of his city. However, although he is like Hector in this respect, he is also comparable with Patroclus in others. Meghanāda's death in *MBK* 6 sets in train a revenge killing, just as Patroclus' death sets in train Hector's and so, on this schematic level, Meghanāda's role resonates with that of the Greek rather than the Trojan hero. Furthermore, some finer textual resonances serve to align Meghanāda with Patroclus. For example, at *MBK* 6.651ff., Meghanāda makes a dying prophecy to his slayer, Lakṣmaṇa, foreseeing Rāvaṇa's untiring efforts to exact revenge for his death. This dying prophecy brings to mind very specifically the last words of Patroclus to Hector (*Il.* 16.852–4) to the effect that fate will soon bring down the latter at the hands of Achilles. Meghanāda's

[78] Cf. Dasgupta (1933–5) 128.

dying prophecy to Lakṣmaṇa is more like that of Patroclus to Hector than that of Hector to Achilles. At *Il.* 22.356–60 Hector foretells the death of Achilles at the hands of Paris and Apollo, a killing that will take place at a point in time beyond the scope of the *Iliad*'s narrative. Hector's prophecy is, then, an 'external prolepsis'.[79] In the case of the dying prophecies of both Meghanāda and Patroclus, what we have is 'internal prolepsis': the killing foreseen will occur later in the same narrative. Indeed in both cases the slayer foreseen is a single character (Achilles and Rāvaṇa respectively). Hector, on the other hand, foresees a pair slaying Achilles. Meghanāda, though he is in many ways a Hector figure, is at the point of death more closely aligned with Patroclus than with the Trojan hero.[80] Madhusudan's alignment of Meghanāda with both Hector and Patroclus, two of the most sympathetic heroes in the *Iliad*,[81] is yet another tactic used in his reversal of the reader's sympathy for Rāma, and towards the traditional villains of the story.

MBK 7, following immediately after the slaying of Meghanāda in *MBK* 6, is in turn a compression of *Il.* 18–22. It has already been noted that some critics have seen Rāvaṇa as analogous to Priam, which is the most obvious interpretation: he is the king of a beleaguered city, the father of a hero slain while protecting his people. However, by extension of Meghanāda's dual identification with both Hector and Patroclus, his father Rāvaṇa is not only a Priam but also an Achilles. Rāvaṇa's revenge killing of Lakṣmaṇa in *MBK* 7, following the latter's slaughter of Meghanāda in *MBK* 6, is analogous to Achilles' revenge killing of Hector in *Il.* 22. The comparison of Rāvaṇa's actions with those of Achilles begins with the delivery of the news of Meghanāda's death. The manner in which Rāvaṇa learns of his son's death is more akin to that in which Achilles hears of Patroclus' death than to that in which Priam learns of Hector's.

[79] See de Jong (1987) for this and other narratological terms.

[80] The slaying of Meghanāda, a character aligned with both Patroclus and Hector, thus implies the comparison of the two Iliadic slayings at *Il.* 16.829–63 and 22.330–367. This comparison would be endorsed by recent criticism of the *Iliad,* which has identified structural and thematic connections between the two episodes. See Richardson (1993) *ad Il.* 22.330–67, 830–63, Fenik (1968) 217f., and Schadewaldt (1959) 262 and 323.

[81] See Janko (1992) 317 for the narrator's 'sympathetic' apostrophes to Patroclus, and *Il.* 11.804–12.2, 16.21-45, 19.282-300 for episodes in which Patroclus' sympathetic characteristics are emphasized; *Il.* 6.242–493 and 22.430–515 for intimate portrayals of Hector's family life, and *Il.* 24.267ff. for his (unique) kindness to Helen.

Indeed, Priam does not need to be told of Hector's slaughter, for he witnesses it first hand (see *Il.* 22.408), and it is made clear that he is a spectator of the whole event (cf. *Il.* 22.25–8 where Priam is the first to see Achilles). Just as at *Il.* 18.2ff. Antilokhus comes as a messenger to tell Achilles of his comrade's death at the hands of Hector, so too at *MBK* 7.95ff. Vīrabhadra comes as a messenger to tell Rāvaṇa of his son's death at the hands of Lakṣmaṇa. Whereas Achilles is prescient about the bad news (*Il.* 18.4), Rāvaṇa erroneously expects good news (*MBK* 7.108–10). However, in both instances the messenger foresees an act of violence in response to the news: Antilokhus fears Achilles may cut his own throat (*Il.* 18.34); Vīrabhadra, imagining that the king's anger would be directed towards him, refuses to relate the news before Rāvaṇa grants him *abhaẏa*, 'assurance of safety' (*MBK* 7.111–4).

Priam's first impulse, in response to his son's death, is to go to Achilles to supplicate for the return of the body (*Il.* 22.418). Rāvaṇa's response to the news is much more akin to Achilles' than to Priam's. Rāvaṇa's response is not desperate, like Priam's, but angry (see *MBK* 7.153ff.) and he exhorts his men to arm for battle to exact revenge (ll. 153ff.). This angry response echoes Achilles' who, after great lamentation, states that he has no wish to live unless Hector is slain by his spear and made to pay for his comrade's death (*Il.* 18.90–3). Indeed this idea, that the sole purpose of the bereaved is to avenge the death of the slain, is echoed clearly in Rāvaṇa's address to his wife. Here, in conversation before going out to battle to avenge his son's death, he states that they live only to exact revenge (*MBK* 7.339ff.).[82]

The parallels between the revenge narrative of *Il.* 18–22 and that of *MBK* 7 extend right up to the revenge killing itself. Lakṣmaṇa, victim of the revenge killing and therefore analogous here to Hector, swears at *MBK* 7.247: *maribo, nahe māribo rābaṇe* . . . , 'Either I shall die or I shall kill Rāvaṇa . . . '. This sentiment echoes Hector's deliberation before facing Achilles, which he concludes by exhorting himself to test which way the Olympian will give victory (*Il.* 22.129f.). In both cases, the hero who will be slain commits himself to mortal combat, conceding that his own death is a possible outcome and an acceptable risk.

[82] Cf. also *MBK* 7.384-6.

The subsequent combat between Rāvaṇa and Lakṣmaṇa is itself reminiscent of that between Achilles and Hector in *Il.* 22. Achilles refuses a pact and insists that he will feed Hector's body to the dogs and birds (*Il.* 22.353). Similarly Rāvaṇa, upon joining with Lakṣmaṇa in fight, addresses his opponent in wrath saying (*MBK* 7.716f.): *māṃso tor māṃsāhārī jībe/ dibo ebe . . .*, 'now I will give your flesh to flesh-eating beasts . . . '. Achilles taunts his victim, telling him that he was wrong not to fear his wrath and to think he could get away with killing Patroclus (*Il.* 22. 331–3). In the same way, Rāvaṇa makes it clear to Lakṣmaṇa that killing Meghanāda was a mistake and that he will pay for it (*MBK* 7.718ff.).

Furthermore, certain rhetorical devices used to describe the revenge killing of *MBK* 7 recall those used in the analogous Iliadic scene. For example, the slaying of Lakṣmaṇa is described through a series of similes.[83] As Rāvaṇa delivers the lethal blow, the narrator ornaments the narrative with four similes (*MBK* 7.736ff.). This concentration of similes to describe the fall of Lakṣmaṇa echoes the similar concentration in the description of Hector's death, not only at the moment of his slaying (at *Il.* 22.306–21 the narrative culminates in two similes), but also in the narrative building up to it (cf. esp. *Il.* 22.162–6 and 189–93).

Another device for focusing attention on the event of Lakṣmaṇa's death is the 'spectatorship' of both men and gods, a markedly Iliadic feature.[84] At *MBK* 7.729-30 the narrator comments: *cāhilā biśmaẏe/ deb naro dōhā pāne . . .*', 'Gods and men looked at them both in wonder . . . '. This device echoes the *Iliad*'s narration of Hector's death. In the *Iliad*'s account of Hector's death there is a 'framing' of the event whereby, both before and after the killing, the spectatorship of both gods and men is described. At *Il.* 22.166 the gods are said to be looking down on the scene; and at the moment of Hector's death the spectatorship of his mother is described (*Il.* 22.407). Like Hector's downfall in the *Iliad*, Lakṣmaṇa's death sequence in the *MBK* is also accentuated and framed by the narrative device of divine and human spectatorship.

The complex relationship between the characters of the *MBK* and their Iliadic counterparts (the overlaying of features of various Iliadic

[83] See above for a treatment of Homeric 'consecutive similes'.

[84] On divine spectatorship in the *Iliad*, see Griffin (1980) Ch.6, esp. 181 *ad Il.* 22.166–70.

characters in the characterization of a single hero of the *MBK*) continues through to the rapprochement that occurs in *MBK* 9.[85] Various critics have noticed striking parallels here between Rāvaṇa and Priam, notably in his successful call for a truce during the funeral ceremonies for his son Meghanāda.[86] Once again, however, this neat correspondence between Rāvaṇa and Priam is disrupted by further Iliadic allusions. The rapprochement between the two characters for the duration of the funeral puts one in mind primarily of *Il.* 24. However, the manner in which the reconciliation is effected recalls not so much Achilles and Priam in *Il.* 24 as the Embassy to Achilles in *Il.* 9, aligning Rāvaṇa in this instance with neither Priam nor Achilles (as in *MBK* 7), but with Agamemnon. For example, whereas the negotiations between Achilles and Priam in *Il.* 24 are conducted in person, the embassy of *Il.* 9 is a negotiation by proxy using third party representatives, a crucial difference that may, to an extent, underlie Achilles' distinct responses to the two requests: sincerity, dear to Achilles (cf. *Il.* 9.312f.), is perhaps more successfully expressed in person.[87] In this respect, Rāvaṇa's overtures to his enemy (see *MBK* 9.70ff.) are more akin to Agamemnon's embassy to Achilles than Priam's supplication: the king does not go in person, like Priam in *Il.* 24, but sends an embassy to Rāma just as Agamemnon sends an embassy to Achilles in *Il.* 9.

The force of this secondary allusion to *Il.* 9 is strengthened at *MBK* 9.103ff. Here Sāraṇa, rather than apologizing or conveying Rāvaṇa's apology for the abduction of Sītā (here more readily identifiable with Briseïs than with Helen),[88] makes excuses for the king instead. Here we are put in mind of Agamemnon's failure in *Il.* 9 to make a sincere and contrite apology to Achilles.[89] Furthermore, at *MBK* 9.115f., Sāraṇa blames Rāvaṇa's folly on the *māyā* ('deception') of Fate. This claim that Fate is responsible for the offender's actions, rather

[85] Recall that *MBK* 8, charting Rāma's descent into the underworld, owes much to *Aen.* 6: see Section 1 above. This canto interrupts the sequence under discussion (slaying, revenge and reconciliation) in the same way that the funeral games of Patroclus in *Il.* 23 effects a narrative break between Hector's death in *Il.* 22 and the 'reconciliation' of Achilles and Priam in *Il.* 24. Moreover, both *Il.* 23 and *MBK* 8 provide a kind of 'closure' that is 'complementary' to the kind provided by the final book (see Macleod (1982) 17, 28–32).

[86] See n. 54 above.

[87] See Taplin (1990) esp. 71.

[88] See n. 54 above.

[89] On Agamemnon's behaviour here, see Thornton (1984).

than the offender himself, recalls Agamemnon's speech at *Il.* 9.115ff. Here, Agamemnon claims to have been blinded (ll. 116), a claim elaborated at *Il.* 19.91f., where, like Rāvaṇa's minister, he claims that it was a divinity who brought about the mistake – namely Ate, the Greek Māẏā.[90]

Rāvaṇa's negotiation with Rāma here in *MBK* 9, as with much of the preceding narrative, uses Iliadic resonances to add layers of complexity to the basic character-correspondences between the two poems. This allusion in a single narrative sequence to both *Il.* 9 and *Il.* 24 represents a subtle reading of the Greek epic; for the two Iliadic scenes, as has been suggested by Macleod, are connected within the Homeric poem itself by a variety of narrative and thematic devices.[91] Furthermore, this alignment of one Indian character with several Iliadic heroes is part of a broader pattern. As we have seen throughout this section, Rāvaṇa is not only aligned with Priam, but also (in *MBK* 7) with Achilles and to an extent (in *MBK* 9) with Agamemnon. Meghanāda is not only a Hector-figure, but (in *MBK* 6) he also recalls Patroclus and Lakṣmaṇa, the aggressor's brother and therefore most obviously equivalent to Menelaus, is also (in *MBK* 6) a Hector-figure. Or to put it another way, Hector becomes two characters in the *MBK*, Meghanāda and Lakṣmaṇa; Agamemnon becomes two characters, Rāma and Rāvaṇa (and so forth).

This technique of combining several Iliadic characters into one, and *vice versa*, represents a sophisticated response to the Homeric model. Indeed, it may put one in mind of the famous response to Homeric epic in Vergil's *Aeneid*. As Knauer has observed, '. . . Vergil has sometimes combined several Homeric characters into one . . . But the reverse too may occur. One Homeric character is split up into three . . .'.[92] Madhusudan's response to the *Iliad* in the *MBK* is not only sophisticated but perhaps even Vergilian in some respects. The Bengali poet's readings of Homer and Vergil are implicated in each other, and his response to both works reveals him to be a highly nuanced reader of the Graeco-Roman epic tradition.

[90] Cf. 105 above for the complexity of Māẏā's relationship with the Iliadic model.
[91] See Macleod (1982) 34f.
[92] See Knauer (1990) 394f. and Gransden (1984).

3. MADHUSUDAN'S GRAECO-ROMAN SAMPLINGS IN CONTEXT

The Bengali poet's response to Graeco-Roman epic in the *MBK* represents an ambitious exercise in literary appropriation; but it is also illustrative—perhaps even emblematic—of the kind of subtle and multi-directional cultural subversion which, as will emerge increasingly in the course of the following chapters, is quite typical of Madhusudan's oeuvre. Homer's *Iliad* and Vergil's *Aeneid* are both marshalled to contribute, in subtle but unmistakable ways, to the bold reversal of sympathies attaching to the figures of Rāma and Rāvaṇa. Rāma becomes a second Agamemnon, and in *MBK* 8 another Aeneas, and the Graeco-Roman resonances diminish the Hindu character in the reader's eyes. Rāvaṇa plays the role of Priam, and Meghanāda is slain while performing Hector's duties towards his own city. The reader is thus left (an effect consciously modelled on Milton's *Paradise Lost*) with a strong sympathy for the villains of this traditional morality tale.

While this reversal represents a striking act of resistance to the cultural hegemony of the Hindu pundits and of Hindu orthodoxy in general, it is not accompanied by a slavish or humourless acceptance of the Graeco-Roman tradition as unassailably authoritative, nor by an uncritical transfer of allegiance from one form of cultural hegemony to another. In particular, Madhusudan's emphatic positioning of his response to the Dios Apate in the second canto of his Bengali epic serves to highlight a surprising generic counter-current within the cornerstone text of the Graeco-Roman canon. The Bengali poet draws the reader's attention to this Iliadic 'bedroom farce', which he not only imitates but even elevates and sanitizes, and thereby makes a proleptic apologia for those aspects of his own epic which do not fit neatly within contemporary Western notions of what an epic should be. Madhusudan impliedly asks: if even the greatest Greek poet permitted himself moments of farce and lightness within his archetypal martial epic, then why not a Bengali poet too? The Bengali poet was aware that the nature of his Hindu subject matter was such that a transplant of Graeco-Roman models into this Indian soil might yield surprising results. Most strikingly, several of Rāma's allies are in fact monkeys rather than men, prompting the Bengali poet to say in a letter to a friend: '. . . if the father of our Poetry [*viz.* Vālmīki] had given Ram human companions I could have made a regular *Iliad* of the death of Meghanad'.[93] Elsewhere, he commented in a similar vein: 'The subject is truly heroic; only the Monkeys spoil the joke . . .'[94] But Madhusudan was a critical reader of the Graeco-Roman classics just as much as he was of the Hindu tradition, and his tendency towards iconoclasm is just as evident in his response to Homer's *Iliad* as it is in his reading of the *Rāmayaṇa*.

Given Madhusudan's knowledge of the English literary heritage and his awareness of the contemporary British literary scene,[95] it is instructive to set his response to the Graeco-Roman epic tradition in this context. Generically, the *MBK* lies somewhere between an epyllion (indeed Madhusudan's epyllion *Tilottamā-sambhab kābya* was a prefiguring of the more ambitious *MBK*) and a full-scale epic. The nine canto structure signals a drawing back from the full scale and scope of Homer's twenty-four-book model and even from Vergil's twelve-book paradigm. However, while Madhusudan described the *MBK* self-deprecatingly as an 'Epicling',[96] in truth the Bengali poem does not fall very far short of the Graeco-Roman models in terms of volume and range. Thus Madhusudan's ambitions stand in marked contrast to contemporary British trends. Full-scale epic was very rarely attempted in the Victorian period, and never by a prominent poet.[97]

[93] See Murshid (2004) 31.

[94] See Murshid (2004) 152. Humour and wit are ubiquitous features of Madhusudan's oeuvre (see, for example, Radice (2010) xxxi–xxxiv): almost any page of the poet's work will testify to the poet's ironic and self-conscious pose. The irony here, though, is perhaps that the poet was in many ways deadly serious about the Iliadic 'joke' of the *MBK*, and was equally serious about his broader project to 'reform' Bengali literary culture.

[95] In this connection we might note that by June 1854 Madhusudan had already read Stowe's *Uncle Tom's Cabin*, first published in book form in March 1852. This is evidence that the Bengali poet was not only interested in contemporary Western literature, but was very much up-to-date in his engagement with it. The rapidity with which Madhusudan had read and assimilated this novel, *viz.* within just over two years of its first publication, is also significant for our understanding of the relationship between the British colonies and the metropolis: lines of cultural communication were evidently such that Madhusudan's awareness in British India of contemporary literary matters in the European metropolis was practically immediate. We infer that he had read Stowe's novel by June 1854 since he alludes to it in his lecture, delivered in Madras in the same month, called *The Anglo-Saxon and the Hindu*. See Chapter 4, n. 3.

[96] See Murshid (2004) 97 and 119.

[97] Note, however, that certain less notable Victorian poets had fewer qualms about direct confrontation with the Homeric model (see Tucker (2008)).

Arnold, Tennyson, and Browning—three celebrated poets of the period who frequently returned to classical themes— by and large avoided emulating Homer in an overt or direct way;[98] likewise they generally eschewed Homeric length and ambition when they did turn to Homeric models.[99] While Madhusudan's *MBK* perhaps shares Arnold's tendency to emulate Homer indirectly rather than directly, by retelling a traditional Hindu narrative in a Homeric fashion (compare Arnold's Homeric treatment of the Persian tradition in 'Sohrab and Rustum' (1853)), it is significant that the Bengali poet felt no such inhibition in his later *Hekṭor-badh* (1871), an ambitious work in which a loose 'Orientalist' version of the first twelve books of Homer's *Iliad* is rendered into experimental Bengali prose.[100]

Indeed, if Madhusudan read Homer through any English lens, it was through Milton's seventeenth-century epic *Paradise Lost*. Speaking of his response to the *Iliad* in the *MBK* Madhusudan noted that 'Homer is nothing but battles . . . I have, like Milton, only one',[101] a comment implying a response to Homer through Milton, or at least a close association in his mind between the two. The *MBK*'s reception of *Paradise Lost* is well documented:[102] Madhusudan's rehabilitation of Rāvaṇa, traditional villain of the *Rāmāyaṇa* story, seems to take Milton's inadvertently sympathetic treatment of Satan as its primary inspiration. And the Bengali poet's use of Iliadic, and indeed Vergilian allusions in the furtherance of his challenge to Hindu orthodoxy figures a contribution towards this Miltonic trope.

Madhusudan's *MBK* is a locus of myriad literary incorporations, both Hindu and European: a thoroughgoing discussion of them all would require a whole monograph. Although this reading of the Bengali epic's response to the Graeco-Roman epic tradition has

[98] See Harrison (2007d) focusing especially on Arnold's reception of Homer in 'Sohrab and Rustum' (1853) and 'Balder Dead' (1855), characterized by 'miniaturization' and indirect imitation. See also Tennyson's 'Ulysses' (1833) which takes the brief episode of *Od.* 11.100–37 and extends it. Though the strategy is different, Tennyson's poem is similar to Arnold's 'Homeric' works in being a brief response to Homer's monumental epics. Indeed we see a similar effect in other poems by Tennyson: see 'The Lotos-Eaters' (1832), 'Oenone' (1832) and (1891), etc.

[99] See Harrison (2007d).

[100] For an examination of this work, see Chapter 6 below.

[101] See Murshid (2004) 171.

[102] The influence of *Paradise Lost* on the *MBK* has been recognized since its first publication, and various studies of the influence have been carried out. See esp. S. Bhattacharya (1962) and Radice (1995).

been necessarily symptomatic, some of the poem's more distinctive aspects have been discussed. It has emerged that the relationship of the *MBK* to its Iliadic and Vergilian models is marked above all by an independence of mind, a freedom in particular from the influence of contemporary British inhibitions in the face of Homer's monumentality, and a tendency towards multi-directional subversion and resistance. In this respect Madhusudan's reception in the *MBK* of Homer's *Iliad* and Vergil's *Aeneid* is emblematic of the Bengali poet's response to the Graeco-Roman classics throughout his oeuvre.

4

Further Receptions of Vergil's *Aeneid*

INTRODUCTION

The two texts considered here, *The Anglo-Saxon and the Hindu* (1854) and the embryonic 'national epic' *Siṃhal-bijay kābya* (*c.* 1861), show a close engagement with Vergil's *Aeneid.*[1] Although both texts are somewhat marginal (the former being a little-studied lecture in English, the latter amounting only to a few verses of Bengali and a brief plan in English), nonetheless each represents an arresting response to Vergil's *Aeneid* worthy of the reader's attention. Furthermore, there is a certain thematic congruity between these two texts, despite their obvious differences, which argues that they should be considered together. Both texts, for example, read Vergil's *Aeneid* in terms of national identity and colonial adventure: one text uses the Roman epic to consider the colonial relationship between Britain and 'queenly Hindustan'; the other to consider Bengali national identity and Bengal's relationship with the rest of India. The responses examined here have a marked and somewhat subversive political aspect, and address themselves to sensitive issues surrounding Britain's presence in India and its effect on Bengali culture.

1. *THE ANGLO-SAXON AND THE HINDU* (1854)

The Anglo-Saxon and the Hindu[2] is a lecture delivered in English during June 1854 in Madras to a British (or predominantly British)

[1] For the Vergilian panel in the *Meghnādbadh kābya* (1861), see the previous chapter.

[2] The edition referred to throughout is Patra (2005) 628ff.

audience (and published soon thereafter).[3] It dates from the time Madhusudan spent in that southern city, mostly alongside British colleagues, teaching and working for English-language journals. The lecture concerns the colonial relationship between India and Britain. Madhusudan states that the 'Anglo-Saxon's' mission is 'to renovate, to regenerate, or—in one word to Christianize the Hindu'.[4] The rise of the 'Anglo-Saxon' is charted, and then the decline of the 'Hindu', and finally the Anglo-Saxon's mission to 'Christianize' the Hindu is stated: the Anglo-Saxon must bring about the Hindu's '*national rejuvenescence*'.[5] The Anglo-Saxon must save the Hindu who, he says, is teetering 'on the verge of a moral grave'.[6] Indeed the author stands, one supposes, as a paradigm for this 'moral regeneration'. The lecture is a learned *tour de force*, full of the European learning and Christian zeal that might 'restore' his ailing people.

The lecture has received little attention from Indian scholars, in no small part because of its ostensibly pro-British attitude, and the desire to construct Madhusudan as an early 'nationalist'.[7] Though Indian nationalism as such did not really gain ideological traction until the 1870s,[8] Madhusudan was in many ways a proto-nationalist, and in this lecture he pins his patriotic colours unambiguously to the mast: 'believe it not that *we* have no love of country—that our heart strings do not cling round the land of our fathers!'.[9] For Madhusudan the embrace of Western 'high' culture was not incompatible with profound Indian patriotism, rather the former was a necessary consequence of

[3] The first of four lectures, only the first of which survives. Seely (2004) 27 places the lectures 'in 1854 or possibly somewhat before'. This lecture, the first of four lectures, is said by Seely (2004) 27 to have been delivered in '1854 or possibly somewhat before'. In fact I have discovered four advertisements for the lectures in the *Madras Athenaeum*, appearing in consecutive weeks during June 1854 (on 6, 15, 17, and 22 June). Presumably, then, this first lecture in the series was delivered on or around 6 June of that year. One infers that the audience was British, or at least included Britons, from his repeated apostrophes to his audience as 'the sons and the daughters of the Anglo-Saxon'. Indeed, the lecture was dedicated to Charles Egbert Kennet and, while in Madras, Madhusudan associated almost exclusively with European or 'Eurasian' Christians: see Murshid (2003) 104f.

[4] Patra (2005) 643: the climax of the final paragraph of the lecture.

[5] A phrase used twice, both times in italics see Patra (2005) 638.

[6] Patra (2005) 637.

[7] This, at least, is the reason suggested by Murshid (2003).

[8] See Chapter 1 above. Note, however, that Bankim, the Bengali nationalist and novelist, in his obituary of Madhusudan in 1873, celebrated him as a *jātīyo kabi* or 'national poet'.

[9] Patra (2005) 634. Emphasis original.

the latter, a vital tool for the promotion and advancement of Indian culture.

In this context, the Vergilian allusion, with which the lecture is prefaced, radically complicates our interpretation of the lecture's entire argument, and is strongly suggestive of proto-nationalist and xenophobic sentiment.[10] The work is prefaced with a citation, in the original Latin, of *Aen.* 4.10: *quis novus hic nostris successit sedibus hospes!* (rendered into English by Madhusudan, with a bathetic question mark, as 'Who is this stranger that has come to our dwelling?'). On the basis of this verse (cited repeatedly throughout the lecture), and following the familiar trope of gendering the European power as masculine and the colonized Indian as feminine,[11] Madhusudan constructs a metaphor whereby Aeneas stands for the 'Anglo-Saxon' and Dido for 'queenly Hindustan'.

Such a citation of *Aen.* 4.10, aligning Britain with Aeneas and India with Dido, is a surprising place to begin an apparently pro-British tract. After all, Aeneas is not fated to remain in Carthage, his proper business being elsewhere;[12] and Aeneas' treatment of Dido leads to her suicide at the end of *Aen.* 4. In its context, Dido's exclamation at *Aen.* 4.10 is a moment of dramatic irony, preparing for one of the poem's most tragic episodes. Indeed the tragic discourse of the *Aeneid*, nowhere more in evidence than in the fourth book, may be said to 'counterbalance' its 'nationalist and imperial teleology'.[13] And one can hardly forget that Dido's suicide is the aetiology of the eternal enmity between Carthage and Rome.[14]

Madhusudan immediately qualifies the metaphor, though the back-pedalling in fact complicates the matter further still:

[10] Radice (1998) 147 argues that 'to trace the nationalist or xenophobic strain in Madhusudan requires subtlety and empathy: one must be prepared to read between the lines sometimes, to look for the deeper implications of his writing'. In the case of the *Anglo-Saxon and the Hindu*, an otherwise markedly pro-British work, a 'xenophobic strain' may certainly be seen in the lecture's Vergilian metaphor.

[11] A trend explored particularly well by Bandyopadhyay (2004) 381ff., who remarks that the 'effeminacy' of Indian society, as supposed by the discourse of colonial politics, 'justified' its loss of independence.

[12] Mercury relays Jupiter's command to Aeneas telling him to leave Carthage (4.265ff.) and remember Italy (ll. 275f.). See Austin (1955) *ad loc.*

[13] See Harrison (2007a) 208ff. for the particular resonances with Attic tragedy (Sophocles' *Antigone*) at the beginning of *Aen.* 4. See also Hardie (1997). See Nisbet (1990) 378 for Aeneas as a 'proto-Augustus' who '[prefigures] the ideology of Virgil's own patrons'; also Kennedy (1997) 150.

[14] A fact explored, for example, by Griffin (1986) 87.

> Now—though I cannot conscientiously say that the Anglo-Saxon stranger has created in the bosom of this magnificent land of the sun, this queenly Hindustan—that profound, that fervent, that all-absorbing feeling of love, which immolated the hapless Dido on the blazing pyre,[15] and sent her to Hades, an unblest, a melancholy ghost[16]—yet well may she ask—well may this queenly Hindustan—ask in the language of the love-sick Phoenician[17]—'*who is this stranger that has come to our dwelling?*'[18]

In some respects, of course, this qualification of the metaphor makes the Anglo-Saxon appear even worse. 'Queenly Hindustan' is like Dido to a certain extent, but her Aeneas inspires less love: her feelings for this 'pale-faced stranger',[19] the Anglo-Saxon Aeneas, are insufficient to 'immolate' her on the 'blazing pyre'.[20] And the Anglo-Saxon, unlike the Trojan, 'has bound us, as it were, with chains of adamant, and [his] bright sword gleams before our eyes like a fiery meteor—terrifying us into submission and humbling us to the dust'.[21] Dido's love is replaced by the Hindu's violation, guest-friendship with intrusion. The Anglo-Saxon Aeneas has not simply visited but has conquered and humiliated this Hindu Carthage. The conventional metaphor of Britain's relationship with India as a successful union between masculine and feminine cultures, a marital metaphor commonly used throughout the nineteenth century to legitimate Britain's colonial role in India,[22] is replaced with intimations of violation and rape.

Furthermore, the Anglo-Saxon Aeneas is *novus* in a sense alien to the original context of *Aen.* 4.10 (where Aeneas is 'newly arrived' in Carthage): Madhusudan describes him as 'the nameless vagrant of the other day, the pale-faced stranger from the west'.[23] The Anglo-Saxon

[15] Reference to Dido's suicide at *Aen.* 4.663ff. In the Indian context of this lecture—especially given Madhusudan's personal interest in and support of the Widows Remarriage Act—we might detect an oblique reference here to the Hindu practice of *suttee*.

[16] See *Aen.* 6.456ff. The language of 'unblest' and 'melancholy' suggests Aeneas' description of Dido's shade as *infelix* ('unhappy'): see *Aen.* 6.456, a passage of Aeneas' *katabasis* which, as was seen in Chapter 3 above, Madhusudan took as a model for his own *katabasis* in *MBK* 8.

[17] Note the language of 'sickness' and 'wounds' at *Aen.* 4.1ff—this is the language of Roman love elegy. For Dido's 'love-sickness' and its relation to Roman love elegy, see Harrison (2007a) 210ff. and Keith (2000).

[18] Patra (2005) 628. [19] Patra (2005) 629.

[20] Patra (2005) 628. [21] Patra (2005) 628.

[22] See Bandyopadhyay (2004). [23] Patra (2005) 630.

here is *novus* in the sense of 'newly arrived' on the scene of history, 'nameless' before his arrival in India. Vergil's Aeneas is hardly without renown before coming to Carthage; indeed Aeneas asks Achates, as they gaze upon an engraving on the new Carthaginian temple (*Aen.* 1.459f.): *quis iam locus . . . quae regio in terris nostri non plena laboris?*, 'Is there a place . . . is there a land on earth not full of our suffering?'[24] For the Anglo-Saxon, however, it was the very act of subduing India's 'Carthage' that made his name. If we reflect on the Vergilian metaphor we might wonder whether India resonates more clearly, at least in this respect, with Italy than with Carthage. Glory acquired through interracial collaboration is a Vergilian theme, but not one connected with Carthage: *sit Romana potens Itala virtute propago . . .*, 'let the stock of Rome be made mighty by the manly courage of Italy . . . ' (Juno's words to Jupiter at *Aen.* 12.827).[25]

The idea of the 'Anglo-Saxon' as another Aeneas entails the further, more familiar metaphor of imperial Britain as another Roman Empire.[26] Indeed this implication is made explicit in the course of the lecture. Having described Rome's rise to imperial power and her capacity to 'civilize' her subjects, Madhusudan turns to his 'Anglo-Saxon' audience and exclaims: 'Such was the mission of imperial Rome. See ye not on whom the mantle has fallen?'[27] His plea that Britain oversee India's 'national rejuvenescence' is reinforced by the *exemplum* of the civilizing mission of Imperial Rome, and an insistence that Britain take on that imperial 'mantle'.

However, we should remember, as Vance observes, that '[for] the mid-Victorians connections between Rome and ideas of empire were disquieting rather than stimulating'.[28] Roman Empire still had connotations of a European and religious tyranny which posed a threat to British sovereignty and it was not until later in the century

[24] Indeed it is this sense that Dido already knows and feels for the Trojan sufferings which draws Aeneas so urgently to her: see Austin (1971) 151.

[25] See also Anchises' words in Elysium (*Aen.* 6.756f.). Indeed note the poet's sympathy with the Italian peoples, above all in the catalogue at *Aen.* 7.641ff. See also Williams (1973) 497.

[26] See esp. Goff (2005) and Vance (1997) 133ff. for the ambiguity surrounding the Roman model for imperial Britain in the mid-Victorian period.

[27] Patra (2005) 640. Note that Madhusudan's call to arms here echoes the notion expounded by Charles Trevelyan (1807–1886) that Britain should bring European civilization to India just as the Romans had once 'Romanized' the rest of Europe (including Britain) (see Mantena (2010)).

[28] Vance (1997) 141.

that advocates of British Empire would turn to this model with enthusiasm.[29] Indeed one of the most awkward aspects of the Roman model was Rome's extension of 'a common citizenship and common purpose' to its subject peoples.[30] Many British writers argued that the 'backwardness' of Britain's subject peoples was something with which the Romans (apparently) did not have to contend.[31] Nations such as India posed a modern problem to Britain for which ancient Rome had no answer. But Madhusudan stood before his 'Anglo-Saxon' audience as an aspiring *civis Britannicus*,[32] arguing that the advantages of British acculturation (educational, religious, and so on) should be extended to all Hindus just as they had been extended to him. Madhusudan's implicit claim throughout the lecture was that he had assimilated the best of Anglo-Saxon culture. Nowhere, indeed, was this claim more compelling than in his citation, in the original Latin, from Vergil's *Aeneid*; no intellectual currency had a higher cultural value in Victorian Britain than the ability to cite Augustan poetry in the original Latin.[33]

When it came to thinking about the British Empire in the mid nineteenth century, as recent studies have shown, Rome could be used 'on both sides of the debate'.[34] The Roman past meant Empire but also its decline; and if Britain was playing Rome's role in the nineteenth century, it was hard to forget that Britain itself had been defeated and colonized by Rome in the past.[35] Moreover, Britain's status as an erstwhile Roman colony raised questions about what

[29] Vance (1997) 141. See Vasunia (2005b) for an analysis of several late Victorian and early twentieth-century works in which the Roman model is used to legitimate the idea of the British Empire.

[30] See Vance (1997) 233 and Goff (2005) 17.

[31] Majeed (1999) 105.

[32] An expression used in the dedication prefacing N. Chaudhuri (1951) ('*Civis Britannicus Sum*'); also R. Chaudhuri (2002) 87, n. 4.

[33] Vergil and Horace in particular: see Vance (1997) 133ff. Madhusudan also had a penchant for citing Horace in Latin. He cited, for example, *Odes* 1.16.1 (*O matre... pulchrior*) in the preface to Sonnet 72 (1866), *Odes* 3.3.18-21 (*Ilion, Ilion... in pulverem*) in a footnote to *The Captive Ladie* (1849), and *Satires* 1.10.73-4 (*neque... paucis lectoribus*) in preface to the *Tilottamā-sambhab kābya* (1860). In the nineteenth century Horace provided 'the route into the gentlemanly club': see Harrison (2008). I consider this issue in greater detail in Section 3 below.

[34] Goff (2005) 17; and Vance (1997). See also Vasunia (2005b) who considers some late Victorian works connecting the Roman and British Empires.

[35] Goff (2005) 17. See, further, Bradley (2010b) for the British reception of Tacitus' *Agricola* in the nineteenth-century, its 'ambivalent interpretation of Romanization', and the potential of that Latin work to be a 'sourcebook for British nationalism'.

Britain's own colonies might one day become.[36] The unsettling parabola of Rome's fortunes (from humble beginnings to imperial might, and finally to decadence) served as a *memento mori* for imperial power. Again, this unsettling aspect of the Roman paradigm is one highlighted rather than avoided in Madhusudan's lecture. In the context of describing Britain's swift rise to imperial power, the author reminds his Anglo-Saxon audience of Rome's origins as 'a rude and scanty collection of lowly huts'.[37] Elsewhere in the lecture, Madhusudan alludes to that most troubling aspect of the Roman paradigm, its eventual decline. Describing India's 'degenerate' state, he quotes from Felicia Hemans' 'Roman Girl's Song' (1828), '. . . thou art no more, what thou hast been—on thy seven hills of yore, thou sat'st as queen!'.[38] Although Rome is compared here with contemporary India rather than with imperial Britain, nonetheless the audience is reminded explicitly of the possibility of imperial decline. Indeed, throughout the lecture, Madhusudan foregrounds the theme of the 'instability of human grandeur':[39] a nation, like a man, 'has its infancy, its youth, its manhood, its age'.[40] Such, he argues, is the 'burden of the song of the Muse of History'.[41]

Madhusudan's identification of contemporary India with Felicia Hemans' Rome is itself striking. Indeed in an otherwise markedly Anglicist lecture, the idea of India as once great, just as Greece and Rome were once great, figures a clear admixture of Orientalist thought.[42] Given that Madhusudan compares India with Rome in

[36] See Macaulay's fantasy, imagining a time 'when some traveller from New Zealand shall . . . sketch the ruins of St Paul's': cited in R. Jenkyns (1980) 53; see also Goff (2005) 17.

[37] Patra (2005) 639. Again, perhaps an idea drawn from Vergil: see Evander's Pallanteum on the future site of Rome (*Aen.* 8.1–369, 454–607). See Williams (1973) *ad loc.*

[38] Patra (2005) 637.

[39] Patra (2005) 636; see also 632 and 634. Madhusudan's theme of imperial decline is redolent of Edward Gibbon's eighteenth-century interest in the themes of Roman imperial decline. See esp. Rogers (2010) 189–209.

[40] Patra (2005) 636.

[41] Patra (2005) 638. Indeed, this is a basic theme expounded by Herodotus and Thucydides. See Herodotus *Histories* 1.5.4 and Asheri (2007) *ad loc.* See also Thucydides *Histories* esp. 1.2–3 and Hornblower (1991) 7ff. Indeed, both of these Greek historians are referred to in the conclusion to Madhusudan's lecture.

[42] For the lecture as a blend of Anglicist and Orientalist ideologies, see R. Chaudhuri (2002). See Chapter 1 above for an introduction to the Orientalist/Anglicist controversy.

this way (and given the Vergilian metaphor underpinning the lecture), his recurrent and emphatic prayer for the 'national rejuvenescence' of India may take on further Vergilian meanings. Madhusudan argues that, though 'History telleth not of *national rejuvenescence*',[43] with Britain's help 'queenly Hindustan' may prove a signal exception. However, we might recall just such a case of 'national rejuvenescence' (literary and mythological rather than strictly historical), namely the famous notion of Rome as *Troia recidiva*. The *Aeneid* itself is underpinned by this Roman myth of origins, which claimed that Ascanius, son of Aeneas, founded Alba Longa, the state which would later be superseded by Rome.[44] Rome was a second Troy, destined even to surpass the first in glory. Thus, even in the very story of Rome's origins (and in the narrative arc of Vergil's *Aeneid*) we find another respect in which the Roman paradigm might be unsettling for imperial Britain. The Trojan Aeneas—symbolizing the potential for past glory to be rekindled, and for complete military defeat to become unbounded *imperium*—offered more comfort to the Hindu than the Anglo-Saxon in the mid nineteenth century.

2. THE *SIṂHAL-BIJAY KĀBYA* (*c.* 1861)

If comparisons between Rome and India, and of Aeneas with the 'Hindu', are secondary in the *Anglo-Saxon and the Hindu* (1854), then they are foregrounded unambiguously in the *Siṃhal-bijay kābya* (*SK*) (*c.* 1861), Madhusudan's planned Bengali 'national epic'.[45] In 1860, Madhusudan's friend Rajnarain gave the poet the idea of writing a 'national epic', the *SK*, on the theme of the invasion of Simhala (contemporary Ceylon, present-day Sri Lanka) by the Bengali King Vijaya. According to Pāli sources, King Vijaya, whose

[43] Patra (2005) 638.

[44] A recurrent theme in the *Aeneid* and Augustan poetry generally. See: *recidiva . . . Pergama* (*Aen.* 7. 322), *Troia nascens* (*Aen.* 10.27, 74f.: here referring to the 'new Troy' of Aeneas' camp: see Harrison (1991) 65), *Troiae renascens . . . fortuna* (Horace *Odes* 3.3.61–2, a rather gloomy formulation of the idea), and see Nisbet (2004) 51). See also Livy *Hist.* 1.3 and Dionysius of H., *Rom. Ant.* 1.66; also Fowler (1931).

[45] Madhusudan's own description of the project, see Murshid (2004) 118. In the words of Murshid (2004) 129, n. 8: '[Rajnarain] thought [the poem] would enhance the national pride of Bengalis'.

ancestors came from Bengal and Orissa, conquered Simhala in 543 BCE, and the present-day Sinhalese population of the island trace their ancestry back to him.[46] Madhusudan first mentions the idea in a letter to Rajnarain written on 24 April 1860.[47] However, the poet's work on the *MBK*, among other projects, intervened before the poet again returned to the idea of the *SK* in the summer of 1861 (as we infer from another letter, dated 29 August 1861). By this time, so the poet claimed, he had 'forgotten the story and do not know in what work to find it . . . '.[48] His correspondent must have enlightened him since by February 1862 he had 'written 20 or 30 lines of the new Epic', but had 'laid it by,—only for a time, I hope.'[49] Madhusudan never, in fact, returned to the *SK*, but we do have those '20 or 30 lines' (24 to be exact), together with a brief plan written in English for the first three books of the poem. In Appendix 5 below the reader may consult my translation of these 24 Bengali verses and transcription of the English plan.[50] Although the poem was never executed, this was not, from what one can tell, because the poet rejected the plan: it was just one of the many poetic projects which he began but set aside for want of time.[51] Despite its embryonic state Madhusudan's plan for the *SK* is indicative of a most interesting and surprising reading of the *Aeneid*, and therefore deserves to be examined in detail.

The English sketch and the few extant Bengali verses are sufficient to show that Madhusudan was preparing a Bengali *Aeneid*.[52] Just as the *MBK* had, in effect, made an *Iliad* of an episode drawn from the

[46] The story is first related in the famous Pāli *Mahāvaṃśa*, first translated into English by Turnour (1836). The account is related in digest by Knighton (1845), in his history of Ceylon. This English history, or perhaps Turnour's translation of the Pāli account, seems the most likely source for Madhusudan's *SK*.

[47] See Murshid (2004) 118; see also 128 and 153.

[48] Murshid (2004) 175f.

[49] See Murshid (2004) 177. Note that these verses, which have survived, are composed in Madhusudan's 'blank verse' (like the *MBK*, the *BK* (1862), and the *Tilottamā-sambhab kābya* (1860)) and not, as he had contemplated in 1860 (see Murshid (2004) 153), in Tasso's *ottava rima*.

[50] The text consulted is that printed in Basu (1893, 1993 reprint) 357f. Basu claims erroneously (ibid.) that the plan was modelled on the *Iliad*.

[51] Interestingly, the idea of composing a *Siṃhal-bijay kābya* was not taken up by Madhsudan alone, and in 1875 we find the art historian and nationalist ideologue Shyamacharan Srimani also composing an epic by the same name and treating the same themes. See Guha-Thakurta (1995) esp. 73.

[52] For the *Aeneid* as a 'national epic', the term used by Madhusudan to describe the planned *SK*, see R. Williams (1990) 21ff.

Rāmāyaṇa tradition, so the *SK* was to make an *Aeneid* of an episode taken from Bengali history. Book 1 of the *SK*, as the English sketch describes it, seems to correspond to *Aen.* 1.1–313. The poem was to begin with an 'invocation' (compare *Aen.* 1.1–11), and a 'description of the voyage': perhaps this 'description' might have corresponded, in abbreviated form, to Aeneas' narration of his voyage to the Carthaginians in *Aen.* 2–3.[53] The sketch of Book 1 continues: 'They near Ceylone [*sic*], when Murajā excites Pavana to raise a storm which disperses the fleet.' Indeed, the 24 Bengali verses of the embryonic *SK* completed by Madhusudan relate this very episode. The passage is strongly reminiscent of *Aen.* 1.34ff. Murajā's angry outburst at ll. 7–20 recalls Juno's words and actions at *Aen.* 1.36ff. Both goddesses are outraged to see a hated mortal making a journey which they resent (compare *Aen.*1.37–9 and ll. 7–9) and both vow to inflict gales on the travelling heroes. They turn to the god of winds, Aeolus and Pavana respectively, to effect this plan (compare *Aen.* 1.50ff. and ll. 17ff.).[54] In both cases, the outburst is prefaced by a narration of the merry progress of the ship in question: compare *Aen.* 1.34f. ('they spread their sails seaward and were happily ploughing the briny foam with bronze prow') and ll. 3f. ('a beautiful vessel was floating, her sails fluttering up into the sky, filling all directions with an auspicious sound'). Much emphasis is laid on the anger felt by the goddesses: compare *Aen.* 1.36, 50–2 (Juno's speech is prefaced and followed by references to her anger)[55] with Murajā's words at l. 13: *jvale rāge deho*, 'my body is ablaze with anger'.

Murajā's words here and her attitude towards the poem's principal hero align her unmistakably with Vergil's Juno. Contrast the *PN* (1860) where it was the goddess Śacī rather than Murajā who stood for Juno (see Chapter 2), and the *MBK* where Durgā stood for the Iliadic Hera (see Chapter 3 above). Note also that the poem's counterpart to Carthage is rather ambiguous. Murajā asks rhetorically

[53] Note that the compression (or elision) of *Aen.* 2 and 3 speaks to the basic differences between Aeneas' story and King Vijaya's: the Bengali hero is not part of the way through a journey to a new home, nor has he fled a fallen *patria*, and so he has no Vergilian *apologoi* to narrate. For echoes of *Od.* 9–12 (the so-called '*apologoi*') in *Aen.* 2 and 3, see Camps (1969) 81.

[54] On this episode of the *Aeneid*, see Feeney (1991) 129ff., Otis (1964) 227ff., Quinn (1968) 98ff., and O'Hara (1990) 130ff.

[55] See Feeney (1991) 132ff., following Hardie (1986) 90ff., for further allegorical (non-anthropomorphic) aspects of Juno's fury.

(ll. 11f.): *udyān svarūpel sājānu siṃhale ki lo dite parajane?*, 'Did I adorn Simhala [*viz.* Ceylon, Sri Lanka] like a garden only to give it away to another?' Similarly Juno loved Carthage above all other lands, holding Samos itself less dear (*Aen.* 1.15f.), and even at this time she had hopes that this would be *regnum . . . gentibus*, 'the capital of nations' (ll. 17–18).[56] But if Simhala is the Indian Carthage, then the Vergilian model is somewhat disrupted: for Simhala is to be conquered by King Vijaya, not just visited for a brief interlude (contrast Aeneas' time in Carthage), and indeed is the very object of the hero's mission. To this extent, in fact, Simhala stands for Italy rather than Carthage.[57]

We should note also that Murajā expresses anger at the goddess Lakṣmī, wife of the great god Viṣṇu and primary divine supporter of Vijaya. She complains of Lakṣmī's arrogance and her ability to calm her father Jaladhi (*viz.* Ocean) through supplication (ll. 14–7).[58] Just as Juno acts in defiance of the will of Neptune (he expresses his anger at Juno's actions at *Aen.* 1.132ff.),[59] so at ll. 16f. Murajā proposes to inflict a storm on Vijaya against the will of Jaladhi ('Ocean').

Lakṣmī, as King Vijaya's principal divine supporter, stands for Vergil's Venus. But from the point of view of comparative theology, the more natural Hindu 'counterpart' to Venus would be Rati, goddess of love: indeed, as we saw earlier in Chapter 2, Rati played Venus' role in the Judgement of Indranīl in the *PN* (1860). But Lakṣmī is indeed identifiable with Venus in one crucial respect. Just as Venus is

[56] For Juno's traditional (Ennian) predilection for Carthage, and her identity with the Carthaginian Tanit, see Feeney (1991) 130f.

[57] For Italy's status as the proper destination for Aeneas' journey, see Jupiter's words to Mercury at 4.229ff. (and Mercury's to Aeneas at 4.272ff.) and 5.82 (Italy's *fatalia . . . arva*, 'destined fields').

[58] Note that this relationship between Lakṣmī and Jaladhi perhaps echoes Neptune's assertion (*Aen.* 5.800f.): 'You have every right, Venus, to trust in this my realm, whence you were born'. Indeed Venus' complaint to Neptune here (5.781ff.) might be compared with Lakṣmī's supplications to Jaladhi at ll. 16f.

[59] Neptune is *graviter commotus* (1.126) upon seeing Aeneas suffering at sea: after all, Aeneas carries the hopes of Neptune's city (we are reminded of this at 2.625). But, as Venus puts it so acerbically, Neptune himself has a hand in destroying Troy (2.610). See Austin (1964) *ad loc.* Note that Neptune directs his rage at the winds (1.132f.), but he is not unaware of his sister's (Juno's) hand in stirring up the storm (1.130). For an interesting reading of Juno's wrath at *Aen.* 1.50–123, see Feeney (1991) 132ff. and, for a reading of Vergil's gods in general, see esp. Quinn (1968) 300–7 and Heinze (1993) 291ff.

the patron goddess of Rome (ROMA:AMOR),[60] the *Aeneadum genetrix* of Lucretius' *DRN* 1.1,[61] so Lakṣmī has a comparable role of patronage for Bengal. In Sonnet 3 (*Baṇga bhāsā* or 'The Bengali Language'), for example, Madhusudan refers to the goddess as Bengal's *kulalakṣmī* or 'tribal Lakṣmī' (see l.9):[62] in this role of national sponsorship the Hindu goddess is a fitting counterpart to the Vergilian Venus.

The plan for Book 1 of the *SK* continues: 'The ship, with Vijaya and his immediate followers, is wrecked on an unknown island.' This unknown land, which it will transpire is Andaman island, corresponds to Carthage to the extent that the Bengali Aeneas is driven there by the poem's opening storm. We might compare this episode with *Aen.* 1.157–79: the storm has been quelled by Neptune and Aeneas lands on the Libyan shore. Thereafter, the sketch continues: 'The hero lands and after worshipping the *debatā* [*viz.* godheads] of the place, and eating *prasād* [*viz.* food offerings] wanders out alone to explore the island.' This passage corresponds with *Aen.* 1.305ff.: Aeneas determines to set out *locosque/ explorare novos*, 'and explore the strange land' (ll. 306f.).[63] Furthermore, Lakṣmī's prayer to Viṣṇu ('Lakṣmī prays to Viṣṇu . . . ') recalls Venus' supplication to Jupiter (*Aen.* 1.227ff.): the goddess complains that her Trojans have borne many disasters (ll. 231ff.) and that Jupiter's promise that they shall enjoy great glory (l. 250) seems far from being delivered.

Book 2 seems to correspond roughly with *Aen.* 1.314–end and 4.1–197: *Aen.* 2 and 3 have no analogue here but, as was suggested above, they may have been incorporated in abbreviated form within Book 1. Of the contents of Book 2 we are told: 'Murajā on finding Vijaya separated from his companions, sends a Yakṣa to lead him to the city of the king of the island.' The Vergilian model is again unmistakable but complicated. Having ventured forth from the Libyan shore, Aeneas meets his mother, the goddess Venus, disguised as a huntress (*Aen.* 1.319). The goddess, keeping up the pretence of

[60] For a comprehensive study of the role of Venus in Roman religion, see Schilling (1954, reprinted 1982).

[61] A phrase often recycled by later poets: see esp. Ovid *Tristia* 2.261f., *Fasti* 4.90ff., etc. see Ernout (1962) *ad DRN* 1.1. On the *DRN* in the context of Roman politics and history, see Schiesaro (2007).

[62] For an interesting reading of this sonnet, see A. Chaudhuri (2008).

[63] Indeed, the first book of the *Aeneid*, as Jenkyns (1998) 389 notes, has 'an exploratory air'.

being a huntress, urges him to go to Dido (l. 389): *perge modo atque hinc te reginae ad limina prefer*, 'only proceed and make your way from here to the queen's palace'.[64] In *SK* 2, the instruction to proceed to the royal city will come not from Vijaya's divine ally but from an agent sent by Murajā, the goddess who loathes him.

The rest of the plan for Book 2 recalls Homer's *Odyssey* more obviously than Vergil's *Aeneid*. Vimohinī, being the daughter of the king of an island state, recalls Nausicaa rather than Dido, who is a queen rather than a princess. Odysseus, like Vijaya, has been washed up on an island (*Od.* 5.460ff.), and having spent the night on the beach, he meets the princess Nausicaa (6.110ff.). Nausicaa is evidently interested in Odysseus as a potential husband (her words to him at *Od.* 6.276ff. are especially suggestive),[65] but the hero eventually manages to disentangle himself (*Od.* 8.461ff.).[66] To this extent, then, King Vijaya's marriage to Princess Vimohinī represents an alternative *nostos,* or homecoming, for Odysseus, one in which the Phaeacian princess got her way and married the Greek hero.[67]

Book 3, so far as the English plan sketches it, seems to correspond with *Aen.* 4.198–583. Just as Jupiter, beseeched by Dido's brother Iarbas (*Aen.* 4.198ff.), sends Mercury to Aeneas with a message to leave Carthage (*Aen.* 4.219ff.), so too Lakṣmī sends Vijaya a 'vision' and he consequently prepares to leave Andaman island. The language used in the expression 'the Island Kingdom, promised to him and his descendants' is highly suggestive of Vergilian themes. The plan for the poem ends abruptly at this point, though presumably it would have continued to relate King Vijaya's invasion of Simhala. Just as Jupiter has 'promised' (*pollicitus*: *Aen.* 1.237) the future glory of Rome to Aeneas' descendants, so too the Island Kingdom of Simhala (Ceylon, Sri Lanka) is 'promised' to Vijaya and his descendants.

[64] The negotiations between Venus and Juno over the fates of the Trojan and Carthaginian stocks are rather complex: at 4.90ff. Juno proposes a Trojan-Carthaginian alliance, since Dido has conceived passionate love for Aeneas as a result of a measure taken by Venus to pre-empt Juno harming Aeneas in Carthage (1.657ff.). On these negotiations see Horsfall (1990) esp. 131, and Austin (1971) and (1955) *ad loc.*

[65] Indeed Aristarchus (the Alexandrian scholar) found these lines un-maidenly (see Hainsworth (1988) 311): she obliquely reveals her eligibility to the hero.

[66] Nausicaa's 'farewell' to Odysseus marks the hero's successful disentanglement: she tells Odysseus to remember her when he returns home, which implies that she envisages him departing rather than staying with her.

[67] For Nausicaa as one in a series of potential (female) threats to Odysseus' successful *nostos*, see esp. Cohen (1995).

Once again, however, the Vergilian model is complicated. Vergil's poem celebrates the arrival in Italy of Rome's Trojan forefather: it is a Roman poem about the mythological origins of Rome. *Aen.* 8, for example, lavishes detail on locations within Evander's Pallanteum which will one day be the site of Roman landmarks.[68] But the *SK* is conceived, as it were, from the Trojan perspective. King Vijaya is the founding father not of Bengal but of the people of Simhala (Ceylon, Sri Lanka): Bengal is the Troy to Simhala's Rome. Indeed, the figure of King Vijaya, and the foundation myth of his invasion from the north, still loom large in the self-image of the present-day Sinhalese population of Sri Lanka.[69] To this extent, the *SK* represents more of a 'national epic' for Ceylon than one for Bengal, where Vijaya is still remembered but is hardly a central component of ethnic identity. Madhusudan himself had to be reminded (or perhaps just affected the need to be reminded) of the details of the story by his friend Rajnarain.

However, as an account of an ancient Bengali king's conquest of another part of India, the *SK* is evidently a celebration of Bengal, an attempt to 'enhance the national pride of Bengalis'.[70] Indeed, a full analysis of the *SK* must look to the context of the colonial politics of British India. It is important to note that the Bengali *bhadralok* were cultivated by the British from an early stage of colonial contact; that they were co-opted by the British into positions of authority, and found themselves in other parts of British India as administrators, teachers, clerks, and so on.[71] Madhusudan himself served as a teacher, lecturer, and journal editor in the British Presidency of Madras, and he spent his time there almost exclusively in the company of British or 'Eurasian' friends.[72] This was the context in which *The Anglo-Saxon and the Hindu* (1854) was conceived and delivered. Therefore, Madhusudan's reference to Ceylon as 'the Island Kingdom, promised to [Vijaya] and his descendants' resonates with Bengal's place within the colonial power structures of contemporary British India. Just as it

[68] See R. Williams (1973) 245ff., W. Fowler (1931), and Camps (1969) 98f.

[69] So much so that, for example, the first, and for a while only warship in the navy of post-independence Sri Lanka was the HMCyS Vijaya, an Algerian class mine-sweeper.

[70] See n. 45 above.

[71] See P. Sinha (1978) and Mukherjee (1977), and See Kejariwal (1988); also Chapter 1 above.

[72] See Murshid (2003) 104f.

was Aeneas' fate to rule *tota Italia*,[73] the *Aeneid* being a canonical expression of the aetiology for Rome's contemporary hegemony over the rest of Italy (as well as a foreshadowing of a more global *imperium*), so too the *SK* may be read as an historical precedent for the contemporary influence of Bengal over other parts of India. Moreover, from a postcolonial perspective, it is interesting that this Bengali poet's patriotism expressed itself not in explicit resistance to British *imperium* but in fantasizing about Bengali dominion over the rest of India: it is well-documented that this generation of Bengali intellectuals aspired to Western culture and mores, but it is striking (perhaps even somewhat pathetic) to observe Madhusudan's implicit aspirations to copy the colonial practices of the British.

It is important to set the *SK* in its particular historical context. By the late 1850s, the Bengali *bhadralok*, although pre-eminent among Indians within this colonial power structure, began to feel that their relationship with the British had run aground. Whereas earlier generations of Britons had taken a sympathetic interest in Bengali and Hindu culture, by the mid nineteenth century the British were rapidly losing that 'patrimonial' and 'affective' knowledge which they had once cultivated (see Chapter 1 above).[74] This aloof disdain for Hindu culture now shown by British residents in Calcutta raised issues of Bengali pride and self-esteem. Bankim, the famous Bengali novelist writing a little later than Madhusudan, articulated this anxiety:

> There is no Hindu history. Who will praise our noble qualities if we do not praise them ourselves? . . . When has the glory of any nation ever been proclaimed by another nation? The proof of the warlike prowess of the Romans is to be found in Roman histories . . . The Hindus have no such glorious qualities simply because there is no written evidence.[75]

By the 1860s, Madhusudan had returned to Calcutta from Madras and had fallen in with a Bengali intelligentsia beset by such anxieties and keen to boost Bengali self-esteem by celebrating the glories of the Hindu past. In Madras in the 1850s, Madhusudan had pleaded with the 'Anglo-Saxon', figured ambiguously as a latter-day Aeneas, to champion the Hindu's cause as earlier generations of Britons had done. The imagination of the Hindu as Dido perhaps pointed to the

[73] See F. Cairns (1989) 109ff.
[74] See also Bayly (1996).
[75] Cited by R. Chaudhuri (2002) 147f.

futility of the plea. By the 1860s, having returned to Calcutta, Madhusudan had begun to champion that cause himself by composing literary and dramatic works which, so he hoped, might form the foundations of a 'national' literature for Bengal.[76] Had he not left Calcutta for London in June 1862, an ill-fated journey that would interrupt his literary output, this corpus of works might have included a Bengali *Aeneid.*

3. MADHUSUDAN AND VERGIL'S *AENEID*: WIDER CONTEXTS

Of all of Madhusudan's classical appropriations, his response to Vergil's *Aeneid* in these two works is by far the most overt in its political content, and the most obviously subversive of the British colonial presence in India. The shift in Aeneas' identity between these two receptions, from a symbol for Britain's cruel treatment of an Indian Dido to a literary model for a Bengali hero with his own colonial ambitions, indicates both the different roles adopted by the Trojan hero in Vergil's epic and indeed the ambiguity of identity attaching to the hero himself: a Trojan fugitive who became Rome's forefather, a vanquished founder of a victorious imperial power. As Majeed has argued, early Victorian Britain's attitude towards Rome was marred by a strong anxiety regarding its own former status as a Roman colony and the 'fearsome capacity' of both Rome and India 'to assimilate British national identity on different levels'.[77] Madhusudan's response to Vergil's *Aeneid* goes to the quick of this anxiety and exposes some uncomfortable colonial ambiguities.

Furthermore, the hybridity of Aeneas in these Bengali responses is oddly reflective of the status of 'Westernized' intellectuals like Madhusudan in colonial Bengal. As was noted above, the opening words of the lecture *The Anglo-Saxon and the Hindu*, words of Latin rather than English, signal a claim to membership of an elite Western club. Familiarity with the Graeco-Roman classics was a marker of the

[76] For Madhusudan's rhetoric about laying the foundations for a 'national' literature and theatre, see esp. Murshid (2004) 118 (Madhusudan's first letter to Rajnarain), and 153.

[77] Majeed (1999) 108. See also Goff (2005) 14f.

British ruling classes in both the eighteenth and nineteenth centuries, and citations in Latin were common even in the Houses of Parliament, the seat of British national and imperial power. Vergil and Horace were the classical authors most often on the lips of parliamentarians.[78] Indeed, Gladstone's exchanges with Robert Lowe in 1866 were so laden with Vergilian quotations, 'almost [exhausting] the Second Book of the *Aeneid*', that they 'did not leave the Trojan Horse a leg to stand on'.[79] Madhusudan addressed his Anglo-Saxon audience in Madras rather as a British parliamentarian might have addressed the House of Commons in London.[80] However, despite his educational credentials, Madhusudan inevitably failed to gain complete access to this elite British world. Likewise, 'Westernized' Bengalis, especially Christian converts like Madhusudan, were considered to fall outside traditional Hindu society, deemed in orthodox terms to be tainted by impurity, and effectively outcaste. Thus the hybridity of Madhusudan's identity as a 'Westernized' Bengali, the 'third space' he came to occupy,[81] was a cultural no man's land. Moreover, in his literary works, the Bengali poet created a comparably hybrid imaginary space, and peopled it with characters who straddled both cultures just like him: a Homeric Rāma, Ovidian Hindu heroines, a Bengali Aeneas.

And yet, while the position occupied by intellectuals like Madhusudan was isolated, both the lecture and the poem examined above argue that there is a heroism in such hybridity: just as the Bengali King Vijaya is aggrandized through his association with Aeneas, and colonial Calcutta is thereby sublimated to the status of an imperial Rome, so Madhusudan presents himself in the *Anglo-Saxon and the Hindu* as a champion of Westernized Bengalis, his phenomenal hybrid erudition deployed to impress his British audience and provoke them towards a greater commitment to Macaulay's Anglicist educational ideology. Thus, as with much of Madhusudan's creative

[78] Majeed (1999) 108.

[79] See Vance (1997) 133ff. Note, incidentally, that Gladstone himself reached for the beginning of *Aen.* 4 when he joined the Liberal Party, comparing himself with the shipwrecked Aeneas being welcomed by Dido, and commenting that he hoped the consequences for the Liberal Party would be better than they were for Dido. See ibid.

[80] And one might observe, as was noted above at n. 33, that Madhusudan's penchant for quoting Horace in Latin also maps on to this feature of upper-class British culture: see esp. Harrison (2008).

[81] For a study of the hybridity of colonial identities, see esp. Boehmer (1995).

practice in sampling from the Graeco-Roman classics examined elsewhere in this book, the two responses to Vergil's *Aeneid* examined above shed a revealing light on the attitudes of the Westernized Bengali intelligentsia towards their colonial experience and on the complex identity in which that experience resulted.

5

The *Bīrāṅganā kābya* (1862) and Ovid's *Heroides*

INTRODUCTION

The *Bīrāṅganā kābya* (1862) (henceforth *BK*) is, in a sense, Madhusudan's most antinomian and mischievous reception of the Graeco-Roman classics. In its interest in Ovid, let alone in his *Heroides*, it is certainly a most unexpected mid-nineteenth-century response to the Graeco-Roman canon.[1] In early February 1862, Madhusudan wrote to his friend Rajnarain:

> within the last few weeks, I have been scribbling a thing to be called Birangana Kabya, i.e. Heroic Epistles from the most noted Puranic women to their lovers or lords. There are to be twenty-one Epistles, and I have finished eleven. These are being printed off, for I have no time to finish the remainder.[2]

The *BK* (see Appendix 6 for a synopsis of the poems), literally 'Poems of the Women of Heroes', takes Ovid's *Heroides* as a generic literary model.[3] Indeed, the very word *bīrāṅganā*, Madhusudan's own

[1] For the depths plumbed by Ovid's reputation in the nineteenth century see, for example, Hardie (2002a) 1ff. See also Vance (1997) 154ff., who notes the complexity of Ovid's profile at the time: at once seen as 'a degenerate in a degenerate age' (156) and yet a staple of elementary classical education (154), and clearly an inspiration to prominent early-nineteenth-century poets such as Keats, Shelley, and Byron (174).

[2] See Murshid (2004) 177.

[3] Madhusudan probably first read Ovid in Latin at Bishop's College Calcutta where he studied Latin and Greek literature between 1844 and 1847: see Chapter 1 above. There he would most likely have encountered the old eighteenth-century Delphine edition of Ovid: Bishop's College library was stocked mostly with copies of those classical editions which were in print at OUP and CUP in 1822 (see Chapter 1 above). It was not until 1825–6 that OUP brought out its first post-Delphine edition of Ovid's

Sanskritic coinage, which is etymologically capable of meaning 'war-like women' or 'heroes' women',[4] attempts a rendering into Bengali of the Greek term *heroides*, hence 'i.e.' in the quotation above. Various scholars have acknowledged the influence of Ovid on the *BK*, though none has analysed it in any depth.[5] The *BK* is a collection of poems treating the elegiac themes of love and the plight of women separated from their beloved. But, more fundamentally, the *BK* uses Ovid's *Heroides* to say something about the nature of illicit readership, to challenge the very idea of what makes a 'classic', and to resist literary authority—both European and Hindu. The poems recognize the status of Ovid's *Heroides* as an 'anti-classic', a countervailing force at the heart of the Graeco-Roman canon. The *BK* appropriates Ovid's subversive work as a springboard to making implicit comments about colonialism and classicism, and the troubled relationship of both these concepts to gender identity.

Above all, the collection represents the fruits of a reading of the Graeco-Roman classics that was itself somewhat illicit. This is a reading not just against the grain of contemporary Western classical taste,[6] but against the very spirit of contemporary Western notions of the 'classical'. In Ovid, Madhusudan found a perfect mentor in subversion, a paradigm for resisting literary authority residing, paradoxically, at the very heart of the hegemonic Graeco-Roman canon. But the Bengali poet's attraction to Ovid turns on personal as well as more abstract associations: this is a collection of poems about the

works (with Bentley's notes on Burmann's text): see Appendix 2. However, in 1849, Madhusudan was gifted a 'most valuable number of classical works' by George Norton (Murshid (2004) 74) and so it is possible that, by the time he came to compose the *BK*, Madhusudan had also encountered this rather better OUP edition of the *Heroides*. The editions of Ovid's *Heroides* referred to in this chapter are Knox (1995) (for *Her.* 1–2, 5–7, 10–11, and 15), Kenney (1996) (for *Her.* 16–21), and Dörrie (1971) (for the rest).

[4] For an explanation of the construction and semantics of this type of Sanskritic compound ('dependent determinative'), see Kale (1961) 121ff.

[5] See, for example, Basu (1893) 512, Dasgupta (1933–5) 130, Bandopadhyay (1945–51) [introduction] 1f., Banerjee (1952) 75f., Dasgupta (1969) 65, Radice (1987) 164, and Murshid (2004) 2 and 92. This Ovidian debt, when it has been observed, has not always been seen in a positive light. Dasgupta (1933–5) 130, for example, remarks: 'it is a pity that Ovid's eroticism and frank sensibility influenced Madhusudan . . . '. The otherwise excellent commentary of Banerjee (1952), the most thoroughgoing study of the *BK* to date, only touches on the Ovidian influence rather cursorily in the introduction (ibid. 74–7), and not in the commentary itself.

[6] See n. 1 above.

abandonment of women composed by one who had abandoned his own wife and children in Madras in the 1850s.[7]

1. THE *BK*: A HINDU *HEROIDES*

The *BK*,[8] written in 1861 and published in 1862,[9] is a collection of eleven epistolary poems composed in 'blank verse' like the earlier *Tilottamā-sambhab kābya* (1860) and *MBK* (1861). Each of the eleven poems is notionally 'written' by a female character from traditional Hindu epic or drama to her (sometimes prospective) husband or lover. However, while the substance of the *BK* is thus drawn from the Hindu tradition, its basic generic architecture is markedly Ovidian.[10] As was intimated above, the poet's choice of title for the collection, *Bīrāṅganā kābya*, that is 'warlike women' or 'heroes' women', is itself suggestive of Ovidian inspiration. Moreover, the poet's own reference in his correspondence to the poems as 'Heroic Epistles'[11] speaks for itself as an allusion to English descriptions of the Ovidian work, and indeed to its common Latin title *Epistulae Heroidum*.[12]

[7] For this personal dimension of the *Bīrāṅganā kābya* see esp. Murshid (2003) and Radice (1987).

[8] The edition referred to throughout is Bandyopadhyay (1945–51).

[9] See Bandyopadhyay (1945–51) *BK* [Introduction] 3.

[10] *Pace* Banerjee (1952) 75, whose otherwise excellent commentary misleadingly states: 'All Madhusudan learned from Ovid was the possibility of composing poetry in letter form, nowhere did he borrow anything substantive from his work'. Banerjee's commentary, like many mid-twentieth-century Bengali studies of Madhusudan's work, is somewhat sidetracked by the nationalist discourse, as in its emphasis on Madhusudan's 'originality' and 'independence' from Western models: 'Although Madhusudan's *Bīrāṇganā* is comparable with Ovid's Heroic Epistles, it has no lack of originality [*maulikatā*]' (ibid.). The *BK* is indeed most original but the springboard for this originality lies, to a large extent, in its engagement with Ovid's *Heroides*.

[11] See n. 2 above.

[12] It seems plausible that they were called this by Ovid, using a title that had previously been used (*Heroinai*) by the Greek poets Philochorus and Theocritus (cf. *Suda ad loc*, for works now lost). As pointed out by Knox (1995) 5, Ovid's poems are cited under this title by Priscian (*Inst.* 10.54) and the scholia to the *Ibis* (357, 589). Ovid himself refers to one of the poems in his own collection as an *epistula* (*Ars* 3.345); see Kraus (1968) 89, Horsfall (1981) 107, Knox (1995) 5. See also Kennedy (2002) 218f., who prefers to think they were first published as the *Epistulae Heroidum*. For the historical background of Graeco-Roman letter writing, out of which the genre of the elegiac epistle emerged (apparently Propertius' innovation: see Prop. 4.3), see

Furthermore, many of the fundamental formal features of the *BK* recall the Ovidian model. The very number of epistles is suggestive: although only eleven poems were published in 1862, it is clear that twenty-one, the number of poems in Ovid's *Heroides*, were intended for a second edition.[13] The poet wrote to a friend: 'There are to be twenty-one Epistles, and I have finished eleven'.[14] Although the rest of the poems were never published, there remain notes written by the poet for a further six epistles.

There are occasional moments in the *BK* when Ovid emerges in the Bengali text almost verbatim, as when the Latin metaphor *inque tua est vitaque morsque manu* ('[my] life and death are in your hands') becomes Madhusudan's Bengali *jīban maraṇ mamo āji tabo hāte!* ('my life and death are now in your hands').[15] Indeed, it is telling that such a moment should strike so elegiac a note: Ovid emerges in plain view at a moment of heightened elegiac tension. However, the generic influence of Ovid's work is also detected in much subtler structural respects. The individual poems of the *BK* are, for example, of a comparable length to Ovid's elegiac epistles.[16] Madhusudan's letter-poems follow Ovid's apparent law of composition for *Her.* 1–15 that 'each individual epistle be autonomous'.[17] As in *Her.* 1–15, every Bengali

the introduction to Trapp (2003). For comments on the relationship of Ovid's *Heroides* to Prop. 4.3, Arethusa's elegiac epistle, see esp. Hinds (2006) 418ff. (and ibid. for further bibliography).

[13] The question of the publication of the *Heroides* as a collection/collections is itself rather vexed. At *Am.* 2.18.19–26, Ovid refers to a collection of poems taken by many critics to refer to *Her.* 1–15 (that is, everything before *Her.* 16–21); see Knox (1995) 6. The other six poems, which are generally regarded as authentically Ovidian (see ibid. 7ff.), are thought to have been published at a later date. The principal difference of *Her.* 16–21 from *Her.* 1–15 is that they are 'double epistles', comprising three male letters plus a female 'response' to each. Many critics also consider *Her.* 1–15 to fall into two or three discrete groups, perhaps *Her.* 1–5, 6–10, and 11–15. See esp. Pulbrook (1977), who considers *Her.* 1–15 to be much too long for a single Ovidian book; also Stroh (1991) 205 and Heinze (1997) 36f. For the nature of the 'publication' of literature in the Roman world, cf. Knox (1995) 6, n. 9, and Kenney (1982) 15–22.

[14] See n. 1.

[15] *Her.* 12.74 and *BK* 2.167 (the end of *BK* 2). Translations from Latin and Bengali are my own throughout.

[16] Ovid's single epistles are, on average, 161 lines; the mean length of the complete Bengali poems is 145 lines, very close to the Roman model. In terms of structure, the *BK* as we have it seems to model itself only on the single epistles. Ovid's 'double epistles' are generally longer than the others, and are set apart in this and certain other respects; see esp. Knox (1995) 7ff.

[17] Barchiesi (2001) 29; cf. Barchiesi (1992) 15.

poem is shaped in such a way that it bears all the information necessary to make it intelligible, so as 'not to call for any response or supplement'.[18] Furthermore, in the *BK*, we find an Ovidian distribution between obscure and famous writers, and between epic and dramatic sources:[19] just as some of the Latin epistles are written by obscure figures such as Phyllis and others by famous characters like Penelope,[20] so too some of the Bengali poems are written by obscure heroines such as Janā (*BK* 11) and others by prominent literary heroines like Śakuntalā (*BK* 1). And just as some of the *Heroides* are written by figures from epic and others by characters from drama, so too the literary provenance of the writers of the *BK* is split between Hindu drama and epic. Moreover, the Hindu heroine Śakuntalā may remind one of Ovid's Medea in her dual identity as both epic and dramatic heroine.[21]

A comparison of the distribution of the Hindu source texts in the *BK* and the *Heroides* also reveals an Ovidian presence in the Bengali work.[22] In the *BK*, as in the *Heroides*, some of the heroines inhabit the same source text, and this can lead to rather ironic contrasts of perspective. For example, we find Bhānumatī's epistle to Duryodhana in *BK* 7 immediately after Draupadī's epistle to Arjuna.[23] The two addressees, Arjuna and Duryodhana, are arch-enemies and the greatest warriors on their respective sides of the great war of the Hindu epic *Mahābhārata*. This ironic juxtaposition resonates with Ovid's positioning of Briseis' epistle to Achilles (*Her.* 3), the 'best of the Achaians',[24] in close proximity to Oenone's epistle to Paris (*Her.* 5), the Trojan shepherd prince. Indeed, just as Paris' seduction of the Achaean Helen sparked the Trojan War, so it was Duryodhana's shameful treatment of Arjuna's wife Draupadī, notional author of the letter in *BK* 6, which sparked the great war of the *Mahābhārata*.[25]

[18] Barchiesi (2001) 29.

[19] For a tabulation of these distributions (epic/drama; famous/obscure), see Appendix 7 below.

[20] Cf. Barchiesi (2001) 123.

[21] Cf. Bessone (1997) 20; for the 'two Medeas'; cf. Wilamowitz-Moellendorff (1924) 214 and 200, and *contra* Paduano (1986) 21f. See also Hinds (1993) for a treatment of Medea as an 'intertextual' heroine.

[22] See Appendix 7 for a tabulation of these source texts.

[23] See Appendix 6 for synopses of the poems of the *BK*.

[24] An Iliadic expression, ambiguously attaching to both Achilles and Agamemnon: see Nagy (1979).

[25] For the cause of the war of the *Mahābhārata*, see van Buitenen's introduction to the first volume of his translation of the Sanskrit epic (1973).

There is a further Ovidian resonance in the juxtaposition of the letters to Daśaratha and to Lakṣmaṇa (*BK* 4 and 5), father and son, who are addressed by Kekayī and Sūrpaṇakhā respectively. Daśaratha has already treated Kekayī callously, and Lakṣmaṇa is about to treat Sūrpaṇakhā even more high-handedly: this 'genetic' propensity towards mistreating women is brought out by the juxtaposition of the two epistles. This example finds a close analogue in the letters addressed to Demophoon and Theseus (*Her.* 2 and 10): though not juxtaposed, these two epistles express the feelings of women abandoned by father and son respectively, and the inclusion of both poems in the *Heroides* brings out a family resemblance, the tendency to thwart the hopes of the women who wait for them. Madhusudan points up the very same genetic tendency in two of his addressees, making the connection even more explicit through juxtaposition.

One should also observe that there are important general differences between Ovid's *Heroides* and Madhusudan's *BK*. For example, some of the Indian females are divine, whereas Ovid's are all human, save for the somewhat complicated exception of Helen.[26] And all of Madhusudan's eleven epistles (and all six incomplete poems) are from female characters: there are no double epistles, letters accompanied by their responses, and no male voices. It is unclear from the extant notes for the planned but aborted second edition of the *BK* whether Madhusudan planned to include any double epistles on the model of *Her.* 16–21.

However, notwithstanding such differences, it is quite evident that Ovid's influence lies beneath the *BK's* generic surface. Ovid is not only present in the *BK* in an architectural, formal sense: the Latin epistles are refracted throughout the Bengali collection. Two fundamentally Ovidian features, the *BK's* 'epistolarity' and its process of 'translation into elegy',[27] will be examined in detail in Section 2 below. However, a close reading of individual poems also reveals myriad

[26] Note that divinity in the Sanskrit epic is a complex issue; many of the characters, though apparently human, are in various passages held to be avatars of certain gods: see Smith (1980) esp. 66–77. So, for example, Rāma is a hero (*bīra*), but also an avatar of Viṣṇu. Rukmiṇī (of *BK* 3) is in many ways a powerless human female, forced by her brother to marry king Śiśupāla, but is also considered to be an avatar of the goddess Lakṣmī. For an overview of Helen's status according to Graeco-Roman tradition, transcending the distinction between divine and mortal, see Cancik (2005) 62f. See also Chapter 2, Section 3 above.

[27] The expression of Knox (1995) 23.

moments of Ovidian theme, situation, or motif. Indeed, features of various Ovidian epistles sometimes appear in the same Bengali passage. Kekaẏī's emphatic denunciation in *BK* 4 of Daśaratha's faithlessness provides such an example (see ll. 59ff.):

kām-made māti yadi tumi
bṛthā āśā diẏā more chalilā, tā kaho;—
nīrabe e duḥkh āmi sahibo tā hale!
kāmir kurīti ei śunechi jagate . . .

> If it was raving with the intoxication of desire that you deceived me, giving me vain hope, tell me so;—I will endure this woe in silence if that is the case! I have heard that this is the wicked custom [*kurīti*] of the lustful the world over . . .

The *Heroides*, many of which are reproaches written by jilted women,[28] are full of such accusations of infidelity. But the ferocity of Kekaẏī's rebuke—'the lord of the Raghu clan is the greatest exponent of heretical wickedness [*adharma*!]', she says repeatedly, for example at l. 93—is perhaps especially reminiscent of Oenone's epistle to Paris (*Her.* 5).[29] However, as a wife forsaken for another, Kekaẏī perhaps recalls Hypsipyle (*Her.* 6)—though it is not her husband, Daśaratha's, polygamy, so much as his treatment of Kekaẏī's son that is at issue.[30] Furthermore, Kekaẏī's reference to making false oaths as the *kurīti*, or 'wicked custom', of the lustful (l. 62) might prompt the reader to consider that this *kurīti* is not only well-documented but in fact expounded in another Ovidian work, the *Remedia Amoris*.[31]

Draupadī's epistle at *BK* 6 is perhaps most naturally comparable with *Her.* 1. Penelope and Draupadī await the return of their respective husbands, and both worry that they may remain abroad willingly (compare *Her.* 1.80 and *BK* 6.21).[32] However, whereas Penelope just

[28] In particular, *Her.* 2, 5–7, 8-10, 12, 13.

[29] Note that Oenone's status as Paris' first wife is not known to us from Homer or tragedy (see Knox (1995) 140) and is therefore an obscure legend. For our sources before Ovid, see Lycophron's *Alex.* 57–68, Bion 2.11, and Hellanicus, *FGrH* 4 F 29; also Stinton (1965) 40–50. Note that Madhusudan relates the story of Oenone in his 'back-story' (2–3) to the *Iliad* in his *Hekṭor-badh* (1871): see Chapter 6 below.

[30] For the relationship and contrasts between the epistles of Medea and Hypsipyle, Jason's first and second loves respectively, see Bessone (1997) 18f., esp. n. 17.

[31] Note especially its plot of 'escape from love' and the status of Lethaeus Amor (ll. 549–78) as its 'presiding spirit'; see Hardie (2006) esp. 178; also 176ff.

[32] Note that the fears of Ovid's Penelope are made more credible by the non-Homeric tradition: for Odysseus as a wandering philanderer, see Philetas *Hermes* (*CA*,

alludes to possible extra-marital affairs, Draupadī seems fully aware of Arjuna's activities in Vaijayanta. Indeed, her readiness to welcome him home despite infidelity may remind us of Oenone in *Her.* 5 (compare *BK* 6.173f. and *Her.* 5.157f.).[33] And so, once again, we find not one but two or more Ovidian situations refracted in this Bengali epistle.

Of all the Bengali epistles, the locus most resonant with Ovidian influence is Śakuntalā's epistle in *BK* 1. Being the first in Madhusudan's collection of 'Epistles', *BK* 1 resonates most obviously with *Her.* 1, Penelope's letter to Ulysses. Both heroines are eminent figures in their respective mythologies and their stories are not entirely dissimilar: each suffers the absence of a husband with whom she will ultimately be reunited. By the time of 'writing' her epistle each heroine has been urged, Penelope by her father Icarius (ll. 81ff.) and Śakuntalā by her female companions (ll. 155ff.), to give up hope of her husband's return. But, one might also say that, like Phyllis in *Her.* 2, Śakuntalā has been caused by (thwarted) hope to imagine her lover's arrival: compare *Her.* 2.11f. and *BK* 1.6–10. And like Phyllis in *Her.* 2,[34] and indeed like Hypsipyle (*Her.* 6) and Medea (*Her.* 12), Śakuntalā will be betrayed by her love (see *Mahābhārata* 1.7b.30ff., *Abhijñānaśakuntalam*, Act 4, 1ff.), though in Śakuntalā's case the betrayal will be followed by reconciliation. Furthermore, like Medea in *Her.* 12 Śakuntalā, as was noted above, has received treatments in both epic and drama. Her depiction in the *BK*, like Medea's in *Her.* 12, focuses on a crisis common to both treatments (resolved differently in each),[35] namely her abandonment by Duṣmanta.[36] Moreover, the heroine's account at ll. 19ff. of visiting old haunts where she and her love once courted, figures a further Ovidian resonance: compare Sappho's account at *Her.* 15.137f.[37]

p. 91); Parthenius *Erot.* 3; and Soph. fr. 203 Radt; also Knox (1995) 103 and Barchiesi (1992) 91f.

[33] Note that Quintus of Smyrna (10.425-7) also attributes this sentiment to Oenone; see Knox (1995) 170.

[34] See Barchiesi (1992) 123 and Knox (1995) 111 for a study of the relationship between *Her.* 2 and its source texts.

[35] On the different consequences and treatments of this abandonment see Emeneau (1962) 41–4.

[36] Ovid, as noted by Bessone (1997) 20, focuses on the comparably critical moment of the 'imminenza della vendetta'.

[37] Sappho's frenzied wanderings are themselves reminiscent, for example, of Phaedra's (Eur. *Hipp.* 215–22); see Knox (1995) 302.

Throughout Madhusudan's Bengali epistles, one may detect myriad resonances of this kind. In *BK* 5, to take a final example, Sūrpaṇakhā's predicament recalls that of Helen (*Her.* 17), Ariadne (*Her.* 10), and her sister Phaedra (*Her.* 4). Like the Cretan Ariadne's love of the Athenian Theseus, Sūrpaṇakhā's love of Lakṣmaṇa crosses the lines of enmity,[38] both women being attracted to their kinsmen's sworn enemy. But in Sūrpaṇakhā's case, unlike Ariadne's, this enmity is only prospective: the irony lies in the reader's knowledge of the consequences of the heroine's letter.[39] Moreover, as a confession of love destined to fall on deaf ears, *BK* 4 also recalls *Her.* 4, the epistle of Ariadne's sister Phaedra. Just as Phaedra's love has overwhelmed her and driven her to a confession (see esp. l. 161), so the love confessed by Sūrpaṇakhā is overpowering (see esp. l. 62); and in each case the confession is ill-judged. As the *aition* for a great epic war, Sūrpaṇakhā's situation here in *BK* 5 perhaps recalls Helen's in *Her.* 17; but, whereas it is Paris' abduction/seduction of Helen that leads to the Trojan War, it is Lakṣmaṇa's cruel rejection of Sūrpaṇakhā, by contrast, that leads to the War of Laṅkā.

There are further examples of this kind of multiple Ovidian resonance, too many to treat fully here: Tārā in *BK* 2, for example, in some respects reminds the reader of Helen (*Her.* 17) and in others of Phaedra (*Her.* 4). Bhānumatī in *BK* 7 brings to mind the predicament of Laodamia and her plea to Protesilaus in *Her.* 13, but in other respects recalls Hero's letter to Leander (*Her.* 19). In any case it is clear that the *BK*, in a manner that recalls, for example, the subtle use of the Iliadic model in the *MBK* (see Chapter 3 above), incorporates aspects of the Ovidian model without letting the influence descend into mere pastiche or even overt imitation. Indeed, we might recall here Madhusudan's description of his own attitude towards literary appropriation: 'In matters literary, old boy, I am too proud to stand before the world, in borrowed clothes. I may borrow a neck-tie, or even a waist coat, but not the whole suit.'[40] There are moments in Madhusudan's oeuvre when his classical appropriations may be fittingly described as a kind of literary transvestism, as in the Vergilian

[38] For the paradigmatic, even proverbial, status of Ariadne's story of seduction and betrayal, see *Aetna* 21–2: *quis non periuriae doluit mendacia puppis,/ desertam vacuo Minoida litore questus?*; also Cat. 64, which is very much the 'source' text for the epistle (see Knox (1995) 233 and Conte (1986)).

[39] See Section 2 below for an analysis of such literary ironies in the *BK*.

[40] Murshid (2004) 107.

katabasis of *MBK* 8 or the Judgement of Paris scene 'Indianized' in the *PN*; but in the *BK* one must look carefully to see the Ovidian cut of his literary cloth.

2. EPISTOLARITY, THE HINDU TRADITION, AND 'TRANSLATION INTO ELEGY'[41]

Madhusudan's interest in Ovid's *Heroides* as a literary model had much to do with the subversive possibilities entailed by the Latin work's generic identity. The aspects of the *BK* considered in Section 1 go only so far as to indicate that the *Heroides* was a source of literary influence, but the further Ovidian themes and tropes under analysis now in Section 2 are suggestive of some of the literary and cultural purposes for which Madhusudan may have turned to Ovid in the first place. In particular, the *BK* uses Ovid's *Heroides* as a vehicle for a twofold challenge to received literary wisdom. The Bengali poet imitates Ovid's subtle assault on Graeco-Roman literary authority in the *Heroides* to launch his own attack on the hegemony of traditional Hindu literary perspectives. However, by a deft sleight of hand, Madhusudan also accommodates the Ovidian genre of epistolary elegy to the poetics of the indigenous Hindu tradition. In this way the Bengali poet impliedly suggests that the seeds of such a genre are present in the Sanskrit literary tradition, or at least that its rigid rules need not necessarily preclude it. Hereby, the poet furthers a contention made implicitly throughout his Bengali oeuvre, namely that the Graeco-Roman and the Hindu literary traditions have much more in common than might be visible at first sight.

The 'epistolarity' of the *BK*, its use and thematization of the epistle form,[42] is generically Ovidian in much more than a superficial sense. Not only are Madhusudan's epistles of an average length modelled on the Ovidian 'single epistle', an observation made in Section 1 above, but they even thematize this Ovidian generic marker. Towards the end of *BK* 6, at 223 verses the longest epistle in the Bengali collection, the heroine Draupadī breaks off at l. 146 and then explains (l. 147):

[41] The expression of Knox (1995) 23.

[42] For a broad exploration of 'epistolarity' in Ovid's *Heroides*, see esp. Kennedy (2002); also Spentzou (2003) and Fulkerson (2005).

eto dūro likhi kāli, phelāinu dūre/ lekhanī . . . , 'So much did I write yesterday, then I flung the pen far off . . .'. The mimetic effect of breaking the poem into two days' worth of writing (ll. 1–146 and 147–223) thematizes the average length of a *BK* epistle (which stands at 145 lines) by imagining it as the amount a heroine can write in a single day.[43] Indeed the thematization of epistolary length is already present in Madhusudan's Ovidian model: at *Her.* 20.241, for example, Acontius states that he will stop writing: *longior infirmum ne lasset epistula corpus* . . . , 'so that too long a letter may not weary your weakened body . . .'.[44] Madhusudan takes this trope a step further by introducing and thematizing the notion of the daily letter writing output of his heroines.

There are various other respects in which Madhusudan thematizes his characters' imagined act of letter writing that bring the Ovidian model to mind. In both collections, for example, it is common for the heroine to draw attention to her act of letter writing at the beginning or end of her epistle.[45] This effect underlines the generic conceit that a literary epistle is at once a letter (intended for a fictive addressee) and a work of poetic fiction (intended for a 'real' readership). As Kennedy advises: 'We need to keep these two levels of authorship, and their interaction, in mind . . .'[46] We might compare, for example, Urvaśī's statement that she has written her letter on the banks of the Mandākinī in heaven (10.94f.), or Tārā's confession that she has written her epistle sitting alone in the forest trembling with fear (2.162ff.), with Cydippe's allusion to her letter at *Her.* 21.243–end,[47] or with Penelope's reference to her act of writing (*Her.* 1.62: 'the sheet marked by my fingers').[48]

[43] Compare *BK* 7 where Bhānumatī apologizes at l. 106 (39 lines short of the average) for the length of her letter.

[44] Cf. also *BK* 5.119–23.

[45] See esp. *BK* 1. 67, 2. 5ff., 158, 162–5, 3.10–12, 5.78, 119–23, 6.147, 7.106, 8.124, 10.85. Cf. *Her.* 3.1ff., 4.10ff., 5.21–30, 6.7–16, 7.183, 10.3f., 11.1–6, 13.164–end, 14.21, 131f., 15.1–4, 97–8, 17.265–end, 18.1–20, 217–end, 19.9f., 20.33, 93f., 20.171f., 209–14, 21.1ff. 25ff., 207f., 225f., 21.243–end. For an exploration of epistolarity in the *Heroides*, see Spentzou (2003) esp. Chapter 5.

[46] See Kennedy (2002) 222.

[47] For an exploration of this passage see Spentzou (2003) 128ff. and *passim*; and Kenney (1996) *ad loc.*

[48] For the resonance between this verse and *Pont.* 4.3.26 and *Am.* 1.11.14, see Barchiesi (1992) 88.

Madhusudan foregrounds other aspects of the heroines' letter writing activities in a manner reminiscent of Ovid's work. For example, the *BK* thematizes the pen and the fingers that use it;[49] and the fatigue of writing.[50] These too are epistolary features found in the Ovidian model.[51] But, of course, the principal effect of the frequent allusions to letter writing in both the Bengali and the Latin epistles, somewhat paradoxically, is not to convince the external reader that the fictive writing is real but rather to draw attention to the generic conceit of that fictive writing. This is Roman poetry at its most 'artificial', and one should bear in mind that Madhusudan's interest in it came at a time when in Britain it was precisely for its artificiality—as opposed to the supposedly natural purity of Greek culture—that Latin literature was then largely out of vogue.[52]

It is, however, in the thematization of the letter recipient's anticipated reading, rather than of the heroine's act of writing, that the epistolary form may be seen to lend itself so fittingly to the elegiac genre. The vehicle of the epistle necessarily entails a spatial and temporal separation between the writer and the anticipated reader:[53] the distance between them is what makes the letter necessary,[54] and this separation is ripe with elegiac possibilities. References to a heroine's anticipation of her intended recipient's reading of the epistle are strewn throughout both the *Heroides* and the *BK*.[55] And the separation between writer and anticipated reader is illustrated in both works in spatial and temporal terms with references to what the

[49] See, for example, *BK* 2.164f., 3.10–2, 6.147f. and 8.124.

[50] See, for example, *BK* 3.10–2.

[51] For pens and fingers, see *Her.* 11.3, 17.265f., 20.241, and 21.27 and 245 (and Kenney (1996) 248, *ad loc.*). For fatigue, see *Her.* 21.27, and note the elucidation of this verse by Kenney (1996) 219, who emphasizes the tone of agitation; cf. also *Her.* 3.2, 14.131f., and 15.1f.

[52] See, for example, Vance (1997).

[53] See Kennedy (2002) 221 for an analysis of both kinds of separation in the *Heroides*.

[54] Penelope (1), Briseis (3), Hermione (8), and Laodamia (13) have been separated from their loved ones by forces outside their control, such as war or 'politics' (see Kennedy (2002) 221), as have Rukmiṇī (3), Draupadī (6), Bhānumatī (7), Duḥśalā (8). Others feel in some way abandoned by their addressee, such as Phyllis (2), Dido (7), Deianira (9), Ariadne (10), Medea (12); as do Śakuntalā (1), Kekayī (4), and Janā (11). And others are 'separated' from their loves by 'social' convention, such as Phaedra (4) or Canace (11). Compare Tārā (2) or Urvaśī (10).

[55] We might especially compare *BK* 5. 119ff. and Ūṣa's letter (second draft poem) ll. 3–5 with, for example, *Her.* 3.1–4, 4.2–5, 175–end, 5.1f., 10.3, 11.1–6, 15.1–4, 17.1f., 18.1–4, 201–3, 20.3–6, and 241–end. But see also *BK* 5.94f. and *Her.* 4.2.

reader can look upon but the writer cannot,[56] or to the wait which the writer has so far endured or must still endure before being able to look upon the reader again.[57] In both collections the heroines express anxiety as to how her epistle will be able to navigate the distance between herself and the recipient. How the epistle itself is to negotiate the physical distance between writer and addressee is also a theme in both the *BK* and the *Heroides*. The epistles of Draupadī (*BK* 6) and Leander (*Her.* 18) face particular difficulties transcending this distance.[58] Leander's letter has to cross a dangerous sea, and only one seaman is brave enough to serve as courier (*unus, et hic audax*... 18.9f.); similarly Draupadī's epistle must transcend the distance between earth and heaven, and so the heroine enlists the help of the virtuous son of a virtuous sage who is (by asceticism and lineage) sufficiently 'pure' to make the journey (ll. 224f.).[59]

Furthermore, the heroine's anxiety regarding her epistolary correspondence takes on a physical presence in the letter itself when the letter writer imagines the 'page' to be blotted with her tears.[60] Just as Draupadī apologizes for her letter becoming wet with profuse tears (*BK* 6.142f.), so Sappho draws Phaon's attention to the tear 'blots' on her letter.[61] Indeed these blots may speak as loud as the words they obscure, as Briseis observes at *Her.* 3.4: *sed tamen et lacrimae pondera*

[56] In *BK* 6, Draupadī, who remains on earth while Arjuna is visiting the abode of the gods, emphasizes that her husband now sees things in heaven that she has only ever heard about (ll. 29f.). Compare Laodamia in *Her.* 13.137ff., who envies the Trojan women for being close enough to their husbands to be able to see them.

[57] Bhānumatī and Phyllis are cases in point, both referring to the anxiety of waiting: compare *BK* 7.1f. and *Her.* 2.11f. For further references to a wait, either to be endured or already endured, see, for example, *Her.* 1.1f. and *BK* 1.27ff., 3.80ff., 6.172 and 177ff., 7.1f., and 10.100ff.

[58] But cf. also Śakuntalā (*BK* 1) and Penelope (*Her.* 1): Penelope says that whenever someone comes to her shores, she asks him about Ulysses and gives him a letter (l. 61); Śakuntalā refers to entrusting her writings to the winds and to stags in the vain hope that they may take them to Duṣmanta (ll. 67ff.).

[59] Hinduism has the notion of *tapas* (literally 'heat' or 'energy') which refers to the practice of acts of austerity with a view to accruing spiritual energy: the energy thus accrued may be used by an ascetic to achieve feats, even ascend to heaven. For an overview of this idea, see Klostermaier (1989) esp. 51f.

[60] A trope borrowed by Ovid from Propertius 4.3 (apparently Ovid's model for his own epistles); see also *Tristia* 1.1. On the trope of blotting tears in the *Heroides* see esp. Merklin (1968) 472ff. and Baca (1971) 195-201.

[61] For this trope of blots on the page, see esp. *Her.* 3.1–4, 11.1–6; *BK* 5.138f. Farrell (1998) 336, n. 58 notes that the word *litura* 'blot' can also mean 'erasure' or 'editorial correction', which may treat the Ovidian author as a kind of scholarly editor (and thus reader) of his own works. See also Kennedy (2002) 229f.

vocis habent . . . , 'but nonetheless even tears have the weight of words . . . '.[62] Moreover, the *lacrimae* ('tears') of the lover are a distinguishing feature of the Roman genre of love elegy, and of the *Heroides* itself.[63] The *BK* picks up this generic marker very clearly, not only in the trope of the tears blotting the page, but elsewhere too. The elegiac first person, in almost every single poem of the Bengali collection, describes herself as 'weeping'. Amid these references to tears in the *BK* there are some close parallels to the *Heroides*. Compare, for example, *BK* 6.150: *hāẏ re, titinu, nāth, naẏan-āsare!*, 'O, alas, O lord, I have grown wet with tears!'; with *Her.* 6.70: *lacrimis osque sinusque madent*, 'my face and breast are wet with tears'. Indeed, such sentiments litter both collections:[64] weeping characterizes the elegiac plight of the Bengali as much as the Ovidian *Heroides*?.

The behaviour that provokes them is of a piece with this elegiac motif of tears. In *Her.* 4, for example, Hippolytus is described as *ferreus*, 'made of iron' (l. 14), *durus*, 'hard' (l. 85), *rusticus*, 'uncooth' (l. 102): all adjectives that derive from the stock terminology of Roman love elegy.[65] The Bengali addressees are often described in comparable terms of disapprobation: note the tone adopted by Janā, at *BK* 11.107f., when she says to her husband: *bām mamo prati/ tumi*, 'you treat me with antipathy'. Similar accusations are levelled at the

[62] This theme of tears blotting the page is modified in both the *Heroides* and the *BK*, though in different ways. At *BK* 5.138f., for example, the tears that blot Sūrpaṇakhā's letter are of joy rather than anguish; whereas at *Her* 11.2 Canace says that if Macareus sees any blots on the letter then it is because the little roll has been stained by its mistress' blood.

[63] See esp. Huxley (1956) 78ff.; also Pichon (1902) 202 and Kenney (1982) 423. At least from the fifth century BCE, Greek elegy tended to be a genre of lamentation: see Page (1936) 206–30 who discusses the 'elegy of lament' with special reference to Euripides' *Andromache*. Whereas Greek elegy tended to express the lamentations of the bereaved (threnody), Augustan elegy—including Ovid's *Heroides*—typically gives voice (in the first person) to the lamentations of a lover (see Huxley (1956) 78ff.). For the relationship of the *Heroides* to the 'Origins of Latin Love Elegy', see Barchiesi (2001) 123–7.

[64] Weeping (*kādā*) and tears (*aśrujal*) are mentioned in the following *BK* passages: *BK* 1.17, 18, 50, 59, 86, 107, 128; 2. 81; 3.119, 120; 5. 10, 90, 138; 6.102, 103, 146, 148, 150, 186; 7.17, 94, 112; 8.25 (twice), 44 (twice), 78; 9.2 (reversal: addressee's tears); 11.119f., 124. Other expressions of distress are found at: *BK* 1.3, 12, 46, 62, 80, 84, 109, 141, 159; 2.85, 96, 113, 130, 147–8; 3.91, 97, 102; 4.52ff., 100, 126; 5.5, 7, 12; 6.36, 41, 45, 51, 106, 113, 128, 129, 153ff., 185, 188; 7.1 (first word), 79; 8.1, 43; 9.30 (reversal: addressee's distress); 11.21, 119, 121.

[65] See: Knox (1995) 29; Kenney (1982) 423; Pichon (1902) 202.

addressees of three of the poems in the Bengali collection.[66] And just as the Ovidian Herois tends to urge love over war, once again recalling the world of elegiac love (compare *Her.* 3.117–20 with *Am.* 2.11.31f.),[67] so too many of the Bengali epistles concur with Bhānumatī's sentiment at *BK* 7.140: *eso tumi, prāṇanāth, raṇ parihari!*, 'Come, O lord of my life, and abandon the battlefield!'[68]

Of course, the Hindu tradition of erotic poetry also has its own provisions for treating unhappy love, and the *BK* shows marked signs of a simultaneous engagement with this indigenous tradition too. In the *BK* we find, in addition to motifs specifically connotative of Roman love elegy, various markers of the Sanskritic 'flavour' of 'love-in-separation', or *vipralambhaśṛṅgārarasa*. As noted in Chapter 1 above, Hindu aestheticians considered there to be various *rasas* or 'flavours/sentiments', literary quintessences of real-life emotions, one of which was the 'erotic flavour' or *śṛṅgārarasa*. A subdivision of this 'erotic flavour' was the *vipralambhaśṛṅgārarasa*, the 'flavour of love-in-separation'. In many works of Sanskrit erotic poetry we find a period of separation before and/or after the union (or reunion) of two lovers. During this period of separation, the heroine may, according to the Sanskrit aesthetician, undergo ten stages of experience connoting this 'flavour' of 'love-in-separation'.[69] In the *BK*, besides the *locus amoenus* imagery generally connotative of the 'erotic flavour' and the language specifically denoting 'separation' (*viraha*, etc.),[70] we also find examples of these ten stages of 'love-in-separation':

(1) longing (*abhilāsa*) in *BK* 1, 2, 3, 5, 6, 7, 8, and 10;
(2) pondering (*cintana*) throughout all eleven epistles;
(3) remembrance (*smṛti*) particularly at 1.19ff., 2.73ff., 6.99ff., and 10.30ff.;

[66] See, for example, *BK* 1.39, 83, 84, 85, 148, 155f.; 2.150; 3.39, 90, 93 (which is identical to 98, 103, 105, 107, 111), 121 (ironic praise), 11.26, 43, 94, 100.

[67] See Knox (1995) 29.

[68] See, especially, *BK* 1.160–end, 7.140–end, 8.100 and 125. Note the exception of 3.148–end and 11.20: these Bīrāṅganā (like the women of *Her.* 3 and 8) urge their men to fight for them.

[69] For these ten stages of 'love-in-separation', see esp. Dhanañjaya's *Daśarūpaka* 4.51cd-52; and Vasudeva (2006) 31.

[70] For *locus amoenus* imagery, see esp. *BK* 1.19ff., 110ff., 2.35ff., 2.62, 2.85ff., 3.129ff., 5.50–9, 111–8; 6.6-33. For the language of 'love-in-separation', see esp. *BK* 1.59–75; 2.62, 147; 6.53–5, 82–98 (as at 1.59–75), 172, 217ff., 218; 9.5, 30, 50.

(4) praising (*guṇa/kīrtana*) at 1.130ff., 2.37ff., 3.23ff., 5.60ff., 6.192ff., 8.127ff., 9.16ff. 10.40ff.;

(5) agitation (*udvega*) at 1.4ff., 2.5ff.,, 3.7ff., 4 (throughout), 6.148ff., 7.1ff. and 109ff., 8 (throughout), 11 (throughout);

(6) babbling (*pralāpa*) at 1.66ff. (addressing inanimate objects), 3.139–42, 4.78–86, 5.39–60, 6.129ff. (excused at ll. 147ff.);

(7) madness (*unmāda*) at 1.4ff., 3.80ff., 4.91ff., 6.41ff., 11.21;

(8) fever (*saṃjvara*) at 2.147ff. and 7.16ff.;

(9) torpor (*jaḍatā*) at 1.104 and 8.69; and finally

(10) death (*maraṇa*) at 6.152ff. (threatened) and 11.130ff. (foreshadowed).

Indeed it is significant that Śakuntalā, the first 'heroine' of the *BK*, should come from Kālidāsa's Sanskrit drama, *Abhijñānaśakuntalam*, the most famous exposition of the Sanskrit 'flavour' of 'love-in-separation'.[71]

Madhusudan's very accommodation within the *BK* of tropes from both Sanskrit erotic poetry and Roman love elegy figures an implied comment on the similarity of these two traditions. This is an instance of aesthetic syncretism to mirror the mythological and theological Indo-European syncretism pervading much of Madhusudan's oeuvre. In this connection it is interesting to note that Madhusudan in fact prefaces the *BK* with a citation from the *Sāhityadarpaṇa*, a Sanskrit treatise composed by the Bengali or Orissan aesthetician Viśvanātha (an abridgement of Ch.3, 127):[72] *lekhyaprasthāpanaiḥ—nāryā bhāvābhivyaktir iṣyate*, 'It is agreed [by the learned] that women may reveal their feelings—by the sending of letters'.[73] Although the Hindu tradition has no genre of 'epistolary' poetry as such, Madhusudan cites this passage from a Sanskrit aesthetics treatise to imply that the potential for such a genre is embedded in the indigenous tradition. Madhusudan's import of a Roman genre, Ovidian epistolary elegy, into Bengali poetry is 'excused' in the preface of the *BK* as an extension of an idea already present in the Hindu tradition.

There are, then, various respects in which the *BK* responds to the aesthetic discourses of the Hindu tradition and accommodates the

[71] See Vasudeva (2006) esp. 31ff.

[72] He cites from the same work in preface to the *PN* (1860) too.

[73] Madhusudan writes *lekhya-*, but the correct reading is probably *lekha-*; both mean 'writing', 'letter(s)'. See Kane (1923), the edition referred to here.

Ovidian model to them. Nonetheless, we may detect further respects in which these Bengali poems engage with the model of Ovidian epistolary elegy. As Knox observes, 'Ovid's creation of an "elegiac voice" in the *Heroides* is effected by the separation of his heroines from their "literary bases"'.[74] The Bengali poet's creation of an 'elegiac voice' is also effected by just such a separation:[75] like the *Heroides,* the *BK* takes characters from both epic and drama and 'translates' them into elegy.[76] Echoes and foreshadowings of events from outside the moment of the letters' composition (but from within the narrative of the epistles' 'source' texts) are operative in our response to the poems *qua* elegy.[77]

As Barchiesi notes, '[we] are frequently struck by a feeling of foreknowledge while reading Ovid's *Heroides*'.[78] A poignant case in point is that of Oenone in *Her.* 5, and this finds a particularly close analogy in *BK* 5. Oenone appeals to her erstwhile husband in the hope of rekindling his love and of removing him from the dangers of the Trojan War. Both hopes are implied at l. 15: *non ego cum Danais arma cruenta fero*, 'I do not bear bloody arms with the Danaans'. Unlike Dido, whose words to Aeneas in Vergil's epic are recalled here,[79] Oenone later gives the lie to this statement. It is clear from the epistle's extant sources[80] that the nymph will later render important help to the Danaan invasion in revenge for her abandonment. In this way we, the external readers, know something that the internal writer does not, namely that her love will soon evaporate and be replaced with hatred; and we know something that the internal addressee does not, namely that his response to this letter will determine much weightier issues than at first appear.

[74] Knox (1995) 23.

[75] See above for details of the Hindu 'source' texts, underlying the poems of the *BK*. Madhusudan prepares his readers for this 'separation' of his heroines from their 'literary bases' by prefacing his epistles with notes on the poems' literary contexts.

[76] Cf. Knox (1995) 23.

[77] Indeed, that the reader is 'meant' to recall the literary contexts of the Bengali epistles (the history behind and the consequences entailed by each letter) is implied by comments in Madhusudan's brief prose introductions to each poem; note, for example, the comment at the end of the preface to *BK* 3: *rukmiṇī-haraṇ-bṛttānto e sthale byakto karā* ***bāhulyo***, 'It is **unnecessary** here to give details of the story of Rukmiṇī's rescue.' (Emphasis mine.)

[78] Barchiesi (2001) 107.

[79] For the resonance between this and Dido's words at *Aen.* 4.425f., cf. Barchiesi (2001) 109.

[80] Cf. Stinton (1965) 40f.

Just such an irony, predicated, as elsewhere, on a kind of suppressed foreshadowing of events to come later in the epistle's 'source' text, is also very much in evidence in *BK* 5. Sūrpaṇakhā, in her declaration of love for Lakṣmaṇa, not only assures her addressee that she does not bear arms against him, but that she will bear arms with him. If you have been defeated by some foe, she says (ll. 23f.), *kaho śīghro; dibo senā bhab-bijaẏinī,/ rath, gaj, aśbo, rathī—atul jagate!*, 'tell me [so] at once; and I will give you a world-conquering army, chariots, elephants, horses, charioteers—without match in the whole world!' Sūrpaṇakhā promises a great military alliance, and thus gestures towards a future in which their love and his success will go hand in hand. Just as in *Her.* 5, the promise made by the Herois in *BK* 5 is given the lie by the external reader's knowledge of a 'source' text, in this case *Rāmāyaṇa* (B) 6,9.13f. We know from the Sanskrit epic that Lakṣmaṇa, having dismissed Sūrpaṇakhā's declaration and humiliated her for it, will provoke her wrath. As a result Sūrpaṇakhā's brother, Rāvaṇa, will provoke war with the Rāghavas by abducting Sītā, Lakṣmaṇa's sister-in-law. A rather uncomfortable irony, akin to that at *Her.* 5.15, is triggered by our knowledge of the poem's epic 'source'.

Intertext, or more accurately the 'separation' of the female writers from their 'literary bases', may thus play a part in the 'translation into elegy' by activating literary ironies.[81] However, as Barchiesi stresses, elegy's contribution to the *Heroides* (and the same may be said of the *BK*) 'cannot be reduced . . . to long lists of influences and interferences', nor just to the intertextual business of suppressed foreshadowing.[82] In addition, perhaps in particular, elegy teaches the heroine to

[81] Most of the epistles of the *Heroides* and the *BK* alike are underpinned by such elegiac ironies, though there is no space to discuss them all in depth. But note esp. Bhānumatī's unwitting prophecy of her husband's death (*BK* 7.138) and Briseis' expression of hope at *Her.* 3.44 ('and does not a gentler hour come once woes have begun?'), which figures an allusion 'conjugated in the future tense' (Barchiesi (2001) 108) to *Il.* 19.290 ('evil always follows on evil').

[82] But note that further examples of (external) analepsis and prolepsis, that is, flashback and flash forward, in the *BK*, or of resonances with passages earlier and later in a 'source' text, are as follows: [analepsis] 1.47, 60ff., 145ff., 153ff.; 2.35–106 (lengthy narration of first meeting with love object); 3.1ff., 28–75 (narration of birth of Kṛṣṇa); 4.56ff., 75, 78ff.; 5.14ff., 123; 6.37ff., 64f., 69–134 (narration of speaker's past), 190f., 105ff.; 7.1ff., 25ff., 31ff.; 8.86ff., 128ff., 133ff.; 9.4ff., 46ff.; 10.9ff., 30ff.; 11.13ff., 104ff., 122ff.; [prolepsis] 1.110ff., 153ff.; 5.25ff., 133; 6.192ff.; 7.78ff., 115ff., 8.46ff., 83ff.; 9.32ff., 64ff.; 10.81ff.; 11.9ff., 130ff.

bring back 'every external reality... to the *persona* of the lover'.[83] This elegiac shift of perspective—from universal to particular, from objective to subjective, from masculine to feminine[84]—is also seen in the *BK*.

In fact, the Bengali collection emblematizes this elegiac shift of perspective in two tableaux. In *BK* 7 and 8, Madhusudan exploits the narratological complexities of the *Mahābhārata*. Much of the epic is narrated in reported speech by secondary or tertiary speakers who are also, therefore, characters in the poem.[85] One of these internal narrators is Sañjaya, a bard at the court of the Kaurava king, Dhṛtarāṣṭra, who narrates the events occurring on the battlefield of Kurukṣetra to the royal court of Kuru. The female authors of *BK* 7 and 8 are the wives of Kaurava warriors, and thus in attendance at the court of Dhṛtarāṣṭra while the battles fought by their husbands are reported by the bard. In both poems, Sañjaya's epic narrative is itself related and in both, the female authors gloss the narration with their own elegiac responses. So at *BK* 7, Bhānumatī, the wife of Duryodhana, describes herself listening to the news of the battle from Sañjaya (l. 13), and then relates her response to it thus (ll. 17f.): *pařiyā kãdi, śāśuřīr pade,/ nayan-āsare dhauto kari pā dukhāni!* 'I fall down and sob, at my mother-in-law's feet, and wash them both with the tears from my eyes!' We might compare Duḥśalā bursting into tears at *BK* 8.44. Both elegiac heroines give a response to epic narrative expressed in tears, the clearest marker of elegy's lamentatory tone.[86] Just as Briseis' elegiac tears stand in for linguistic communication at *Her.* 3.4, so too Bhānumatī says at *BK* 7.19: *nāhi sare kathā mukhe, kãdi mātro khede!* 'I cannot get words out of my mouth, I only weep in sorrow!'

One might also note the disparity of knowledge and power between the male epic narrator and the female elegiac voice.[87] Bhānumatī, for

[83] Barchiesi (2001) 32.

[84] Many of the *Heroides* may be said to figure not only a markedly elegiac response to martial themes, but also a markedly feminine response to epic. For a study of *Her.* 3 and 8 with this in mind, see Fulkerson (2005) Ch.4.

[85] For the embedding structures underpinning the narration of the *MBh*, see esp. Minkowski (1989) 401–20. On the phenomenon of 'frame stories' in Sanskrit literature more generally, see Witzel (1987) 380–414.

[86] See n. 63 above.

[87] For an exploration of these gender issues and power relations in the *Heroides*, see Kennedy (2002) 225ff.; also Fulkerson (2005).

example, says of Sañjaya's epic narration at *BK* 7.15: *ki ye śuni, nāhi bujhi—āmi pāgalinī!* 'What I hear I cannot comprehend—I am a simple woman!' The account given by the *Mahābhārata* seems unassailably 'authoritative' and, in the face of it, the female describes herself as ignorant and powerless. However, despite this avowed weakness and ignorance, both *BK* 7 and 8 figure an appropriation of the epic narrative, and an attempt by the women to affect the events related to them. Like Briseis and Hermione in *Her.* 3 and 8, Bhānumatī and Duḥśalā thrust their elegiac (feminine, subjective) point of view on to their male addressees.[88] Indeed, the Hindu women go one step further than Ovid's heroines by mediating their husbands' 'reading' of their own epic story: Duryodhana and Jayadratha will hear their wives' elegiac interpretations of Sañjaya's epic narrative before being able to consider it for themselves.

These Bengali epistles, which are imagined to have taken place before the narrative of the *Mahābhārata* was composed, seem (just like Ovid's *Heroides*) to have the paradoxical advantage of 'temporal priority' over their 'source' texts.[89] The 'source' texts both of the *BK* and the *Heroides* come to look like 'later . . . appropriations or recuperations of the legendary authors' words'.[90] The epistle thus becomes a vehicle for elegy to challenge the authority of epic. Indeed, it was perhaps the special capacity of epistolary elegy to challenge the authority of epic in this way that attracted Madhusudan to Ovid's *Heroides* as a model for the *BK* in the first place. As was seen in the reading of the *MBK* given in Chapter 3 above, Madhusudan was keen throughout much of his Bengali oeuvre to challenge Hindu religious doctrine in his revisions of the Hindu epic tradition. While, in the Sanskrit and mediaeval Bengali *Rāmāyaṇa* poems, the hero Rāma is identified with the god Viṣṇu, and is still worshipped by Hindus today as an avatar of this supreme deity, the Christian Madhusudan famously asserted 'I despise Ram and his rabble'.[91] In the *MBK* Madhusudan presented Rāma as a man rather than a god and played down

[88] For Briseis' appeal to Achilles to 'reinvent himself as an epic hero who is *also* an elegiac lover', see Fulkerson (2005) 96f. For Hermione's emulation of this appeal, see ibid. 97ff. Indeed, whereas Briseis may be described (as by Knox (1995) 19) to have 'read, so to speak, the *Iliad*', Bhānumatī and Duḥśalā have literally heard their 'source' text being composed.

[89] Kennedy (2002) 226.

[90] Kennedy (2002) 226.

[91] Murshid (2004) 168f.

his heroic qualities while rehabilitating his Rākṣasa enemies (in part using Homeric and Vergilian models to do so: see Chapter 3 above).[92]

In the *BK*, Madhusudan pursues this same end—the demotion of Rāma from perfect god to flawed man—by exploiting the capacity of epistolary elegy to challenge epic.[93] The heroines Kekaẏī in *BK* 4 and Sūrpaṇakhā in *BK* 5 take it in turns to cast doubt on the probity and heroism of Rāma's father and brother, respectively. In *BK* 5 Madhusudan draws attention to, and exacerbates, the cruelty of Rāma's brother Lakṣmaṇa: the poet allows Sūrpaṇakhā, Rāvaṇa's sister, who fell in love with Lakṣmaṇa, to portray herself not in the disgusting terms used in the earlier tradition (see Preface to *BK* 5 ll. 1ff.) but in terms suggesting that she was most unworthy of being rejected, let alone in the humiliating way Lakṣmaṇa did so. And, in *BK* 4, we find a much more overt attack against Rāma's father Daśaratha: his second wife Kekaẏī takes him to task for his preferential treatment of Rāma (her step-son) over Bharata (her son), accusing him of breaking his word and thus of behaving in an 'irreligious' manner (see esp. ll. 86–115). The 'temporal priority' of these two epistles, a generic conceit afforded by the model of Ovid's *Heroides*, makes the epic *Rāmāyaṇa* itself look like a later revision of these elegiac denunciations of Rāma's family.

3. WIDER PERSPECTIVES: SUBVERSION THROUGH GENDER AND GENRE

Madhusudan's reception of Ovid's *Heroides* shows a great sensitivity to the generic implications of the Latin work. The generic capacity of Ovid's *Heroides* to challenge literary authority evidently appealed to

[92] Indeed, Madhusudan's 'secularization' of the *Rāmāyaṇa*, his removal of Hindu theological doctrine from the Hindu epic tradition, figured something of a return to origins: scholars have shown that the divinity of the hero Rāma was a later Brahmanical addition to an earlier, purely warrior caste epic tradition. See esp. Brockington (1998).

[93] Note that in *BK* 11 Madhusudan goes even further: here he addresses a theological issue of the *Mahābhārata*, the other of the two great Hindu epics, by having the heroine Janā challenge the truth of *Naranārāẏaṇa*, the Hindu doctrine which holds that the hero Arjuna is in fact the deity Nara (conjoined with the god Kṛṣṇa as Nārāẏaṇa). See esp. *BK* 11.42ff.

Madhusudan, and this is certainly an aspect of his Ovidian model that the Bengali poet exploits in the *BK*. Ovid's *Heroides* represents something of an 'anti-classic', a model for the deconstruction of hegemonic literary authority. To this extent, we might not be surprised by the Latin work's appeal to a Bengali poet who once proudly characterized himself, and not without justification, as a 'tremendous literary rebel'.[94]

Another explanation sometimes offered for Madhusudan's interest in Ovid's *Heroides* is of a more personal nature. During his period of living in Madras in the late 1840s and early 1850s, Madhusudan married Rebecca McTavish, an Anglo-Indian student at the school where he was then teaching, and went on to have four children by her.[95] However, by 1855 he had begun an affair with an Englishwoman, Henrietta White. And when, on 28 January 1856, Madhusudan left Madras permanently, he effectively abandoned Rebecca (for reasons that are not entirely clear),[96] and he never saw her or their four children again.[97] Two and a half years later Henrietta would join him in Calcutta, later following him to Europe in 1862 along with their children and, though unmarried, they spent the rest of their lives together. The very fact that Madhusudan 'married out' in this way was met with disapproval among many Europeans and Indians alike and is itself an anomaly of some historical interest.[98] It has been suggested by certain scholars that Madhusudan's literary interest in abandoned women, which we see not only in the *BK* (1862) but also in his contemporary *Brajāṅganā kābya* ('Poems of the Women of Braja'),[99] had its personal genesis in the poet's own abandonment in 1856 of his wife and their children.[100] Certainly, Śakuntalā's opening words in *BK* 1 ('Even though you have forgotten her, can this wretch

[94] Murshid (2004) 130. See Radice (1987), a doctoral dissertation which takes this expression as its title, for an exploration of the sobriquet.

[95] See Murshid (2003) 107.

[96] Murshid (2003) 57.

[97] Murshid (2003) 57.

[98] For an excellent history of interracial marriage in British India, see Ghosh (2006).

[99] These poems, 'odes' as Madhusudan called them, are written in the persona of Rādhā (consort of the god Kṛṣṇa) in honour of Kṛṣṇa, and they are all written during her 'separation' (*viraha*) from Kṛṣṇa. Throughout this work, Madhusudan repeatedly plays on the *śleṣa* ('paronomasia') of *madhu*, which may denote any or all of 'honey', the god 'Kṛṣṇa', or 'Madhusudan' (the poet's own name).

[100] See Murshid (2003) and also Radice (1987).

ever forget you?') and perhaps Duḥśalā's plea at *BK* 8.124f. that Jayadratha return for their child's sake even if not for hers, may seem to speak to the poet's own turbulent love life rather poignantly.

However, in addition to the poet's personal interest in the theme of abandoned women, there are also certain broader contexts relevant to a full understanding of Madhusudan's literary interest in Ovid's *Heroides*, above all the discourses of contemporary colonial and gender politics. Recent studies have explored the way in which, even from a very early stage, the discourse of colonial politics in British India was gendered: the colonized society was 'feminized' and 'its "effeminate" character, as opposed to "colonial masculinity", was held to be a justification for its loss of independence'.[101] This gender dichotomy, moreover, found expression in the specific caricature of the 'effeminate Bengali'.[102] It was observed in the previous chapter that, in his lecture 'The Anglo-Saxon and the Hindu' (1854), Madhusudan reflected this gender discourse in his characterization of the 'Hindu' as a Dido figure contrasting with the 'Anglo-Saxon' Aeneas.

Furthermore, in the West a 'civilizational critique' of India was constructed on the basis of the 'women's question', with intellectuals like James Mill taking the 'degraded' condition of Indian women as an 'indicator of India's inferior status in the hierarchy of civilisations'.[103] This goes some way towards explaining why the status of women became the focus of the reformist agenda among the modernizing Bengali *bhadralok* who, as Bandyopadhyay observes, 'imagined a golden past where women were treated with dignity and honour ... [and] urged reforms of those customs, which they considered to be distortions or aberrations.'[104] In this way (most notably) female education was promoted, the Widow-Remarriage Act was passed, and the practice of suttee was outlawed. All of these reforms were legitimated among the Hindu community on the authority of revisionist readings of the Sanskrit *śāstras* (treatises).[105] Indeed it is well known that Madhusudan himself took a strong view on all of these social issues: he contributed monetarily ('one half of my pay') towards

[101] Bandyopadhyay (2004) 381; see n. 198 for further bibliography. For a broader reading of the status of women in nineteenth-century Indian society see Sarkar (1987) and (2002).

[102] See esp. Sinha (1995).

[103] Bandyopadhyay (2004) 381.

[104] Bandyopadhyay (2004) 381.

[105] Bandyopadhyay (2004) 381.

the construction of a statue of Vidyasagar in honour of his work as the 'Promoter of Widow-Remarriage';[106] and earlier in his life he had written an English prize essay on the importance of educating Hindu women.[107]

Madhusudan's reception of Ovid's *Heroides* in the *BK* may be seen to mirror these processes of social 'reform' in the domain of literature. It is significant, in this connection, that Madhusudan used the language of 'reform' in his discussions of his own literary aspirations: 'I would sooner reform the Poetry of my country than wear the imperial diadem of all the Russias'.[108] In the *BK* Madhusudan revisits the famous heroines of Hindu mythology, many (though not all) of whom are denied a voice in traditional accounts,[109] and implicitly 'corrects' the Sanskrit literary tradition by allowing them to speak for themselves. Contemporary Bengali social reformers would cite the authority of the Sanskrit *śāstras* (treatises) to legitimate their promotion of women's 'rights' in the social domain;[110] similarly, as was seen in Section 2 above, Madhusudan cited his own Sanskrit *śāstra*, Viśvanātha's *Sāhityadarpaṇa* (a work of *alaṅkāraśāstra* or 'poetics'), to legitimate his privileging of the female voice in the literary domain. Furthermore, just as in the sphere of social reform, this restoration of a Hindu tradition to its supposed 'original' state went hand in hand with, and to some extent disguised, the underlying appropriation of a Western paradigm.

One criticism levelled at Ovid's *Heroides* by feminist scholars in recent years is that the 'female' voices of the Epistles are mere projections of the male poet, that Ovid 'usurps' his heroines' voices and fails to write authentically 'like a woman'.[111] However, as post-

[106] Murshid (2004) 135.

[107] For a discussion of this essay, see Radice (2010) lxxii–lxxiv.

[108] Murshid (2004) 118; see also 78, 106f., 111, 114f. Indeed, literary reform, such as Madhusudan was attempting, may of course be seen as a type of social reform. Note that a similar process of literary 'reform' (a return to an Indian classical past tempered by the 'high' literature of the West) was being attempted by other *bhadralok* artists at the time, most notably the poet and playwright Rangalal. This process would be taken forward a little later (from the mid 1860s onwards) in the realm of the novel by Bankim, the famous Bengali novelist and intellectual.

[109] Certainly, Rukmiṇī (*BK* 3), Kekaẏī (*BK* 4), Sūrpaṇakhā (*BK* 5), Bhānumatī (*BK* 7), Duḥśalā (*BK* 8), and Janā (*BK* 11) are all marginal characters in their respective 'source' texts; and the elegiac epistle gives them a platform to articulate views which they are prevented from articulating in the Hindu tradition.

[110] See Bandyopadhyay (2004) 381.

[111] For charges of 'female ventriloquism' levelled against Ovid, see esp. de Jean (1989), Harvey (1989), and Rimell (1999). For a post-feminist critique of this feminist position see esp. Fulkerson (2005) 5ff. but also Spentzou (2003) 1–3 and 25.

feminist scholars like Fulkerson and Spentzou have argued, Ovid has managed to 'write like a woman' inasmuch as 'he has seemed to do so to many of his readers throughout the ages, both male and female'.[112] In any case, the biological woman, an 'increasingly disputed category', has no automatic monopoly over the feminine.[113] Indeed, the distinction between sex (a function of biology) and gender (a cultural construct) is nowhere more evident than in the gender-troubled discourse of colonial politics: as was noted above, contemporary Indian society itself was traditionally gendered feminine by contrast to the masculine colonial power. Given that Madhusudan, while of course being biologically male, may thus be seen as a colonial-feminine reader, it is significant that the Bengali poet was attracted to Ovid's *Heroides* as a literary model. Remember that Dido, with whose Vergilian incarnation Madhusudan once identified the 'Hindu race' (see Chapter 4 above), in fact 'authors' *Her.* 7. One might wonder whether Madhusudan also read this Ovidian Epistle, as he once read Vergil's *Aeneid* 4, as an articulation of his (feminine) colonial society's attitude towards the (masculine) Anglo-Saxon.

Ovid's oeuvre in general, and his *Heroides* in particular, were largely out of favour in mid-nineteenth-century Britain for his perceived moral decadence and aesthetic artificiality. In the eighteenth-century Augustan period of English poetry, however, Ovid enjoyed a much higher reputation. Dasgupta has suggested the epistolary poem 'Eloisa to Abelard' (1717) by Alexander Pope as a possible further influence on Madhusudan's *BK*. Pope was certainly one of Madhusudan's favourite poets and he was firmly within the English literary canon as it stood in the nineteenth century. As Byron wrote: 'Thou shalt believe in Milton, Dryden, Pope . . . ' (*Don Juan*, 1.205). Indeed, one might note that Pope also published a translation of Ovid's *Her.* 15 under the title of 'Sappho to Phaon'. Many of the Ovidian themes and tropes of Madhusudan's *BK* find parallels in Pope's 'Eloisa to Abelard': here, as in the Bengali collection, we find the Ovidian motif of the 'first meeting'; the thematization of reading and the anxiety concerning how the reader will respond; the trope of the blotting tears.

However, such points of comparison between Madhusudan's *BK* and Pope's Augustan poetry are faint echoes rather than deep

[112] Fulkerson (2005) 5. [113] Fulkerson (2005) 5.

resonances. Certainly, Madhusudan's interest in Ovid—especially his *Heroides*—went very much against the fashion of contemporary British literary tastes. In this context, it is interesting to note that Madhusudan was joined in his against-the-grain attraction to Ovid's *Heroides* by Emma Garland, a female poet from Liverpool, who in 1842 composed her own English translation of the Latin collection, one of very few to be published in England in the nineteenth century.[114] There is no evidence that Madhusudan had read or knew of Garland's translation, though his citation of Felicia Hemans' *Roman Girl's Song* in 'The Anglo-Saxon and the Hindu' (1854) (see Chapter 4 above) suggests that he took an interest in contemporary female British poets. In any event, it is an engaging case of literary happenstance, if nothing more, that both poets—roughly contemporary—imagined themselves to be interpreting Ovid's *Heroides* for the benefit of readers of their own kind (English women and Bengalis respectively), that in so doing they were conscious of their status outside the definition of the typical classical reader (the white male). As a woman, albeit an English one, Emma Garland was not expected by the standards of Victorian society to know any Latin. Indeed her rather apologetic introduction to the work, in which she meekly excuses her audacity in attempting a translation from Latin,[115] suggests that she was in fact expected not to know the language. Women with literary inclinations were meant to read works not of Latin but Italian—Dante, for example—a 'feminine' language by contrast with Latin's 'masculinity'.[116] Similarly, as an Indian colonial, Madhusudan was not 'supposed' to have learned Latin or Greek, let alone be an able and sensitive reader of Western classical literature (see Chapter 1 for a treatment of this educational context). In both cases, then, the very fact that these two poets could read Latin in the first place was itself somewhat illicit.

Just as Madhusudan sought through his *BK* to bring Ovid, albeit obliquely, to a Bengali readership, so too, in the introduction to her Ovidian translation, Garland made clear that her purpose was to interpret Ovid for women and expressed the hope that her translation

[114] For a full treatment of nineteenth century versions and imitations of Ovid in English, see esp. Gillespie (2004) 207–18.

[115] See Garland (1842) v, and Vance (1988) 224.

[116] See Bayley (1992) esp. 364.

would be 'agreeable to her own sex'.[117] In both cases, the poets' illicit readership of the Western classics revealed a feminine counter-current within this quintessentially masculine discourse. Here was a classical text that arguably belonged more readily to subaltern readers like Garland (women) or Madhusudan (Indians) than to the traditional readers of the Graeco-Roman classics (white men). In their different ways, both poets attempted to recover for their own communities a text which embarrassed the Victorian classical discourse with its subversive and artificial femininity. Moreover, Madhusudan's reception of Ovid's *Heroides* in the *BK* may thus be seen as the apogee of a tendency which has already been noted in earlier works. For example, in the *Meghnādbadh kābya* (1861) examined in Chapter 3 above, it was seen that the Bengali poet highlighted the presence of a 'bedroom farce' at the heart of Homer's *Iliad*, the weighty cornerstone text of the Graeco-Roman canon. The *BK* demonstrates this same tendency to emphasize classical counter-currents, and takes it to its logical conclusion.

[117] Cf. Garland (1842) vi.

6

The *Hekṭor-badh* (1871) and Homer's *Iliad*[1]

INTRODUCTION

By the time the *BK* was published in February 1862, Madhusudan had already begun to turn away from literary enterprise:

> I suppose my poetical career is drawing to a close. I am making arrangements to go to England to study for the Bar and must bid adieu to the Muse![2]

Later that year, on 4 June, just five days before embarking on the steamer *Candia* bound for 'Albion's distant shore',[3] Madhusudan wrote again to Rajnarain about forsaking 'the Muse': 'an early triumph is ours, and I may well leave the rest to younger hands, not ceasing to direct their movements from my distant retreat'.[4] In fact, whilst he was in Europe, Madhusudan composed the majority of his 'Sonnets', the very fine *Caturdaśpadī kabitābalī*, which would be published to wide acclaim in August 1866. However, aside from this notable exception, his 'poetical career' had indeed drawn to a close, and he achieved no major literary success between his return to Calcutta and his tragic death in June 1873. Although he had been called to the Bar by Gray's Inn before his return to Calcutta, he

[1] An embryonic version of this chapter appeared as a chapter in Hall (2010): see Riddiford (2010).

[2] Murshid (2004) 178: letter to Rajnarain, early February 1862 (*BK* published later that month).

[3] As a youth, Madhusudan wrote an English poem expressing his desire to go to England: 'I sigh for Albion's distant shore'. At last, in the summer of 1862, he finally got his chance to fulfil this dream, though in the event his sojourn in Europe turned out to be ill-fated.

[4] Murshid (2004) 180.

proved to be a poor barrister, no doubt largely because of his advanced alcoholism. In this context, and in a desperate attempt to earn a little money, Madhusudan eventually turned again to writing. Thus, at the request of a publisher, he composed some short narrative poems for children, and he wrote a play called *Māẏākānan* ('The Forest of Illusion'), a tragedy (first performed posthumously in 1874) in which the hero Ajay and heroine Indumatī are compelled by Fate to sacrifice their own lives. Like his earlier play, *Kṛṣṇakumārī nāṭak* (1861), this tragedy seems to owe more to Shakespeare than to Attic tragedy, and appears to owe less to the Sanskritic tradition than his first Bengali plays, *Śarmiṣṭhā nāṭak* (1859) and *Padmābatī nāṭak* (1860). In addition to these works, he also published the *Hekṭor-badh*, 'The Slaying of Hector' (1871), which is the subject of this chapter.

The *Hekṭor-badh* (henceforth *HB*) is an abridged version, composed in six *paricched* or 'chapters' of Bengali prose, of Homer's *Iliad* 1–12, two Homeric books per Bengali chapter. The work was in fact composed in 1867/8: ill health seems to have been why, to the author's embarrassment, the *HB* was published despite being only half-finished.[5] Bandyopadhyay, a twentieth-century editor of the *HB*, refers to the work as *gadyakābya* or 'prose poetry'[6]—Sanskritic *kābya*, which can be rendered into English somewhat imperfectly as 'poetry', may be either *padya* (verse) or *gadya* (prose)[7]—and this is an apposite formal description of the work. The *HB*, Madhusudan's only extended work of Bengali *gadya*, is in many ways very curious. The experimental prose style adopted in the work was not received well, at least not at first:[8] even Yogindranath Basu, Madhusudan's first biographer (1893), could not find much to say in its favour.[9] In particular, Madhusudan's rendering of Homeric epithets, for which he coined rather cumbersome and opaque Sanskritic compounds, and his neologistic coinage of compound verbs (like *gaman karā*, 'make a movement', instead of the simple *yāoẏā*, 'go'), give the work a density that some have found unattractive and

[5] See Bandyopadhyay (1945–51) [Introduction] 1.

[6] See Bandyopadhyay (1945–51) [Introduction] 1.

[7] For this and other such distinctions in Hindu literary aesthetics, see De (1960).

[8] Later critics, especially Maitra (1975), have praised Madhusudan's prose, describing it as *dhrupadī* ('majestic', 'solemn') and have noted that it seems to have been influenced by German prose (Madhusudan had learned German whilst in Europe): see Radice (2010) lxxxvii.

[9] Cited by Radice (2010) lxxxvii.

inaccessible.[10] Indeed, it was partly in response to the heaviness of Madhusudan's style that Rabindranath Tagore later went on to develop the lightness of style that so distinguished his Bengali prose and verse.

Despite such aesthetic issues, the *HB* is a fascinating work from the point of view of its reception of Homer's *Iliad*. As its name implies ('The Slaying of Hector' rather than 'The Iliad'), the *HB* is a very loose and transformative version of the Homeric original, such that it is really a new work in its own right.[11] Above all, the *HB* figures a kind of implicit commentary on Homer's *Iliad*, a translation strewn with implied glosses on the work translated. In addition to numerous elisions of Homeric passages, there are also various interpolations in the Homeric narrative representing Madhusudan's authorial comments on his Iliadic model. Madhusudan's 'version' of Homer's *Iliad* is especially similar to Alexander Pope's English 'translation' in this respect. But the Bengali 'commentary' is, first and foremost, a comparative Indo-European one: throughout the *HB*, Homeric gods, customs, and religious practices, are frequently glossed with Hindu 'equivalents', rather than being translated or transliterated in a straightforward manner. Thus Homer's Apollo becomes Sūrya, Hindu god of the sun, and Ares the Hindu god of war becomes Skanda. The nexus of Indo-European comparisons underpinning Madhusudan's *HB* seems to be inspired not by the contemporary (and more scientifically credible) Indo-European comparativism of Friedrich Max Müller, but by the scholarship of the early British Orientalist Sir William Jones.

1. MADHUSUDAN'S *HB*: A HINDU COMMENTARY ON HOMER'S *ILIAD*

The status of the *HB* as something other than a straightforward translation[12] of Homer's *Iliad* is indicated by its very title *Hekṭor-*

[10] This, at any rate, is the criticism of Basu (1893) 470; see also Radice (2010) lxxxvii.

[11] In fact, though Madhusudan seems unaware of it, a translation of the *Iliad* into Bengali had already been composed, in *pāẏār* verse (the traditional meter of Bengali poetry), by Ananda Chandra Mukhopadhyay in 1863: see Sen (1932) 187.

[12] Of course there is perhaps no such thing as a 'straightforward' translation: as Hardwick (2005) argues, any translation of a text from one language into another will

badh ('The Slaying of Hector' rather than 'The Iliad'); indeed the title itself figures the work's first implicit comment on the Homeric original. The Bengali title, throwing the emphasis on to the death of Hector (and away from the 'wrath of Achilles', the theme introduced at *Il.* 1.1), implies a reading of Homer's *Iliad* as a celebration, above all, of Hector's death. Madhusudan thus fulfils the wish expressed by Hector at *Il.* 22.304f. that he not die without a struggle, nor without glory, but in the accomplishment of some great deed that men yet to be born may hear about.[13] The very title of the *HB* marks the *kleos* ('glory') of the Trojan hero at the moment of his death in *Il.* 22, which is in many ways the climax of the poem. As was seen in Chapter 4 above, the *MBK*, Madhusudan's earlier response to Homer's *Iliad*, aligns the sympathetic Rākṣasa hero, Meghanāda, with the Iliadic Hector. Indeed, in the preface (*upakramanikā*) to the *HB*, Madhusudan once again compares Hector with Meghanāda: [*hekṭorke*] *troysvarūp laṅkār meghnād balā yāite pāre*, '[Hector] could be said to be the Meghanāda of his Trojan Laṅkā'.

Furthermore, the structure of the *HB* is itself indicative of a certain reading of Homer's *Iliad*. The division of the half-finished *HB* into six chapters (relating twelve books of Homer),[14] which would have come to a total of twelve chapters if Madhusudan had finished the work (relating all twenty-four books), recalls the number of books in Vergil's *Aeneid* (itself an exercise in Homeric compression).[15] It was seen in Chapters 3 and 4 above that, in some of his earlier Bengali works—the *MBK* but also his embryonic national epic *SK*—Madhusudan's reading of Vergil was implicated in his reading of Homer.

inevitably entail a 'translation of cultures' too. However, it is possible to translate a text with more or less attention to the details of the original, and in this sense the *HB* represents a very loose 'version' of the *Iliad* rather than a translation as such.

[13] See Richardson (1993) *ad loc.* for the climactic nature of Hector's words here.

[14] The Homeric book divisions sometimes even fall mid-paragraph in the *HB*: *HB* 3, 19 (Chapter 3, paragraph 19), for example, corresponds to *Il.* 5.907–6.4. This feature perhaps suggests that Madhusudan was alive to the occasional arbitrariness of the Homeric book divisions (see Taplin (1992)). Indeed he may have gleaned this insight from the *scholia* printed in the editions of Heyne (1821) or Dindorf (1856). For the editions of Homer's *Iliad* available to Madhusudan see Chapter 1 above and Appendix 2 below. It is clear from various *scholia* on the Homeric epics that the book divisions are an Alexandrian rather than original convention. Throughout this chapter, as in Chapter 3 above, all line references to and citations from the original Greek text are based on the recent edition of M. West (1998) and (2000) (two volumes).

[15] The classic study of the Homeric aspects of Vergil's *Aeneid* is Knauer (1964) but, for Vergil's reception of the *Iliad* in particular, see also Gransden (1984).

The very number of Bengali chapters in the *HB* may reflect a similarly Vergilian reading of the *Iliad*.

The *HB* is an abridgement of the *Iliad* and much of what is excised comprises lengthy battle narratives.[16] This is perhaps unsurprising in light of Madhusudan's comment on the *MBK*: 'Homer is nothing but battles. I have, like Milton, only one'.[17]

The implicit comments on the *Iliad* made by Madhusudan in the *HB* fall into three main categories: the explanatory, the moralizing, and the comparative. In the *HB* there are a number of interpolations, passages not present in the Greek original, designed essentially to set the scene for the Bengali reader. Indeed the very opening of the *Iliad*, the Muse-invocation at *Il.* 1.1ff., is excised in the *HB* and replaced[18] by a lengthy prose preface (*upakramaṇikā*) in which the backstory to the Homeric poem, as Madhusudan imagined it, is related in detail (see Appendix 8 for my translation of this preface). Madhusudan's preface assumes in its Bengali readership a near absolute ignorance of the ancient Greek world and adopts a rather patronizing tone (Preface, Section 2):

> There is a small region in the west of the Asian continent called Asia Minor. Once upon a time, there was a very famous city in this region called 'Ilium' or 'Troy'. The king of the city was called Priam

One might compare the patronizing tone of Madhusudan's preface with, for example, that of Kingsley's *The Heroes* (1855), one of the mythological digests written for children in the mid nineteenth century (Story 1, Part 1):

[16] Battle narrative excised: *Il.* 5.144–65 (cf. *HB* 3, 4), *Il.* 5.517–89 (*HB* 3, 14), *Il.* 5.609–710 (*HB* 3, 15), *Il.* 6. 414–30 (*HB* 3, 23), and *Il.* 8.253–349 (*HB* 4, 9). Battle narrative compressed: *Il.* 5.38–85 (*HB* 3, 3) and *Il.* 12.329–470 (*HB* 6, 11). Other passages excised by Madhusudan include, most notably, catalogues and all four of the Muse invocations of *Il.* 1–12 (*Il.*1.1–7; 2.484-93, 761f.; 11.218–20). Madhusudan thus eliminates a major complexity of Homeric narration. Our first acquaintance with the Homeric narrator, as de Jong (2004) 13 observes, is 'deceptive': he 'steps forward openly', suggesting an 'overt narrator' but after the proem he 'largely withdraws into the background'. See also de Jong (1987) 41–53 and Richardson (1990). Madhusudan's excision of catalogues and invocations to the Muses is perhaps especially curious given that in his earlier works, especially the *Tilottamā-sambhab kābya* (1860) and the *MBK* (1861), Madhusudan was celebrated for his mastery of the catalogue; and that he also adapted Western Muse invocations in these works.

[17] Murshid (2004) 171.

[18] I say 'replaced' since the preface ends mid-sentence ('. . . whereupon . . .') and with punctuation suggesting that *Il.* 1.12ff. follow on from it syntactically.

> Once upon a time there were two princes who were twins. Their names were Acrisius and Proetus, and they lived in the pleasant vale of Argos, far away in Hellas.[19]

Madhusudan's target readership, Bengalis ignorant not only of ancient Greek but also of English,[20] are addressed by the author rather as children might be addressed by an adult. Madhusudan's voice here may be contrasted with the tone he adopted in *The Anglo-Saxon and the Hindu* (1854) where he addressed a British audience, the 'masculine' colonial master (figured as Aeneas), speaking on behalf of Britain's 'feminine' Hindu subjects (figured as Dido). In *The Anglo-Saxon and the Hindu* Madhusudan speaks 'up' to a British audience (assumed to be well-versed in the classics); in the *HB* he speaks 'down' to a Bengali readership (assumed to be entirely ignorant of Western culture). In each case, Madhusudan represents one community to the other and, in each case, it is knowledge of the Graeco-Roman classics that marks Madhusudan out most clearly as a Westernized Indian speaker. The contrast in tone between these two works speaks to the ambiguous status of Westernized Bengalis like Madhusudan who occupied a 'third space' between Western and Indian communities, regarding themselves 'as mediators between [the two] . . . cajoling both towards correct conduct',[21] while of course not being a true member of either.

In his preface to the *HB*, Madhusudan separates the backstory of the *Iliad* into three strands and he narrates them in three discrete sections: Helen's marriage to Menelaus (Section 1); the birth of Paris and his love for Oenone (Section 2); and the Judgement of Paris, as a

[19] For a study of popular children's literature on classical mythology and its role in promoting knowledge of the classical world in Victorian Britain (especially the works of Kingsley and Bulfinch), see Feldman (1972) esp. 555ff.

[20] In his letter to Bhudeb Mukherjee, the dedicatee of the *HB*, Madhusudan explained his reason for composing it: 'the thought came to me to write a chronicle of this unprecedented poem [the *Iliad*] in order to bring it to the knowledge of those of our countrymen who do not know the language of England'. (My translation from Bengali and see Bandyopadhyay (1945–51) [Introduction] 1.) Note that from the early nineteenth century, the English-speaking Bengali could easily pick up a copy of Pope's *Iliad* even from 'the native bazaars of Calcutta', as noted by Richardson (1840) 1542. It is ironic, if Madhusudan's aim in composing the *HB* really was to bring Homer's *Iliad* to a readership of Bengalis ignorant of English, that its prose style was condemned even by Madhusudan's earliest biographer as unintelligible to Bengali readers ignorant of Western languages, and barely intelligible even to Western-educated Bengali readers: see Basu (1893) 470.

[21] Bayly (1996) 180.

consequence of Strife's umbrage at not being invited to the wedding of Peleus and Thetis (Section 3). This threefold backstory is itself rather distinctive. Helen's marriage to Menelaus is described in Section 1 as a *svayaṃvara*, or 'own-choice' marriage, the same nuptial rite undergone by the 'Indian Helen' Padmābatī in Madhusudan's *Padmābatī nāṭak* (1860). The Judgement of Paris, which was the model for Madhusudan's 'Judgement of Indranīl' in the *Padmābatī nāṭak*, is related in full in Section 3, although in the *Iliad* it was only alluded to once and even then rather obliquely (see Section 1 of Chapter 2). The preface to the *HB* thus serves, among other things, as a retrospective commentary on Madhusudan's earlier receptions of Graeco-Roman literature. In this connection, Madhusudan's emphasis on the story of Oenone, the focus of Section 2 of the Preface, is particularly striking. The story of Paris's first marriage to the nymph Oenone is rather obscure, and it may be relevant that Ovid's *Heroides*, which Madhusudan used as a model for his *BK* (1862), is one of our main sources for it.[22] Not only is Madhusudan looking back to his earlier Bengali works in the preface to the *HB*, he also seems to be reading Homer's *Iliad* through the lens of Ovid's *Heroides*.

In a programmatic passage spanning the first six paragraphs of *HB* 1 (roughly equating to *Il.* 1.12–100) Madhusudan interpolates a number of his own authorial comments, serving further to set the scene for the Bengali reader. At *HB* 1, 6, for example, Madhusudan inserts four lengthy Bengali sentences in order to unpack *Il.* 1.94f. In the Greek original (*Il.* 1.94f.), Calchas briefly asserts that the Achaeans are suffering because Agamemnon has dishonoured the priest Chryses. The Bengali Calchas, by contrast, narrates in careful detail how Agamemnon came to dishonour Chryses and his daughter (*HB* 1, 6). While Madhusudan offers such explanatory glosses throughout the *HB*,[23] they are most apparent in the first few paragraphs of *HB* 1 and may be seen as an extension of the scene-setting function of the preface.

[22] See also Knox (1995) 140. Note that Tennyson's 'Oenone' (1832, 1842 (two versions)) might of course represent a contemporary source of inspiration.

[23] *HB* 1, 6 goes on to unpack *Il.* 1.96f. (Calchas states that Apollo will continue to give the Greeks woe) with a lengthy and rather rhetorical account of precisely how Apollo will do this. At *HB* 1, 7, Madhusudan inserts into Agamemnon's mouth a reflection on the nature of kingship (as it were between *Il.* 1.117 and 118). Similarly, for example, *Il.* 1.530f. is unpacked at *HB* 1, 25; and *Il.* 10.8 at *HB* 5, 9.

In addition to such explanatory glosses, Madhusudan also interjects, from time to time, authorial comments of a more moralizing nature. One of the most striking examples is a comment placed in the mouth of Athena at *HB* 1, 12 (a comment replacing *Il.* 1.198–200). The Greek passage replaced by Madhusudan's gloss comes immediately after the goddess seizes the hero's blond hair in the assembly, a famous passage of *Il.* 1, and has the primary narrator relating that Athena appeared to Achilles alone and that the hero was seized with wonder. The *HB* instead has Athena address Achilles in direct speech: *re barbar! tui e ki karitechis?* 'O barbarian! What is this that you are doing?' Madhusudan has Athena call Achilles a *barbar*, a Bengali word derived from the Sanskrit *barbara* (used in the Sanskrit epics to refer to the 'non-Aryans, barbarians'),[24] which in turn is either cognate with or came directly from the Greek *barbaros*.[25] Indeed Madhusudan might have used the Sanskritic synonym *mleccha* for 'barbarian': his choice of *barbar* is deliberate. This interpolation leaps off the page: Madhusudan's Athena describes Achilles, the 'best of the Achaeans',[26] using a word recalling the Greek *barbaros*, a derogatory term used by Greeks to describe non-Greeks (though note that the derogatory sense of the word is post-Homeric).[27] By the fifth century BCE, the word *barbaros* had become central to a discourse regarding Hellenic ethnicity and was used to designate the non-Greek 'Other'.[28] Madhusudan's use of this ethnically derogatory term to describe the archetypal and greatest Greek hero underscores the ambiguity of Homeric heroism (at once noble and savage), and indeed the hypocrisy inherent in classical Greek ideas of ethnicity. More to the point, given the colonial context in which the *HB* was composed, Madhusudan's description of the greatest hero of the

[24] See Monier-Williams (1872) *ad loc.*

[25] In any case, the similarity of the Greek and Sanskritic words can hardly have been lost on the polyglot Bengali poet. The antiquity of the word's usage in Sanskrit texts raises questions about its Indian pedigree: *barbara* may be an Indo-European cognate with the Greek *barbaros*, or a direct borrowing from the Greek. Dating the Sanskrit epics (where the word first occurs) is difficult but, given that the Sanskrit epics reached their final form no earlier than the beginning of the Common Era, it is possible, if not likely, that the word *barbara* entered the Sanskrit lexicon after contact with the Greeks led to India by Alexander in the fourth century BCE.

[26] See Nagy (1979) for this complex Iliadic theme.

[27] See Hall (1989) 11f., esp. n. 37.

[28] See Hall (1989) esp. 1ff. For the special role of Attic tragedy in forming the new 'vocabulary' of the barbarian discourse, see ibid. 101ff.

greatest European epic[29] as a 'barbarian' also has implications for the legitimacy of contemporary European claims to cultural and racial superiority.[30]

Interpolations like these, offering moral or ethical glosses rather than straightforward explanatory information, occur throughout the *HB*. But perhaps the most striking example of all occurs at *HB* 3, 20: Madhusudan's narration of Menelaus' slaying of Adrestus (cf. *Il.* 6.37–65). Menelaus is poised to slay Adrestus, when the latter begs for his life. The Greek hero relents and decides to spare him. Hereupon, Agamemnon arrives to tell his brother not to take pity on the enemy, but to despatch him without mercy. The Homeric narrator approves the advice (ll. 62f.): 'so spoke the hero and turned his brother's mind, for his advice was justified'.[31] Madhusudan disagrees with this matter of fact assertion and, instead of rendering the Greek original, he interpolates his own comment, couched in markedly Indian terms (*HB* 3, 20): *sahodarer ei byaṅgo rūp nidāghe bīrbar mānilyuser hṛtsarobarastho karuṇārūp mukulito kamal śuṣko hailo*, 'Under the heat of this mockery from his brother, the lotus of compassion that had blossomed on the lake of the heart of Menelaus, the excellent warrior, dried up'. Homer simply notes sound advice; Madhusudan laments a war crime. Since the *Iliad* is a cornerstone text of European high culture, and given the custom persisting into the nineteenth century of seeking political and moral guidance from texts like Homer's *Iliad*,[32] it is significant that this Bengali 'version' should take issue with such points of Homeric morality.

Madhusudan's technique of encoding explanatory and moralizing glosses into his Bengali rendering of the *Iliad* finds an analogue in

[29] Note Madhusudan's description, in his letter to Bhudeb Mukherjee (the dedicatee of the *HB*), of Homer's *Iliad* as the greatest epic: see Bandyopadhyay (1945–51) [Introduction] 1.

[30] As Radice (1998) notes, though one must be prepared to read between the lines of Madhusudan's work to detect his 'xenophobia' and 'nationalism', these qualities are certainly present. Note further that the emergent concepts of racial theory in the nineteenth century were bound up, to some extent, with notions of the intellectual and physical purity of the ancient Greeks (see esp. Challis (2010) 94–120).

[31] The Greek *aisima* (*Iliad* 6.62), translated 'justified' here, refers to what is 'apportioned' or 'destined'. Thus it implies not a moral judgement but an invocation of regular heroic attitudes; see Kirk (1990) 161.

[32] The classic, and most high profile, example of Iliadic consultation in political and moral issues is that of Gladstone, who propounded Homer's moral and political uses in addition to his aesthetic qualities: see esp. Bebbington (2004) 149ff.; Turner (1981) esp. 234f.

various translations and versions of the Homeric poem. However, we may perhaps be reminded especially of Pope's *Iliad*.[33] As one recent critic of Pope's *Iliad* has noted:

> [Pope] negotiates the details he thinks may bore us rapidly, and sets others he would not wish us to miss in what he called 'the strongest point of light'.[34]

Pope's fidelity to Homer 'in the large rather than the small',[35] his encoding of an implicit commentary in the fabric of his 'translation', is precisely what we find in Madhusudan's *HB*.

Indeed, in the striking case of *HB* 3, 20 noted above—Madhusudan's disagreement with Homer over the soundness of Agamemnon's advice to Menelaus at *Il.* 6.62f.—we find a striking precedent in Pope's *Iliad*. While Homer states simply that Adrestos persuaded (*epeithe*, 'persuaded': *Il.* 6.51) Menelaus to spare him (before Agamemnon later persuaded him otherwise), Pope adds an explicit reference to Menelaus' compassion (ll. 63ff.): 'compassion touch'd the hero's heart/ He stood, suspended with the lifted dart'. If Pope brings Menelaus' compassion explicitly into the scene (it is left implicit at *Il.* 6.51), then Madhusudan takes the idea a step further by having Menelaus' compassion desiccated by Agamemnon at *HB* 3, 20 (see above), and by adding the markedly Indian metaphors of the 'lake of the heart' and the 'lotus of compassion'. Madhusudan leads his Bengali reader to Homer through Pope, adding the Indian stamp of the lotus metaphor.

Aside from such explanatory and moralizing glosses, which may to some extent have been inspired by Pope's technique in 'translating' Homer, the *HB* represents above all an Orientalist and 'syncretistic'[36] commentary on Homer's *Iliad*. Throughout the *HB*, Madhusudan

[33] It is worth recalling here the comment made in 1840 by Richardson, Madhusudan's teacher at Hindu College, that 'Pope's translation is already in almost every hand and is easily and cheaply procurable in the native bazaars of Calcutta': see Richardson (1840) 1542, and above Chapter 1, Section 2.

[34] Rosslyn (1985) xii. See also Mason (1972) and C. Williams (1993).

[35] Rosslyn (1985) xii.

[36] By 'syncretism' I refer to that practice which goes beyond the identification of similarities between different cultures and attempts to reconcile disparate or even mutually contradictory cultural practices and ideas: the identification of Roman deities with Greek counterparts (Minerva with Athena, Mars with Ares), despite their obvious differences (historical, iconographic, functional), is an example. For a good introduction to the long history of religious syncretism, and for a further bibliography on the subject, see Leopold (2004).

glosses Greek cultural and religious terms, including the names of gods, with Hindu 'equivalents'. Thus Homeric sacrifices become acts of Hindu *pūjā* or 'worship' (with the narrations of sacrifice themselves elided).[37] Rituals are divided into *nitya* and *naimittika* types (the Hindu distinction between 'habitual' and 'occasional').[38] Offences against a godhead are referred to as *adharma* or 'irreligion', or 'heresy' (implying a sense of orthodoxy alien to the orthopraxy of Homeric religion).[39] The sea is described as a purifying *mahātīrtha* or 'sacred ford' (which evokes a particular discourse regarding Hindu pilgrimage and the sanctity of certain bodies of water).[40] All such terms, going beyond a literal translation of the Homeric original, imply distinctively Hindu ideas which, though they may be comparable with Greek notions, are hardly identical to them. Thus the Greek and Trojan heroes of Madhusudan's *HB* are made to practise a kind of Homeric Hinduism. At the same time the Bengali reader is alerted to the close, if not perfect, comparability of Hindu and Homeric religious practices.

Madhusudan's glossing of Homeric religious practices with such Hindu vocabulary might seem to be just the kind of 'cultural translation' inevitable in any rendering of a text from one language to another.[41] However, the syncretism underpinning his treatment of the Homeric pantheon is unequivocal and deliberate.[42] For example,

[37] For references to Homeric worship as acts of *pūjā*, see esp. *HB* 1, 22; 1, 23; 4, 9; 5, 4. The notion of *pūjā* as a term within the broader discourses of Hindu theology is examined by Flood (2003) 6f.

[38] For example, Chryses' roofing of shrines and burning of sacrificial thigh pieces, mentioned at *Il.* 1.39ff., becomes *nitya naimittika sebā*, 'acts of habitual and occasional worship' (*HB* 1, 3): presumably the thigh-burning is a 'habitual' ritual, something done on a regular basis regardless of circumstances, whereas the roof-building is 'occasional' or 'caused' by the particular circumstances in which Chryses finds himself.

[39] See especially *HB* 2, 16 (≈ *Il.* 3.365ff.); also *HB* 2, 26; 3, 12. For the Hindu notion of *dharma* ('religious or moral law'), and its antonym *adharma*, see esp. Rocher (2003) 102–4.

[40] See esp. *HB* 1, 16 (≈ *Il.* 1.314ff.). For the history of the *(mahā)tīrthayātrā*, or 'pilgrimage to the (great) fords', see esp. Brockington (2003) 118. For a thoroughgoing treatment of Greek notions of purity and pollution, which are to some extent analogous to notions found in Hinduism, see esp. Parker (1983).

[41] For 'cultural translation' as an inevitable corollary of linguistic translation, see esp. Hardwick (2005).

[42] Radice (1987) 213 notes Madhusudan's description of Zeus as Mahādeva (a name of the god Śiva) in the *HB*, but he does not consider the wider syncretistic pattern underlying Madhusudan's treatment of the gods in the *HB*.

Madhusudan could render the Greek Apollo into Bengali by simply transliterating his name (this is his method for the names of human characters) but, instead, he chooses to call him by the various names of Sūrya,[43] the Hindu god of the sun: 'Ravideva' ('God Ravi'),[44] 'Bhāskara Deva' ('Illuminating God'),[45] 'Marīcimālī Ravideva' ('Sun-Garlanded God Ravi'),[46] and so on. Nowhere is Apollo's name simply transliterated; instead the Hindu sun god plays Apollo's part, as it were, throughout the *HB*.[47]

Most of the other Homeric deities are treated similarly in the *HB*, their names being replaced either all or most of the time by those of Hindu deities. For example, the Greek god, Hephaistus, is replaced in every case by the Hindu Viśvakarmā,[48] the 'heavenly architect'.[49] Hades is similarly replaced in every case by Yama (sometimes also known as Kṛtānta, Śamana, or Kāla),[50] the Hindu god of death.[51] And when Greeks and Trojans die in the *HB*, they are sent to the abode not of Hades but of this Hindu deity.[52] Other Greek deities replaced in this way by Hindu 'equivalents' include: Eos replaced by Uṣādebī, a

[43] Ravideva, or Sūrya as he is more usually known, is an ancient Hindu god. For his Vedic antiquity, see Witzel (2003) 72f. He remained an important god, being one of the five gods worshipped in the *Bhāgavatas* (for which See Colas (2003) 239), an important literary source for some of Madhusudan's other works.

[44] See *HB* 1, 7; 1, 8; 1, 16; 2, 13; 2, 28; 3, 12; 4, 3; and 4, 5.

[45] See *HB* 1, 1.

[46] See *HB* 1, 3.

[47] Note that the idea underlying Madhusudan's identification of Apollo with Sūrya—that Apollo is essentially a 'sun god'—was widely held until the late nineteenth century but is now discredited. See, for example, Müller (1859) (vol. 2) 83 (article first published 1856) and Roscher (1884–1890) 422. For the discrediting of the idea of Apollo as a 'sun god', and that the Greek deities stand for different forces of nature, see Guthrie (1949) 74.

[48] Cf. *HB* 1, 26; 3, 2; 3, 3; and 4, 8.

[49] Again note that the choice of this Hindu god reflects a distinctive evaluation of Hephaistus' divine role, one that emphasizes his status as a 'smithy god', but which elides his association with fire: note that his name is used metonymically for 'fire', for example, at *Il.* 2.426 (See Cancik (2005) 140ff.). Given his association with fire the *HB* might instead have represented him as the Vedic god Agni.

[50] For the godhead Yama, a deity especially important in Sanskrit epic, see Brockington (2003) 118.

[51] Yama at *HB* 2, 17; 3, 3; 3, 7; 3, 20 (twice); 5, 4; and 6, 5. Kṛtānta at *HB* 4, 5; 5, 2; 5, 7; and 6, 6. Śamana at *HB* 2, 5; 3, 6; 5, 14; and 6, 4; and Kāla at *HB* 3, 2; 3, 20; 3, 23 (twice); and 5, 14.

[52] For examples of heroes entering, or being sent to, the 'house of Yama', see *HB* 2, 5; 2, 17; 3, 2. 3, 3; 3, 6; 3, 7; 3, 20 (twice); 5, 4; 5, 14; 6, 4 (twice).

Vedic goddess of dawn;[53] Eos' consort, Tithonos, by Aruṇa,[54] Hindu mythology's 'charioteer of the sun';[55] and Gaia ('Earth') by Vasumatī,[56] Hindu goddess of the earth. Poseidon, referred to just twice in the *HB*, appears as Varuṇa, Hindu lord of the waters;[57] and even the minor god, Paean, makes his single appearance in the *HB* as Dhanvantarī,[58] the divine physician of Hindu mythology.

In addition to these cases of the wholesale replacement of a Greek with a Hindu deity, there are other more complex instances of theological syncretism. For example, Ares and Athena are occasionally referred to by their Greek names, but more usually by names of 'equivalent' Hindu deities: thus Athena is also *vidyādebī*,[59] 'goddess of wisdom', one of the names of the Hindu goddess Sarasvatī;[60] and Ares is also referred to as Skanda or Devasenānī ('leader of the army of the gods'),[61] alternative appellations of the Hindu war god Kārtikeya.

However, the most complex examples of theological syncretism in the *HB* concern Madhusudan's treatment of Zeus and his wife Hera, the king and queen of the gods. In some cases, these deities are referred to by their Greek names transliterated into Bengali: *jyus* (the closest Bengali can get to 'Zeus');[62] and *hīrī* (the Bengali long vowel [i:]in the latter reflects, one suspects, the Victorian British pronunciation of the Greek letter *eta*, which, these days, British

[53] See *HB* 1, 28; 4, 2; 4, 12; and 6, 1. For Ūṣa's special place in the Vedic pantheon, see Witzel (2003) 72.

[54] See *HB* 6, 1.

[55] For a typical image (from a Shaiva Temple in Varanasi) showing Aruṇa as driver of Sūrya's chariot, see Nagar (1995) 3.

[56] See *HB* 2, 10; 2, 29; 3, 23 (twice); and 4, 2. For the Vedic origins of Vasumatī as a Hindu goddess, see Witzel (2003) 72–3.

[57] See *HB* 4, 8 (twice).

[58] See *HB* 3, 18.

[59] See *HB* 1, 11; 1, 12; 1, 35; and 6, 1.

[60] For Sarasvatī as patron goddess of the sciences (*vidyā*) and arts, and her place within the divine hierarchy, see Michaels (2004) 223. Note that this reading of Athena as a 'goddess of wisdom' is not especially consonant with the depiction of the goddess within the *Iliad* but agrees with one of Athena's extra-Homeric roles, and with the allegorical interpretations of the *Iliad* by the Hellenistic critics (who took Athena to stand, allegorically, for 'wisdom'; Hera for 'air'; Hephaistus for 'fire'; and so on). See Kairns (2004) 71.

[61] For Ares as 'Skanda', see *HB* 2, 4; 2, 5; 2, 8; 2, 16; 2, 21; 2, 23; 2, 25; 2, 27; 3, 7; 3, 14; 3, 20; 4, 9; 5, 10; 6, 5; 6, 8; as 'Devasenānī' (or similar), see *HB* 2, 27; 3, 10; 3, 11; 3, 12 (twice); 3, 14 (twice); 3, 15; 3, 16 (thrice); and 3, 19.

[62] See: *HB* 1, 21; 1, 24; 4, 2; and 5, 3.

classicists tend to pronounce as the long vowel [e:]).[63] However, elsewhere in the *HB*, Zeus is aligned with not just one Hindu god but with three. When, at various points, Zeus' role regarding fate and creation is emphasized, the Greek god is referred to by one of the names of Brahmā,[64] the Hindu god of creation. At other points, when Zeus is depicted in his role as king of the gods, he is referred to as Indra,[65] the name of the king of the Hindu gods. By extension Hera is sometimes referred to as Indrāṇī,[66] one of the names of Śacī, the wife of Indra. When Zeus is behaving destructively (see esp. *HB* 4, 11), or is pictured sitting on top of Mount Olympus (see esp. *HB* 1, 24), he is referred to as Mahādeva, one of the names of Śiva, the mountain-dwelling Hindu god of destruction.[67] Similarly, when Hera becomes angry, she is referred to in terms connoting the wrathful Hindu goddess Durgā,[68] Śiva's consort.[69]

This complex example of theological syncretism, whereby Zeus and Hera are identified with multiple Hindu deities, turns on the historically layered complexity of Hindu theology. According to an early tradition, as evidenced most famously in the Sanskrit epics, the king of the Hindu gods is considered to be Indra (who in the Vedic religion, an even earlier stage of the Hindu tradition, had just been a powerful warrior god).[70] But, as the Hindu tradition developed, the

[63] See, for example: *HB* 1, 25 (twice); 1, 32; 2, 24; 2, 25. For a study of classical education in Victorian Britain, plus further bibliography, see Stray (1998).

[64] See: *HB* 1, 14; 1, 21 (twice); 1, 31; 2, 2–3; and 4, 9.

[65] See: *HB* 1, 5; 1, 12; 1, 24; 1, 25 (thrice); 1, 26; 1, 27 (thrice); 1, 31; 1, 34; 2, 13; 2, 16; 2, 24 (thrice); 2, 25; 3, 3; 3, 12; 3, 18 (thrice); 3, 21 (twice); 4, 5; 4, 7; 4, 9 (twice); 4, 10; 4, 11; 5, 2; 5, 9; 5, 10; 5, 11; 6, 1; 6, 4; 6, 10; and 6, 11.

[66] See *HB* 1, 11; 1, 26; 1, 27; 2, 22; 2, 24 (twice); 2, 25 (twice); 3, 15; 3, 16; and 6, 1.

[67] This particular resonance, between Zeus and Śiva in the *HB*, is noted by Radice (1987) 213.

[68] As Michaels (2004) 223 notes, when Śiva's wife appears as Durgā, rather than in her more benevolent aspects (such as Pārvatī, Gaurī, or Umā), she is a wild and dangerous goddess.

[69] As when, for example at *HB* 1, 27, Hera is described with the epithet *ugracaṇḍā*, a description connotative specifically of Durgā. See *Samsad Bengali-English Dictionary* (Third Edition, Sixth Imprint: 2003) 144: 'ugra-caṇḍā, *n. fem.* an appellation of Goddess Durgā when conceived as the goddess of wrath'. Note also that Durgā is often represented as 'not very close' to her consort Śiva, and as a goddess independent of her husband's will: see Michaels (2004) 223. Durgā's attitude towards Śiva is thus very similar to Hera's towards Zeus in the *Iliad*: see esp. Griffin (1980) 66.

[70] Indra is the warrior god of the Vedic pantheon (i.e. at the earliest stage of attested 'Hindu' religion), associated with storms and thunder (Michaels (2004) 202–5). In the later 'Puranic' stage of Hinduism, and especially in the Sanskrit epic

god Indra was eclipsed by three gods (considered to be the 'three embodiments', or the *trimūrti*, of the same transcendant and supreme godhead): Brahmā, the creator of the universe; Viṣṇu, the maintainer; and Śiva, the destroyer.[71] Thus Zeus is Śiva when he behaves like that Hindu god; he is Brahmā when his role as creator and settler of fate is invoked; and he is Indra when his anthropomorphic role as 'king' of the gods is emphasized.

Indeed, perhaps the most revealing exegetical comment implied by Madhusudan's subtle characterization of Zeus in the *HB* is the very fact that he is nowhere referred to in terms connoting Viṣṇu, the second of the three gods of the *trimūrti*, the 'sustainer' of the universe. The Iliadic Zeus controls fate (like Brahmā) and destroys men (like Śiva), but he rarely displays the gentle benevolence associated with Viṣṇu.[72] Furthermore, Zeus' connections with Śiva, the Hindu god of destruction, are especially marked in the *HB*. At one point, when Zeus upbraids his wife (*HB* 1, 26; compare *Il.* 1.545f.), he is even imagined in terms recalling Śiva's role in the esoteric rites of Tantra: *āmār maner kathā tomāke ki karaṇe khuliẏā balibo? āmār rahasyamaṇḍale tumi keno prabeś karite cāho?* 'Why should I tell you openly what is in my mind? Why do you wish to enter my secret-circle?' This 'secret-circle' (Sanskrit *rahasyamaṇḍala*) alludes to the secret 'energy grids' of Tantra,[73] a cultic phenomenon closely associated with Shaivism (the branch of Hinduism which venerates the god Śiva above all

Mahābhārata, Indra is represented as king of the gods and is still remarkable for his valour. However, his importance seems to be declining in the Sanskrit epic (see Gonda (1962) and Gajendragadkar (1946)), and his kingship over the gods seems really to be a kind of guardianship of the universe (see Michaels (2004) 213), rather than a transcendent power. In later stages of Hindu belief, Indra's status is increasingly sidelined.

[71] See Matchett (2003) 139 and Michaels (2004) 205. This notion of the *trimūrti* has not yet crystallized in the Sanskrit epic *Mahābhārata* but is strongly foreshadowed there, and is certainly connected with the decline of Indra's pre-eminence in later layers of the poem: see Brockington (2003) 118f.

[72] As is noted by Kairns (2004) 67, Zeus says at *Il.* 20.21 of mankind in general: 'I care for them, mortal though they are'. And yet so often, though the most powerful of the gods, he is unable to save even his favourites (Sarpedon, Hector) from gruesome deaths. Inasmuch as Zeus is the god who determines Fate, and since his 'thought is identical with future happenings' (Lloyd-Jones (1983) 5), he is indeed ultimately responsible for all the terrible destruction related in the *Iliad*. To this extent he is certainly more comparable to Śiva and Brahmā than Viṣṇu.

[73] For a treatment of Tantra, and of the term *maṇḍala* as a key term within this tradition, see White (2000) 9–14.

others).[74] Thus Zeus is not only named as the Hindu god of destruction, but he even speaks in the esoteric accents reminiscent of that Hindu deity.

It almost goes without saying that Madhusudan's syncretistic identification of Homeric gods with Hindu counterparts in the *HB* invokes the discourse of Indo-European comparative mythology.[75] Indeed, around the time of the composition of the *HB* (1867/8) popular interest in Indo-European comparative mythology was being rekindled in Britain thanks largely to the scholarship of the dynamic Friedrich Max Müller.[76] His collected essays, *Chips from a German Workshop* (1867), were published some eighty years after Sir William Jones' revolutionary suggestion of the kinship between the ancient languages and mythologies of Europe and India.[77] In one essay Müller debunks (with the greatest tact) some of the wilder connections made by Jones in his 1788 article ('*On the* GODS *of* GREECE, ITALY, *and* INDIA'), and suggests alternative (and more scientifically plausible) connections between the cognate traditions.

However, the syncretistic method underlying Madhusudan's *HB* is inspired not by Müller's contemporary scholarship but by the original work of 'Oriental Jones' himself. In fact, the very article (Jones (1788) which was challenged by Müller in one of his collected essays (1867), seems to have been the inspiration for Madhusudan's system of Indo-European correspondences in the *HB*.[78] The most distinctive point of overlap between Jones (1788) and Madhusudan's *HB* lies in the

[74] But Tantra is also a Buddhist phenomenon; see White (2000) esp. Chs. 2, 6, and 30. For a brief overview of Shaivism, and of Tantra's place within it, see Flood (2003) 219ff.

[75] This field of intellectual inquiry was inaugurated by the early British Orientalists, particularly Sir William Jones. The fields of Indo-European comparative philology and mythology are still very much alive: recent works of Indo-European comparative mythology include Watkins (1995) and West (2007).

[76] See Stone (2002) xiii.

[77] For an overview of the importance of the work of Sir William Jones, see esp. Cannon (1964).

[78] Madhusudan was evidently interested in contemporary European Indology: his Sonnet 83, composed in the early 1860s while he was in Europe, is entitled 'Pundit Theodore Goldstucker' (1821-1872) and is a celebration of the Professor of Sanskrit at University College London whom Madhusudan met whilst studying in the city. Therefore the Bengali author's reversion to late-eighteenth-century 'Orientalist' ideas, instead of engaging with contemporary Western Indo-Europeanism, seems to be a conscious choice rather than implying his ignorance of contemporary European Indology.

association of Zeus with multiple Hindu deities: like Madhusudan, Jones associates Zeus with more than one Hindu god, namely Brahmā, Śiva, Indra, and Viṣṇu;[79] and, like Madhusudan, Jones suggests points of similarity not only between Hera and Śacī (Indra's consort) but also between Hera and Durgā (Śiva's consort).[80] Müller (1867), by contrast, undermines some of these comparisons: the Greek Zeus, for example, is said to be cognate not with the Sanskrit Śiva (*contra* Jones (1788) 248), but with the Vedic Dyaus Pitṛ (see also Latin Diespiter).[81] As my Appendix 9 makes clear, all of the Indo-European correspondences between Graeco-Roman and Hindu deities underpinning the *HB* (Apollo as Sūrya, Ares as Skanda, and so on) recall the intuitive, and rather unscientific, connections made by Jones (1788).

Madhusudan's interest in the early British Orientalists may have been out of step with contemporary British culture, where Müller's new theories were attracting public attention, but it was by no means idiosyncratic in the context of mid-nineteenth-century Calcutta. As Rosinka Chaudhuri has observed, the early Orientalist scholars, like Jones and Colebrooke, enjoyed an almost 'mythical' status among mid-nineteenth-century Bengalis.[82] This earlier generation of British colonial administrators had shown a profound and flattering interest in Indian culture that contrasted starkly with the increasingly indifferent attitude of the contemporary British administration. In some of his early poems and plays, Madhusudan mentions by name certain works of British Orientalist scholarship, including one work by Jones himself.[83] By the time he composed the *HB*, Madhusudan may have dropped the Orientalist convention of writing scholarly footnotes to his own literary works, but he had not ceased to engage with Orientalist scholarship. For Madhusudan, the historical identity of the gods

[79] See Jones (1788) 242 (Zeus as Brahmā); 248 (Zeus as Śiva); 241 (Zeus as Indra).

[80] Jones (1788) 241 (Hera as Śacī); 252 (Hera as Durgā).

[81] See Stone (2002).

[82] R. Chaudhuri (2002) 149.

[83] For example, in Madhusudan's scholarly footnotes to his own English poem, *The Captive Ladie* (1849), he cites: 'Sir W Jones' preface to "Sacontola" and Wilson's Hindu Theatre' (note 'h' *ad* Canto 1); and 'Wilson, As. Res. [*Asiatick Researches*] xvii, 609' (note 'r'). In his notes on Canto 2, he observes that '[like] Neptune Sheva wears a trident called in Sanskrit Trisulum' (note 'i'), an observation made in Jones (1788), which Jones published in the first volume of his journal *Asiatick Researches*. For the inclusion of scholarly footnotes in works of poetry as an 'Orientalist convention', and one taken up by mid-nineteenth-century Bengali poets, see R. Chaudhuri (2002).

of ancient Greece and Rome with the deities still worshipped by contemporary Hindus was perhaps not so much a trope borrowed consciously from Jones' scholarship as an ingrained and unconscious mentality, but the genesis of this mentality clearly lies in Jones' work rather than more recent varieties of Indo-European comparative scholarship.

Finally, it is to be noted that there may be a racial aspect to Madhusudan's intense and sustained interest throughout his oeuvre in the Indo-European discourse, especially in light of the links between Orientalism and the rise of racial science in the mid nineteenth century. This issue is an especially complex one and must be teased out with subtlety. Discussion of this aspect of the Bengali poet's Orientalist interest is therefore deferred to the concluding chapter, where it may be set in the context of other broader modes of interpreting Madhusudan's classical appropriations.

2. HOMERIC CONTROVERSIES: TRANSLATION AND RELIGION

While Madhusudan explicitly compares the Hindu epic tradition with Homer's *Iliad* in his preface to the *HB*, he is quite clear as to his estimation of their relative value. In his letter to Bhudeb Mukherjee, the dedicatee of the *HB*, Madhusudan asserts:

> It is known to everyone that, among the composers of *mahākāvya* ('epic'), the composer of the *Ilias* is pre-eminent. Our *Rāmāyaṇa* and *Mahābhārata* are only *jīvana-carita* ('[linear] biographies') of Blessed Rāma and the five Pāṇḍavas.[84]

Here the Bengali author expresses a view that would have been quite uncontroversial in mid-Victorian Britain: the status of Homer as the greatest epic poet had endured in the West since earliest antiquity,[85] and his towering importance for various cultural debates can hardly be overstated.[86] Indeed, the genius of Homeric form (an idea implicit

[84] Bandyopahyay (1945–51) [Introduction] 3. My translation from Bengali.

[85] On the early reception history of Homer, see esp. Porter (2004) 326ff.

[86] In particular, as we shall see below, discussions of Homeric epic and of the Bible became inextricably intertwined at this time.

in Madhusudan's contrast between Homeric 'epic' and Hindu '[linear] biography') was precisely what the Bengali poet attempted to bring to the Hindu epic tradition in his Iliadic reworking of the *Rāmāyaṇa* in the *MBK*.

However, the view here expressed by Madhusudan, himself a Christian convert steeped in Western culture, is a markedly un-Hindu one. It may perhaps have been shared by Bhudeb Mukherjee (Madhusudan's Western-educated dedicatee), but certainly not by all, or even most, Hindu Bengali readers. Then, as now, the Sanskrit epic *Rāmāyaṇa* remained a sacred Hindu scripture, some of its characters worshipped as gods by devout Hindus. Indeed Madhusudan claimed to have precisely this Hindu, non-Westernized readership in mind: the *HB* was, in his own words, an attempt to bring the *Iliad* 'to the knowledge of those who do not know the language of England'.[87] Madhusudan, who had once toyed with the idea of becoming a Christian missionary,[88] thus imagines himself as a kind of cultural missionary, preaching the gospel of Homer to a Hindu readership.

Indeed, one may see the Bengali author's systematic substitution of Hindu religious and cultural concepts for Greek as something akin to a missionary tactic. It was the practice of certain Christian missionaries in nineteenth-century India to bring their Hindu students to Christianity by using and building on the ideas and terms already present in the Hindu tradition.[89] Ready and sympathetic appreciation

[87] Bandyopahyay (1945-51) [Introduction] 3.

[88] Murshid (2004) 10ff.

[89] Note the example of the missionary Ballantyne, who used the language of the Hindu tradition of *Nyāya* ('Logic') to teach Western logic to his indigenous students: See Bayly (1996) 224f. Intriguingly, an unpublished work, written on three pages (six sides) of manuscript at Bishop's College Calcutta in 1846 (i.e. while Madhusudan was studying there) and entitled, 'Thesis on ways of convincing Hindoos of the error of their ways', encourages the analogous technique of disabusing Hindus of their 'pagan' 'superstitions' (rather than leading Hindus to Christianity) by deconstructing them on their own terms. The work is preserved in the USPG archive: see Rhodes House Archive, Oxford, C Ind. I. (1) 48. The thesis is anonymous. However, there are various reasons to think that it was written by Madhusudan himself. In particular, the hand is very similar, in various distinctive respects, to other extant examples of Madhusudan's hand. Various features (such as the distinctive punctuation combination '!–') are indicative of Madhusudan's style. Madhusudan was one of the few students attending the college in 1846 to have come originally from the Hindu community, and the work is written from the perspective of the Hindu convert (it appears to have been commissioned by the British missionaries so that they might gain insight into the mindset of those they sought to convert). Furthermore, the views expressed are not inconsistent with, for example, Madhusudan's later lecture 'The Anglo-Saxon and the

of Homer's *Iliad* might come to the Hindu reader more quickly if presented in terms familiar to him, especially if the similarities between the Homeric and Hindu religions were placed front and centre. In any case, it is significant for our interpretation of the *HB* that Madhusudan approached Homer's *Iliad* from the Western point of view (that Homer is the *kabipitā*, 'father of poets')[90] rather than the Hindu (the traditional view being that Vālmīki was the *ādikabi* or 'first poet'). Madhusudan's entire Bengali oeuvre is suspended between the hegemonic standards of two cultural traditions (Hindu and European), which are often in conflict with each other. Where conflict does arise, as in the question of whose 'first poet' trumps the other, it is significant that Madhusudan takes the European view.[91]

However, it is interesting to note that, once again, Madhusudan was markedly independent of the trends in Homeric interpretation which prevailed in contemporary Britain. Indeed, at least in some respects, the *HB* represents a rather eighteenth-century approach towards rendering Homer, evoking, in particular, the technique and licence of Pope's Homeric 'translations'. Madhusudan thus adopts an English Augustan mode of reading Homer's *Iliad,* whilst entirely ignoring a famous controversy that was underway in contemporary Britain: the public and rather acrimonious debate between Newman and Arnold over how best to translate Homer.[92] Madhusudan's use in the *HB* of prose rather than verse sidesteps one of the central terms of the Arnold-Newman controversy. Newman favoured the indigenous

Hindoo' (1854), examined in Chapter 4 above, in which Madhusudan expatiates on the advantages that Christianity and Western high culture would bring to the Hindu. The concluding remark of the thesis gives a flavour of the audacity with which the thesis is written and suggests the author's pique at being asked to answer some rather patronising and arrogant questions. It reads: 'The Missionary must show the Christian & unlearn the mere Englishman as much as he can.' There is insufficient space to transcribe this work in full in this book. However, I intend to publish a full transcription of the thesis in a forthcoming article, arguing that the author of the thesis is Madhusudan.

[90] Madhusudan's phrase: see Bandyopadhyay (1945–51) [Introduction] 3.

[91] Madhusudan evidently thought that the forms and genres of the Western classics provided aesthetically superior models. In various letters to friends, Madhusudan expresses frustration at the limitations of the conventions of the Hindu tradition. See esp. Murshid (2004) 118, 130, 134, but esp. 179: 'as for the old school, nothing is poetry to them which is not an echo of Sanscrit—they have no notion of originality'.

[92] On which see esp. Porter (2004) 338; also 'Homeric Translators and Critics', *The Saturday Review* (July 27, 1861) p. 96, cited in Bermann (2005) 250.

forms of Anglo-Saxon prosody, while Arnold passionately advocated the cultivation of English hexameters; but both Englishmen agreed, at least, that verse rather than prose was the better medium for translating Homer.[93] Perhaps the issues debated so hotly by Arnold and Newman were particular to the English literary discourse and less relevant to a Bengali translator of Homer. After all, questions regarding which metrical forms best suit Homeric translation, and other subtle matters of this kind, rather assume a prior tradition of translating Homer. Madhusudan's *HB* represents only the second attempt to render Homer's *Iliad* into Bengali (and Madhusudan seems to have been unaware of the first);[94] whereas twenty-five English translations of Homer had been published between 1800 and 1860 alone.[95] The basic need for any Bengali version at all of this hegemonic work of Western classical literature, and for communicating the appeal and importance of Homeric poetry to a Bengali readership assumed to be ignorant of it,[96] no doubt seemed more pressing to the Bengali author than such subtle questions of prosody. Furthermore, as will be considered in greater depth in the final chapter of this book, Madhusudan's reversion to Augustan modes of reading the classics (rather than imitating his Victorian contemporaries) is a part of a broader trend in the Bengali poet's reception of Graeco-Roman literature.

Another key debate regarding Homer in mid-nineteenth-century Britain concerned religion, the relationship between Homeric epic and Christianity. The sense that there was a 'peculiar historical and cultural relationship between the Homeric poems and the Bible',[97] which was promoted by Christian scholars and translators of Homer (see especially the influential 1830 commentary by Hartley Coleridge, the poet's nephew),[98] became axiomatic for many Victorian readers.[99]

[93] See Turner (1981) and Bermann (2005).

[94] See n. 11 above.

[95] See Porter (2004) 338, n. 71; indeed by the end of the century a total of sixty-four had appeared (see ibid.). See also France (2006) for an encyclopaedic treatment of contemporary English Homeric translations.

[96] Note Madhusudan's emphasis, in his letter to Bhudeb Mukherjee the dedicatee of the *HB*, on wishing not to eclipse the brilliance of Homer: 'If in places and from time to time I eclipse the brilliance of this moon [*viz.* Homer] like a cloud with the darkness of my ignorance, then I have only one basis for excusing myself, that my affection for our lovely mother tongue is so great that I cannot resist dressing her up in her literary ornaments . . . ' (see Bandyopadhyay (1945-51) [Introduction] 3f.).

[97] Turner (1981) 155.

[98] Coleridge (1834), cited by Turner (1981) 155.

[99] Turner (1981) 155. See also Alford (1841) 17f.

This interpretative trend, a reflex of the anxiety of Victorian Christians about the 'secularization of history'[100] by non-Christian writers, turned the Homeric epics into a key battlefield in the war between religious scepticism and Christian faith.[101] Of course, the most famous and influential participant in this debate was Gladstone himself, whose own syncretistic contention was that 'certain Greek divinities represented an original illumination by God at the dawn of history'.[102]

Madhusudan's reading of Homer seems to pull in the opposite direction to this contemporary British discourse, away from religion and towards the secular domain. Whereas important cultural figures like Gladstone attempted to appropriate Homer as an essentially Christian poet (or at least a proto-Christian one), Madhusudan's comparisons between Homer and Hinduism seem to point instead to the secular nature of Homeric epic. The very first words of Madhusudan's preface concern the nature of Homeric religion (see Appendix 8 below for a translation of this quotation in its original context): 'In the past the people in ancient Hellas—that is Greece—used to practise an idolatrous religion believing in various gods and goddesses'. The non-Christian nature of Homeric religion could not be signalled more plainly. Nor, indeed, could Madhusudan have indicated more clearly the comparability of Homeric and Hindu religion: the ancient Greeks, like the modern Hindus, worshipped idols and venerated many gods and goddesses. Indeed, the analysis of the previous section demonstrated just how extensively Madhusudan elaborated this syncretistic vision in the *HB*. The *HB* thus seems to further an end pursued earlier in the *MBK* and other works, namely the indication of a secular way of reading the Hindu canon. Just as the *MBK* attempts to 'secularize' the *Rāmāyaṇa* tradition, a cornerstone text of Hindu scripture, so too the *HB* challenges Hindu orthodoxy by signalling its close similarities to Homeric religion.

[100] Turner (1981) 155.

[101] The yoking of Christian doctrine and Homeric scholarship at this time is famously emblematized in Mrs Browning's *Aurora Leigh*: '. . . Wolff's an atheist;/ And if the Iliad fell out, as he says,/ By mere fortuitous concourse of old songs,/ We'll guess as much, too, for the universe.'

[102] Bebbington (2004) 155; see also Turner (1981) 163–70. Gladstone's most thoroughgoing and famous treatment of such topics is his three-volume *Studies on Homer and the Homeric Age*, first published in 1858. See Bebbington (2004) for further bibliography.

Conclusion: 'Above all Greek, above all Roman Fame'[1]

1. BROADER IMPLICATIONS OF MADHUSUDAN'S CLASSICAL READINGS

In a letter to his friend Rajnarain, written in May 1860, Madhusudan stated his desire for literary fame in terms evoking Alexander Pope's Augustan taste for the Roman as well as the Greek classics:

> What a vast field does our country now present for literary enterprise! I wish to God, I had time. Poetry, the Drama, Criticism, Romance—a man would leave a name behind him, 'above all Greek, above all Roman fame.'[2]

This appeal to Pope, whose loose version of Horace *Epistles* 2.1 is cited here, is evocative of Pope's Augustan taste in the Graeco-Roman classics and, simultaneously, of the literary world view of Horace (Augustan in the original sense). Madhusudan's attraction to Pope has been shown to be evident at numerous junctures in his literary career (especially in his *Bīrāṅganā kābya*, the collection of elegiac epistles, and in his technique for 'translating' Homer in the *Hekṭor-badh*). It is symptomatic of the Bengali poet's tendency to read the Graeco-Roman classics through the lens of later figures in the Western literary canon (his reading of Milton and Vergil, for example, was implicated in the *MBK's* response to Homer's *Iliad*). Madhusudan's

[1] The phrase of Alexander Pope (l. 26 of his 'version' of Horace *Epistles* 2.1) quoted by Madhusudan (see Murshid (2004) 122).

[2] Murshid (2004) 122: letter to Rajnarain dated 15 May 1860.

specific attraction to Pope's Augustan ambitions, as expressed above, seems to turn on the latter's identification of Horace as a voice for his own time and culture.[3] In the 'Advertisement' to his Horatian *Epistle* 2.1, Pope remarked: 'The Reflections of *Horace*, and the Judgments past in this Epistle to *Augustus*, seem'd so seasonable to the present Times, that I could not help applying them to the use of my own Country.' Madhusudan, reading the Augustan Horace through the English Augustans, makes a similar appropriation of the Roman poet on behalf of his own country. In the preface to his *Tilottamā-sambhab kābya* (1860), the *epyllion* that prefigured Madhusudan's epic *MBK* (1861),[4] Madhusudan cites (in Latin) Horace's *Satires* 1.10.73f.: *neque te ut miretur turba labores, contentus paucis lectoribus*, 'do not work that the crowd might admire you, be happy with few readers'.[5] Madhusudan's habit of citing Horace and Vergil in Latin, examples of which abound in the margins of his texts, represented a claim, as was noted in Chapter 4 above,[6] to the status of a well-educated English gentleman. But Madhusudan's citation of Horace in the preface to the *Tilottamā-sambhab kābya* also serves to align the community of Madhusudan's Bengali readers with the elite and exclusive literary culture of Augustan Rome (*odi profanum vulgus et arceo* . . .),[7] even though Madhusudan's disdain for public approval was arguably as affected as Horace's.[8] The Bengali poet desired Augustan fame for himself as a poet ('above all Greek, above all Roman fame'),[9] but he also claimed an Augustan identity for the elite literary community to which he belonged.

Madhusudan's imagination of an Augustan community of Bengali readers and artists is to be seen in the context of the emergence in

[3] For Pope's relationship with Horace, see Stack (1985).

[4] See Chapter 3 above.

[5] This Horatian tag is set alongside another prefatory citation of Milton (*Paradise Lost*, 7.31): 'fit audience tho' few'. For Madhusudan's reception of Milton, see Radice (1995).

[6] See Chapter 4, n.33 and 3.

[7] 'I hate the uninitiated crowd and keep them at a distance . . . ' (Horace, *Odes* 3.1.1).

[8] For Horace's ambiguous attitude towards his public, see, for example, Rutherford (2007) esp. 257.

[9] In this connection, note the fitting—and witty—homage to Madhusudan's Augustan ambitions in 'The Argument/ [*as supply'd from beyond the grave by* Mr. Alexander Pope]', which prefaces Radice's recent translation of the *MBK*: Radice (2010) cxvii–cxxi.

nineteenth-century Bengal of the idea (or ideal) of a national literary culture. In this connection, it is instructive to recall a striking editorial that appeared in a Calcutta journal a generation before Madhusudan composed his oeuvre. On 8 March 1824 (a few weeks, incidentally, after Madhusudan's birth), Dr. John Grant, a British classical scholar and editor of the *India Gazette*, commented with caustic wit on the proliferation of English poetry published by Bengalis in Calcutta's newspapers (a result of the recent introduction of the English-style education examined in Chapter 1 above):

> Calcutta ought to have its name changed. Instead of being called the City of Palaces, it should be denominated the city of Poets. Parnassus is no longer the haunt of the Muses. They have fled to Calcutta, and the Hooghly has become the Castalian stream. Like the Rustic mentioned by Horace, we have at times supposed that the poetic stream would run itself out—but no—*Labitur et labetur in omne volubilis aevum*... Yea, this is truly the Augustan age in Calcutta.[10]

Madhusudan followed very much in this Bengali tradition of intense and uninhibited literary appropriation of Western culture and, indeed, may with good reason be seen as the apogee of this trend. Forty years after this editorial was published, Madhusudan turned Grant's witty hyperbole into a serious literary ambition. A Bengali poet had emerged so consummately steeped in Western high culture—both modern and classical—that he had made it his business to 'engraft the exquisite graces'[11] of Graeco-Roman culture on his own. Moreover, he imagined this project in markedly Augustan terms.

What is perhaps most striking about Madhusudan's Augustan literary ambitions, from the perspective of the history of classical reception, is his catholic taste for both classical cultures: 'Above all Greek, above all Roman fame'. The Bengali poet's attraction to Vergil and Ovid, topics examined in Chapters 4 and 5 above, came at a time when in Britain these Roman authors were largely out of favour and when British Hellenism was at its zenith. In the course of the close readings of Madhusudan's oeuvre in Chapters 2 to 6 above, certain

[10] *India Gazette*, dated 8 March 1824 (emphasis original); cited in R. Chaudhuri (2008) 9. The Latin cited by Grant is taken from Horace's *Epistles* 1, 2, l. 43: '[the stream] runs and will run copiously for all time'. Horace refers to the fable of the simple 'rustic' who waits for the river to finish running, whereas, of course, it continues and will continue to run for ever: see Mayer (1995) *ad loc.*

[11] Murshid (2004) 125.

possible resonances have emerged from time to time between the Bengali poet's response to the Western classics and the classical receptions of contemporary British poets such as Tennyson or Arnold. And yet such moments are fleeting and serve to reinforce the sense that, in the main, this Bengali response to Graeco-Roman culture was markedly independent of such influences. Madhusudan's emphasis, despite his interest in Roman authors, on Homer's *Iliad* (see Chapters 3 and 6) is an aspect of his classical readership which may strike one as a reflex of Britain's contemporary Hellenism, and the cultural obsession with Homer in particular. However, even this may be explained without reference to the contemporary British phenomenon. The *Hekṭor-badh* (1871) evidences explicitly a mentality that impliedly underpins many of Madhusudan's Greek appropriations (the *Meghnādbadh kābya*, but also the *Padmābatī naṭak* and other works), namely a fascination for the common origins of the Hindu and Greek traditions as hypothesized by the Indo-European scholarship of the early British Orientalists. While Latin is no less a linguistic cognate of Sanskrit than Greek, it is Greek rather than Roman mythology that is the richer and more obvious source of Indological comparisons. The antique Hellenic mythology embodied in Homer's *Iliad* represented for Madhusudan not only the cornerstone of elite Western culture but also the form of Western culture closest to the Indo-European source shared by his own Hindu tradition. The poet's recurrent responses to the Greek epic may be explained, at least in part, by his eagerness to indicate the particular comparability of the ancient Hindu and Greek cultures.

Madhusudan's taste in Western classical texts, which may seem idiosyncratic from the point of view of the scholar of contemporary British receptions of the Graeco-Roman tradition, was certainly not a function of his ignorance of British literary trends—there is ample evidence that he was well-informed in this respect—but represents a conscious decision to depart from contemporary British norms. As to why he decided to do so, the answer may lie, in part, in the classical world's status as an elite branch of Western culture with no living constituents, and unable therefore to criticize or censure the Bengali author's appropriations. Madhusudan turned away from English and towards Bengali as his chosen literary language in the 1850s, partly in response to the high-handed advice of the British civil servant Bethune (see Chapter 1 above).

Simultaneously he also turned away from contemporary British influences and towards Graeco-Roman and earlier English ones. His retreat into the Graeco-Roman world may perhaps be seen as a recoiling from the disappointments of a failed career as an English-language poet, and from the scornful attitudes of some in the British establishment towards his literary pretensions. One might compare the sentiment of another non-white classicist, the black American intellectual and activist W.E.B. Du Bois (1868–1963), who wrote at the beginning of the twentieth century of his relationship with the West's cultural past:

> I sit with Shakespeare and he winces not. Across the color line I move arm in arm with Balzac and Dumas... I summon Aristotle and Aurelius and what soul I will, and they come all graciously with no scorn or condescension.[12]

The Bengali poet chose to access the West's cultural past unmediated by contemporary British taste in part because this enabled him to cross the 'colour line', or at least the boundary between colonized subject and colonial power, with less inhibition.

It is instructive also to compare Madhusudan's nineteenth-century Bengali attitude to the Graeco-Roman world, marked by a simultaneous embrace of the Western past and a reaction against the British present, with that of other non-white colonial poets. For example, despite the many differences in context (linguistic, historical, cultural), the experience of the contemporary West Indian poet Derek Walcott bears salient similarities with Madhusudan's, and yields a critical vocabulary that can be fruitfully applied to an analysis of the Bengali poet and his context. In an account of West Indian education under the British administration, Walcott has expressed the view that literature was 'the greatest bequest the Empire made'.[13] Describing the educational experience of the West Indian colonial subject, he has observed that the 'spiritual death' of an artist living under colonial conditions was something he avoided in part because of this literary bequest:

> The grounding was rigid—Latin, Greek, and the essential masterpieces, but there was this elation of discovery. Shakespeare, Marlowe, Horace,

[12] Du Bois (1965 [1903]) 69; see also Greenwood (2009).
[13] Walcott in Hamner ([1993] 1997) 50.

> Vergil—these writers weren't jaded but immediate experiences. The atmosphere was competitive, creative... It was cruel, but it created our literature.[14]

Madhusudan's experience chimes with Walcott's, at least to the extent that it was precisely the West's literary 'bequest' that, despite the cruel realities of the British present, nonetheless animated his ambitions for a literary reform of Bengali culture. In Walcott, Madhusudan finds an apt successor in creative hybridity, a fellow 'mulatto of style'[15] who, like the protagonist of Walcott's 'The Schooner *Flight*', aspires boldly but anxiously to forge a new identity out of borrowed parts:

> I'm just a red nigger who love the sea
> I had a sound colonial education
> I have Dutch, nigger and English in me
> and either I'm nobody, or I'm a nation.[16]

Notwithstanding the resonances between Walcott's colonial experience and Madhusudan's, a distinctive aspect of the Bengali poet's cultural project was the tension between Western high culture and the elite status of the existing Hindu tradition in contemporary Bengal. Walcott's use of the West's literary heritage is fundamental to his attempt to address what he perceives to be the 'broken tradition'[17] of West Indians of African descent. The colonial deracination caused by the slave trade entailed an estrangement from ancient cultures and a breaking of traditions, and so the Western literary past is called upon to yield paradigms for a modern literary aesthetic. In Madhusudan's case, by contrast, the Graeco-Roman classics are called upon to reform and bring a perceived generic discipline to the vast and complex pre-existing Hindu tradition. The Bengali poet's recourse to the West's ancient literary paradigms is in large part an attempt to subvert Bengal's indigenous elite culture, as embodied in and promulgated by the Hindu pundits, a culture that Madhusudan

[14] Walcott in Hamner ([1993] 1997) 50.

[15] Walcott's illuminating self-description in the essay 'What the Twilight Says: an Overture' (see Walcott (1970)). For a discussion of Walcott's cultural hybridity, see esp. Breslin (2001) and Ramazani (2001).

[16] Derek Walcott, *The Schooner 'Flight'*, ll. 40-3. see Walcott (1986) 346.

[17] See, for example, Walcott's 'Ruins of a Great House': 'Stones only, the *disjecta membra* of this Great House...'.

viewed as ossified and reactionary. In his lecture, *The Anglo-Saxon and the Hindu*, examined in Chapter 4 above, not only do we find a strong and explicit statement of this view (the 'Hindu' is teetering 'on the verge of a moral grave'),[18] but it is also clear that Madhusudan's excoriation of indigenous elite culture is not inconsistent with the most ardent patriotism: 'believe it not that *we* have no love of country—that our heart strings do not cling round the land of our fathers!'[19]

Madhusudan conceived of his pronounced literary transvestism, his assimilation of the best of European culture (as he saw it) to the best of his own, as a patriotic rather than a craven or treasonable act: 'In matters literary, old boy, I am too proud to stand before the world in borrowed clothes. I may borrow a neck-tie, or even a waist-coat, but not the whole suit'.[20] If this study of Madhusudan's oeuvre has any impact on broader scholarly discourses then may it be as a corrective to the commonly held postcolonial assumption that Indian cultural resistance during the nineteenth century was aimed invariably at the colonial oppressor. This Bengali poet's work was arguably a reaction, above all, against those forces within his own culture that he perceived as a hindrance to Bengali culture's revival and progress. Moreover, these forces included not only the indigenous elite culture of the Hindu pundits but also the intellectually corrosive effects, as he saw them, of so-called 'popular' culture, especially the popular drama dubbed by him as *alik kunāṭyo*, 'false, bad theatre'.[21] Madhusudan's love of country was not only consistent with his attempt to appropriate what he perceived to be the best of Western culture, it seems, in fact, to have demanded that he do so. Thus for the Bengali poet, Western high literary culture, and the Graeco-Roman classics in particular, served the dual purpose of helping to oust elite Hindu taste from the apex of Bengali literary culture, and of elevating the modern Bengali vernacular from what was in his view the base and unsophisticated culture of the Hindu masses. There has already been reason in earlier chapters to comment on the ambiguous status of Westernized Bengalis, like Madhusudan, who occupied a 'third space' between Western and Indian communities, regarding themselves 'as

18 Patra (2005) 637.
19 Patra (2005) 634. Emphasis original.
20 See Murshid (2004) 107; also Radice (1987) 239.
21 See Chapter 1, n.110 above.

mediators between [the two] . . . cajoling both towards correct conduct',[22] while of course not being a true member of either. This ambiguity of cultural identity, and the self-appointed role as mediator between both the cultures to which he belonged (and from which he was simultaneously excluded), have emerged again and again in the course of this study of Madhusudan's response to the Graeco-Roman classics.

In addition to Madhusudan's undoubted patriotism, various moments of embryonic nationalism have been observed in his oeuvre. The language of nationalism and the concept and ideal of an India independent of British control did not fully emerge in Bengal until the 1870s, some years after Madhusudan's most productive period. Nonetheless, we see from time to time a subversion of Western values both in his Graeco-Roman appropriations and in broader aspects of his oeuvre. We might consider, for example, the distinctive and unexpected sympathy in the *Meghnādbadh kābya* with the besieged city of Laṅkā, and the antipathy towards Rāma, leader of the foreign force investing that city and the divine hero of traditional accounts of the myth. We might wonder whether this reversal of the traditional roles of hero and villain attests, on one level, to the poet's identification with Meghanāda and Rāvaṇa as victims of foreign aggression.[23] As was seen in Chapter 4 above, Madhusudan insinuated, through Vergilian allusions, that the Anglo-Saxon invader was akin to Aeneas and that the hapless Hindu was not only the Anglo-Saxon's Dido but a Dido who lacked any love for her Trojan guest. There is even something subversive of Western values, as was seen in Chapter 5 above, in the Bengali poet's extensive and imaginative reworking of Ovid's *Heroides*. This collection of poems figures an act of appropriation which highlights the presence at the heart of the Western classical canon of a text going against the grain of contemporary British notions of what constitutes the classical. It also suggests that some Western classical texts speak much less obviously for those in power than for those who try to resist it. Moreover, the Bengali poet's emphatic treatment in the second canto of the *Meghnādbadh kābya* of the *Iliad's* 'Dios Apate', Hera's deception of Zeus, serves to highlight the presence of unexpected and farcical generic strands even within the weighty cornerstone text of the Graeco-Roman canon.

[22] Bayly (1996) 180.

[23] See Radice (1998) for an analysis of Madhusudan's implied 'xenophobia'.

Such subtle but bold and antinomian appropriations of the Western classical tradition act to deflate the pomposity of the view commonly held by mid-nineteenth-century British commentators that the Western classics were an uncomplicated monument to European high-mindedness to be contrasted with the light, frothy, and ultimately inconsequential decadence of Indian art.[24]

At its most resistant to contemporary British cultural norms, Madhusudan's independent and distinctive appropriation of the Graeco-Roman classics might suggest a resonance for some readers with, for example, the twentieth-century Nigerian poet and playwright Wole Soyinka. Like Madhusudan, Soyinka used the Western classics both to address problems in his own society and to challenge the British intelligentsia's presumed ownership of those ancient artifacts.[25] Like Soyinka, Madhusudan did not wish so much to share the Graeco-Roman classics with his contemporaries in the West, showing due deference to European canons of taste, as to take them outright and accommodate them to his own cultural context without reference to that contemporary Western readership.[26] Certainly, Madhusudan stands at the very beginning of a long line of non-white artists who have challenged or altogether bypassed modern Western attitudes in their appropriation of the Graeco-Roman classics and in so doing have made them fully their own.

Madhusudan's proto-nationalism emerges readily enough if one reads the poet's work attentively,[27] but the question of his engagement with the mid-nineteenth-century preoccupation with race, and with Aryanism in particular, is a more contentious aspect of his response to Graeco-Roman literature. In the eighteenth century the terms 'nation' and 'race' were virtually synonymous, but the 'politicization' of the former and the 'biologization' of the latter[28] came to dominate (and in the case of 'racial science', to blight) various nineteenth-century discourses. While it may be relatively uncontroversial to

[24] See, for example, Macaulay's highly influential debunking of eastern literature as essentially worthless in his 'Minute on Indian Education' (1835). He confessed readily to not knowing any oriental languages.

[25] See, for example, Okpewho (1999) 52.

[26] See Soyinka's comments on the matter in *Art, Dialogue and Outrage: Essays on Literature and Culture* (1988).

[27] A point noted quite rightly by Radice (1998).

[28] For this idea of the bifurcation of these two concepts, see especially Trautmann (2004) xxiii.

suggest that Madhusudan's patriotism shaded from time to time into a kind of early Bengali nationalism, the role of race in his oeuvre must be drawn out with some subtlety, though it is arguably just as important. The poet himself experienced racialist taunts and abuse throughout his life, especially while married to a white woman in Madras in the 1850s and while training for the Bar in London in the 1860s, accompanied by his white partner Henrietta. These experiences are to be set in the context of the virulent popularity in the West of so-called 'racial science', which emerged in the early to mid nineteenth century and grew exponentially thereafter.[29] Moreover, racial theories of history began to flourish especially after the mid-nineteenth-century disjunction of ethnology from philology. As was seen in Chapter 1 above, the discoveries of Sir William Jones in the late eighteenth century marked the birth in the Indian context of a belief in a necessary connection between language and race, specifically that the status of Sanskrit as a linguistic cognate with Latin and Greek (among other European and non-European languages) entailed necessarily a special ethnic kinship, a shared Indo-European or Aryan identity, between the Indian and the European. This connection, or the 'tyranny of Sanskrit', as it was referred to by its critics, was unpicked in the 1850s by works like Gobineau's notorious *Essai sur l'inégalité des races humaines.*[30] From this moment onwards the western racialist discourse could feel disabused of the notion that Sanskrit's kinship with European tongues entailed any kind of meaningful racial kinship between Indians and Europeans. In this context, although Madhusudan never explicitly cited race as a motive for his intense Indo-European interests, it is hard not to read Madhusudan's almost obsessive enthusiasm for the comparability of ancient India and Europe as a comment on the very contentious and live racial debate surrounding this Indo-European discourse. The works of Madhusudan, studied in the preceding chapters, return again and again to eighteenth-century Orientalist comparisons between ancient Hindu and Graeco-Roman (especially Greek) culture. The Bengali poet has traditional Hindu characters behave like Greek or Roman heroes. In his *Meghnādbadh kābya* and *Bīrāṅganā kābya,* in particular, but

[29] See generally Trautmann (2004), but also Poliakov (1977), Lincoln (1999), and Olender (1992).

[30] Notorious in no small part for its influence on the development of twentieth-century ideologies of racial hatred: see Trautmann (2004) xxv and Poliakoff (1974).

also in the *Padmābatī nāṭak*, Hindu characters are manipulated so as to speak and behave like Greek or Roman counterparts. Indeed, in the *Hekṭor-badh*, this trope is inverted so that the Greek gods of the *Iliad* morph kaleidoscopically into various Hindu deities, and the Trojans and Achaeans find themselves at the mercy of Śiva's wrath and Durgā's caprice. Madhusudan's achievement in this context is to have created an aesthetic space in which characters from ancient Indian and European traditions could blend seamlessly into each other, their cultural differences momentarily invisible and their separate Indian and European categories collapsed into one. It might be a step too far to claim that this feature of Madhusudan's work represented a desire on his part to install such cultural—and racial—equality among his own generation of Indians and Europeans; but it may certainly be read as a highly romanticized vision of the common identity once supposedly shared by the two peoples, in whose place now prevailed the West's growing sense of its own racial, religious, and cultural superiority.[31]

In the context of Madhusudan's sense of his own cultural tradition's kinship with the Graeco-Roman world (via the Indo-European discourse), it is interesting to compare Madhusudan's response to the Graeco-Roman classics with the psycho-geographies posited by scholars working in the field of 'Classica Africana'. In this African context, as was observed in Chapter 1 above, Goff and Simpson have constructed the 'Black Aegean' as a 'triangle . . . projected from within the Black Atlantic and symmetrical with it, but with its third point radiating eastwards so that it links Africa to ancient Greece'.[32] By contrast, the Indo-European discourse adopted and developed so distinctively in Madhusudan's Bengali classicism is suggestive of a literary space with a fourth dimension, a space in which the cognate status of Hindu and European culture is indicated by pointing backwards in time to a point at which the two cultures were one and the same. According to this model, the relationship between Hindu India and the European classical world is one of horizontal kinship, the sharing of a common ancestor, and the conceit of Madhusudan's

[31] Moreover, in light of the role of notions of the intellectual and physical purity of the ancient Greeks in the development of racial theory in the nineteenth century (see esp. Challis (2010)), it is significant that Madhusudan was particularly interested in aligning the Hindu with the ancient Greek.

[32] Goff (2007) 38f.

classicizing works is to turn the clock back to a time when the family resemblances were more readily visible. Whilst Madhusudan's identification with the Graeco-Roman past via the Hindu tradition was of course a historically contingent one and to be understood in terms of its particular context, it is nonetheless interesting to note that the posited linguistic and cultural links between ancient India and ancient Europe still enjoy scientific credibility today.[33] In any case, Madhusudan's reception of the Graeco-Roman classics should serve as an interesting point of comparison for scholars working in the new field of black classicism, since the obvious differences in cultural context (British India rather than Africa or African American culture) make those similarities that may exist (centring on the plight of the non-white reader in negotiating the encoded bigotries of Western scholarship and high culture) all the more striking and significant. Some of these points of comparison have been highlighted above, but it is hoped that this book will provoke other scholars to suggest further comparative insights.

While Madhusudan's oeuvre may stand as an interesting point of comparison, or indeed of contrast, for various distinct scholarly discourses, it is important not to lose sight of what makes this Bengali poet distinctive and his poetry so immediate in its appeal. The quality which most distinguishes Madhusudan, the feature of his oeuvre which has won him so many Indian admirers (and a fair few critics as well), is the tremendous amplitude and fervour of his literary enthusiasms. Madhusudan's immersion in what he perceived to be the best of Western and Hindu culture was almost fanatical: 'There never was a fellow more madly after the Muses than your poor friend! Night and day I am at them.'[34] His assimilation of myriad literary influences, the fruits of years of linguistic and literary toil, and his deployment of these in the service of the perceived literary 'reform' of the Bengali language, have granted Madhusudan a long-established and controversial place in the history of Indian literature. These aspects of the Bengali poet's work also make for a surprising early

[33] This may be contrasted with the controversial (indeed largely discredited) vertical relationship of African (i.e. Egyptian and North African) precursors and Greek successors postulated in the African context most notably by Bernal in *Black Athena* (1987).

[34] Murshid (2004) 130.

chapter in the history of the non-Western reception of the Graeco-Roman classics.

2. FURTHER QUESTIONS AND FUTURE RESEARCH

The ambit of this book has been circumscribed to include only Madhusudan's Graeco-Roman samplings. This theme has been selected since it not only sheds a distinctive light on the Bengali poet's oeuvre and context but it also contributes to the flourishing discourses surrounding the reception of Western classical texts. It has not been possible here to give a focused and free-standing analysis of the Bengali poet's reception of Sanskrit and mediaeval Bengali literature (let alone his other Western literary influences such as Tasso, Shakespeare, and Milton). Although such themes have emerged recurrently throughout the book, and the notion of the Sanskrit canon as a 'classical' tradition has been interrogated and found wanting (see Chapter 1 above), this potential vein of inquiry is just as rich and complex as Madhusudan's reception of the Graeco-Roman classics and requires another monograph of its own.[35] Various compilations of Madhusudan's Sanskrit and mediaeval Bengali sources have been made by Indian scholars,[36] though the most thoroughgoing works have themselves been written in Bengali and so are unavailable to most Western readers. It would be desirable to see a work in English dedicated to Madhusudan's response to the various rich Hindu traditions, and examining the extent to which this aspect of his oeuvre reveals the kind of subversion of contemporary elite and popular Hindu cultures that has been revealed in the present study. The aesthetic developed by the Bengali poet was a remarkably cosmopolitan one, and this analysis of his Graeco-Roman appropriations would be enriched immensely by companion explorations of the other cultural strands that are brought together in his oeuvre.

Of course, the most pressing concern for scholars of Madhusudan's oeuvre is the lack of English translations. Two translations of the

[35] See, however, the Source Notes in Radice (2010), the excellent new translation of the *MBK*, where many of the Hindu literary influences on Madhusudan's epic are helpfully observed and examined.

[36] See esp. Bhattacharya (1962) and Bhattacharya (1972).

Meghnādbadh kābya have been published since the beginning of the new millennium,[37] and the general reader will gain a very helpful impression of Madhusudan's poetry from either of these works. In the appendices to this book, I have included my own translations of excerpts from other works (the *Padmābatī nāṭak*, *Hekṭor-badh*, and *Siṃhal-bijay kābya*: see Appendices 3, 5, and 8 below), and detailed synopses of the *Padmābatī nāṭak* and *Bīrāṅganā kābya* (Appendices 4 and 6). However, these appendices necessarily offer only a piecemeal and partial introduction to his works. Madhusudan's Bengali oeuvre could offer scholars from various disciplines some extremely distinctive and surprising material. Madhusudan stands as the apogee of various trends in the development of nineteenth-century Bengali culture and his work attests to a fascinating and ambiguous moment immediately before the dawn of Indian nationalism. The Anglophone academy is limited in its ability to comment on these themes without direct access to the Bengali poet's oeuvre. For this reason alone, and quite apart from the great inherent beauty and charm of Madhusudan's Bengali works, it would be most desirable for works other than the *Meghnādbadh kābya* to find good English translations. His very fine collection of sonnets, the *Bīrāṅganā kābya*, the *Brajāṅganā kābya*, and his plays, especially his farces, would be the most obvious candidates for such treatment, and it is very much to be hoped that good English translations of these and other works will emerge in due course.

There are various other topics which it would be desirable for future studies to address. One that stands out as being of potentially great value is a study of the first translations of classical texts into Indian vernacular languages. Classical scholars have begun to consider the question of the reception of Graeco-Roman texts in modern India, and the present study follows in a tradition established by works such as Goff (2005), Hardwick (2007), and Hall (2010). However, it would be very instructive to know when, why, by whom, and for whom the texts of the Western classical canon were first translated into the various Indian vernacular languages, and indeed to discover which were the texts first selected for translation. It is well-documented that the translation of the Bible into Bengali and other

37 Seely (2004) and Radice (2010).

languages of the subcontinent, both modern and ancient,[38] was an abiding preoccupation of the nineteenth-century missionary effort in India,[39] and it would be interesting to compare this phenomenon with the dissemination of the most hegemonic texts of the West's secular canon. The story of the dissemination and reception of the Graeco-Roman classics in India is only beginning to be told. This book will have achieved its basic aim if it is received as a surprising early chapter in that story.

[38] See the 'Preface to the New Edition' of Sir M. Monier-Williams' Sanskrit-English Dictionary (1899), which he states (at ix): 'I have made it the chief aim of my professorial life to provide facilities for the translation of our sacred Scriptures into Sanskrit'.

[39] See, for example, Vishwanathan (1990); see also Pascoe (1901) for a near-contemporary account of this and other aspects of nineteenth-century missionary practice.

APPENDICES

Appendix 1

Madhusudan's New Testament Examination Script (9 June 1847)

This appendix presents a transcription of the New Testament examination answer script (plus the corresponding question paper),[1] previously unpublished,[2] which the student 'M. Dutt' or 'Modhoo Sooden Dutt'[3] (as Madhusudan still referred to himself at the time, without the Christian name Michael) wrote on Wednesday 9 June 1847 at Bishop's College, Calcutta. The document, which is significant in various respects, is especially illuminating, in the context of the present study, for its evidence of Madhusudan's confident handling of Biblical Greek.

Madhusudan's answer paper is a response to the New Testament examination set by the College at the end of the academic year in the summer of 1847. The answer paper comprises seven leaves, with Madhusudan's answers written on both the recto and the verso sides of the manuscript. It was written by Madhusudan at the age of twenty-three during his last year at

[1] The answer paper, and the question paper to which it corresponds, both belong to The United Society for the Propagation of the Gospel. This USPG archive is housed at the Bodleian Library of Commonwealth and African Studies at Rhodes House, where the question and answer papers are catalogued as C.Ind.I(6)32 and C.Ind.I(6)32G, respectively. Madhusudan's answer paper and the question paper are transcribed and published here with the kind permission of the USPG and the Bodleian Library of Commonwealth and African Studies at Rhodes House.

[2] This document was originally discovered by Ghulam Murshid, to whom I am greatly indebted for directing me to it, during his researches for his biography of the poet (Murshid (1995; 1997)). A photographic picture of the verso side of the fifth page of this script, the beginning of question XVIII, is printed on p. 81 of the Bengali version of Murshid's biography.

[3] The answer paper is signed at the end (page 7 verso) in the student's own hand as 'M. Dutt', and the same page is marked in another hand (presumably in Prof. Rev. Street's, and seemingly for the benefit of the English recipient of the batch of examination scripts to which Madhusudan's script belongs) with the words: 'New Testament/ Modhoo Soodden Dutt/ Senior Division/ 145/ (native lay student)'. The number '145' seems to refer to the mark awarded to the answer paper: see below for further analysis of this mark.

Bishop's College, Calcutta,[4] the summer before he moved to Madras. Madhusudan's examination script is one of ten included in the archive's collection, of which seven respond to a New Testament examination and three to an Old Testament examination.[5] Three copies of the New Testament question paper are also included in the archive (but no copies of the Old Testament question paper), and so the seven New Testament answer papers, unlike the other three, may be considered in light of the exact questions to which they respond.

The reason why these examination scripts were sent to England is itself rather interesting. In a dispatch dated 29 December 1847, Prof. Rev. Street, the Principal of the College at the time, sent the scripts to a certain Mr. Rogers in Oxford in an effort to dispel rumours circulating in England: 'it has been said at home . . . that at Bishop's College, the students know nothing of their Bibles' (the indignant underlining is Street's own).[6] The letter not only makes a claim that Bishop's College students knew their Bibles well, but also stands as a flamboyant display of the Professor's own academic credentials. Profesor Street presents himself to Mr. Rogers at the beginning of the letter in the following way: 'I think you acted as *'Ερμῆς Πομπαῖος* into the regions of *vivâ voce*, when I had the audacity to present myself at an examination at Oriel.'[7] Reminding his addressee of their earlier acquaintance in Oxford, Professor Street speaks in the language of the Victorian English gentleman (strewn with witty classical allusions)[8] in order to proclaim his own academic experience: he has taken examinations at Oriel College, Oxford. His classical learning is displayed in a striking way: the Graeco-Roman allusions are humorous but also a little forced, speaking perhaps to a degree of colonial insecurity (is Street's use of the word 'audacity' modest or bitter?). This correspondence thus sheds interesting light on the cultural and intellectual climate of Bishop's College at the time of Madhusudan's attendance, and in particular it suggests that the British clergymen who taught there felt the need to justify their colonial endeavours to their masters in the British metropolis, and to draw attention not only to their students' intellectual accomplishments but also to their own.

[4] For an account of Madhusudan's experiences at Bishop's College, Calcutta, see Murshid (1995) 73-90. See above, Chapter 1, nn. 3–4, for the controversy surrounding Madhusudan's assumption of the Christian name Michael.

[5] The seven New Testament answer papers are catalogued in the USPG archive from 'A' to 'G'. The collection also includes the Old Testament scripts of three of the students whose New Testament scripts are in the archive.

[6] Prof. Street's letter to Mr. Rogers, which evidently accompanied the examination scripts in the dispatch to England, is included in Rhodes House USPG archive at C.Ind.I.13.140.

[7] *'Ερμῆς Πομπαῖος*, or in Roman transliteration 'Hermes Pompaios', is the Greek god who conducted souls to the underworld.

[8] See esp. Griffin (1992) and Vance (1997) 133ff.

In a report sent to a Mr Fagan in England, roughly a month after the examinations of summer 1847, Street tabulated the twenty-five students then in attendance at the College, providing details about, for example, their age and ethnicity, and ranked the top three 'in order of standing'.[9] Madhusudan stands out in this tabulation in various respects. He was ranked third in the College overall, the highest position attained by a non-English student, and was one of only two 'lay students' then in attendance, that is to say, students not intending to enter the ministry. Indeed, we know from other documentation that he was the very first lay student to be admitted to the college.[10] While his ranking in the College was third overall, one might note that he attained only the fifth highest mark of the seven New Testament papers sent back to Mr Rogers. Madhusudan's script was marked at '145' (perhaps 145 out of 200?), whereas William Nichols achieved the top mark with 190 and Henry Cockey the lowest of the seven with 94. Madhusudan's rather average ranking in the New Testament examination is therefore markedly under par in the context of Madhusudan's aggregate ranking of third in the College overall. Madhusudan must have performed rather better in some or all of the other papers he sat that year and, in this connection, one may recall the high proportion of the College syllabus set aside to the Graeco-Roman classics and speculate that this was the area in which the student excelled. Street's comment in his letter to Fagan that Madhusudan was 'very intelligent, a good Greek & Latin scholar',[11] may lend some support to this speculation. In any case, Madhusudan's handling of Greek terms in the answer script transcribed below is confident, and his observance of Greek accentuation, a marker of mastery over the language,[12] is of a fairly high standard.

It is interesting to consider Madhusudan's relatively poor performance in the New Testament examination in the context of Street's evaluation of the student's attitude towards Christianity. In correspondence, Street stated that Madhusudan was 'obedient, honourable, moral, and I believe religious':[13] the qualification—'I believe'—seems to hint at a niggling doubt, perhaps not altogether unjustified. Madhusudan refused to be provided for as a Foundationer on the basis that he would have to wear 'native' clothes like the other Indian students at the College, whereas Madhusudan was very attached to his habit of dressing in Western clothes. Both Professor Street and the Bishop of Madras could not help feeling that 'it was a case of a coat and allowances in one scale against the Missionary calling in the other'.[14] Indeed, we may detect a

[9] USPG Archive, C.Ind.I.13.134.
[10] USPG Archive, C.Ind.I.12.111.
[11] USPG Archive, C.Ind.I.13.134.
[12] Citation or composition of Greek without accents was referred to in the Victorian period as 'ladies' Greek': see Stray (1998) 81.
[13] USPG Archive, C.Ind.I.13.134.
[14] USPG Archive, C.Ind./I/13.

certain flippancy in some of the answers given by Madhusudan to the questions in the New Testament examination. As noted in Chapter 1, Madhusudan stated in his response to Question 11 (part of which asked for the original Greek for a passage of St. John's Gospel (xiii. 10)): 'As I cannot remember the words as they are in the Greek text, I refrain from translating these sentences in my own way.' There is a hint of flippancy in Madhusudan's tone here: a New Testament examination is arguably not the place to boast that one could translate, if one so wished, the King James Bible back into one's own Biblical Greek prose. Moreover, the general attitude of this 'very intelligent' student towards the New Testament examination seems to have been strikingly lackadaisical. Many of his answers are remarkably brief and, although he demonstrates a good knowledge of the Gospels, he cannot quote from them chapter and verse. Compared with the answer paper of William Nichols (who beat Madhusudan in this exam quite convincingly), and even that of Henry Cockey (whom Madhusudan beat comfortably), the brevity of some of Madhusudan's answers is striking. It is significant that at this stage in his career at Bishops' College, Madhusudan had abandoned any missionary ambitions he may once have had,[15] and was on the verge of leaving Calcutta for Madras where he would find secular employment as a schoolteacher and newspaper editor.

What follows is a transcription of Madhusudan's answer paper and the corresponding New Testament question paper. In bold, above each of Madhusudan's answers, I transcribe the question to which it responds, and in the answers themselves I preserve the author's own superscript corrections as they are found in the manuscript. To help the reader who lacks Greek, I add my own translations and comments on the relevant Greek passages in the footnotes below. It is unclear what is indicated by the asterisk preceding some of the question numbers. The asterisked questions are possibly more difficult than the others, and so it may be that students of the Senior Branch of the college (including Madhusudan) were to answer all of the questions, while students of the Junior Branch were only to answer non-asterisked questions. No answer papers written by students of the Junior Branch are to be found in the collection, and so it is impossible to be certain on this point.

The Examination Script Transcribed

1. —*I lay down my life, that I might take it again. No man taketh it from me, but I lay it down of myself. I have power to lay it down, and I have power to take it again.* St. John x. 17, 18. Prove from these words the verity of the two Natures in our Lord's Person, and confirm the doctrine by other texts.

[15] Noted by Street in his letter to Fagan: see USPG Archive, Rhodes' House Oxford, C.Ind.I.13.134.

The first clause of the 1ˢᵗ sentence proves his humanity
for the expression 'lay down my life'. means that he was
going to die—if our Savior had no human nature,
being God he cᵈ not die and consequently there
wᵈ be no meaning in his saying.—The second
clause shows his Divinity because none but God
cᵈ revivify the dead—From these facts we can
verity of the
infer the ⋏ union of two natures in Him.—The
following are a few texts showing the union of the
two natures of our Savior.—John chap. I. 'The <u>Tabernacle</u>'
plainly alluding to the presence of God in the Law
      The Deity dwelling in the human body.
called the S̶e̶c̶h̶i̶n̶a̶ Shechinah. ⋏—St. Paul—'Who being
in the form of a servant thought it not robbery
'being equal with God he was God & yet he had the form of a servant
to be equal with God.—⋏ The whole life of our
Savior—during which he showed so many
instances of his being both God and Man—
Weeping at the Grave of Lazarus—his agony
in the Garden &cᵃ

2. Show that when our Lord laid down His life, there was no interruption of the union of His Godhead with either His soul or His body.

If there had been any interruption of it our Savior
         if
cdn could not have risen from the dead—For ⋏ his
Divinity was with-drawn from his humanity—tho'
it was the purest—he cᵈ not be said to have raised
himself.

3. Ἐγένετο δὲ τὰ ἐγκαίνια ἐν τοῖς Ἱεροσολύμοις, καὶ χειμὼν ἦν.[16]
What festival was this?

This was the festival instituted by Judas
Maccabaeus on the occasion of the purification
of the temple from the heathens.—

4. Ἐγὼ καὶ ὁ Πατὴρ ἕν ἐσμεν. St. John x. 30.
What kind of unity does ἕν denote?[17]
Adduce other texts in proof,
 i. Of the Unity of the Father and the Son;
 ii. Of the Unity of the Father, Son, and Holy Ghost.

---

[16] 'And a festival took place in Jerusalem, and it was winter.'
[17] This Greek phrase "Ἐγὼ καὶ ὁ Πατὴρ ἕν ἐσμεν" means 'I and the Father are One'. The Greek word ἕν, which is repeated in the following line, is the word for 'One'.

iii. Of the distinct Personality of all three;
iv. Of the procession of the Holy Ghost from the Father;
v. Of His procession from the Son also.

and
Unity of Substance — will — ^ operation.
(I) 'As my father worketh so I work.'
'What are mine are thine and what are thine are mine.'
(II) 'There are three that bear witness in heaven +ca
and these three are one.'
(III) 'Go ye unto all nations — making them disciples in the
the
name of the Father ^ Son, and the Holy Ghost.'—
In which text ~~are~~ the three are mentioned as
distinct persons.—In St Matthew we read of
the ~~exclusive~~ a blasphemy exclusively against
the Holy Ghost.—Our Savior says 'he [the father]
will send another comforter'. 'he [κειvος-][18] shall
testify of me.
(IV) 'And he will send another Comforter'
(V).'And I will send him' See also XVI.7 (John)
Whom [Sc. the Comforter] I will send unto you'.

5. His *disciples say unto him, Master, the Jews of late sought to stone thee; and goest thou thither again? Jesus answered, Are there not twelve hours in the day? If any man walk in the day, he stumbleth not, because he seeth the light of this world. But if a man walk in the night, he stumbleth, because there is no light in him.
St. John xi. 8, 9, 10.
On what occasion was this said?
Explain the argument,
i. With reference to Our Lord.
ii. -to the disciples.

When our Savior was going up to the Village
of Lazarus — (1) The argument with reference
to our Lord is that he himself being
the Light ~~he~~ and seeing every thing cd
not stumble. i.e. Knowing the Past, present
and the future he knew all that the
Jews cd do + therefore there was

[18] Madhusudan cites the Greek word κειvος-, which means 'that [man]' (nominative, masculine, singular of the demonstrative adjective). With proper accentuation the Greek should in fact read κεῖνος.

no necessity for him to be afraid of them. (II) With
referrence to the disciples—If they walked in his
light—they, too, c$^{\underline{d}}$ not stumble like those
who walk in the night—i.e. behave not as
the son of man.—This shows that the disciples
were under the protection of our Lord as he
himself said in his prayer to the Father, 'I have
preserved
~~protected~~ them' +$^{\underline{ca}}$.

6. Point out the several particulars in which the Resurrection of Lazarus was plainly miraculous.

It was miraculous (I) because it took place three
his
days after his death and burial, when ~~he had~~
system had
already begun ~~to xxxxx~~ to putrify. (~~II~~) which
circumstances plainly show that there c$^{\underline{d}}$
have been no vitality in ‸any degree in him. (II)
because it was done by no external application
of any thing, ~~which~~ but Jesus only from
a distance spoke 'Lazarus arise' and he that
was dead arose.—

7. How many other Resurrections from the dead are mentioned?
i. In the Old Testament.
ii. In the Gospels.
iii. In the rest of the New Testament.

(I) The widow's Son who fed Elijah—The woman's Son in
whose house Elisha lodged.—The man who was
let down into Elisha's grave.—(II) The daughter of Jairus.
The Centurion's se‸rvant or Son [παις][19] The Widow's Son
+ Lazarus. (III) The man who fell down from
the window.—and another by St. Peter

8. Show that nevertheless our Lord alone was the firstfruits of them that slept.

~~Because~~ Our Savior was the the firstfruits of
them that slept in as much as he rose himself
by his own power for our justification and

[19] The Greek word παις means simply 'child', 'boy', or 'son'—as the context here makes quite clear. With proper accentuation the Greek should in fact read παῖς.

went up to the Father as an acceptable sacrifice for
our sins—

9. What was the result as regards the Jews at large, of the raising of Lazarus?

Some it confirmed more in their wish [. . .][20]
~~belief~~
our Savior, others in their ~~wavering~~ belief.
~~For instance~~, When this fact was reported to
some
them, ^ instead of investigating its truth and
~~then~~ examining the pretensions of the man who
went
performed such a stupendous miracle, ~~whe~~
about to prevent the displays of that power
which must have at times convinced them
that Jesus was no ordinary man. While others
with that humility which such an awful
miracle must have inspired believed in him.

***10. —*this spake he not of himself: but being High Priest that year, he prophesied that Jesus should die for that nation.* St. John xi. 51. Mention the various uses in Scripture of the words 'prophet' and 'to prophesy.'**

Prophecy in S.S. has various meanings—one is
the ~~us~~ general acceptation attached to the
word: i.e. to foretell future events as the
prophets did of our Savior—of Babylon
the Persian empire +ca Which events
took place long after they had been
spoken of ~~as about to happen~~. The other,
used in the New Testament is to mention
a thing past, as when the servant
struck our Savior in the house of
the high-priest he said *προφητευσον*.[21]
The word 'prophet' is used in S.S. to signify

[20] Text uncertain here.

[21] Madhusudan cites the word *προφητευσον*, the second person singular of the aorist imperative: 'prophesy!' Note that an acute accent on the upsilon (the letter [*υ*]) is struck through twice, indicating Madhusudan's hesitation over accenting his Greek. Properly accentuated the Greek should in fact read *προφήτευσον*. Note, however, that in the first person singular present active of the verb, *προφητεύω*, there is an acute accent on the upsilon. This may be what caused Madhusudan's confusion.

a foreteller of Future Events—also Jesus
Balaam was a prophet.

11.** ***If I wash thee not, thou hast no part with me. **St. John xiii. 8.**
Jesus saith to him, He that is washed needeth not save to wash his feet, but is clean every whit: and ye are clean, but not all. **St. John xiii. 10.**
Give the Greek of these passages.
What general lesson did our Lord inculcate by washing his disciples feet.

ds stand

* It [As I cannot remember the work as they ~~are~~ in the Greek text, I refrain from translating these sentences in my own way.]

The general lesson taught by our Lord is 'humility'—If he our Lord and Master be so humble as to c^d ~~so far~~ ^ condescend to wash the feet of his own disciples—we surely ought to be very humble.—

***12. What other doctrines seem indicated by the gracious act?**
The one entire purification by the rite of baptism, for in answer to Peter's request that he sh^d wash not only his feet but head +ca our Lord says ὁ λελουμένος[22] i.e. a person once baptized needeth it not again.—because he is (as the Gr. word in the text means) thoroughly washed—
The word νίπτειν shows that although baptized and washed we need the washing—(so to call it) of the sacramental ordinances of the Church cleansing for ~~keep off~~ the impurity which we must contract by our intercourse with the world.

13. ***A new commandment I give unto you, That ye love one another; as I have loved you, that ye also love one another.*** **St. John xiii. 34.**
Show how this was a *new* commandment.
This was ~~xxx~~ a new Commandment, for although the duty of loving our fellow creatures is distinctly

[22] Madhusudan uses the Greek words ὁ λελουμένος ('he who has bathed [himself]': perfect middle participle) and νίπτειν ('to wash'). Madhusudan's observance of accentuation is sound here.

inculcated in the Law, yet we are never
~~tol~~ told to love each other with the depth
of affection which our Savior means.—
the
~~because we~~ commandment is ‘that ye
love one another καθὼς ἐγὼ’[23]—We must
love our brother with the love which he bore
towards us and which even made him lay
down his life for those he loved.—It is this
that makes it a new commandment.

14. ***‘Abide in me and I in you.’***
What is meant by our abiding in Christ?
What is the proof that we abide in Him?
Can we be *in* him and yet unfruitful?

Remain steadfast in the Faith.—~~xxxx xxxx that~~
~~in the sense in which we use the ‘temples’~~
~~of the Holy Ghost’~~
Our works—as the course of life we lead for
whoever abideth in X^{t} is in the light
and stumbleth not:

ays
No: For St. John says ‘If any one s~~aith~~
he hath fellowship with him + still walketh
in darkness—he is a liar.’ Epist.

15. ***But when the Comforter is come, whom I will send unto you from the Father, even the Spirit of truth, which proceedeth from the Father, He shall testify of me.* St. John xv. 26.**
What points of the doctrine of the Trinity can be proved from these words?

(I) The existence of the three persons—I, The Father,
and The Spirit—(II) The ἐκπορεύσις[24] of the latter both

[23] The Greek cited by Madhusudan, καθὼς ἐγὼ, is taken from St. John xiii, 15, i.e. καθὼς ἐγὼ ἐποίησα ὑμῖν, which means ‘just as I did for you’. Again Madhusudan’s observance of accentuation is correct in the given context. Note, however, that the word ἐγὼ only takes the grave accent if followed by a word like ἐποίησα (in final position it should be written ἐγώ with an acute accent on the omega); therefore it might have been more stylistically attractive if Madhusudan had given the full citation (καθὼς ἐγὼ ἐποίησα ὑμῖν).

[24] The Greek ἐκπόρευσις means ‘procession’, and refers to the concept that the Holy Spirit proceeded from the Father (and from the Son, if one accepts the Roman Catholic ‘filioque’ version of the Nicene Creed). Madhusudan makes a slip in accentuation similar to that found in his answer to Q. 10, placing the acute accent on the upsilon (ἐκπορεύσις) rather than on the omikron (again, the accent is indeed on the upsilon in the first person singular present active of the verb, i.e. ἐκπορεύω).

'Whom
from the Father and the Son. '^ I will
~~him~~
send^' says our Lord, intimating the procession
of the Spirit from himself. 'Which proceedeth
from the Father.'—The Holy Ghost being
the 'Spirit of Faith' in God for god is
Truth.'—If our Savior c^d have power to send
God the Holy Ghost—he must be God himself.

Union of operation: because we see God the Father Son and Holy Ghost all engaged with work of man's salvation.—

16. What is the Greek for 'Comforter?'
Is it used any where of the Lord Himself?

παρακλητος[25]—yes—Christ is called our
'comforter'.—

17. How is the Holy Ghost our Paraclete?
How is the Son our Paraclete?

The Holy Ghost is our παρακλητος because
he comforts us—in that he maketh intercession
for us with groanings which can not
be uttered—as well as dwelleth in us
as his temples turning our hearts from the
despondency ~~of~~ and despair of Sins to the
Comforts of Religion.

The Son is our παρακλητος because he says
ye
~~Come~~ 'Come unto me all that faint and are
heavy-laden and I will give you rest.'—
and because by his Passion—Resurrection
and ascension he hath ~~the~~ effected the
Salvation of sinners.—

18. *And when he is come, he will reprove the world of sin, and of righteousness, and of judgment: of sin, because they believe not on me; of righteousness, because I go to my Father, and ye see me no more; of judgment, because the prince of this world is judged.*
St. John xvi. 8, 9, 10, 11.

[25] Madhusudan uses the word παρακλητος, 'comforter', repeatedly throughout his answers to Questions 16 and 17. The word is the correct Greek term, but Madhusudan omits the accent: it should read παράκλητος.

Explain this passage briefly.

When the Holy Ghost will come he will reprove
[convict or convince] the world of Sin. In the first
some
place—^ commentators say that the word 'world'
means the Jewish nation only, but the Greek
word *κοσμος*[26] is always used in S.S. to signify
'<u>mundus</u>' whereas we find the expression *οἰκουμένη*
(sc. *γῆ*) used for Judea. [See Luke III—The
Temptation]. again ~~th~~ if we admit this
interpretation of the 'world' here signifying
only the Jewish nation, we confine the
operations of the Spirit which are universal
to locality.—The word *ἐλεγξει* may be rendered
in three ways ~~as the version~~. If we attach
the meaning 'Convict' to it, it will mean
that the Holy Ghost will condemn the whole
for
world ^ ~~of~~ the crime of rejecting the true
Messiah—if 'Convince'.—it will mean, that
contrasting
by ^ the purity of the ~~lives~~ lives of disciples
with those of the unbelieving world he will 'convince'
~~of~~ them of the truth of the Religion of him whom
they reject.—as also—by the triumph of Christianity
tho' lowly and humble in its beginning over all
other religions.—If 'reprove' it will mean that
he will by revivifying, as it were, their dead
consciences invest them with more than ordinary
force to accuse them for their rejection of the
Savior:
'Of righteousness because I go to my Father.'
If Christ had not risen from the Grave—and
had not ascended up to the father he w$^{\underline{d}}$ not
have been righteous.—But his resurrection +
ascension proves that he was righteous else how
c$^{\underline{d}}$ one who was not righteous go up to

[26] The Latin word *mundus* ('world', 'earth') is used to render Greek *κόσμος* (note Madhusudan's omission of the accent): the Greek word, transliterated into English as 'cosmos' has broader connotations of 'order' and 'universe'. The Greek '*οἰκουμένη* (sc. *γῆ*)' (accentuation observed correctly) means, literally, 'inhabited (viz. earth)'. The Greek term *ἐλέγξει* (the accent is omitted in the script) is exegeted sufficiently by Madhusudan's answer.

Heaven to the Father? Our Savior's resurrection
showed that he was righteous See Rom: 1.4.
'Of Judgement' +ca. The price of this world—i.e.
Satan has fallen from heaven like lightening [sic]—
The humiliation of his power is a sure indication
to those who follow the ways that their Judgement
is ~~h~~ at hand.—

19. ***—for their sakes I sanctify myself that they also might be sanctified through the truth.*** **St. John xvii. 19.**
What is to be understood by our Lord's *sanctifying* Himself? Prove your answer.

~~Αγο αγι~~ ἁγιαζειν[27]—the word used in the Greek
text, means to set apart any thing for any
hence
religious purpose.—~~for instance~~ τὰ ἁγια were ~~what~~
for
~~the Latin~~ things set apart ~~for to~~ the service of the
Deity. Our Savior by ἁγιαζειν here means —
that he offers 'himself to God—for the sake
of his ~~af~~ disciples.—St Paul in the Ephes. uses
the word in a similar sense.—'Which he hath
sanctified'—

20. ***—that it might be fulfilled which was spoken by the prophets, He shall be called Nasarene.*** **St. Matthew ii. 23.**
Where is this prophecy found? In how many ways does it appear to have had its fulfilment?

called
In Isaiah:—In his having been ~~called~~ himself ^ a
for having been brought up ~~at~~ in Nazareth
Nazarene ^ + in giving his name to the Religion
he taught. Christians are to this day called
Nazarenes by Mahomedans and others.

21. **Enumerate in order the several appearances of our Lord recorded in the New Testament between his Resurrection and Ascension.**

It is a disputed point—but many commentators
generally believe that he appeared ten times.—
1st To Mary Magdalene: —

[27] The words ἁγιάζειν ('to sanctify') and and τὰ ἅγια (literally '[things] sanctified', 'sacred things'), are cognates. Madhusudan omits most of the accentuation in the script.

2nd To the other women:—
3rd To Peter:—
4th To the two going to Emaus:—
5th To the disciples assembled together:—
6th Do and to Thomas:—
7th To James
8th To Peter, John +ca ~~at~~ catching fish:—
9th To the 500
10th At the time of his ascension to all assembled together—

P

[If I mistake not, the ~~principle~~ principles gave us the order of our Savior's appearances as here stated above]

***22. *Who was delivered for our offences, and was raised again for our justification.* Romans iv. 25.**

Give the Greek of these words, and explain them concisely.

Our Savior was delivered for our offences—that is he came to suffer for us + by one oblation of himself—satisfy the offended majesty of God.—as he says—Sacrifice and offerings thou w^dst not then ǂ said I lo ! I come +ca 'And was raised again' +ca 'If Christ be not risen { again then is all in vain. for his resurrection is the most important point and is the foundation of Religion. for by rising from the dead he was passed into Heaven + therefore we have a 'high-priest'.

23. *Καὶ τοῦτο εἰπὼν ἐνεφύσησε, καὶ λέγει αὐτοῖς· Λάβετε Πνεῦμα Ἅγιον. Ἄν τινων ἀφῆτε τὰς ἁμαρτίας ἀφίενται αὐτοις. ἄν τινων κράτητε κεκράτηνται.*[28] St. John xx. 22, 23.

Reconcile this with the fact that the Holy Ghost was not given until Christ was glorified. Also state what has been considered the special import of out Lord's act of breathing on the Apostles.

By *λάβετε πνεῦμα ἅγιον* our ~~Savior breathed~~ Savior ~~on them~~ prepared them for the ^public reception of the Spirit on the pay of Pentecost:—
First, that the spirit proceeds also from him and

[28] 'And saying this he breathed on them and said, "Receive the Holy Spirit. If you forgive anyone his sins they are forgiven; if you do not forgive them they are not forgiven."'

cause
~~recove~~
second that the ~~fact~~ of our recoving [sic] the Gifts of the Holy Spirit was the incarnation of our blessed Lord:—

M. Dutt

APPENDIX 2

Editions Of Classical Texts Possibly Encountered By Madhusudan

See Chapter 1 for the methodology for compiling the table below (Table A.1.). The contents of Bishop's College library seem not to have survived, as such. However, it is known that in 1822 both Oxford University Press and Cambridge University Press made donations to Bishop's College of a copy of every work in print that year. On this basis, it is possible to infer which editions of the works were dispatched to Bishop's College by OUP and CUP, and which were likely therefore to have been available to the students during the 1840s when Madhusudan was in attendance. The following is a tabulation, *inter alia*, of the editions of the classical works stipulated in the college's various extant 1840s syllabuses, plus of those classical works which influenced Madhusudan's later literary oeuvre.

Resources used to compile the following table:

- Lowndes (1864) [six volumes];
- Orders and Accounts of the Delegates of the Clarendon Press 1811–1853; and
- The British Library Databases.

Table A.1. Classical texts available to Madhusudan

Context in which Madhusudan encountered a given text	**Classical Text**	**Edition(s) that are likely to have been kept in the Bishop's College library during Madhusudan's studies there (1844–1847)**	**Edition(s) that Madhusudan could have encountered after leaving Bishop's College (i.e. after 1847)**
Texts on Bishop's College syllabus (1844)	Herodotus *Histories*	Historiarum libri, Gr. cum notis Reizii et Schaeferi, Oxon. 1814, 2 vols.; Oxon 1817, 2 vols.; Oxon 1820, 2 vols.	
	Juvenal *Satires*	Juvenalis Satirae XVI a Georgio Alex. Ruperti. Oxon. 1808./ Juvenalis, ex Editione G. A Ruperti. Oxon. 1814.	
	Lucretius *De Rerum Natura*	T. Lucretii Cari de Rerum Natura Libri sex cum Interpretatione et Notis Thomae Creech. Accedunt variae Lectiones IV Edd antiquiss. necnon Annotationes R. Bentleii. Oxon. 1818.	
	Plato *Crito* and *Phaedo*	Platonis Dialogi V. (Amatores, Euthyphro, Apologia Socratis, Crito et Phaedo) Gr. et Lat. ex Recensione Nath. Forster. Oxon. 1745, 1765, 1772, 1800.	
	Vergil *Eclogues* & *Georgics*	Phineas Pett & Christian Gottlob Heyne , P. Virgilii Maronis Opera, locis parallelis ex antiquis scriptoribus et annotationum delectu illustrate in usam iuventutis, Oxon. 1820.	
	Horace *Odes* & *Epodes*	Thomas Kidd, ed. (1817), Horatii Flacci Opera (Cantab.)	
	Xenophon *Cyropedia*	Schneider, J. (1812), Xenophontis de Cyri Disciplina (OUP) [republished in 1820: see OUP Orders and Accounts, 19 May 1820].	

Cicero *De Senectute* & *Somnium Scipionis*	Opera omnia, ex Recensione J. Aug. Ernesti cum ejusdem Notis et Clave Ciceroniana. Oxonii, 1810, 8 vols. Opera, cum Indicibus, variis Lectionibus, et Clave. Oxon. Clarend. 1783, 10 vols. [A reimpression of the text of Olivet (1749, 20 vols.), with various readings, but without notes. . . . A volume of notes 'Oliveti Delectus Commentariorum in M. T. Ciceronis opera omnia. Oxonii, 1821' was printed to accompany this edition.]
Euripides *Medea*	Euripidou Mydeia (Euripidis Medea) (1818, Clarendon Press), ed. P. Elmsley.
Sextus Aurelius Victor *Historia*	[I can find no Oxon. or Cantab. editions in print in the early 1820s. Perhaps printed in a school text (as Eutropius was), or an older edition of the work donated by Bishop Middleton.]
Eton *Exempla Minora*	Eton Exempla Minora: Morel, Thomas (1787), Exempla Minora, or, New English Examples, to be rendered into Latin, adapted to the rules of Latin Grammar, lately printed at Eton; for the use of the Lower Forms. [A new revised edition] Reprints: 1794, 1803, 1810, 1821, etc.
William Neilson *Greek Composition*	Greek Exercises: In Syntax, Ellipsis, Dialects, Prosody and Metaphrasis, William Neilson (Edinburgh, 1814, 4th edition).

Continued

Table A.1. *Continued*

Context in which Madhusudan encountered a given text	**Classical Text**	**Edition(s) that are likely to have been kept in the Bishop's College library during Madhusudan's studies there (1844–1847)**	**Edition(s) that Madhusudan could have encountered after leaving Bishop's College (i.e. after 1847)**
Works used as literary models in Madhusudan's Bengali poems and plays (late 1850s onwards)	Homer *Iliad*	Clarendon Press, 1821, Homeri Ilias cum brevi annotatione, curante C.G. Heynio, Accedunt Scholia minora passim emendante, 2 vols.	Homeri Iliad, Dindorfii. Gr. Oxon. 1856.
	Homer *Odyssey*	Homeri Iliad et Odyssea, Batrachomyomachia, &c. Gr. cum Scholiis Didymi. Oxon. 1780, 4 parts in 2 vols.	Odyssea cum scholiis et variis Lectionibus; accedunt Bach., Hymni, fragmenta; ex recensione Buttmani. Oxon. 1827, 2 vols.
	Horace *Odes*	(As above)	Horatii Opera, cum not. In usum Delphini, with Annotations in English, and the Delphin Ordo in the margin, by the Rev. Pemble. Lond. 1832. Horatii Opera ex recensione Doering, with explanatory Notes in English, by Anthon. Lond. Priestley, 1835. Editio nova. Lond. Tegg, 1845,1846 (with Index). Again, Lond. 1855.
	Vergil *Aeneid*	Virgilii Opera, Locis parallelis ex antiquis Scriptoribus ex Annotationum Delectu illustratu (a Phinnea Pett.) Accedunt Tabulae Geographiae et Index Maittairianus. Oxon. 2 vols. 1795, 1820, &c.	Virgili Opera, ex recensione T. Connington (Cambridge Greek and Latin Texts), Camb. 1859.
	Ovid *Heroides*		

	Opera, ex Editione Burmanni. Lond. 1815. 3 vols. The Regent's edition. Opera ex edit. Burmanniana, cum Notis in usum Delphini et Variorum curante Valpy. Lond. 1821, 9 vols . . . Epistolarum Heroidum Liber, cum interp. & Notis, ad Usum seren. Delphini. Lond. 1702, Reprinted 1714, 1722 &c. [Note that neither OUP nor CUP brought out their own editions of this work until 1825 (see next item).]	P. Ovidii Nasonis Opera, e Textu Burmanni; cum Notis Bentleii hactenus ineditis, necnon Harlesii, Giergii, Burmanni, Lemairii, et aliorum selctissimin. Oxonoo, 1825, 5 vols.
Ovid *Metamorphoses*	Opera ex edit. Burmanniana, cum Notis in usum Delphini et Variorum curante Valpy. Lond. 1821. 9 vols . . . Metamorphoseon Libri XV. Interpretatione & Notis, ad Usum serenissimi Delphini. Lond. 1708, 8vo. Reprinted 1719, 1730, 1810, &c.	P. Ovidii Nasonis Opera, e Textu Burmanni; cum Notis Bentleii hactenus ineditis, necnon Harlesii, Giergii, Burmanni, Lemairii, et aliorum selectissimis. Oxonii, 1825, 5 vols.
Euripides *Iphigenia at Aulis*	Tragoediae, Graece at Latine, ex nova recognitione Aug. Mattiae. Oxon. 1821. 3 vols. IPHIGENIA in Aulide, et in Tauris, Gr. cum Notis Marklandi integris, et aliorum selectis. Oxon. 1810.	

APPENDIX 3

Judgement Scene in *Padmābatī nāṭak*

Act One

Mount Vindhya, grove of the gods

Enter King Indranīl at speed, bow and arrow in hand

KING: [*looking around in all directions, as an aside*] Which way did that stag go so suddenly? Amazing! Am I draped in sleep, beholding a dream?[1] Then how is it that I still speak? The blessed Mount Vindhya still stands here as a mountain in front of me. [*thinking*] Given that using a chariot in this mountainous terrain is quite a hindrance, and granted that pursuing a stag on foot is a miserable business, is it true then that, at length, my sole achievement is to have ended up all alone in this deserted forest? In the desert, mirages seem like water to people; is that what has given me so much distress and sorrow here, a deer mirage? Be that as it may, now I must rest here awhile, I must put this fatigue behind me. [*walking about*] My word! What a delightful place this is! It must be the grove of some Yakṣa or Gandharva, I think. Nature, cause of mankind's visual joy, bears nowhere such incomparable beauty. Let me sit down on the rock by this spring. With this murmuring sound, it seems to voice a summons for me. [*sitting down, startled*] What is this? This garden has suddenly filled up with an uncommonly pleasant odour. [*a sweet instrumental music in the sky*] Ah! What a sweet sound! What—? [*suddenly, draped in sleep, he falls on the rock*]. (1)[2]

Enter Śacī and Rati

ŚACĪ: Friend, why keep asking questions about Indra? He is always and forever contemplating how to wreak the complete destruction of the wicked Daitya clan. For the enjoyment of what other pleasure does he have any thought? Goddess Rati, how fortunate you are. You see, your Manmatha does not forsake you even for half a moment. Ah! Just as sweet fragrance remains ever fixed as it clings to a *parijat* flower, so too is Madana under your control. (2)

RATI: Friend, that is indeed true. I have almost forgotten what people call the flame of separation. [*both walk around*] How amazing! Goddess Śacī, see how your jasmine, as if it were irritated at the arrival of the *Malaya* wind, forbids one with a nod to approach it. (3)

[1] Patra (1989) notes *ad loc.*: 'In the *Śakuntalā*, Kālidāsa's play, after the prologue Duṣyanta entered bow and arrow in hand, chasing after a stag. Here we can observe a clear imitation of that.'

[2] Note that this numbering is my own, simply so that reference may be made more easily to particular speeches.

ŚACĪ: Why should it not? See, it has spent all day in amorous sport with the lotuses in that excellent, pellucid water, and this is all that comes. Is there not in this an offence to the jasmine's pride?

Enter the goddess Murajā

Ah, is that our friend Murajā? Come. Come. Why do you wear such a dispirited look today? (4)

MURAJĀ: [*letting forth a deep sigh*] Friend, whom else shall I tell of my grief? (5)

RATI: Why? Why? What has happened? (6)

MURAJĀ: Almost fifteen years ago Pārvatī cursed my daughter Vijayā to be born on Earth; since that time I have been unable to make any further progress in my search. (7)

ŚACĪ: What's that? Blessed Pṛthivī [*viz.* Earth] didn't agree to bear her in her own womb? (8)

MURAJĀ: Yes, she did and she still holds her. But ever since the birth she has not wanted to tell me on any terms into whose hands she placed her to be reared and brought up. How much have I wept as I grasped her feet! What more shall I say about it? (9)

RATI: Did the Reverend One tell you that? (10)

MURAJĀ: She said—'Child, in time you yourself will be able to know everything. Now you must check your tears and go to Alakā. Your Vijayā is in extreme bliss. (11)

ŚACĪ: Then, friend, it is in no way appropriate for you to be perturbed about this. And take thought and reflect: on Pṛthivī [*Earth*] the sport of a human's life, like a bubble of water, comes to an end most swiftly. (12)

MURAJĀ: Friend, my mind in separation from Vijayā is constantly bursting forth in grief! Alas! The Lord of All, though he has made us immortal, has made us subject to grief. (13)

ŚACĪ: Friend, what fruit is there in the Creator's vast creation that a worm cannot enter? (14)

Enter Nārada at a distance

NĀRADA: [*aside*] I was travelling through the air to the hermitage of the great sage Pulastya. Suddenly, having seen these three female goddesses in this grove of the gods, I desired to see if I could do something to introduce a quarrel between them—that is why I have come down to this mountain plateau. Through what opportunity shall I bring this desire of mine to fruition? [*thinking*] Yes, I've got it. Using this golden lotus that I have picked from lake Mānasa I will bring my intention to fruition. [*moving forward*] May you fare well! (15)

ALL: Great sage, we all make obeisance to you. [*bowing*] (16)

ŚACĪ: [*aside*] This blasted man is forever the cause of strife; he has come again, and where from this time?—O my! What am I doing? That man is competent to know the minds of others. If he is aware of the whole contents of my mind, what is there still kept from him? [*openly*] Reverend one, what an auspicious day it is for us today! Having seen your blessed feet, all our desires have been fulfilled. So where are you heading to? (17)

NĀRADA: [*aside*] There is no shame at all in that vile woman. What is this? With her what is sweet to the mouth may be poison to the belly. She is a *makal* fruit.[3] The eye is made happy upon seeing its golden hue, but inside—ash! While the capacity is still in me I must in no way leave this place without first doling out condign punishment. [*openly*] Upon seeing your moon-like faces I have entered extreme bliss. Why ask any more about me? Having met a most grievous misfortune, I travel flitting between the three worlds. (18)

RATI: What are you saying? (19)

NĀRADA: Need I go on? Some time ago, having seen Hara and Gaurī on Mount Kailāsa, I was returning to my own hermitage, when I arrived by a trick of Fate, striken by thirst, at the excellent lake Mānasa—(20)

ŚACĪ: Then what, good sir? (21)

NĀRADA: Arriving at the bank of the excellent lake, I saw that there was blossoming in its waters a golden lotus. (22)

RATI: Divine sage, what happened then? (23)

NĀRADA: Seeing the beauty of the lotus, I forgot that I was afflicted by thirst, and with great effort I picked it. (24)

ALL: Then what? Then what? (25)

NĀRADA: All of a sudden there came this divine voice from the sky—'O Nārada, this is the lotus of the reverend Pārvatī; it is not your proper business to pick this. Now if you fail to give this flower to the most beautiful female among all the females of the three worlds then you will be burnt by the flame of Girija's anger.' Woe, what a pretty fix this is!—(26)

ŚACĪ: [*a smile on her face*] Reverend one, you mustn't be worried about this any longer. Why don't you just give the lotus to me? (27)

MURAJĀ: Why, why should he give it to you? Divine sage, give me the lotus. (28)

RATI: Great sage, take thought now. What female is there in the three worlds more worthy of this god-made golden lotus than me? (29)

NĀRADA: [*aside*] Here, my desire is coming to fruition. Before this storm begins I'd better leave this place right now. [*openly*] It is not right for you to make entreaties to me in this matter. Look, I am old, a forest-dwelling ascetic—you are all divine females. Which one is the most beautiful among you, this I am not able to calculate. Therefore I left this golden lotus on the very summit of the reverend mount Vindhya; anyone other than she who is the most beautiful among you, immediately upon touching this flower, will turn to stone and spend a thousand years in this grove. Now I bid you farewell. [*exit*] (30)

ŚACĪ: [*a little angrily*] What woman is there more brazen than you two? (31)

BOTH: Why? In what way, exactly, do you see brazenness in us? (32)

ŚACĪ: Why? Do you really need to ask that? To see your vanity is just fearful. Oh my! For shame! Do you really preen yourselves so vainly in front of me? (33)

BOTH: Why? Why? Are we preening ourselves? (34)

ŚACĪ: Do you not know that I am the Indrāṇī of Indra? (35)

[3] A lovely-looking fruit with offensive-smelling, inedible pulp; cf. colocynth.

Murajā: Pah, that may be so. Do you not know that I am Murajā, the mistress of the lord of the Yakṣas? (36)

Rati: Listening to you two makes me laugh. Have you forgotten that I am Rati, she who bewitches the mind of Anaṅga, who in turn beguiles the minds of everyone? (37)

Śacī: Ha! Don't tell me any more about your Manmatha! Since he was incinerated by the fire of Hara's anger, what is left of him? (38)

Rati: Why, what is missing? If you forbid me to speak of my Manmatha, then you can't let the name of Indra pass your lips again either. Everyone knows how much affection the Lord of Gods has for you. If he didn't continue to feel such affection for you would he still be the God of a Thousand Eyes?[4] (39)

Śacī: [*angrily*] What great worthiness do you have? You find fault with the Lord of the Gods! Just to look at your face is a sin. (40)

Enter Nārada again, unseen

Nārada: [*aside*] Aha! What a quarrel I've sent their way. I wish I could sound the *vina*, raise my hands in sheer delight, and do a dance. [*thinking*] Be that as it may; this flame of anger, hard to conquer, ought now to be extinguished. [*exit*] (41)

Murajā: Ah! Why are you brawling in vain? (42)

In the sky: O, you female divinities! Why must you engage in this futile quarrel, and bring blame on yourselves among the other gods? Look, on a rock by that spring there lies asleep the great Indranīl, king of the city of Vidarbha. Call on him to mediate in this matter. (43)

Murajā: Did you hear that? What point is there in continuing our quarrel? Come on then, may the great King Indranīl be awoken. (44)

Śacī: King Indranīl has remained enshrouded in sleep thanks to my *maya*. Come, let's go and stand by the mountain peak over there and release the Great King from the net of *maya*. [*exeunt all, sweet instrumental music in the sky*] (45)

King: [*getting to his feet, aside*] Aha! What a marvellous dream I was having! [*heaving a deep sigh*] O goddess sleep, have I been so sinful that you have now become so unfavourable towards me? Woe! No sooner did I begin to experience the delights of heaven, body intact, than you dragged me down again in this net of unconquerable *samsara*! Mother, is this the *dharma* of a mother! Ah! What a marvellous dream I was having! I fancied I was sitting in the Assembly of the Gods listening to the lovely songs of the gathered Apsaris, and from all four directions there fell a rain of fragrant nectar—to describe it would be impossible for a mortal. [*startled*] Now what's this? Who are all these people?—Goddesses or humans?

Enter Śacī, Murajā, and Rati again

Their eyes are unblinking, their bodies without shadow, even if I did have doubts about their divinity, my hesitation would be dispelled by the loveliness of their incomparable beauty. If he catches the smell of a lotus, even a blind man knows that there is a lotus in bloom nearby. Is the loveliness of such incomparable beauty possible on the Earth? (46)

[4] Patra (1989) notes: 'An allusion to the Puranic story of Indra's abduction of the guru's wife.'

ŚACĪ: Victory to the Great King. (47)

MURAJĀ: Long life to you, O Great King. (48)

RATI: O Great King, may auspiciousness attend you in everything. (49)

ŚACĪ: O lord, I am Queen Śacī. (50)

MURAJĀ: O Great King, I am Murajā, wife of the Yakṣa King. (51)

RATI: O lord of men, I am Rati, partner of Manmatha. (52)

ŚACĪ: [*as an aside to Murajā and Rati*] Let just one of us speak. Why make such a racket? If you do that what will be achieved? (53)

KING: [*bowing*] Having seen your blessed feet my life has obtained its goal. Now what command do you issue to this slave? (54)

ŚACĪ: O Great King, give that golden lotus, which you can see atop that mountain peak, to the one of all three of us whom you consider to be the most beautiful. (55)

RATI: O Great King, have you properly understood what Goddess Śacī has said? The most beautiful of all—(56)

ŚACĪ: Hey, why don't you quieten down? (57)

KING: [*aside*] What a terrible mishap this is! I'm looking at all these female divinities—which of them shall I satisfy? Which shall I anger? [*openly*] Please absolve your slave from this responsibility. (58)

ŚACĪ: That can never be. You are an avatar of *dharma* on Earth.[5] You must of necessity make this judgement. (59)

MURAJĀ: If you do not make this *mimamsa* [*viz.* religious interpretation] then who else will? (60)

RATI: What have you got to fear in this matter? Just take a good look at us. (61)

KING: [*aside*] What a disaster! Whom shall I live to tell that I made this journey at an inauspicious time! (62)

ŚACĪ: O lord of men, are you still keeping quiet? Does your mind have any doubts in this matter? Look, I am the chief queen of Indra, if I so wished I could in an instant appoint you as the Lord of the whole Earth and the Oceans. (63)

MURAJĀ: Goddess Śacī, my friend, that is an idle boast. See how you remain as if dead day and night in Amaravatī through fear of the mighty Daitya clan. How, then, will you grant overlordship of the Earth and the Oceans? [*to the King*] O lord of men, consider carefully: I am the lawful wife of the Lord of Wealth; the Earth, this Mine of Jewels, is mine—all the masses of priceless jewels that there are in it, I am the one who possesses them all. (64)

RATI: [*aside*] Pah, as I can see that these two are prepared to give the judge a bribe, then why should I keep quiet any longer? [*openly*] Great King, what joy there is to be found in the office of Lord, the Lord of Gods himself knows. The falcon, king of birds, indeed sits proudly on a lofty mountain peak; but when a storm begins it is his destruction that occurs before anyone else's. And what shall I say about wealth? The jewel that lives on a snake's head remains ever hidden in its hole. And if ever, afflicted with hunger, it comes out into a ferocious and gloomy night, then who, upon seeing the loveliness of its jewel, will not try to destroy its life? Look, moreover, at him whose desire is the acquisition of wealth: his condition is ultimately that of a mulberry-worm.

[5] Kings are traditionally considered to embody *dharma*.

This foolish worm builds a splendid house with great toil, and he is bound within it, squandering his life in hunger and thirst, and other people dress themselves in his silk. (65)

ŚACĪ: Ah! What keen reasoning goddess Rati has! Who on Earth, then, has pleasure? (66)

RATI: How would you know about it? In my opinion the bee has most pleasure of all. He has no other business than drinking the flowers' honey. Great King, all the women that, like flowers, bloom here on earth—they all worship me. (67)

KING: [*aside*] What should I do now? Where shall I find deliverance from this disaster? (68)

ŚACĪ: O lord of men, your delaying further in this matter is not fitting. (69)

KING: What a command. [*taking the golden lotus*] You have appointed me of your own volition as judge in this matter; if I give my true opinion about it as it seems to me, will any of you be angry with me? (70)

ALL: Why should we be? (71)

KING: Then I give this golden lotus to the goddess Rati. In my opinion Rati, who bewitches Manmatha, is the queen of all females. [*gives the lotus to Rati*] (72)

ŚACĪ: [*angrily*] You horrible man, have you succumbed to desire and destroyed *dharma*? I shall on no account fail to mete out a fitting punishment to you for this. [*exit*] (73)

MURAJĀ: [*angrily*] When you were born into the royal caste, did you undertake to act in your greed for women like an untouchable? You will receive condign punishment for this in due course, of that there is no doubt. [*exit*] (74)

RATI: [*face glowing with joy*] Great King, you need be afraid on no account. I will protect you, and I will not forget to reward you as is fitting. With my blessing you will come to enjoy supreme pleasure. For now I bid you farewell. (75)

KING: [*aside*] Who can rescind the decree of the Creator? What is to be remains unseen by me; I have survived the disaster that has just happened. I have achieved a great thing in not being turned to ashes by the fire of the anger of Śacī and Murajā. (76)

[*End of the Judgement scene; the Act continues with the entrance of the Jester and conversation between him and the King.*]

APPENDIX 4

Synopsis of the *Padmābatī nāṭak*

Act One

The play begins with Indranīl, the King of Vidarbha, hunting on Mount Vindhya; suddenly he hears sweet music emanating from the sky, smells a sweet fragrance, and is lulled to sleep (Act 1, 1). Enter Rati and Śacī, Hindu goddess of love and the queen of the gods respectively (2), the latter complaining to the former about her husband's neglect of her (2–4). Then enters the goddess Murajā, wife of Kubera, the god of wealth (5), who complains about her fruitless search for her daughter Vijayā, an avatar of whom has been born on earth in mortal form (5–14). Hereupon Nārada, the mischievous *debarṣi* or 'divine sage', descends to the mountainside (15). The sage tells the audience, as an aside, that whilst flying through the air he observed the goddesses and conceived the desire to set them quarrelling with each other (15). Nārada tells the goddesses about a golden lotus he has found on lake Mānasa (20ff.). Upon picking the flower, so the sage claims, a divine voice told him that it belonged to the great goddess Pārvatī, and that if he failed to give it to the most beautiful female in the three worlds (hell, earth, and heaven) then he would be scorched by the flame of Śiva. Any unworthy female to touch the flower, so Nārada continues, is doomed to turn to stone for a thousand years (30).

Even before Nārada finishes his story, the goddesses begin to quarrel (27ff.), much to Nārada's satisfaction, and they each appeal in turn to the sage to give the lotus to her. The sage demurs, arguing that as an old ascetic he is unqualified to make such a judgement, and says that he has left the lotus on the very summit of Mount Vindhya (30). Nārada departs and the goddesses continue to argue; he enters again, this time unseen (41). A voice 'in the sky', emanating from the invisible Nārada, advises the goddesses to cease quarrelling, indicates the sleeping Indranīl, King of Vidarbha, and tells them to appoint him as judge (43).

The goddesses find King Indranīl, and Śacī commands him to take the 'golden lotus' and to give it to the goddess he thinks most beautiful (56). Śacī offers him, as a bribe, 'the overlordship of the earth and the oceans' (64). Murajā, decrying Śacī's bribe, implies that she will give him 'all the masses of priceless jewels' on earth (65). And Rati, casting aspersions on both goddesses' bribes, declares that all women worship her, leaving the precise nature of her offer a little ambiguous.

Indranīl, hesitant and afraid, foresees and tries to forestall the goddesses' anger (71). In unison the three goddesses assure him that, whatever the outcome, they will not be angry. Hereupon Indranīl awards the lotus to Rati, the goddess of love. At once, and despite the promise not to be angry, Śacī angrily exclaims that she will punish Indranīl for his snub (74). Śacī exits soon followed by Murajā who also threatens 'condign punishment' for the insult (75). The King and Rati are left alone onstage, and the goddess assures him that she will protect him from the other goddesses' anger, and adds that, at her blessing, he will come to enjoy supreme pleasure (76). Exit Rati (78), and enter the King's charioteer, whereupon follows a comic set-piece involving the jester to diffuse the tension of the judgement scene (79ff.).

Act Two

Act Two is split into two Scenes. Act Two, Scene One is set in the city of Māheśvarī, home of the beautiful Princess Padmābatī, and begins with the Princess in conversation with her friend. The goddess Rati comes to Padmābatī disguised as a *citrakari* or 'picture seller' (15) and sets about arranging for King Indranīl to marry Princess Padmābatī (17). Rati shows Padmābatī a picture of Indranīl and it causes the Princess to swoon (37): Padmābatī has seen the man pictured on the canvas in her dreams (60). *Exeunt omnes* and enter the goddesses Śacī and Murajā (65), both bent on thwarting Rati's plans. Murajā expresses concern that Śacī means to ruin Padmābatī as well as Indranīl (83), a concern which figures an ironic foreshadowing of Murajā's discovery in Act Five that Padmābatī is in fact her own daughter. But Śacī defends her plans and Murajā acquiesces in them (86). Act Two Scene Two, set like Scene One in Māheśvarī, gives some comic relief after Scene One. A conversation between Padmābatī's friend and the venal old Kañcuki ('Brahmin Supervisor of the Royal Chamber') dominates the scene: the former attempts to extract information from the latter about Padmābatī's upcoming *svayaṃvara*, the 'wedding competition' whereby various suitors compete for a princess' hand. The Kañcuki finally yields and tells her that it will happen soon (2, 2, 19). The friend is happy for Padmābatī but sad at the prospect of losing her friend to marriage: she and a female servant begin to weep; the Kañcuki insults them; the two girls depart. The Scene ends with a song sung offstage by some *vaitalaka* (panegyricists) praising the city of Māheśvarī.

Act Three

Act Three is also split into two Scenes, and is again set in Māheśvarī. Scene One begins with the entrance of King Indranīl (with his Jester), who has come to the city disguised as a merchant and on the pretext that he wishes to observe the *svayaṃvara*, or 'wedding contest', of the Princess (3, 1, 3). The Jester tells the audience, during the King's brief absence to fetch water, that Indranīl has seen a girl in a dream and has sworn that he will marry either that girl or nobody (8). The King and Jester leave to look more closely at the *svayaṃvara* preparations (19). Enter Padmābatī's friend and servant (20), who have been going about incognito with the picture of Indranīl, trying in vain to find a match for it among the suitors (24–5). Padmābatī has sworn the same oath as Indranīl, to marry the figure from her dreams or nobody (34). Enter Indranīl (40), and the girls have a match for the picture; but the servant notes anxiously that Indranīl is not dressed as a King (44). The servant fetches Padmābatī (50). The Princess sees Indranīl (now offstage) and swoons with excitement (62). The King rushes onstage to help Padmābatī and at once recognises her (70). Padmābatī is introduced to the King (deceptively) as just a friend of the Princess (79); Indranīl claims to be a companion of the King of Vidarbha (86). Padmābatī and her retinue depart (100), and the Scene ends with the King rejoicing that he has found the girl of his dreams (101), but lamenting that she is apparently not the Princess herself (106). Act Three, Scene Two begins with the Priest and the Kañcuki revealing that the *svayaṃvara* has not taken place (3, 2, 1–8): Padmābatī has become faint and has been instructed by the royal physician to remain indoors; the auspicious moment for the *svayaṃvara* has passed and so the suitors have had to go home (6). Padmābatī's friend and servant enter and reveal that the Princess is ill because the man of her dreams is apparently not a King (13). The girls depart, Indranīl enters lamenting (16): the goddesses Śacī and Murajā, so he thinks, have conspired to make it impossible for him to marry the girl given to him by Rati. The Jester enters fleeing from guards (22): Indranīl's royal identity is revealed since the guards will only release the Jester if they know he is a King (29). The Priest and the Kañcuki, followed by Padmābatī's friend and servant, return to discover Indranīl's true identity (36, 44). The Princess' retinue go to tell the Princess the good news (46).

Act Four

Between Act Three and Act Four, Indranīl and Padmābatī have married. Act Four is split into three Scenes. Scene One is set at the gate of Indranīl's city Vidarbha. The vicious god Kali begins the scene with a soliloquy (4, 1, 1): the god has gone to the failed suitors and told them of Padmābatī's marriage to

Indranīl, and these kings are now outside Vidarbha taking counsel. Indranīl is outside the city fighting, while Padmābatī is inside the city. Kali has come to snatch Padmābatī away in the hope that Indranīl will commit suicide from grief (3). Padmābatī and her friend converse, observed by Kali who has become invisible, and the Princess laments for all those who will die on her account (5). Kali comes onstage, this time visibly and dressed as a charioteer. He convinces the two women that Indranīl has instructed him to remove them to a mountain fortress (16). Padmābatī eventually agrees and she mounts Kali's chariot with her friend (24). The rest of the Scene is a comic passage, diffusing the tension of the Scene so far: the Jester comes on stage (26), apparently covered in blood, but in fact just covered in red dye so as to appear to have been fighting. Scene Two again begins with Kali, this time atop a wooded mountain, telling the audience that he has brought Padmābatī here at Śacī's command (4, 2, 1). Śacī and Murajā enter to interview Kali (2): Murajā finds Kali's glee at Padmābatī's suffering distasteful (6), again foreshadowing the denouement where it will be revealed that Padmābatī is Murajā's daughter. After Kali has left, Murajā questions Śacī's justification for ruining a blameless girl for another man's transgression (12). Murajā spots Padmābatī (16); the goddess' breasts swell with milk and her heart trembles (18), which will prove to be the goddess' bodily recognition of Padmābatī as her daughter (see 5, 1, 16ff.). Murajā storms off (22) when Śacī proposes worsening Padmābatī's plight, and the other goddess follows. Enter Padmābatī and her friend (24), the latter lamenting and complaining that Indranīl must have turned against her (30). Kali enters again (42), this time disguised as a wounded soldier, and gives the false report that the King has been vanquished and Vidarbha put to the torch (46). Kali exits gleefully, and Rati enters dressed as a woodcutter (54), complaining of Śacī's treachery. Rati proposes to send Padmābatī to stay with some 'great sages' while she goes herself to report Śacī's behaviour to the great goddess Pārvatī who will, Rati feels sure, rectify the situation. The Scene ends with Padmābatī and her friend being taken by Rati to safety. Act Four, Scene Three, a brief Scene, mirrors the previous Scene: King Vidarbha has defeated the angry suitors, but is inconsolable over his separation from Padmābatī (4, 3, 1). The Jester attempts to cheer the King but fails.

Act Five

Act Five, the last of the play, is split into two brief Scenes. Scene One is set at the *tīrtha* or 'sacred ford' of Śacī; the goddess recounts her abduction of Padmābatī and tells gleefully of how Indranīl, distraught by his wife's absence, has taken to roaming from place to place trying to find her (3). After a brief conversation between Śacī and Rambha, one of the goddess's *apsarīs* or 'nymphs', Murajā enters weeping (11), and accuses Śacī of visiting absolute destruction on her (12). Murajā reveals what has been liberally foreshadowed in earlier Scenes: 'Padmābatī is my Vijayā' (16). The goddess Pṛthivī ('Earth') gave birth to Vijayā (that is, gave birth to a mortal avatar of Murajā's daughter) and left her on the summit of *śrīparvata* (the Blessed Mountain) (20). Yajñasena, King of Māheśvarī, found her and raised her as his own. Enter Nārada (24), the mischievous 'divine sage' of Act One, bringing good tidings. Pārvatī (27), the 'Great Goddess', commands that Śacī and Murajā desist from their mischief (33). Padmābatī is safe in an *ashram* and the two goddesses are to go there at once (37): Śacī laments that Pārvatī's command is inexorable and that Rati has been victorious after all (36). The two goddesses duly depart (38–9). Act Five, Scene Two, the final scene of the play, is set at the *ashram* of the Great Sage, Angira, on the banks of the river Tāmasa. Gautamī, Aṅgira's wife, tries to comfort Padmābatī saying that Indranīl will soon come for her (5, 2, 1) but Padmābatī is not convinced and believes that her husband has forgotten her (8). Then Padmābatī's friend comes to tell Padmābatī that Indranīl has arrived (15) and Padmābatī, initially incredulous, finally believes her (18). The women depart and Gautamī returns with Indranīl and the Jester (20). Indranīl tells the sage's wife of his grief at being separated from Padmābatī (20–24). Gautamī departs to fetch the Queen (26), leaving the King and the Jester alone. Hereupon, we have the grand entrance of the three goddesses (Śacī, Murajā, and Rati) with Gautamī, Padmābatī, Vasumatī, Nārada, and Angira (41-42): all hail the king (42); Nārada compares Indranīl's recovery of Padmābatī with Rama's recovery of Sita (43); Aṅgira hands Padmābatī over to the king (44); and Śacī gives him her blessing (44). Finally a song is sung wishing the king well, flowers shower down onto the stage, and Nārada bids Indranīl to tread the path of *dharma* and compares Padmābatī to Śarmiṣṭhā, the heroine of Madhusudan's first Bengali play (47).

APPENDIX 5

Siṃhal-bijay kābya

The following is Madhusudan's brief English plan for the first three books of the *SVK*. I transliterate Indian names, originally written in Bengali characters, into Roman script.[1]

Book I.—Invocation; description of the voyage. They near Ceylone, when Murajā excites Pavana to raise a storm, which disperses the fleet. The ship with Vijaya and his immediate followers is wrecked on an unknown island. The hero lands and after worshipping the *devatā* [*viz.* godheads] of the place, and eating *prasād* [*viz.* food offerings] wanders out alone to explore the island. Lakṣmī prays to Viṣṇu to defeat the ill designs of Murajā. He consoles her and by a favourable gale directs the other ships to the same port. The chiefs, alarmed by the absence of the prince, send out messengers all around to seek him. On the return of the messengers without the prince, they set sail and retire to a neighbouring island and encamp there.

Book II.—The adventures of Vijaya. Murajā, on finding Vijaya separated from his companions, sends a Yakṣa to lead him to the city of the king of the island [Andaman]. He marries Vimohinī, the king's daughter, and has a castle in a distant wood assigned to him for his residence. In the society of his wife, he forgets the purpose of his voyage, as well as his companions.

Book III.—Lakṣmī sends Vijaya a vision. He prepares to leave his new home, in search of the companions of his voyage, as also of the Island Kingdom, promised to him and his descendants.

This English sketch is complemented by 24 Bengali verses, presumably from the passage following the 'Invocation' in Book 1 ('They near Ceylone, when Murajā excites Pavana to raise a storm . . . '). I translate these verses as follows:[2]

> In her golden palace Murajā who showers nectar and bewitches the Lord of Yakṣas, hearing that sound in the city of Alakā, cast her gaze and looked towards the ocean in astonishment, a beautiful vessel was floating, her sails fluttering up into the sky, filling all directions with an auspicious sound. In her rage, the good lady said to her moon-faced friend;—'Open your eyes, moon-faced lady, and look over here, Vijaya is proceeding to Siṃhala in his desire to acquire that kingdom,

[1] From Basu (1893, 1993 reprint) 357–8 (the best edition available to me).
[2] Translated from Basu (1893, 1993 reprint) 357–8.

leaving behind his own country at Lakṣmī's command. (10) What shame! While I have breath I shall not let that man take the kingdom, my friend. Did I adorn Siṃhala like a garden only to give it away to another? My body is ablaze with anger when I call to mind Lakṣmī's arrogance, O moon-faced lady, how am I to look upon Lakṣmī handing over my land to her devotee! Her father is the Ocean, so she calms him through supplication. Go, my friend, and summon the charioteer to bring Puṣpaka [*viz.* Kubera's chariot] here; as the King of Winds is graciously aboard, I will go at once with a storm. (20) I will restrain the miscreant, then I shall see what happens.' The chariot, effulgent with golden brilliance, came rattling to the gate, the horses whinnied with stomping of feet, scattering sparks all about. The beautiful lady mounted the chariot with joy, fitting it out with bewitching equipment.'

APPENDIX 6

Synopsis of the Poems of the *Bīrāṅganā kābya*

The first poem in the Bengali collection, Bk1, is *Duṣmanter prati Śakuntalā* ('Śakuntalā to Duṣmanta'), based on the story made famous by Kālidāsa's drama *Abhijñānaśakuntalam,*[1] but originally related (in a simpler version) at *Mahābhārata* 1.7b.62–69.[2] Śakuntalā is the adopted daughter of Kaṇva, a forest-dwelling hermit. In Kaṇva's absence, Śakuntalā is approached by king Duṣmanta, while the latter is hunting in the forest. They marry, but then the king leaves and comes to forget her, though at length the two are reunited. The letter is written after a certain period of separation (placing the poem, as it were, at *Mahābhārata* 1, 7b.20 or between Acts 3 and 4 of *Abhijñānaśakuntalam*), and Śakuntalā has started to believe she has been forgotten (*BK* 1.2f.). The letter is a plea to Duṣmanta that he return (especially at ll. 160–*fin.*), but is mostly concerned with giving details of Śakuntalā's wretched life in the forest without her husband (ll. 4–159).

BK 2 is a letter written by the goddess Tārā ('Star'), wife of the chief god Bṛhaspati, to the moon-god, Soma, whom she plans to seduce. Soma has been studying in the house of Bṛhaspati, the *guru* of all the gods, during which time Tārā has fallen in love with him. The narrative, as related in the *Brahmapurāṇa* (chs. 9 and 152.5–9b), lays emphasis on Soma's passion for and abduction of Tārā; but *Matsyapurāṇa* (ch. 23) is closer to the Bengali poem in presenting Tārā as the instigator of the affair.[3] The Bengali poem is Tārā's confession of love and, in addition to her attempt to persuade Soma to elope with her, she recounts how she first fell in love with him (ll. 35ff.). In both Puranic accounts the elopement results in a war between Soma and Bṛhaspati, ultimately won by the betrayed husband.

BK 3 is the letter of Rukmiṇī, daughter of King Bhīṣmaka, to Dvārakanātha. According to the Puranic accounts (see especially *Mahābhārata* 2.42) Rukmiṇī is an avatar of goddess Lakṣmī, and is therefore devoted from birth

[1] As noted by Banerjee (1952) 87f. For an introduction to this most celebrated of Sanskrit dramas, see Vasudeva (2006).

[2] Line references are to the 'Critical Edition' of the epic, Sukthankar (1919–1966).

[3] For an interesting comparison of the story of Tārā and Soma as related here and in other narratives, see Kirfel (1952).

to Dvārakanātha (god Viṣṇu's avatar). When her brother tries to marry her to Śiśupāla against her will, Rukmiṇī sends for Dvārakanātha to rescue her, which he subsequently does. This letter is Rukmiṇī's request for help,[4] but she also gives an extended account of the miraculous life of her divine addressee (ll. 28ff.), which owes much to Bengali Vaiṣnava devotional poetry.

BK 4 is a letter from Kekaẏī, the second of king Daśaratha's three wives and the youngest, to her husband. The king, whose son Rāma is the eponymous 'hero' of the *Rāmāyaṇa*, is about to install the hero as his successor. This angers Kekaẏī, Rāma's stepmother, since the king had vowed that her son would succeed him to the throne.[5] This letter is a written petition to the king, reminding him of his binding oath (ll. 40ff.). Kekaẏī punctuates her petition with the threat of denouncing him throughout the world, a theme developed especially at ll. 86–115.

In *BK* 5 we find the letter from Sūrpaṇakhā, sister of Rāvaṇa, to Rāma's brother Lakṣmaṇa. At *Rāmāyaṇa* 6.9.13f., Sūrpaṇakhā falls in love with Lakṣmaṇa but, to her great humiliation, is rejected.[6] This humiliation provokes Rāvaṇa to abduct Sītā, Rāma's wife, which in turn causes the great war of the epic. In the *Rāmāyaṇa,* Sūrpaṇakhā, whose name means literally 'shovel-nails', is a grotesque and ugly figure. But in the *BK* (just as in Madhusudan's epic *MBK*), Rāvaṇa's family is depicted with no such antipathy, a fact noted in the preface to *BK* 5 (preface, ll. 3f.). The letter of *BK* 5 figures Sūrpaṇakhā's tentative confession of love to Rāma's brother. In the Bengali poem, Sūrpaṇakhā makes full confession of her love (ll. 1–38), followed by a brief contemplation of the idea that Lakṣmaṇa might not reciprocate her love (ll. 39–59), and then concludes with more words of love and a full introduction of herself as the sister of Rāvaṇa (ll.104ff.).

BK 6 is Draupadī's letter to Arjuna, her (principal) husband, who has gone to *Vaijayanta* (Indra's heaven) to acquire weapons and knowledge from the gods. This locates the letter at some point during *Mahābhārata* 3, 32.43–79, the narration of Arjuna's journey, and is therefore set in the broader context of the Pāṇḍavas' exile in the forest (*Mahābhārata* 3). Draupadī is distressed by their separation, tormented by the notion that Arjuna might be tempted by one of the immortal females (ll. 1–40). Hereupon, she reminds Arjuna of their first meeting (ll. 69ff.), and their wedding (l. 108), and tells him about how she and the family are passing the time in their forest-exile (ll. 177ff.).

BK 7 is addressed to Duryodhana, general of the Kaurava army and Arjuna's arch-enemy, by his wife Bhānumatī. It is sent within a few days (according to l. 2 of the poem's preface) of Duryodhana's departure for the

[4] For a treatment of this Sanskrit epic narrative, and of the *Viṣṇupurāṇa* and *Bhāgavatapurāṇa* where the story is also related, see Hospital (1978).

[5] For Daśaratha's vow to Kaikeẏī, cf. Deshpande (1966).

[6] For an overview of this story's place in the Sanskrit epic, see Bulche (1964).

battlefield of Kurukṣetra, which locates the letter between the end of *Mahābhārata* 5 (at 5,56.152.1-30 Duryodhana arrays his army) and the first few chapters of Book 6. Bhānumatī pleads with her husband to abandon the battlefield (see especially ll. 141ff.), warns of all the foes he will have to face (ll. 31ff.), and relates a dream she has had foreshadowing the deaths of various Kaurava warriors (ll. 78–139).

BK 8 is another plea from a wife to her husband, this time from Duḥśalā to the Kaurava Jayadratha, to abandon the battlefield of Kurukṣetra. The letter is sent upon Duḥśalā's discovery of Arjuna's oath that he will slay Jayadratha, which places the letter shortly after *Mahābhārata* 7,60. Jayadratha has just slain the young Abhimanyu (7,32–51), thereby incurring Arjuna's wrath (7,52-60), and he will in due course be slain by him (7,61–121). The letter expresses Duḥśalā's dismay at hearing of the curse (ll. 1–15), followed by a lengthy narration of the misery with which news of the war is received at home (ll.16–156). The epistle is rounded off with a plea that Jayadratha return in disguise and that husband and wife abscond together (ll. 157–end).

BK 9 is the letter of Jāhnavī to Śāntanu, an apology from a divine wife to the mortal husband whom she has abandoned. The goddess has borne Śāntanu eight children, seven of whom she has had to kill: her seven enemies were fated to be reincarnated as her own children, and so she has been obliged to kill them. But the eighth is a normal child, and she nurtures him carefully (ll. 28ff.): this child, Devavrata, will bring glory to Śāntanu's family (ll. 21ff.). Her letter is full of praise for Śāntanu (ll. 47ff.), and is intended as an explanation for her behaviour (ll. 1-20), and to disabuse the mortal of his misconception that Jāhnavī is his wife (ll. 46). The story of Śāntanu and Jāhnavī is related at *Mahābhārata* 1,92–3, and the letter is therefore imagined as occurring at 1,92.48–55 (Jāhnavī's explanation of her infanticide): Madhusudan transforms a face-to-face theophany into an epistle.[7]

BK 10 is the letter of the goddess Urvaśī to the mortal Pururavā, which (as is noted in the preface to the poem) is a response to the *Vikramorvaśī*, Kālidāsa's famous Sanskrit *troṭaka* drama.[8] But note that the story of this love affair had already been narrated at *Mahābhārata* 1,70 and *Matsyapurāṇa* 24 and 115–20, as well as in the earlier Vedic *Śatapathabrāhmaṇa* 11, 5.1.[9] As a confession of love conveyed from the goddess by her sister Citralekhā to Pururavā, the epistle stands, as it were, as an alternative to Act 2, 10–23: in the play Citralekhā mediates a conversation between the two rather than

[7] For a comparison of this marriage between man and goddess with that of Peleus and Thetis, see Arora (1971).

[8] The *troṭaka* is a variation of the Sanskrit *nāṭaka*, the term denoting a particular kind of dance and confused speech; indeed we should note that it is only in the Bengali recension of Kālidāsa's *Vikramorvaśī* that the Sanskrit play is classified as a *troṭaka* (elsewhere it is considered a straightforward *nāṭaka*). See Keith (1924) 350f.

[9] For these earlier treatments of the story, cf. Post (1984) 11–26, and Janaki (1975).

conveying a letter. In her epistle, Urvaśī first confesses her love (ll. 1–29) and relates the mirth of the gods upon hearing of it (ll. 12f.). Then she narrates Pururavā's rescue of Urvaśī (ll. 30ff.), as related in Act 1 of the *Vikramorvaśī*, and finally vows to come to earth and submit to Pururavā as her husband (ll. 78–end).

BK 11, an epistle of exceptional vitriol, is the letter of Queen Janā to King Nīladhvaja on the subject of avenging their son Prabīra, whose death is narrated at *Mahābhārata* 14 (as noted explicitly in the poem's preface). Arjuna has killed Prabīra, but Nīladhvaja has made peace with him, much to Janā's dismay. As Janā notes (l. 42), Nīladhvaja has made peace because he has recognized the divinity of Arjuna, and does not wish to fight the god (i.e. Viṣṇu). The letter is a plea that Nīladhvaja avenge Prabīra (ll. 1–20), and an attempt to persuade the addressee that he is mistaken: Arjuna, so she argues, is not a god at all (ll. 43–99). After further lament for her son (ll. 100–24), Janā tells her husband (sarcastically) to enjoy his friendship with his son's killer (l. 125), and that she will commit suicide by drowning herself in the Ganges (ll. 126–end).

APPENDIX 7

Sources Of The *The Bīrāṅganā kābya* And The *Heroides*

Distribution of the principal source texts in the *BK* and the *Heroides*: the symbol '(O)' in the table below stands for a story or characters which are obscure, or at least outside of the mainstream. The description 'obscure' is, of course, subjective and the following reflects my own subjective view.

Table A.2. Sources of the the *Bīrāṅganā Kābya (BK)* and the *Heroides*

Number	*Heroides*	*BK*
1	*Odyssey*	Drama / *MBh*
2	?Callimachus (O)	*Matsyapurāṇa* (O)
3	*Iliad*	*MBh* / other *purāṇas* (O)
4	Euripides	*Rāmāyaṇa*
5	?Lycophron/Hellanicus (O)	*Rāmāyaṇa*
6	Euripides / *Argonautica*	*MBh*
7	*Aeneid*	*MBh*
8	Euripides	*MBh* (O)
9	Sophocles	*MBh* (O)
10	Catullus *inter alios*	Drama / *MBh* / *purāṇas*
11	? (O)	*MBh* (O)
12	Euripides / *Argonautica*	
13	Euripides / *Iliad*	
14	? (O)	
15	Sappho/ Attic Comedy	
16	Epic Cycle	
17	Epic Cycle	
18	? (O)	
19	? (O)	
20	Callimachus (O)	
21	Callimachus (O)	

APPENDIX 8

Preface to the *Hekṭor-badh*

Preface[1]

(1)

In the past the people in ancient Hellas—that is Greece—used to practise an idolatrous religion believing in various gods and goddesses. When Zeus, the Lord of the divine clan, had fallen in love with a young human girl called Leda, and had taken on the form of a swan and slept with her, Leda produced two eggs. From one of the eggs were born two offspring; from the other was born an exceptionally beautiful girl called Helen. The king of Lacedaemon, Leda's husband, knew that these three offspring were born of a god's seed, and set about raising them with great care. Just as our beautiful Śakuntalā was raised in the hermitage of the sage Kaṇva, just so was Helen in due course raised to maturity in the royal house of Lacedaemon. Our Śakuntalā, by dint of an evil fate, remained within the hermitage of her adoptive father, and was like a gem in the womb of a mine; but the kingdoms of Hellas very quickly became full of the sweet aroma of the glory of Helen's beauty. Very many young princes, desiring to win this jewel of a girl, continually frequented the royal city of Lacedaemon, and the great splendour of a kind of *svayaṃvara* then took place there.[2] The custom of *svayaṃvara* was not a common practice in Greece, and if it had endured it would have been a wondrous thing.

After Helen had chosen in marriage a certain prince called Menelaus, her adoptive father shared some words with the princes: 'O princes! Now that my daughter has placed, of her own will, the garland around the neck of this young prince, it is not proper for you to display any anger in this matter; rather make a promise, calling on Zeus the father of the gods as your witness,

[1] Patra (1989) notes *ad loc.*: 'The preface is not a part of the translation (sic): it is an independent work. For those who do not know the background history of Greek myth, the tale of the *Iliad* will not be comprehensible, so Madhusudan has said a few words in our own language by way of a summary.'

[2] The *svayaṃvara* is a form of wedding ritual, appearing frequently in Hindu epic, in which a maiden chooses (*vara* = 'choice') a husband for herself (*svayam* = 'oneself') from a field of princes, often after various contests.

that if at any time some calamity befalls this newly married bride and groom, then you will all join together on their behalf and rescue them from peril.'

The princes heeded the king's words, bound themselves by oath, and returned to their respective countries. Menelaus was installed as crown prince of the kingdom of Lacedaemon with his beautiful wife, and passed his time in supreme pleasure.

(2)

There is a small region in the west of the Asian continent called Asia Minor. Once upon a time, there was a very famous city in this region called 'Ilium' or 'Troy'. The king of the city was called Priam. The queen's name was Hecuba. During pregnancy, the queen—like our Gāndhārī, queen of the Kuru tribe—had a dream in which she gave birth to something that seemed to be a firebrand, on account of which one day the royal city would turn to ash. Upon waking from sleep, the queen recalled the narrative of the dream and spent her days in great sorrow. In due course, the entire contents of the dream became common knowledge throughout the city. Then the queen gave birth to an exceedingly handsome prince. King Priam's ministers and friends, like Vidura and the other royal ministers of the Kuru clan, knowing that this child was the bearer of future disaster, advised Priam to abandon him, and the king, unlike Dhṛtarāṣṭra, did just that. His affection for his offspring could not blind King Priam to the future well-being of his kingdom.

As soon as the child had been placed on the ground, a royal servant disobeyed the great king's order; that is, he failed to carry out the child's death sentence and put him on a certain mountain, near to the city, called Ida. A certain shepherd, seeing that the child abandoned there was a wonderfully beautiful child, placed him in the care of his barren wife. The shepherd's wife began to raise the little child with the greatest care, as if he were born of her own womb. Just like our Kārtikeya, the favourite of the Kṛ ttika clan, the young prince in due course grew up, in the shepherd's house, to have beauty and various talents.[3] And like our Puru, Duṣmanta's son, he too laid low the beasts of the forest even at a very young age.

The shepherds, seeing him ward off a number of flesh-eating beasts from the other shepherds, conferred on him the name 'Skandar', meaning 'Protector'. On a part of Mount Ida, there dwelt a certain girl, beloved of all mankind and attractive to the gods, called Oenone. The celestial one became entranced with the prince's incomparable beauty and charm, fell devotedly in love with him, and choosing him as her mate, she spent day and night in supreme delight in this mountainous region.

[3] Cf. Tennyson's *Oenone*, l. 126: 'A shepherd all thy life but yet king-born'.

(3)

There is a region of Greece called Thessaly. Peleus, the crown prince of this kingdom, married the sea-goddess Thetis. Thetis belonged to the god clan, therefore all the gods and goddesses were invited to, and attended, her splendid wedding. Because she was not invited, the young goddess, whose name was Strife and who caused quarrels, contrived on account of her great rage a wondrous device to accomplish her intention of propagating strife. Specifically, she flung down amidst the goddesses a golden fruit, having written on it a few words: 'To her who surpasses all others in beauty does this fruit truly belong'. Hera, the wife of Zeus (that is Śacī the queen of the god clan), Athena, the goddess of wisdom (that is Sarasvatī), and Aphrodite (that is Rati the goddess of love), among these three did a bitter dispute break out, prompted by this fruit, and they went to Prince Skandar on Mount Ida, told him the whole story from beginning to end, and appointed him judge in this matter. Hera said: 'O young prince! I am the queen of the divine clan, if you satisfy me by giving me the fruit, I will give you unbounded wealth and glory. Even though you reside among shepherd people, nonetheless I will raise you, as it were a fire from the ashes, to great brilliance and effulgence.' Athena said: 'I am the goddess of wisdom. If you are able to satisfy me with your devotion, you will obtain pre-eminence among men in knowledge, wisdom, and ability.' Aphrodite said: 'I am the goddess of love, if you propitiate me, I will make the most outstanding woman on earth subject to your love.' After Prince Skandar, drunk on the intoxication of youth, had placed, at this ill-fated moment, the fruit into the hand of Aphrodite, the two other goddesses became blinded by rage and made off for heaven.

The goddess Aphrodite then spoke in great delight and in extremely soft tones: 'Oh imposter! You are no shepherd. The ashes[4] that cover you are a disguise. Your father is Priam, the great king of the mighty city of Troy. Therefore go to him and petition for the honour due to a king's son. What is to be done to effect this boon of mine, which you have received in exchange for giving me the fruit, I shall tell you later.'

When Prince Skandar at the goddess' command had gone up to the royal city and revealed his identity, the old king Priam forgot what had been said

[4] In Hindu culture, an ascetic, an exile, or one of low caste is marked as such by being smeared with ash. Thus Madhusudan has 'Skandar' smeared in ash to designate that he is a shepherd (of low caste). But this is perhaps a *śleṣa* (a Sanskritic double meaning); *bhasmalupta* (which is a Sanskritic compound) means: (1) covered/hidden in ash; (2) destroyed/extinct/abolished in/with ash. The second meaning picks up on the prophecy of Hecabe's dream in which Troy *bhasmasat hailo* ('was turned to ash') by the firebrand born of her womb. Skandar is both covered in ash as a shepherd and destined, along with the whole city, to be covered in ash when Troy falls to the Achaeans.

before on account of his incomparable beauty, charm, and heroic mien. The flame of affection, mitigated by the passing of time, was at once rekindled. Therefore, the king ordered his newly found son to enter the royal family.

Some time later Prince Skandar, in compliance with Aphrodite's command, filled a great number of ships with treasure and tradable commodities and made the journey to the city of Lacedaemon. Menelaus, who was by then the king, invited the young prince into his own home with extreme honour and cordiality. After some time, in order to carry out some particular task, it was necessary for him to go abroad. Queen Helen remained, and was completely devoted in her service to the royal guest.

Queen Helen, her fate destroyed by the snare of the delusion of Aphrodite, became extremely enamoured of the royal guest Skandar, abandoned the *dharma* of a devoted wife, and having abandoned her husband's home, she followed him; and she entered the kingdom of Priam, the crown jewel of kings, as the very Death of that kingdom. King Menelaus, returning to his empty home, at once became extremely agitated and quite furious at separation from his wife.

When this terrible event had become public knowledge throughout Hellas, that is Greece, all of the kings of that country, remembering the promise they had made, assembled to help Menelaus with armed force, installed Agamemnon, his elder brother and king of the land of Argos, as the commander-in-chief of the army, and made a journey over the sea with the intention of attacking the city of Troy. The old king Priam authorized his fifty sons to fight. The great hero Hector (who can be said to be the Meghanāda of his Trojan Laṅkā) assumed overlordship of his foreign allies and of his own royal family's army. A terrible war raged between the two sides for ten years.

Just as the Ganges, Yamunā, and Sarasvatī, a three-pathed trio of rivers, come together as one at the Triple Confluence of the sacred fords, and travel in a single stream bound for arrival in the ocean, in just such a way has the story, with its three divisions as outlined above, come together as one from this point onwards, and headed in the direction of that Ocean of undulating song, the Iliad of the poet *guru* Homer, the Vālmīki of the European continent.

In the world-renowned poem of the poet *guru* Homer, the story of the tenth year is described. The Greeks, being close to Troy, have made an attack on the city, and have brought to their camp the wondrously beautiful daughter of Chryses, a priest of the sun god worshipped in that place. When that incomparably beautiful girl, at the time of dividing up the spoil that had been captured, fell to the lot of Agamemnon, the sovereign king and overlord of the army, he kept her in his camp with great enthusiasm and passion; Whereupon . . .

[Here begins Madhusudan's version of Homer's *Iliad*, beginning with *Il.* 1.12ff.]

APPENDIX 9

Madhusudan's Orientalist Indo-Europeanism

Tabulation of Indo-European comparisons between Greek and Hindu deities made or implied in:

- Jones (1788)
- Madhusudan's *PN* (1860)
- Madhusudan's *MBK* (1861)
- Madhusudan's *HB* (1871)

Table A.3. Greek and Hindu deities in the work of Jones and Madhusudan

Greek Deity	Hindu (Jones)	Hindu (*PN*)	Hindu (*MBK*)	Hindu (*HB*)
Zeus	Śiva, Indra, Brahmā, Viṣṇu		Śiva	Śiva, Indra, Brahmā
Hera	Durga, Śacī	Śacī	Durgā	Durgā, Śacī
Aphrodite	Rati	Rati	Rati	Rati
Thetis	Varuṇinī		Varuṇinī	(Thetis)
Athena	Sarasvatī	(Murajā)		Sarasvatī
Apollo	Sūrya			Sūrya
Hephaistus	Viśvakarmā			Viśvakarmā
Ares	Skanda			Skanda
Poseidon	Varuṇa			Varuṇa
Hades	Yama			Yama
Gaia	Vasumatī			Vasumatī
Tithonos	Aruṇa			Aruṇa
Eos	Uṣā			Uṣā

Bibliography

Archival And Unpublished Material

British Library, London:

Athenaeum Magazine [Madras] (1854)

Bengal Social Science Association Transactions (vol. 2) (1872): 'Some University Matters'

Blackwood's Edinburgh Magazine (1823, 1854)

Richey, J., C.I.E. (1922), *Selections from Educational Records, Part II, 1840–1859* (Calcutta)

Sharp, H., C.S.I, C.I.E. (1920), *Selections from the Educational Records, Part 1, 1781–1839* (Calcutta)

The Gentleman's Magazine (1840)

University of Oxford:

Delegates of the Clarendon Press, Orders and Accounts, 1811–1853 [Archive of Oxford University Press, Oxford]

Radice, W. (1987), *Tremendous Literary Rebel: The Life and Works of Michael Madhusudan Datta (1824–73)* [unpublished D.Phil. thesis, University of Oxford; permission to cite from this work has kindly been granted by the author]

United Society for the Propagation of the Gospel, Archives: C.Ind.I.(1)48; C.Ind.I(6)l; C.Ind.I.12.111; C.Ind.I.13.134; C.Ind.I.13.140 [Bodleian Library of Commonwealth and African Studies at Rhodes House, Oxford]

Bishop's College, Kolkata:

Bishop's College, Kolkata, Archives: Box 1 (labelled 'Library (1839–47)'), 'Report' (dated 1922)

Published Books And Articles

Adhikari, A. (1901), *uttaralipi kābya* (Calcutta)

Ahmad, A. (1992), *In Theory: Classes, Nations, Literatures* (London)

von Albrecht, M. et al., eds. (1968), *Ovid* (Darmstadt)

Alden, M. (2000), *Homer Beside Himself: Para-Narratives in the* Iliad (Oxford)

Alford, H. (1841), *Chapters on the Poets of Ancient Greece* (London)

Allott, K., ed. (1975), *Matthew Arnold* (London)

Allott, K. et al., eds. (1979), *Matthew Arnold* (Oxford)

Anderson, B. (1991), *Imagined Communities: Reflections on the Origin and Spread of Nationalism* (London)

Anderson, W. (1975), 'Arnold and the Classics', in Allott (1975) 259–85

Anderson, W. (2003), *The Youth of Cézanne and Zola: Notoriety at its Source, Art and Literature in Paris* (Geneva)

Arnold, M. (1867), *On the Study of Celtic Literature* (London)

Arnold, M. (1869), *Culture and Anarchy* (London)

Arnold, M. (1960), 'On Translating Homer', in Super (vol. I) (1960) 97–216 (original edition 1861)

Arora, U. (1971), 'The Ganga–Santanu Legend', in *JGJKSV* 27, 3–4: 9–19

Asheri, D. et al. (2007), *A Commentary on Herodotus Books I–IV* (Oxford)

Austin, R., ed. (1955), *P. Vergili Maronis, Aeneidos Liber Quartus* (Oxford)

Austin, R., ed. (1964), *P. Vergili Maronis, Aeneidos Liber Secundus* (Oxford)

Austin, R., ed. (1968), '*Ille ego qui quondam . . .*', *Classical Quarterly* (N.S.) 18, 1: 107–15

Austin, R., ed. (1971), *P. Vergili Maronis, Aeneidos Liber Primus* (Oxford)

Austin, R., ed. (1977), *P. Vergili Maronis, Aeneidos Liber Sextus* (Oxford)

Auty, R. et al. eds. (1980), *Traditions of Heroic and Epic Poetry: The Traditions* (Michigan)

Baca, A. (1971), 'The Themes of *Querela* and *Lacrimae* in Ovid's *Heroides*', *Emerita* 39: 195–201

Ballhatchet, K. (1965), 'Europe's Relations with South and South-East Asia', in Crawley (1965) 552–71

Bandyopadhyay, B. ed. (1945–51), *madhusūdan-granthābalī* (Calcutta)

Bandyopadhyay, S. (2004), *From Plassey to Partition, A History of Modern India* (New Delhi)

Banerjee, A., ed. (1952), *bīrāṅganā kābya* (Calcutta)

Banerjee, S. (1989), *The Parlour and the Streets* (Kolkata)

Barchiesi, A., ed. (1992), *Epistulae Heroidum 1–3* (Florence)

Barchiesi, A. (1997), 'Virgilian Narrative: Ecphrasis', in Martindale (1997) 271–81

Barchiesi, A. (2001), *Speaking Volumes, Narrative and Intertext in Ovid and Other Latin poets* (London)

Barchiesi, A. (2007), '*Carmina*: *Odes* and *Carmen Saeculare*', in Harrison (2007b) 144–61

Barrett, W., ed. (1964), Hippolytus, *Euripides; Edited with Introduction and Commentary* (Oxford)

Basu, Y. (1893), *māikel madhusūdan datter jīban-carito* (Calcutta)

Batstone, W. (2006), 'Provocation, The Point of Reception Theory', in Martindale (2006) 14–22

Bayley, S., et al. (1992), 'Gender, Modern Languages and the Curriculum in Victorian England', *History of Education* 21, 4: 363–82

Bayly, C. (1996), *Empire and Information* (Cambridge)

Bebbington, D. (2004), *The Mind of Gladstone, Religion, Homer, and Politics* (Oxford)
Belfiore, E. (1984), '*Ter Frustra Comprensa*: Embraces in the *Aeneid*', *Phoenix*, 38, 1: 19–30
Bera, M. (2004), 'meghnādbadh kābyer bhāṣāśailī', Majumdar (2004) 450–8
Berger, K. (2000), *A Theory of Art* (Oxford)
Bermann, S, et al. eds. (2005), *Nation, Language, and the Ethics of Translation* (Princeton)
Bernal, M. (1987, etc.), *Black Athena: the Afro-Asiatic Roots of Classical Civilization* (3 vols.) (New Jersey)
Bessone, F., ed. (1997), *Heroidum Epistula XII* (Florence)
Bethe, E. (1914), *Homer, Dichtung und Sage* (vol. 2) (Leipzig)
Bhabha, H. (1994), *The Location of Culture* (London)
Bhatia, N. (2004), *Acts of Authority/ Acts of Resistance: Theater and Politics in Colonial and Postcolonial India* (Oxford)
Bhattacharya, D. (1972), *maikel-samīkṣā* (Kolkata)
Bhattacharya, D., ed. (2008), *Of Matters Modern: the Experience of Modernity in Colonial and Post-colonial South Asia* (Kolkata)
Bhattacharya, S. (1962), *madhusūdaner kābyālaṅkār o kabimānas* (Kolkata)
Bindman, D. (1986), 'William Blake and Popular Religious Imagery', *The Burlington Magazine*, 128, 1003: 712–18
Biswas, S. (2003), *Samsad Bengali-English Dictionary* (Kolkata)
Boehmer, E. (1995; 2nd edition 2005), *Colonial and Postcolonial Literature: Migrant Metaphors* (Oxford)
Boehmer, E. (2002), *Empire, the National, and the Postcolonial, 1890–1920: Resistance in Interaction* (Oxford)
Du Bois, W. (1965 [1903]), *The Souls of Black Folk* (New York)
Bowman, P. (2005), *Post-Marxism Versus Cultural Studies* (Edinburgh)
Bradley, M., ed. (2010a), *Classics and Imperialism in the British Empire* (Oxford)
Bradley, M. (2010b), 'Tacitus' *Agricola* and the Conquest of Britain: Representations of Empire in Victorian and Edwardian England', in Bradley (2010) 123–157
Brandt, E. (1928), 'Zum Aeneisproömium', *Philologus* 83: 331–5
Breslin, P. (2001), *Nobody's Nation: Reading Derek Walcott* (Chicago and London)
Brockington, J. (1998), *The Sanskrit Epics* (Leiden)
Brockington, J. (2003), 'The Sanskrit Epics', in Flood (2003) 116–28
Bryce, J. (1914), *The Ancient Roman Empire and the British Empire in India* (London)
Budelmann, F. (2004), '*Trojan Women* in Yorubaland: Femi Osofisan's *Women of Owu*', in Hardwick (2004) 15–39

van Buitenen, J. (1973), *The Mahābhārata: the Book of the Beginning* (Vol. 1) (Chicago)

Bulche, C. (1964), 'Surpanakha in the Rama-story', *PIntCO* 2, 3 (1): 204–6

Bulfinch, T. (1856), *The Age of Fable, or Stories of Gods and Heroes* (Boston)

Burian, P. (2007), *Euripides Helen* (Bristol)

Burrow, C. (1997), 'Virgils, from Dante to Milton', in Martindale (1997) 79–90

Busteed, H. (1897), *Echoes from Old Calcutta* (London)

Butler, H., ed. (1920), *Aeneid VI* (Oxford)

Buxton, R. (2004), 'Similes and Other Likenesses', in Fowler (2004) 139–55

Cairns, D., ed. (2001), *Oxford Readings in Homer's* Iliad (Oxford)

Cairns, F. (1979), *Tibullus: A Hellenistic Poet at Rome* (Cambridge)

Cairns, F. (1989), *Virgil's Augustan Epic* (Cambridge)

Cameron, A. (1995), *Callimachus and his Critics* (Princeton)

Camps, W. (1969), *An Introduction to Virgil's* Aeneid (Oxford)

Camps, W. (1980), *An Introduction to Homer* (Oxford)

Cancik, H. et al. eds. (2002), *Brill's New Pauly, Antiquity OBL–PHE* (vol. 10) (Leiden)

Cancik, H. et al. eds. (2005), *Brill's New Pauly, Antiquity, HAT–JUS* (vol. 6) (Leiden)

Canning, K. et al. eds. (2002), *Gender, Citizenships & Subjectivities* (Oxford)

Cannon, G. (1964), *Oriental Jones: A Biography of Sir William Jones, 1746–1794* (Bombay)

Carey, W. (1801 1st edition; 1843 5th edition), *A Grammar of the Bengalee Language* (Serampore)

Casali, S., ed. (1995), *Heroidum Epistula IX, Deianira Herculi* (Florence)

Chakrabarty, D. (2000), *Provincializing Europe: Postcolonial Thought and Historical Difference* (Princeton)

Challis, D. (2010), '"The Ablest Race": The Ancient Greeks in Victorian Racial Theory', in Bradley (2010) 94–120

Chatterjee, H. (1961), 'Svayaṃvara, the Ninth Form of Marriage', *The Adyar Library Bulletin* 25: 603–15

Chatterjee, P. (1993), *Nationalist Thought and the Colonial World: A Derivative Discourse* (Minneapolis)

Chatterjee, P., ed. (1995), *Texts of Power* (Minneapolis)

Chatterjee, S. (2007), *The Colonial Staged* (London)

Chaudhuri, A. (2008), *Clearing a Space: Reflections on India, Literature and Culture* (Oxford)

Chaudhuri, N. (1951), *The Autobiography of an Unknown Indian* (London)

Chaudhuri, R. (2000), '"Young India: A Bengal Eclogue', or Meat-eating, Race, and Reform in a Colonial Poem', *Interventions* 2, 3: 424–41

Chaudhuri, R. (2002), *Gentlemen Poets in Colonial Bengal: Emergent Nationalism and the Orientalist Project* (Calcutta)

Chaudhuri, R., ed. (2008), *Derozio, Poet of India: The Definitive Edition* (New Delhi, Oxford)
Cheney, P. et al. eds. (2002), *European Literary Careers: The Author from Antiquity to the Renaissance* (Toronto)
Clader, L. (1976), *Helen: the Evolution from Divine to Heroic in Greek Epic* (Leiden)
Clairmont, C. (1951), *Das Parisurteil in der Antiken Kunst* (Zürich)
Clark, M. (2004), 'Formulas, Metre and Type-scenes', in Fowler (2004) 117–38
Clark, T. (1967), 'Meghnādbadhkābya, Canto VIII: Descensus Averno', *BSOAS* 30: 337–52
Clarke, G., ed. (1989), *Rediscovering Hellenism: The Hellenic Inheritance and the English Imagination* (Cambridge)
Clay, J. (1983), *The Wrath of Athena: Gods and Men in the* Odyssey (Princeton)
Coffey, M. (1957), 'The Function of the Homeric simile', *AJP* 78: 113–32
Cohen, B., ed. (1995), *The Distaff Side: Representing the Female in Homer's Odyssey* (New York and Oxford)
Colas, G. (2003), 'History of Vaisnava Traditions', in Flood (2003) 229–270
Collins, L. (1988), *Studies in Characterization in the* Iliad (Frankfurt am Main)
O'Connor, D., et al. (2000), *Three Centuries of Mission, The United Society for the Propagation of the Gospel, 1701–2000* (London)
Conte, G. (1986), *The Rhetoric of Imitation: Genre and Poetic Memory in Virgil and Other Latin Poets* (Ithaca)
Conte, G. (2007), *The Poetry of Pathos* (Oxford)
Cook, A. (1981), *French Tragedy: the Power of Enactment* (Ohio)
Cook, E. (2003), 'Agamemnon's Test of the Army in *Iliad* Book 2 and the Function of the Homeric *Akhos*', *AJP* 124, 2: 165–98
Cowper, W. (1967), *Poetical Works* [Milford, H., ed.] (Oxford)
Craik, E. et al., eds. (1990), *Owls to Athens* (Oxford)
Crawley, C. et al., eds. (1965), *The New Cambridge Modern History* (Cambridge)
Cronin, R. et al., eds. (2002), *A Companion to Victorian Poetry* (Oxford)
Das, R. (1973), *māikel madhusūdan* (Calcutta)
Dasgupta, H. (1969), *Western Influence on Nineteenth Century Bengali Poetry* (Calcutta)
Dasgupta, J. (1933–5), 'Western Influence on the Poetry of Madhusudan Datta', *BSOAS* 7 (1933–5: 117–31)
Davies, M. (1981), 'The Judgement of Paris and Iliad Book XXIV', *JHS* 101: 56–62
Davies, M. (2003), 'The Judgements of Paris and Solomon', *CQ* 53.1: 32–43
De, S. (1923, 1925), *Sanskrit Poetics* (2 vols.) (London)

De, S. (1960 1st edition; 1976 2nd edition), *Studies in the History of Sanskrit Poetics* (1 vol.) (Calcutta)

Decker, C. ed. (1997), *Edward Fitzgerald, Rubaiyat of Omar Khaiyyam, A Critical Edition* (Virginia)

Deirdre, F. (1995), *Rule Britannia: Women, Empire, and Victorian Writing* (Cornell)

Derrett, J. (1968, 1976), *Religion, Law and the State in India* (New Delhi)

Deshpande, N. (1966), 'Boons and Curses in the *Ramayana*', in Neog (1966) 212–6

Dharwadker, V. (2003), 'The Historical Formation of Indian–English Literature', in Pollock (2003) 199–270

Dhavamony, M. (1982), *Classical Hinduism* (Rome)

Donlan, W. (1971–2), 'Homer's Agamemnon', *CW* 65: 109–15

Dörrie, H. (1968), *Der Heroische Brief; Bestandsaufnahme, Geschichte, Kritik einer Humanistisch-barocken Literaturgattung* (Berlin)

Dörrie, H., ed. (1971), *P. Ovidii Nasonis Epistulae Heroidum* (Berlin)

Douglas-Fairhurst, R. (2003), 'Shakespeare's Weeds: Tennyson, Elegy and Allusion', in Marshall (2003) (vol. 2) 114–30

Duberly, F. (1859), *Campaigning Experiences in Rajpootana and Central India, during the Suppression of the Mutiny* (London)

Duff, A. (1839), *India and Indian Missions, Including Sketches of the Gigantic System of Hinduism, Both in Theory and Practice* (Edinburgh)

Edwards, C., ed. (1999), *Roman Presences: Receptions of Rome in European Culture, 1789–1945* (Cambridge)

Edwards, M. (1991), *The Iliad: A Commentary: Books 17–20* (vol. 5) (Cambridge)

Eliot, T. S. (1919), 'Hamlet and his Problems', reprinted in *Selected Essays* (1950) 121–6

Else, G. (1957), *Aristotle's* Poetics*: The Argument* (Cambridge, MA)

Elton, C. (1814), *Specimens of the Greek and Roman Classic Poets* (3 vols.) (London)

Embree, A. (1963), *1857 in India: Mutiny or War of Independence?* (Boston)

Emeneau, M. (1962), 'Kalidasa's *Sakuntala* and the *Mahabharata*', *JAOS* 82, 1: 41–4

Ernout, A. et al., eds. (1962), *Lucrèce De Rerum Natura, Commentaire Exégétique et Critique* (Paris)

Ewans, M. (1982), *Wagner and Aeschylus: the Ring and the Oresteia* (London)

Farrell, J. (1998), 'Reading and Writing in the *Heroides*', *HSCP* 98: 307–38

Fauche, H. (1864), *Le Ramayana, Poème Sanscrit de Valmiky* (Paris)

Feeney, D. (1990), 'The Taciturnity of Aeneas', in Harrison (1990) 166–90

Feeney, D. (1991), *The Gods in Epic* (Oxford)

Feldman, B. et al. (1972), *The Rise of Modern Mythology, 1680–1860* (London)
Fenik, B. (1968), *Typical Battle Scenes in the Iliad: Studies in the Narrative Techniques of Homeric Battle Description* (Stuttgart)
Flannagan, R., ed. (1998), *The Riverside Milton* (Boston)
Flood, G. (1996), *An Introduction to Hinduism* (Cambridge)
Flood, G., ed. (2003), *The Blackwell Companion to Hinduism* (Oxford)
Fowler, D. (1997), 'Virgilian narrative: Story-telling', in Martindale (1997) 259–70
Fowler, R., ed. (2004), *The Cambridge Companion to Homer* (Cambridge)
Fowler, W. (1931), *Aeneas at the Site of Rome: Observations on the Eighth Book of the Aeneid* (Oxford)
France, P. et al., eds. (2006), *The Oxford History of Literary Translation in English, Volume 4: 1790–1900* (Oxford)
Fränkel, H. (1921), *Die Homerischen Gleichnisse* (Göttingen)
Frazer, J. (1921), *The Golden Bough* (vol. 2) (London)
Fulkerson, L. (2005), *The Ovidian Heroine as Author* (Cambridge)
Galinsky, K. (1996), *Augustan Culture* (Princeton)
Galinsky, K. (1999), '*Aeneid* V and the *Aeneid*', in Hardie (1999) 182–206
Gajendragadkar, S. (1946), 'Indra in the Epic', *PTAIOC* 13: 79–82
Gandhi, L. (1998), *Postcolonial Theory* (Columbia)
Garland, E. (1842), *Ovid's Epistles, in English Verse, with Some Original Poems* (London)
Garvie, A., ed. (1994), *Homer,* Odyssey, *Books VI–VIII* (Cambridge)
Ghali-Kahil, L. (1955), *Les Enlèvements et le Retour d'Hélène dans les Textes et les Documents Figurés* (Paris)
Ghosh, D. (2006), *Sex and the Family in Colonial India, The Making of Empire* (Cambridge)
Gibson, R. et al., eds. (2006), *The Art of Love, Bimillennial Essays of Ovid's Ars Amatoria and Remedia Amoris* (Oxford)
Gilfillan, G., ed. (1851), *The Book of British Poesy, Ancient and Modern; Select Extracts. With an Essay on British Poetry* (London)
Gillespie, S. et al. (2004), 'A Bibliography of Ovidian Translations and Imitations in English', *Translation and Literature* 13: 207–18
Gillespie, S. et al., eds. (2007), *The Cambridge Companion to Lucretius* (Cambridge)
Gladstone, W. (1858), *Studies on Homer and the Homeric Age* (3 vols.) (Oxford)
Goff, B., ed. (2005), *Classics and Colonialism* (London)
Goff, B., et al. (2007), *Crossroads in the Black Aegean—Oedipus, Antigone, and Dramas of the African Diaspora* (Oxford)
Gold, D., ed. (1982), *Literary and Artistic Patronage in Ancient Rome* (Texas)
Goldhill, S. (1991) *The Poet's Voice* (Cambridge)

Gonda, J. (1962), 'A Note on Indra in Puranic Literature', *Purana* 9, 2: 222–61
Goold, G. (1970), 'Servius and the Helen Episode', *HSCP* 74: 101–68
Gransden, K. (1984), *Virgil's* Iliad, *An Essay on Epic Narrative* (Cambridge)
Graziosi, B. (2002), *Inventing Homer, The Early Reception Of Epic* (Cambridge)
Graziosi, D. (2007), *Homer in the Twentieth Century, Between World Literature and the Western Canon* (Oxford)
Greenwood, E. (2009), 'Re-rooting the Classical Tradition: New Directions in Black Classicism', *Classical Receptions Journal* Vol. 1/1: 87–103
Griffin, J. (1977), 'The Epic Cycle and the Uniqueness of Homer', *JHS* 97: 39–53
Griffin, J. (1980), *Homer on Life and Death* (Oxford)
Griffin, J. (1986), *Virgil* (Oxford)
Griffin, J. (1992), 'Virgil', in Jenkyns (1992) 125–50
Griffin, J. (2004), 'The Speeches', in Fowler (2004) 156–70
Griffith, J. (1967–8), 'The Shield of Aeneas', *Proceedings of the Vergil Society* 7: 54–65
Grote, G. (1846–56), *A History of Greece* (12 vols.) (London)
Guha-Thakurta, T. (1995), 'Recovering the Nation's Art', in Chatterjee (1995) 63–92
Gunn, J. (1983), *Beyond Liberty and Property: The Process of Self-Recognition in 18th-Century Political Thought* (Montreal)
Gupt, B. (2006), *Dramatic Concepts Greek and Indian: a Study of the Poetics and the Natyasastra* (New Delhi)
Gupta, K. et al., eds. (1974) *madhusūdan racanābalī* (Calcutta)
Gupta, S. (1959), *ūnabiṃśo śatābdite bāṅgālār naba-jāgaraṇ* (Calcutta)
Guthrie, W. (1949), *The Greeks and Their Gods* (Cambridge)
Haas, G. (1962), *The Dasarupa, A Treatise on Hindu Dramaturgy by Dhanamjaya* (Delhi)
Hainsworth, J. (1988), 'Commentary, Books V–VIII', in Heubeck (1988) 249–408
Hall, E. (1989), *Inventing the Barbarian* (Oxford)
Hall, E., et al. (2005), *Greek Tragedy and the British Theatre 1660–1914* (Oxford)
Hall, E., et al., eds. (2007), *Aristophanes in Performance 412 BCE–2005 CE* (Oxford)
Hall, E., et al., eds. (2010), *India, Greece, & Rome 1757–2007* (London)
Halleran, M. (1995), *Euripides' Hippolytus* (Oxford)
Halliwell, S. (1986), *Aristotle's Poetics* (London)
Hamner, R., ed. (1997), *Critical Perspectives on Derek Walcott* (Colorado)
Hampe, R. (1954), *Das Parisurteil auf dem Elfenbeinkamm aus Sparta* (Stuttgart)

O'Hara, J. (1990), *Death and the Optimistic Prophecy in Vergil's* Aeneid (Princeton)
O'Hara, J. (1996), *True Names—Vergil and the Alexandrian Tradition of Etymological Wordplay* (Michigan)
O'Hara, J. (1997), 'Virgil's Style', in Martindale (1997) 241–58
Hardie, P. (1986), *Virgil's Aeneid: Cosmos and Imperium* (Oxford)
Hardie, P. (1997), 'Virgil and Tragedy', in Martindale (1997) 312–326
Hardie, P. (1998), *Virgil* (Greece and Rome New Surveys in the Classics, 28) (Oxford)
Hardie, P., ed. (1999), *Virgil: Critical Assessments of Classical Authors* (London)
Hardie, P., ed. (2002a), *The Cambridge Companion to Ovid* (Cambridge)
Hardie, P., (2002b), *Ovid's Poetics of Illusion* (Cambridge)
Hardie, P. (2006), '*Lethaeus Amor: The Art of Forgetting*', in Gibson (2006) 166–90
Hardwick, L. (2003), *Reception Studies* (Oxford)
Hardwick, L. (2005), *Translating Words, Translating Cultures* (London)
Hardwick, L., ed. (2007), *Classics in Postcolonial Worlds* (Oxford)
Hardwick, L. et al., eds. (2008), *A Companion to Classical Receptions* (Oxford)
Harrison, S., ed. (1990), *Oxford Readings in Vergil's Aeneid* (Oxford)
Harrison, S. (1991), *Vergil Aeneid 10* (Oxford)
Harrison, S., ed. (1995), *Homage to Horace* (Oxford)
Harrison, S. (2002), 'Ovid and Genre: Evolutions of an Elegist', in Hardie (2002a) 79–94
Harrison, S. (2007a), *Generic Enrichment in Vergil and Horace* (Oxford)
Harrison, S., ed. (2007b), *The Cambridge Companion to Horace* (Cambridge)
Harrison, S. (2007c), 'Horatian Self-Presentations', in Harrison (2007b) 22–35
Harrison, S. (2007d), 'Some Victorian Versions of Greco-Roman Epic', in Stray (2007) 21–36
Harrison, S. (2008), 'Horace and the Construction of the English Victorian Gentleman', in *Helios* 34: 207–22
Harvey, E. (1989), 'Ventriloquizing Sappho: Ovid, Donne, and the Erotics of the Feminine Voice', *Criticism* 31: 115–38
Hatto, A. et al. eds. (1980), *Traditions of Heroic and Epic Poetry* (vol. 1) (London)
Haubold, J. (2000), *Homer's People* (Cambridge)
Hawley, J. (2001), *Encyclopedia of Postcolonial Studies* (Santa Barbara)
Heber, R. et al. (1828), *Narrative of a Journey through the Upper Provinces of India* (London)
Heinze, R. (1993), *Virgil's Epic Technique* (Bristol) (translation of original German (1902))

Heinze, T. (1997), *Der XII. Heroidenbrief: Medea an Jason* (Leiden)
Helgerson, R. (1983), *Self-Crowned Laureates* (Berkeley, London)
Heubeck, A. et al. eds. (1988), *A Commentary on Homer's Odyssey* (vol. 1) (Oxford)
Heubeck, A. et al. eds. (1989), *A Commentary on Homer's Odyssey* (vol. 2) (Oxford)
Hexter, R. (2006), 'Literary History as a Provocation to Reception Studies', in Martindale (2006) 23–31
Hill, R. ed. (1999), *Tennyson's Poetry* (New York, London)
Hinds, S. (1993), 'Medea in Ovid: Scenes from the Life of an Intertextual Heroine,' *Materiali e Discussioni per l'Analisi dei Testi Classici* 30: 9–47.
Hinds, S. (2006), 'Booking the Return Trip: Ovid and *Tristia* 1', in Knox (2006) 415–40
Hohendahl, P. (1989), *Building a National Literature: The Case of Germany, 1830–1870* (Ithaca, NY)
Hornblower, S. (1991), *A Commentary on Thucydides, Books 1–4* (vol. 1) (Oxford)
Horsfall, N. (1981), 'Some Problems of Titulature in Roman Literary History', *BICS* 28: 103–14
Horsfall, N., ed. (1995), *A Companion to the Study of Virgil* (Leiden)
Hospital, C. (1978), 'The Enemy Transformed', *JAAR* 46 (supplement): 200–15
Huddart, D. (2007), *Postcolonial Theory and Autobiography* (London)
Hunter, R. (1989), *Apollonius of Rhodes, Argonautica, Book III* (Cambridge)
Hutchinson, G., ed. (1985), *Seven Against Thebes* (Oxford)
Huxley, H. (1956), 'Roman Elegiac Poetry: its Scope, Status and Decline', *PLPS* 8, 2: 75–82
Ingalls, D. et al., eds. (1990), *The Dhvanyāloka of Ānandavardhana, with the Locana of Abhinavagupta* (Cambridge, MA)
Irschick, E. (1994), *Dialogue and History: Constructing South India* (Berkeley)
Irwin, R. (2003), *For Lust of Knowing: The Orientalists and their Enemies* (London)
Jacobson, H. (1974), *Ovid's Heroides* (Princeton)
Janaki, S. (1975), 'Pururavas and Urvasi', *Sanskrit and Indological Studies: Dr. V. Raghavan Felicitation Volume* (1975) 163–73
Janko, R. (1992), *The Iliad: A Commentary, Books 13–16* (vol. 4) (Cambridge)
Jauss, H.-R. (1967), *Literaturgeschichte als Provokation der Literaturwissenschaft* (Constance)
de Jean, J. (1989), *Fictions of Sappho, 1546–1937* (Chicago)
Jeffrey, L. (1971), 'Homeric echoes in Byron's Don Juan', *SCB* 31, 4: 188–92
Jenkyns, R. (1980), *The Victorians and Ancient Greece* (Oxford)

Jenkyns, R. (1991) *Dignity and Decadence: Victorian art and the classical inheritance* (Oxford)

Jenkyns, R., ed. (1992), *The Legacy of Rome, A New Appraisal* (Oxford)

Jenkyns, R. (1998), *Virgil's Experience* (Oxford)

Jenkyns, R. (2002), 'The Classical Tradition', in Cronin (2002) 229–45

Jensen, M. (1999), 'Dividing Homer: When and Where were the *Iliad* and *Odyssey* Divided into Songs?', *Symbolae Osloenses* 74: 14–22

Johnson, G. (1843), *The Stranger in India, or Three Years in Calcutta* (London)

Jolivet, J.-C. (2001), *Allusion et Fiction Epistolaire dans les Heroides: Recherches sur l'Intertextualité Ovidienne* (Paris)

Jones, W. (1788), 'On the Gods of Greece, Italy, and India', in *Asiatick Researches* 1: 221–75

de Jong, I. (1987), *Narrators and Focalizers: The Presentation of the Story in the* Iliad (Amsterdam)

de Jong, I. (2004), 'Homer', in *Narrators, Narratees, and Narratives in Ancient Greek Literature* (Mnemosyne Supplement 257): 13–24

Joshi, N. (1971), 'Some Kusana Passages in *Harivamsa*', *Indologen-Tagung* (1971) 238–92

Jump, J. (1857), *The Epistles of Ovidius Naso Faithfully Converted into a New Measure of English Verse* (London)

Kairns, E. (2004), 'The Gods in the Homeric Epics', in Fowler (2004) 220–34

Kale, M. (1961), *A Higher Sanskrit Grammar* (Delhi)

Kane, P., ed. (1923), *The Sahityadarpana (Paricchedas I–X)* (Bombay)

Kane, P. (1961 1st edition; 1973 2nd edition), *History of Sanskrit Poetics* (New Delhi)

Karlin, D. (2003), '"The Names": Robert Browning's "Shakespearean Show"', in Marshall (2003) (vol. 2): 150–69

Kassel, R. et al. eds. (1983–95), *Poetae Comici Graeci* (Berlin)

Katzung, P. (1960), *Die Diapeira in der Iliashandlung: Der Gesang von der Unstimmung des Griechenheeres* (Diss.) (Frankfurt am Main)

Kaufman, L. (1986), *Discourses of Desire: Gender, Genre, and Epistolary fiction* (London and Ithaca)

Kaviraj, S. (2003), 'The Two Histories of Literary Culture in Bengal', in Pollock (2003) 503–66

Kaye, J. (1859), *Christianity in India: An Historical Narrative* (London)

Keith, A. (1924), *The Sanskrit Drama in its Origin, Development, Theory & Practice* (Oxford)

Keith, A. (2000), *Engendering Rome: Women in Latin Epic* (Cambridge)

Keith, B. (1924), *The Sanskrit Drama in its Origin, Development, Theory & Practice* (Oxford)

Kejariwal, O. (1988), *The Asiatic Society of Bengal and the Discovery of India's Past* (New Delhi, Oxford)

Kelly, C. ed. (2007), *Mrs Duberly's War* (Oxford)
Kennedy, D. (1984), 'The Epistolary Mode and the First of Ovid's *Heroides*', *CQ* (N.S.) 34: 413–22
Kennedy, D. (1996), 'Imperial History and Postcolonial Theory', *Journal of Imperial and Commonwealth History*, 24, 3: 345–63
Kennedy, D. (1997), 'Virgilian Epic', in Martindale (1997) 145–54
Kennedy, D. (2002), 'Epistolarity: the *Heroides*', in Hardie (2002) 317–232
Kenney, E., et al., eds. (1982), *The Cambridge History of Classical Literature. II Latin Literature* (Cambridge)
Kenney, E., ed. (1996), *Ovid: Heroides XVI–XXI* (Cambridge)
Kinsley, D. (1998), *Hindu Goddesses: Visions of the Divine Feminine in the Hindu Religious Tradition* (Berkeley)
Kirfel, W. (1952), 'Der Mythos von der Tara und der Geburt des Budha', *Zeitschrift der Deutschen Morgenlandischen Gesellschaft* 102: 66–90
Kirk, G., ed. (1985), *The Iliad: a Commentary; Volume I: Books 1–4* (Cambridge)
Kirk, G., ed. (1990), *The Iliad: a Commentary; Volume II: Books 5–8* (Cambridge)
Klostermaier, K. (1989), *A Survey of Hinduism* (New York)
Knauer, G. (1964), *Die Aeneas und Homer* (Göttingen)
Knauer, G. (1990), 'Vergil's *Aeneid* and Homer', in Harrison (1990) 390–412
Knighton, W. (1845), *History of Ceylon* (Edinburgh)
Knox, P. (1986), 'Ovid's *Medea and Heroides* 12', *TAPhA* 90: 207–23
Knox, P., ed. (1995), *Ovid's Heroides, Select Epistles* (Cambridge)
Knox, P., ed. (2006), *Oxford Readings in Classical Studies, Ovid* (Oxford)
Kopf, D. (1969), *British Orientalism and the Bengal Renaissance: The Dynamics of Indian Modernization 1773–1835* (Berkeley/ Los Angeles)
Kraus, W. (1968), 'Ovidius Naso', in von Albrecht (1968) 67–166
Krishnacharya, T. et al., eds. (1911–1913), *Śrīmad Vālmīki Rāmāyaṇa* (3 vols.) (Bombay)
Kundu, P. (2004), 'meghnādbadh kābyer pāṭhāntar', in Majumdar (2004) 494–517
Laclau, E. et al. (1985), *Hegemony and Socialist Strategy: Towards a Radical Democratic Politics* (London)
Lacy, T., ed. (1848–73), *Acting Editions of Plays* (London)
Lane Fox, R. (1973), *Alexander the Great* (Oxford)
Lauber, J. (1968), '*Don Juan* as Anti-Epic', *Studies in English Literature, 1500–1900*, 8, 4: 607–19
Lazarus, N., ed. (2004), *The Cambridge Companion to Postcolonial Literary Studies* (Cambridge)
Lee, D. (1964), *The Similes of the Iliad and the* Odyssey *Compared* (Parkville)
Lee, M. (1979), *Fathers and Sons in Virgil's Aeneid* (New York)

Leeman, A. (1963), *Orationis Ratio: The Stylistic Theories and Practice of the Roman Orators, Historians and Philosophers* (vol. 1) (Amsterdam)
Leopold, A. et al., eds. (2004), *Syncretism in Religion: A Reader* (London)
Lesky, A. (2001), 'Divine and Human Causation in Homeric Epic', in Cairns (2001) 170–202
Lévi, S. (1890), *Le Théâtre Indien* (Paris)
Lincoln, B. (1999), *Theorizing Myth: Narrative, Ideology, and Scholarship* (Chicago)
Lindsay, J. (1974), *Helen of Troy* (London)
Lipking, L. (1981), *The Life of the Poet: Beginning and Ending Poetic Careers* (Chicago)
Lipner, J. (2005), *Anandamath* (Oxford)
Lloyd, R. (1957), '*Aeneid* III: A New Approach', *AJPh* 78, 2: 133–51
Lloyd-Jones, H. (1983), *The Justice of Zeus* (Berkeley)
Lloyd-Jones, H., ed. (1996), *Sophocles: Fragments* (Cambridge, MA)
Lohmann, D. (1970), *Die Komposition der Reden in der Ilias* (Berlin)
Lowndes, W. (1864), *The Bibliographer's Manual of English Literature* (6 vols.) (London)
Lucas, D., ed. (1968), *Aristotle: Poetics* (Oxford)
Lyne, R. (1989), *Words and the Poet* (Oxford)
Lyne, R. (1995), *Horace: Behind the Public Poetry* (New Haven and London)
Macleod, C., ed. (1982), *Iliad. Book XXIV/ Homer* (Cambridge)
Machor, J. (2001), *Reception Study: from Literary Theory to Cultural studies* (New York)
Macintosh, F. (1994), *Dying Acts: Death in Ancient Greek and Modern Irish Tragic Drama* (Cork)
Madan, R., ed. (1982), *Way of Life: King, Householder, Renouncer. Essays in Honour of Louis Dumont* (New Delhi)
Maguire, L. (2009), *Helen of Troy: From Homer to Hollywood* (Oxford)
Maitra, S. (1975), *māikel madhusūdan datta: jīban o sāhityo* (Kolkata)
Majeed, J. (1999), 'Comparativism and References to Rome in British Imperial Attitudes to India', in Edwarids (1999) 88–109
Majumdar, M. (1947), *kabi śrī madhusūdan* (Kolkata)
Majumdar, U., ed. (2004), *meghnādbadh kābya carcā* (Kolkata)
Malamoud, C. (1982), 'On the Rhetoric and Semantics of Purusartha', in Madan (1982) 33–54
Malamud, M. (2010), 'Translatio Imperii: America as the New Rome c.1900', in Bradley (2010) 249–283
Mantena, R. (2010), 'Imperial Ideology and the Uses of Rome in Discourses on Britain's Indian Empire', in Bradley (2010) 54–73
Marg, W. (1956), 'Das Erste Lied des Demodokos', in *Navicula Chiloniensis* (Festschrift Jacoby) (1956) 16–29
Marshall, G. et al., eds. (2003), *Victorian Shakespeare* (Basingstoke)

Martin, C., ed. (1998), *Ovid in English* (London)
Martindale, C., ed. (1984), *Virgil and his Influence* (Bristol)
Martindale, C. (1988), *Ovid Renewed: Ovidian Influences on Literature and Art from the Middle Ages to the Twentieth Century* (Cambridge)
Martindale, C. (1993), *Redeeming the Text: Latin Poetry and the Hermeneutics of Reception* (Cambridge)
Martindale, C., ed. (1997), *The Cambridge Companion to Virgil* (Cambridge)
Martindale, C. et al., eds. (2006), *Classics and the Uses of Reception* (Oxford)
Martini, E. (1933), *Einleitung zu Ovid* (Prague)
Mason, H. (1972), *To Homer Through Pope* (London)
Matchett, F. (2003), 'The Puranas', in Flood (2003) 129–43
May, J., ed. (2002), *Brill's Companion to Cicero* (Leiden)
Mayer, R., ed. (1995), *Horace, Epistles, Book 1* (Cambridge)
McGann, J. ed. (1986), *Byron, the Complete Poetical Works* (vols. 3 and 5) (Oxford)
Meagher, R. (1995), *Helen* (New York)
O'Meally, R. (2007), *Romare Beardon: a Black* Odyssey (New York)
Meckelnborg, C. et al. (2002) Odyssea*: Responsio Ulixis ad Penelopen. Die Humanistiche Odyssea Decurtata der Berliner Handschrift Diez. B Sant. 41. Beiträge zur Altertumskunde 166* (Munich and Leipzig)
Merkelbach, R. (1970, reprinted 1996), *Hestia und Erigone* (Stuttgart)
Merklin, H. (1968), 'Arethusa and Laodamia', *Hermes* 96: 461–94
Metcalf, T. (1960), *Victorian Liberalism and the Indian Empire; the Impact of the Mutiny of 1857 on British Policy in India* (Cambridge, MA)
Metcalf, T. (1984), 'Architecture and the Representation of Empire: India, 1860–1910', *Representations* 6: 37–65
Michaels, A. (2004), *Hinduism Past and Present* (Princeton)
Michalopoulos, A., ed. (2006), *Ovid Heroides 16 and 17: Introduction, Text and Commentary* (Cambridge)
Milbank, A. (1998), *Dante and the Victorians* (Manchester)
Minkowski, C. (1989), 'Janamejaya's Sattra and Ritual Structure', in *JAOS* 109, 3: 401–20
Mitra, H. (1898), *bīrāṅganā patrottar kābya* (Calcutta)
Monier-Williams, M. (1872), *A Sanskrit-English Dictionary* (Oxford)
Moore, T., ed. (1838), *Life, Letters, and Journals of Lord Byron: Complete in One Volume* (London)
Moulton, C. (1977), *Similes in the Homeric Poems* (Göttingen)
Mueller, M. (1984), *The Iliad* (London)
Mukherjee, S. (1977), *Calcutta: Myth and History* (Kolkata)
Mukhopadhyaya, M. (1931), 'Some Notes on Skanda-Karttikeya', *IHQ* 7: 309–52
Müller, F. (1859) *A History of Ancient Sanskrit Literature so far as it Illustrates the Primitive Religion of the Brahmans* (London)

Müller, F. (1867), *Chips from a German Workshop* (Oxford)
Mure, W. (1850–3), *A Critical History of the Language and Literature of Ancient Greece* (4 vols.) (London)
Murshid, G. (1992), *kālāntare bāṃlo gadya* (Kolkata)
Murshid, G. (1995 1st edition; 1997 2nd edition), *āśār chalane bhuli* (Kolkata)
Murshid, G. (2003), *Lured by Hope, A Biography of Michael Madhusudan Dutt* (Oxford)
Murshid, G. (2004), *The Heart of a Rebel Poet: Letters of Michael Madhusudan Dutt* (Oxford)
Musgrave, G. (1865), *The "Odyssey" of Homer Rendered into English Verse* (2 vols.) (London)
Mynors, R., ed. (1972), *P. Vergili Maronis Opera* (Oxford)
Nagar, S. (1995), *Surya and Sun Cult* (New Delhi)
Nagy, G. (1979), *The Best of the Achaeans* (Baltimore, London)
Nauta, R. (2006), *Flavian Poetry* (Leiden)
Nelson, J. (1974), *Sublime Puritan: Milton and the Victorians* (Madison)
Neog, M. et al., eds. (1966), *Professor Birinchi Kumar Barua Commemoration Volume* (Gauhati)
Nisbet, R. et al. (1970), *A Commentary on Horace Odes 1* (Oxford)
Nisbet, R. (1990), '*Aeneas Imperator*: Roman Generalship in an Epic Context', in Harrison (1990) 378–89
Nisbet, R. (2004), *A Commentary on Horace: Odes Book III* (Oxford)
Nutt, A. (1900), 'Cuchalain, the Irish Achilles', *Popular Studies in Mythology, Romance and Folklore* 8: 1–52
Oddie, G. (1999), *Missionaries, Rebellion and Proto-Nationalism: James Long of Bengal 1814–87* (London)
Okpewho, I. (1992), 'Soyinka, Euripides, and the Anxiety of Empire', *R.A.L.* 30.4: 32–55
Olender, M. (1992), *The Languages of Paradise: Race, Religion, and Philology in the Nineteenth Century (trans. Arthur Goldhammer)* (Cambridge, MA)
Olivelle, P. (2004), *The Law Code of Manu, A New Translation Based on the Critical Edition by Patrick Olivelle* (Oxford)
Olivelle, P. (2005), *Manu's Code of Law: a Critical Edition and Translation of the Manava-Dharmasastra* (Oxford)
Otis, B. (1964), *Virgil: A Study in Civilized Poetry* (Oxford)
Paduano, G. et al., eds. (1986), *Apollonio Rodio,* Le Argonautiche (Milano)
Page, D. (1936), 'The Elegiacs in Euripides' *Andromache*', in Toynbee (1936) 206–30
Pal, B. (1932), *Memories of My Life and Times* (2 vols.) (Calcutta)
Palmer, A., ed. (1898), *P. Ovidi Nasonis Heroides with the Greek Translation of Planudes* [completed by L. C. Purser] (Oxford)
Panda, K, ed. (1993), *Nostalgia, An Illustrated History of Hindu-Presidency College* (1817–1992) (Kolkata)

Papponetti, G., ed. (1991), *Ovidio, Poeta della Memoria* (Rome)
Parker, H. (1851), *Bole Ponjis, Containing the Tale of the Bucaneer . . . and Other Ingredients* (London)
Parker, R. (1983), *Miasma: Pollution and Purification in Early Greek Religion* (Oxford)
Parthasarathy, R. (1979), 'Indian-English Verse: The Making of a Tradition', *The Humanities Review* (New Delhi) 1: 14–9
Pascoe, C. (1901), *Two Hundred Years of the S. P. G.; An Historical Account of the Society for the Propagation of the Gospel in Foreign Parts, 1701–1900* (London)
Pathak, M. (1968), *Similes in the Rāmāyaṇa* (Baroda)
Patra, P. et al., eds. (1989, 2004, 2005), *Madhusūdan racanābalī* (Kolkata)
Pelling, C. (1990), *Characterization and Individuality in Greek Literature* (Oxford)
Pichon, R. (1902), *Index Verborum Amatoriorum* (Paris)
Poliakoff, L. (1974), *The Aryan Myth: A History of Racist and Nationalist Ideas in Europe (trans. Edmund Howard)* (New York)
Pollock, S., ed. (2003), *Literary Cultures in History, Reconstructions from South Asia* (Berkeley)
Porter, S., ed. (1997), *Handbook of Classical Rhetoric in the Hellenistic Period 330AB–AD 440* (Leiden)
Porter, J. (2004), 'Homer: The History of an Idea', in Fowler (2004) 324–43
Pöschl, C. (1962), *The Art of Vergil* (Michigan)
Post, K. (1984), 'The Failure of Contract among the Fishes', *ABORI* 65: 11–26
Prendergast, G. (1962), *A Complete Concordance to the Iliad of Homer* (Hildesheim)
Prince, C. (2007), 'A Divided Child, or Derek Walcott's Post-Colonial Philology', in Hardwick (2007) 170–192
Prins, Y. (2005), 'Metrical Translation: Nineteenth-Century Homers and the Hexameter Mania', in Bermann (2005) 229–56
Pulbrook, M. (1977), 'The Original Published Form of Ovid's *Heroides*', *Hermathena* 122: 29–45
Quinn, K. (1968), *Virgil's* Aeneid: *A Critical Description* (London)
Raab, I. (1972), *Zu den Darstellungen des Parisurteils in der Griechischen Kunst* (Bern)
Rabel, R. (1990), 'Apollo as a Model for Achilles in the *Iliad*', *AJP* 111: 429–40
Radice, W. (1995), 'Milton and Madhusudan', in Taneja (1995) 177–94
Radice, W. (1998), 'Xenophilia and Xenophobia: Michael Madhusudan Datta's *Meghnādbadh Kābya*', in Snell (1998) 143–70
Radice, W. (2005), 'Confession Versus the Exclamation Mark: Why Rabindranath Tagore did Not Like the Poetry of Michael Madhusudan Dutt', *Temenos Academy Review* 8 (London): 167–83

Radice, W. (2007), 'What sort of Sonnets did Michael Madhusudan Dutt write?', in *Samaj o Samskriti* [Festschrift for Anisuzzaman] (Dhaka) 409–23

Radice, W. (2008), 'Michael Madhusudan Dutt (1824–1873): A Bengali Poet with Italian Connections', in D. Bhattacharya (2008) 149–72

Radice, W. (2010), *Michael Madhusudan Dutt, The Poem of the Killing Meghnād* (New Delhi)

Raha, K. (1993), *Bengali Theatre* (New Delhi)

Ramazani, J. (2001), *The Hybrid Muse: Postcolonial Poetry in English* (Chicago and London)

Rankine, P. (2006), *Ulysses in Black: Ralph Ellison, Classicism, and African American Literature* (Wisconsin Studies in Classics) (Madison)

Rayan, K. (1965), 'Rasa and Objective Correlative', in *British Journal of Aesthetics*, vol. 5 (1965): 246–60

Raychaudhuri, T. (1988 1st edition; 2002 revised edition), *Europe Reconsidered: Perceptions of the West in Nineteenth Century Bengal* (Oxford)

Reeson, J. (2001), *Ovid Heroides: 11, 13, 14, A Commentary* (Leiden)

Reinhardt, K. (1938), *Das Parisurteil* (Frankfurt)

Reynolds, M. (2001), *The Realms of Verse, 1830–1870: English Poetry in a Time of Nation-Building* (Oxford)

Rhys, J. (1888), *Lectures on the Origin and Growth of Religion as Illustrated by Celtic Heathendom* (London)

Richard, C. (1994), *The Founders and the Classics: Greece, Rome, and the American Enlightenment* (Cambridge, MA)

Richard, C. (2009), *The Golden Age of the Classics in America: Greece, Rome and the Antebellum United States* (Cambridge, MA)

Richardson, D. (1840), *Selections from the British Poets* (Calcutta)

Richardson, F. (1870), *The Iliad of the East: A Selection of Legends Drawn from Valmiki's Sanskrit poem the Ramayana* (London)

Richardson, N. (1980), 'Literary Criticism in the Exegetical Scholia to the *Iliad*: A Sketch', *CQ* 30, 2: 265–87

Richardson, N. (1993), *The Iliad: A Commentary, vol. VI: Books 21–24* (Cambridge)

Richardson, S. (1990), *The Homeric Narrator* (Nashville)

Richman, P., ed. (1992), *Many Ramayanas, the Diversity of a Narrative Tradition in South Asia* (Oxford)

Ricks, C., ed. (1969), *The Poems of Tennyson* (vol. 1) (Harlow)

Ricks, C., ed. (1989), *The Poems of Tennyson* (3 vols.) (London)

Riddiford, A. (2009), 'Homer's *Iliad* and the *Meghanādabadha Kābya* of Michael Madhusūdan Datta', *BSOAS* 72, 2: 335–56

Riddiford, A. (2010), 'The Valmiki of Europe: Homer through Bengali Eyes', Chapter 5 in Hall (2010)

Rimell, V. (1999), 'Epistolary Fictions: Authorial Identity in *Heroides* 15', *PCPS* 45: 109–35
Rocher, L. (2003), 'The Dharmasastras', in Flood (2003) 102–15
Röer, E. (1851), *Sahityadarpana, or, Mirror of Composition: A Treatise on Literary Criticism, by Visvanatha Kaviraja* (Calcutta)
Rogers, A., et al. (2010), 'Edward Gibbon and Francis Haverfield: The Traditions of Imperial Decline', in Bradley (2010) 189–209
Ronnick, M., ed. (2005), *The Autobiography of William Sanders Scarborough: An American Journey from Slavery to Scholarship* (Detroit)
Rorty, A., ed. (1992), *Essays on Aristotle's Poetics* (Princeton)
Roscher, W., ed. (1884–1890), *Ausfürliches Lexicon der Griechischen und Römischen Mythologie* (vol. 1) (Leipzig)
Rosslyn, F., ed. (1985), *Pope's Iliad, a Selection with Commentary* (Bristol)
Rowell, H. (1966), 'The Ancient Evidence of the Helen Episode in *Aeneid* II', in Wallach (1966) 210–21
Rudd, W. (1983), 'The Idea of Empire in the *Aeneid*', *Hermathena* 134: 35–50
Rutherford, R. (2007), 'Poetics and Literary Criticism', in Harrison (2007b) 248–61
Ryals, C. (1973), 'Balaustion's Adventure: Browning's Greek Parable', *PMLA*, 88, 5: 1040–8
Said, E. (1978), *Orientalism* (New York)
Sanyal, D. (c.1917), *meghnād-badh kābya* (Calcutta)
Sarkar, S. (1946), *Bengali Renaissance* (Calcutta)
Sarkar, T. (1987), 'Nationalist Iconography: Image of Women in 19th Century Bengali Literature', *Economical and Political Weekly* 22, 47: 2011–5
Sarkar, T. (2002), 'Enfranchised selves: Women, Culture and Rights in Nineteenth-Century Bengal', in Canning, K. (2002) 120–39
Sastri, H., ed. (1956), *haraprasād racanābali* (vol. 1) (Calcutta)
Schadewaldt, W. (1943), *Iliasstudien* (Leipzig)
Schadewaldt, W. (1959), *Von Homers Welt und Werk* (Stuttgart)
Schiesaro, A. (2002), 'Ovid and the Professional Discourses of Scholarship, Religion, Rhetoric', in Hardie (2002) 62–78
Schiesaro, A. (2007), 'Lucretius and Roman Politics and History', in Gillespie (2007) 41–58
Schilling, R. (1954, reprinted 1982), *La Religion Romaine de Vénus Depuis les Origines jusqu'au Temps d'Auguste* (Paris)
Schmid, W. et al. (1929), *Geschichte der Griechischen Literatur* (vol. 1) (München)
Seely, C. (1982), 'Rama in the Nether World: Indian Sources of Inspiration', *JAOS* 102, 3: 467–76

Seely, C. (1988), 'Homeric Similes, Occidental and Oriental: Tasso, Milton, and Bengal's Michael Madhusudan Dutt', *Comparative Literature Studies* 25, 1: 35–56

Seely, C. (1992), 'The Raja's New Clothes: Redressing Ravana in Meghanadavadha Kavya', in Richman (1992) 137–55

Seely, C. (2004), *The Slaying of Meghanada, A Ramayana from Colonial Bengal* (Oxford)

Sen, K. (2004), 'biśạd ṭīkā o byākhyā', in Majumdar (2004) 103–224

Sen, P. (1932), *Western Influence in Bengali Literature* (Calcutta)

Sen, S. (1959), *madhusūdan – antar-jīban o pratibhā* (Calcutta)

Sen, S. (1971), *History of Bengali Literature* (New Delhi)

Shaw, R. (2007), *Blank Verse: a Guide to its History and Use* (Athens, Ohio)

Sinha, M. (1995), *Colonial Masculinity: The 'Manly Englishman' and the 'Effeminate Bengali' in the Late Nineteenth Century* (Manchester)

Sinha, P. (1978), *Calcutta in Urban History* (Calcutta)

Skulsky, S. (1985), '"Invitus, regina . . .": Aeneas and the Love of Rome', *AJP* 106, 4: 447–55

Smith, B. (2000), 'Who Does, Can, and Should Speak for Hinduism?', *Journal of the American Academy of Religion* 68, 4: 741–9

Smith, J. (1980), 'Old Indian. The Two Sanskrit Epics', in Auty (1980) 48–78

Snell, R. et al., eds. (1998), *Classics of Modern South Asian Literature* (Wiesbaden)

Snipes, K. (1988), 'Literary Interpretation in the Homeric Scholia: The Similes of the *Iliad*', *AJP* 109, 2: 196–222

Snyder, E. (1923), *The Celtic Revival in English Literature* (Cambridge, Mass.)

Sobré, J. (1983), 'The Rise of Modern Catalan', *Ideologies and Literature* 4: 51–65

Solmsen, F. (1961), 'The World of the Dead in Book 6 of the *Aeneid*', in Harrison (1990): 208–33

Som, N. (1916), *madhu-smṛti* (Calcutta)

Sommerstein, A. (2002), *Greek Drama & Dramatists* (London)

Soyinka, W. (1976), *Myth, Literature and the African World* (Cambridge)

Soyinka, W. (1988), *Art, Dialogue and Outrage: Essays on Culture and Literature* (Ibadan)

Spentzou, E. (2003), *Readers and Writers in Ovid's Heroides* (Oxford)

Stack, F. (1985), *Pope and Horace: Studies in Imitation* (Cambridge)

Stahl, H.-P., ed. (1998), *Vergil's Aeneid: Augustan Epic and Political Context* (London)

Stanford, W. (1976), *Ireland and the Classical Tradition* (Dublin)

Stanley, K. (1993), *The Shield of Achilles* (Princeton)

Steiner, G. (2004), 'Homer in English Translation', in Fowler (2004) 363–75

Stinton, T. (1965), *Euripides and the Judgement of Paris, JHS* (Suppl. 11) (1965); reprinted in extended form in Stinton, T. (1990), *Collected Papers on Greek Tragedy* (Oxford)

Stone, J., ed. (2002), *The Essential Max Müller, On Language, Mythology, and Religion* (New York)

Stray, C. (1998), *Classics Transformed: Schools, Universities, and Society in England, 1830–1960* (Oxford)

Stray, C., ed. (2007), *Remaking the Classics, Literature, Genre and Media in Britain 1800–2000* (London)

Stroh, W. (1991), 'Heroides Ovidianae cur Epistulas Scribant', in Papponetti (1991) 201–44

Suerbaum, W. (1980), 'Hundert Jahre Vergil–Forschung', in *ANRW* II, 31, 1: 3–358

Sukthankar, S. et al., eds. (1919–66), *The Mahabharata for the First Time Critically Edited* (19 vols.) (Poona)

Super, R., ed. (1960–77), *The Complete Prose Works of Matthew Arnold* (11 vols.) (Michigan)

Suzuki, M. (1989), *Metamorphoses of Helen: Authority, Difference, and the Epic* (Ithaca, NY)

Taneja, G. et al., eds. (1995), *Literature East and West, Essays Presented to R. K. DasGupta* (Delhi)

Taplin, O. (1990), 'The Earliest Quotation of the *Iliad*?', in Craik (1990) 109–12

Taplin, O. (1991), 'Derek Walcott's Omeros and Derek Walcott's Homer', *Arion*, 3rd series, no.2: 213–26

Taplin, O. (1992), *Homeric Soundings* (Oxford)

Taralankar, J. (1838), *phārsik abhidān* (Calcutta)

Tarrant, R. (1995), '*Da Capo* Structure in Some Odes', in Harrison (1995) 32–49

Tarrant, R. (1997), 'Aspects of Virgil's Reception in Antiquity', in Martindale (1997) 56–72

Taylor, P. ed. (1996), *A Companion to the 'Indian mutiny' of 1857* (Oxford)

Thomas, R. (2001), *Vergil and the Augustan Reception* (Cambridge)

Thornton, A. (1984), *Homer's Iliad: Its Composition and the Motif of Supplication* (Göttingen)

Tinker, C. et al., eds. (1957), *The Poetical Works of Matthew Arnold* (Oxford)

Tod, J. (1829, 1832) *Annals and Antiqputies of Rajasthan* (2 vols.) (London)

Toynbee, A. et al. eds. (1936) *Greek Poetry and Life: Essays Presented to Gilbert Murray on His Seventieth Birthday, January 2* (London)

Trapp, M., ed. (2003), *Greek and Latin Letters, an Anthology with Translation* (Cambridge)

Trautmann, T. (1997), *Aryans and British India* (Berkeley)

Trautmann, T. (2004), *Aryans and British India* (New Delhi)

Trickett, R. (1988), 'The *Heroides* and the English Augustans', in Martindale (1988) 191–204

Trivedi, H. (2007), 'Western Classics, Indian Classics: Postcolonial Contestations', in Hardwick (2007) 286–304

Tucker, H. (2008), *Epic: Britain's Heroic Muse 1790–1910* (Oxford)

Turner, F. (1981), *The Greek Heritage in Victorian Britain* (New Haven, Conn.)

Turner, F. (1989), 'Why the Greeks and not the Romans in Victorian Britain?', in Clarke (1989) 61–81

Turner, P. (1989), *Victorian Poetry, Drama, and Miscellaneous Prose 1832–1890* (Oxford)

Turnour, G. (1836), *An Epitome of the History of Ceylon, compiled from native annals; and the first twenty chapters of the* Mahawanso *[by Mahanama]* (Ceylon)

Vance, N. (1988), 'Ovid in the Nineteenth Century', in Martindale (1988) 215–31

Vance, N. (1997), *The Victorians and Ancient Rome* (Oxford)

Vasaly, A. (2002), 'Cicero's Early Speeches', in May (2002) 71–112

Vasudeva, S., ed. (2006), *The Recognition of Shakuntala* (New York)

Vasunia, P. (2005a), 'Greek, Latin, and the Indian Civil Service', *PCPS* 51: 35–71

Vasunia, P. (2005b), 'Greater Rome and Greater Britain', in Goff (2005) 38–64

Vasunia, P. (2007), 'Dalpatram's *Lakshmi* and Aristophanes' *Wealth*', in Hall (2007) 117–34

Vernant, J-P. (1991), *Mortals and Immortals* (Princeton)

Vishwanathan, G. (1990), *Masks of Conquest* (London)

Walcot, P. (1978), 'Herodotus on Rape', *Arethusa* 11: 137–47

Walcott, D. (1970), 'What the Twilight Says: an Overture', in Walcott, D. (1970), *Dream on Monkey Mountain and Other Plays* (New York)

Walcott, D. (1986), *Collected Poems 1948–1984* (New York)

Wallach, L., ed. (1966), *The Classical Tradition: Studies in Honor of Harry Caplan* (Cornell)

Walters, T. (2007), *African American Literature and the Classicist Tradition: Black Women Writers from Wheatley to Morrison* (New York)

Watkins, C. (1995), *How to Kill a Dragon: Aspects of Indo-European Poetics* (New York, Oxford)

West, D. (1969), 'Multiple-Correspondence Similes in the *Aeneid*', *JRS* 59: 40–9

West, D. (1987), *The Bough and the Gate* (Exeter), reprinted in Harrison (1990) 224–38

West, D. (1993), 'The Pageant of Heroes', *Liverpool Classical Papers* (1993) 283–96

West, D. (2002), *Horace Odes III,* Dulce Periculum (Oxford)
West, M. (1966), *Hesiod Theogony* (Oxford)
West, M., ed. (1998, 2000), *Homeri Ilias* (2 vols.) (Munich)
West, M. (2007), *Indo-European Poetry and Myth* (Oxford)
West, S. (1988), 'Book 4: Commentary', in Heubeck (1988) 192–245
White, D. ed. (2000), *Tantra in Practice* (Princeton)
Wilamowitz-Moellendorff, U. (1924), *Hellenistische Dichtung in der Zeit des Callimachos* (vol. 2) (Berlin)
Wilkinson, L. (1990), 'The Language of Virgil and Horace', in Harrison (1990) 413–29
Williams, C. (1993), *Pope, Homer, and Manliness* (London)
Williams, G. (1983), *Technique and Ideas in the* Aeneid (New Haven)
Williams, R., ed. (1960), *P. Vergili Maronis, Aeneidos Liber Quintus* (Oxford)
Williams, R., ed. (1962), *P. Vergili Maronis, Aeneidos Liber Tertius* (Oxford)
Williams, R., ed. (1973), *Vergil* Aeneid *VII–XII* (London)
Williams, R. (1990), 'The Purpose of the *Aeneid*', in Harrison (1990) 21–36
Wimmel, W. (1960), *Kallimachos in Rom* (Wiesbaden)
Winterer, C. (2002), *The Culture of Classicism: Ancient Greece and Rome in American Intellectual Life, 1780–1910* (Baltimore)
Witzel, M. (1987), 'On the Origin of the Literary Device of the 'Frame Story' in Old Indian Literature', in Falk (1987) 380–414
Witzel, M. (2003), 'Vedas and Upanisads', in Flood (2003) 68–98
Woodruff, P. (1992), 'Aristotle on *Mimêsis*', in Rorty (1992) 73–96
Wright, J., ed. (2007), *Ireland, India, and Nationalism in Nineteenth-Century Literature* (Cambridge)
Zoellner, F. (1892), *Analecta Ovidiana* [University Dissertation] (Leipzig)

Index

Abdul Latif, Nawab 15 n. 50
Abhijñānaśakuntalam (The Recognition of Śakuntalā, Kālidāsa) 24, 51, 80, 85–9, 91–2
love-in-separation 155
and *Padmābaṭī nāṭak* 80, 85–9
recognition scenes 86–7
Aeneid (Vergil)
Aeneid 6 and *MBK* 8: 95–102
The Anglo-Saxon and the Hindu and 122–9, 137, 138–9
Hekṭor-badh and 170–1
and *Padmābatī nāṭak* 74
and *Siṃhal-bijay kābya* 7, 129–37, 138–9
Surrey's translation of 63 n. 5
Aeschylus: *Septem contra Thebas* 84, 87 n. 96
Agricola (Tacitus) 127 n. 35
Anglicists 9, 10, 16–17
Anglicist/Orientalist controversy 16
Anglo-Saxon and the Hindu, The 51–2, 165, 172, 195
and *Aeneid* 122–9, 137, 138–9
gender discourse of colonial politics 124–6, 162
metaphor of Aeneas/Anglo-Saxon and Dido/Hindustan 124–6
Arnold, Matthew
Balder Dead 53, 90
Sohrab and Rustum 53, 90, 120
translation controversy with Newman 186–7
Asiatick Researches (scholarly journal) 12
Asiatick Society, Calcutta 12, 17
Athenaeum, Madras 2

Balder Dead (Arnold) 53, 90
Baṅgo-darśan (journal) 34 n. 135
Basu, Yogindranath 66, 69, 71, 168
Bengali: as literary language 25–7
Bengali elite *(bhadralok)* 11–12, 19, 30, 32, 33, 135, 136
influence of Orientalism on 68
reformist agenda 162
Bengali poetry in English 13–14
Bengal Renaissance 1, 11, 17
Bentinck, William 17
Bethune, J.E.D. 9–10
Bhāgavata Purāṇa 97
Bibidhārtha Saṃgraha (journal) 63 n. 3
Bīrāṅganā kābya: vi, 7, 51, 198–9
abandoned women 161–2
elegiac shift 157–9
epistolarity 149–60
literary ironies 157
and Ovid's *Heroides* 140–66
similarities of content 142–9, 151–4, 156–7
similarities of style 149–60
Rama 159–60
sources 241–2
subversion through gender and genre 160–6
synopsis of poems 237–40
Bishop's College, Calcutta 2 n. 4, 3, 38
foundation of 42–3
library 48–9
possible classical texts available 219–23
syllabus 43–6, 47–8
Black Aegean 57, 199
black classicism 56, 57–8
Blackwood's Magazine 52–3
Blake, William: *The Marriage of Heaven and Hell* 99
blank verse 7, 63
Brahmo Samaj (Society of Brahma) 16, 23
Brajāṅganā kābya ('Poems of the Woman of Braja') 7, 161
Browning, Elizabeth Barrett 60, 120
Buṛo sāliker ghāre roṃ ('New Feathers On The Old Bird') 6, 63
Byron, George Gordon 164
Don Juan 99

Calcutta Cathedral 46, 48 n. 203
Calcutta School Society 17 n. 57

Cambridge University Press (CUP) 48–9
Captive Ladie, The 8, 9, 183 n. 83
Carey, William 26–7
Grammar of the Bengalee Language, A 26
catalogues 171 n. 16
Caturdaśpadī kabitābalī (Sonnets) 5, 7, 165, 167
in honour of Dante 36
Sonnet 78: 19
Chatterjee, Bankim Chandra 32, 34–5, 136
and literary reform 163 n. 108
Chaudhuri, Nirad 103, 112
Chips from a German Workshop (Müller) 182
Clark, T. 97, 100, 101
College of Fort William 17
Colluthus: *Cypria* and *Padmābatī nāṭak* 70 n. 31, 74–5, 76
colonial politics: gender discourse and 124–6, 162
Congreve, William: *The Judgement of Paris* 79
Cratinus: *Dionysalexandros* 79
CUP (Cambridge University Press) 48–9
Cypria (Colluthus): and *Padmābatī nāṭak* 70 n. 31, 74–5, 76

Dasgupta, H. 141 n. 5, 164
deities: comparisons between Greek and Hindu 68–72, 76, 78, 247
De rerum natura (Lucretius) 133
Derozians 20, 39
Derozio, Henry Louis Vivian 8
Dionysalexandros (Cratinus) 79
DLR (Captain David Lester Richardson) 40–2
Don Juan (Byron) 99
Du Bois, W.E.B. 193
Duff, Rev. Alexander 18

East, Edward Hyde 15
East India Company 11, 12
and education 14–16
and missionary work 14–15
education 14–19
classical 38–50
East India Company and 14–16
evangelical movement and 17
Madhusudan's 18, 20, 38–50, 204–18
missionaries and 14–16
see also Bishop's College, Calcutta; Hindu College, Calcutta
Ekei ki bale sabhyatā? ('Is This What You Call Civilization?') 3, 6, 21, 63
Eliot, T.S. 24
'Eloisa to Abelard' (Pope) 164
Epistles (Horace) 191 n. 10
Pope's version of 189, 190
erotic poetry 154–5
Essai sur l'inégalité des races humaines (Gobineau) 31–2, 198
Euripides
Helen 82
Hippolytus 85, 87 n. 96

Gaisford, Thomas 19 n. 65
Garland, Emma 60, 165–6
gender issues 160–6
abandoned women 161–2
colonial politics 124–6, 162
rights of women 162–3
Ghosh, Girish Chundra 31
Ghosh, Manomohan 19
Gladstone, William Ewart 138, 175 n. 32, 188
Gobineau, Arthur de: *Essai sur l'inégalité des races humaines* 31–2, 198
Grammar of the Bengalee Language, A (Carey) 26
Grant, Charles 14
Grant, Dr John 191
Gray's Inn 5

Hare, David 18, 39
Hekṭor-badh ('The Slaying of Hector') 7, 56–7, 76 n. 58, 199
and *Aeneid* 170–1
dedicatory letter 9 n. 24
explanatory commentary 171–3
and *Heroides* 173
and *Iliad* 168–88
moralising commentary 174–6
preface 171–3, 242–5
religious controversy 184–8
structure of 170–1
syncretistic commentary 176–84
Helen (Euripides) 82
Hellenism
British 13, 41, 52
Madhusudan's 52
Hemans, Felicia 60

'Roman Girl's Song' 128, 165
Heroes, The (Kingsley) 171–2
Heroides (Ovid) 51, 60
  Bīrāṅganā kābya and 140–66
  Hekṭor-badh ('The Slaying of Hector') and 173
  Judgement of Paris 67–8
  and *Padmābatī nāṭak* 74, 76, 78
  sources 241–2
Hindu College, Calcutta 3–4, 8, 20, 39–41
  and Christianity 18
  foundation of 15
  syllabus 40–1
Hindu elite 12
  and foundation of Hindu College 15
Hinduism 21–3
  Shaivism 22 n. 81, 181–2
Hindu mythology 28–9
Hippolytus (Euripides) 85, 87 n. 96
Homer
  Iliad 7, 84, 87 n. 96
    Bengali translation 169 n. 11
    Hekṭor-badh ('The Slaying of Hector') and 168–88
    Padmābatī nāṭak and 69–70, 75, 84, 87 n. 96
    Pope's translation of 176
  Odyssey 134
Horace
  Epistles 191 n. 10
    Pope's version of 189, 190
  Odes 104 n. 50, 127 n. 33, 190
  quoted in Houses of Parliament 138
  Satires 190
Hyginus, Gaius Julius: and *Padmābatī nāṭak* 70, 76, 77, 78

Iliad (Homer) 7, 84, 87 n. 96
  Bengali translation 169 n. 11
  Hekṭor-badh ('The Slaying of Hector') and 168–88
  Meghnādbadh kābya and 94–5, 102–17
  Padmābatī nāṭak and 69–70, 75, 84, 87 n. 96
  Pope's translation of 176
India Gazette 191
Indian Civil Service (ICS) 19
Indian Mutiny (Sepoy Uprising) 11, 32–3
Indo-European comparative philology 12
'I sigh for Albion's distant shore' 9

Jones, Sir William (Oriental Jones) 12–13, 169
  On the GODS of GREECE, ITALY, and INDIA 182–3
  translation of Mānavadharmaśāstra 72 n. 38
Judgement of Paris 6–7
  Heroides and 67–8
  Padmābatī nāṭak and 62–92
Judgement of Paris, The (Congreve) 79
Jugement de Pâris et le Ravissement d'Hélène, Le (Sallebray) 79

Kālidāsa
  Abhijñānaśakuntalam 24, 51, 80, 85–9, 91–2, 155
  Meghadūtam 24
Kingsley, Charles: *The Heroes* 171–2
Kṛṣṇakumārī nāṭak 7, 86 n. 91

legal system: and classical languages 19–20
Lucretius: *De rerum natura* 133

Macaulay, Thomas Babington: 'Minute on Indian Education' 16–17, 20 n. 72, 197 n. 24
McTavish, Rebecca 4–5, 161
Madhusudan (Michael Madhusudan Datta) *3*
  alcoholism 6, 167–8
  and Augustan identity 189–91
  biography 2–6
  and colonial dissent 51–2
  conversion to Christianity 42
  cultural identity 195–6
  education 18, 20, 38–50
    1847 examination script 47–8, 204–18
    autodidactic study 49–50
  historical/cultural context 10–37
  legal career 5, 6, 167–8
  literary emblem 36–7, *37*
  nationalism 197–8
  obituary 35
  oeuvre 6–10
    English poems 8–9, 13–14
    prose 168–9
    reaction against contemporary British taste 52–3
    resistance to elite Hindu culture 53–4

Madhusudan (Michael Madhusudan Datta) (*cont.*)
sonnets 5, 7, 19, 36, 165, 167
translations 6 n. 17, 8
see also individual works
patriotism 197–8
tomb *4*
Mahābhārata (Vyāsa) 22–3, 97 n. 23, 144, 158–9, 160 n. 93, 184
Mahommedan Literary Society 15 n. 50
Mānavadharmaśāstra ('Law Code of Manu') 72 n. 38
Māyākānan ('The Forest of Illusion') 7, 86 n. 91, 168
Meghadūtam (Kālidāsa) 24
Meghnādbadh kābya: vi, vii, 5, 6, 28, 50–1, 93–121, 159–60, 198–9
and *Bhāgavata Purāṇa* 97
context 118–21
Daityas/Titans 100–1
and *Iliad* 94–5, 102–17
differences 107–9
similarities 103–7, 109–17
katabasis episode and *Aeneid* 6: 95–102
and *Mahābhārata* 97 n. 23
and *Rāmāyaṇa* 94–5, 98
resistance to elite Hindu culture 53–4
revenge narrative 114–15
similes 110–11, 115
translations of 8, 94
Middleton, Lord Bishop of Calcutta 42, 43, 48 n. 202
Mill, James 162
Milton, John: *Paradise Lost*: vi n. 2, 99, 120, 190
'Minute on Indian Education' (Macaulay) 16–17, 20 n. 72, 197 n. 24
missionaries/missionary activities 16
East India Company and 14–15
and education 14–16
Serampore 14, 16, 17 n. 57, 26
see also Bishop's College, Calcutta
Mitra, Dinabandhu
Nil Darpan 91
Sadhabar Ekadasi 21 n. 77
Mittra, Peary Chand 40
mnestus (marriage suit) 83–4
Müller, Friedrich Max 32, 169, 183
Chips from a German Workshop 182
'My fond sweet blue-eyed maid' 9

nabo-jāgaraṇ ('new awakening') 11, 17
nationalism 196
and national literary culture 33–4
patriotism and 197–8
Newman, John Henry: translation controversy with Arnold 186–7
Nil Darpan (*Indigo Mirror*, Mitra) 91
Norton, George 49, 140 n. 3

Odes (Horace) 104 n. 50, 127 n. 33, 190
Odyssey (Homer): *Siṃhal-bijay kābya* and 134
On the GODS of GREECE, ITALY, and INDIA (Jones) 182–3
Orientalism/Orientalists 12, 14, 192
Anglicist/Orientalist controversy 16
British 13–14, 28–9
influence on *bhadralok* 68
Ovid
Heroides 51, 60
Bīrāṅganā kābya and 140–66
Hekṭor-badh ('The Slaying of Hector') and 173
Judgement of Paris 67–8
Padmābatī nāṭak and 74, 76, 78
sources 241–2
Remedia Amoris 144
Oxford University Press (OUP) 48–9

Padmābatī nāṭak: vi, 6–7, 28, 51, 198–9
and *Abhijñānaśakuntalam* 80, 85–9
Act One: story of golden apple
Indianization of story 65–79
'Judgement of Indranīl' 66–7, 71–3, 78–80, 85, 88–9
and *Aeneid* 74
allegory 71–3, 90–1
Colluthus and 70 n. 31, 74–5, 76
context of 90–2
and *Helen* 82
and *Heroides* 74, 76, 78
Hindu and Graeco-Roman deities, correspondence of 68–72, 76, 78
and *Hippolytus* 85, 87 n. 96
Hyginus and 70, 76, 77, 78
and *Iliad* 69–70, 75, 84, 87 n. 96
and Judgement of Paris 62–92
Judgement Scene 224–9
Padmābatī and Helen 69, 81–3, 84–5
performance history 63–4
recognition scenes 86–7
and Sanskritic dramaturgy 80, 85–9

and *Septem contra Thebas* 84, 87 n. 96
synopsis of 230–4
and *trivarga* 65, 71–3, 90–1
and *Twelfth Night* 85
Paradise Lost (Milton): vi n. 2, 99, 120, 190
patriotism: and nationalism 197–8
Pope, Alexander 169
'Eloisa to Abelard' 164
translation of *Iliad* 176
version of *Epistles* 189, 190
prahasan (farces) 6, 63

racial abuse 197–8
racial science 31–2, 57, 198
racism: in London 5, 9
Rajnarain 35, 129–30
Rāmāyaṇa (Vālmīki): vi, 22–3, 99, 159–60, 184, 185
Meghnādbadh kābya and 94–5, 98
Rangalal 163 n. 108
Ratnābalī 6 n. 17
Raychaudhuri, Tapan 11, 18–19
Remedia Amoris (Ovid) 144
Richardson, Captain David Lester (DLR) 40–2
'Roman Girl's Song' (Hemans) 128, 165
Roman love elegy 153–4, 155
Roy, Raja Rammohun 16, 23

Sadhabar Ekadasi (Mitra) 21 n. 77
Sāhityadarpaṇa (Viśvanātha) 25, 85 n. 91, 155, 163
Said, Edward 58
Sallebray: *Le Jugement de Pâris et le Ravissement d'Hélène* 79
Sanskrit culture 22–9
erotic poetry 154–5
Sanskritic dramaturgy
Padmābatī nāṭak and 80, 85–9
Sāhityadarpaṇa 85 n. 91
Śarmiṣṭhā nātak 85
Sappho 70 n. 32
Śarmiṣṭhā nātak 6, 8, 28
Satires (Horace) 190
Scarborough, William Sanders 56
School Book Society 17 n. 57
Schooner 'Flight', The (Walcott) 194
Selections from the British Poets (Richardson) 40–1
Sepoy Uprising (Indian Mutiny) 11, 32–3
Septem contra Thebas (Aeschylus) 84, 87 n. 96
Serampore College 17 n. 57
Shaivism 22 n. 81, 181–2
Shakespeare, William 168
Twelfth Night 85
Siṃhal-bijay kābya
Aeneid and 7, 129–37, 138–9
Odyssey and 134
plan for first three books 235–6
slave trade 194
Smith, Thomas 42 nn. 174 & 175
Society for the Promotion of National Feeling 35 n. 143
Society for the Propagation of the Gospel in Foreign Parts (SPG) 42
Sohrab and Rustum (Arnold) 53, 90, 120
Soyinka, Wole 58, 197
Stowe, Harriet Beecher: *Uncle Tom's Cabin* 119 n. 95
Street, Prof. Rev. 21 n. 78, 46–7, 205–6
Surrey, Earl of: translation of Vergil's *Aeneid* 63 n. 5
suttee 125 n. 15, 162
svayaṃvara (form of marriage) 83, 84, 173

Tacitus: *Agricola* 127 n. 35
Tagore, Rabindranath 55–6, 169
Tagore, Satyendranath 19
Tagore, Yatindramotan 63
Tennyson, Alfred 120
'Thesis on ways of convincing Hindoos of the error of their ways' 185 n. 89
Tilottamā-sambhab kābya 7, 63, 90
preface: quotation from Horace's *Odes* 190 n. 7
preface: quotation from Horace's *Satires* 190
translation 169 n. 12
Arnold/Newman translation controversy 186–7
Bengali translation of *Iliad* 169 n. 12
Jones's translation of Mānavadharmaśāstra 72 n. 38
by Madhusudan 6 n. 17, 8
of *Meghnādbadh kābya* 8, 94
Pope's translation of *Iliad* 176
Surrey's translation of *Aeneid* 63 n. 5
Trevelyan, Charles 126 n. 27

trivarga (goals of man): *Padmābatī nāṭak* and 65, 71–3
Twelfth Night (Shakespeare) 85

Uncle Tom's Cabin (Stowe) 119 n. 95
United Society for the Propagation of the Gospels (USPG) 43

Vaishnavism 23, 25
Vālmīki 186
  Rāmāyaṇa: vi, 22–3, 94, 98, 99, 159–60, 184, 185
Vergil
  Aeneid 63 n. 5
    Aeneid 6 and *MBK* 8: 95–102
    Hekṭor-badh and 170–1
  quoted in Houses of Parliament 138
Versailles, Paris 5–6
Viśvanātha: *Sāhityadarpaṇa* 25, 85 n. 91, 155, 163
Vivekanda, Swami 32
Vyāsa: *Mahābhārata* 22–3, 97 n. 23, 144, 158–9, 160 n. 93, 184

Walcott, Derek 54–5, 193–4
  The Schooner 'Flight' 194
White, Henrietta 5, 6, 161
Widow-Remarriage Act 125 n. 15, 162–3
Wilson, Bishop of Calcutta 46
Wilson, Horace 91–2
Withers, Professor 38

xenophobia 174–5

Young Bengal movement 3–4, 20–1, 29–30